More Ta___

of a

Highland Minister

by

Rev. Iain Ramsden

Book 2

*This book is dedicated to my lovely wife, Jo,
for all her help, inspiration and support.*

*I am thankful to family members and a number
of good friends for their positivity and
encouragement.*

"Tha mi fadah nad chomain"

'I am very grateful to you'

More Tales of a Highland Minister

This is the second book in the series of 'Tales of a Highland Minister' and it follows on from Book 1 which will gives all the background to the characters and storyline (*worth reading, if you haven't already*).

 It continues the exploits of the Reverend Colin Campbell, a young Church of Scotland Minister who, although being born and bred in Glasgow, fell in love with the beautiful and remote Island of Rhua which is off the West Coast of Scotland, where faith, fun and folklore are interwoven like threads of gold and silver, through the fabric of everyday life.

But more than that, he fell in love with the delightful Lorna MacDonald when visiting the Island to conduct the funeral service of his maternal Grandmother, Mrs Martha McGillivray, some months before.

Many of the tales and incidents in this book are taken from personal experience and others may well have happened, but anyone with even the slightest knowledge of the Highlands and Islands of Scotland will recognize the humour and the antics of the local characters – with a good dram of poetic license added for flavour!

Set in the late 1940's early 1950's, those of a 'certain age' will readily identify with a simpler way of life.

It's been said that Craic and Eccentricity have been superseded by Computers and Electricity, but in many areas of the West Coast, life is still being lived at a slower pace with wit and wisdom at its heart. It is hoped that you will find both of these within the pages of this book.

So, make yourself a cup of tea or coffee *(or something stronger if you wish),* find yourself a comfy seat, and be transported back to a different time and a very different place.

Gabh Tlachd!
Enjoy!

A bit about the Author

The author is from a small village in Argyll and was brought up listening to tales of Scottish folklore, mythology and ancient stories of banshees, fairies, kelpies, mermaids, otters, seals, witches and much more, at his Highland Grandmother's knee.

His first job after leaving school was on the Ballachulish Ferry. He then upgraded to the Royal Navy, travelling the world at Her Majesty's expense.

After leaving the Royal Navy he went home to Argyll where he worked for a number of years in the Forestry, around the West Coast including Ardrishaig, Lochgilphead, Tarbert (Loch Fyne) as well as Mull, Islay and Jura where he acquired a healthy appreciation of the Islay and Jura Malt Whiskies.

In the 1970's he worked as a Navvy on the road between Craignure, Lochdon and Bunessan on the

Isle of Mull where he met many old characters from the Highlands, as well as a number of charismatic Irish Navvies, many of whom had a treasure chest of captivating stories to tell.

After years of rain, midgies and wood wasps he saw an advert in the Oban Times for Revenue Assistants in HM Customs and Excise, ex Servicemen preferred. Being and ex Serviceman he applied, was accepted and soon began working in and around the Distilleries and Whisky warehouses in the Speyside area.
Poacher turned gamekeeper!

As the years passed, he felt an unexpected and yet unshakable 'call' to serve God. This surprised and unsettled him, and after a lengthy conversation with a friend who was a Minister, he applied to the Church of Scotland and was accepted as a Candidate for the Ministry.

He then went to Aberdeen University and 3 years later he Graduated with a Bachelor of Theology Degree. Who would have thought it?

During his final year at university, he spent a summer placement on Britain's most remote, inhabited Island, the Island of Foula which is off the West coast of Shetland.

Foula is also known as "The Edge of the World" after a 1913 film and a 1978 BBC documentary about this fascinating and faraway Island.

He was ordained in 1999 and served as a 'Highland Parish Minister' on the Black Isle for 15 years before retiring to Glasgow where, for a further 7 years, he continued his Ministry as Locum in Ferguslie Park, Carntyne, Easterhouse, Erskine and Kilmacolm until finally retiring in 2021.

Although a faithful Minister, the author still has a healthy respect for the old traditions and beliefs which were passed on to him by his Highland Grandmother, who now rests in peace in Appin Cemetery.

God certainly does work in mysterious ways!

THE CHAPTERS

Chapter 1

Anarchy in Appin

The Rev Colin Campbell was a young Minister of the Church of Scotland who was serving as an Assistant Minister in the Barony Church in Glasgow.

He had excelled at University with a 1.1. Bachelor of Arts (BA) degree and with a Bachelor of Divinity (BD) degree. If he was ever going to be a contestant on 'Mastermind' his specialised subject would be 'Ancient Hebrew,' with honours.

He had always imagined himself as living and serving in and around the Glasgow area working with the poor and the needy, but the past year or so hadn't turned out as he had hoped. Much of his work had been spent in Admin, Management, Personnel and planning meetings with other Clergy in and around the Central Belt. He felt restless and unfulfilled.

There were quite a few churches in Glasgow looking for a Minister, and he had been told by at least three of them, unofficially, that if he were to express an interest in applying, he would be met with a favourable response.

However, he had recently received a letter inviting him to go up for an interview with a view of taking up the position of Minister by the local Church of Scotland on the remote island of Rhua in the Inner Hebrides, off the West Coast of Scotland.

The Vacancy Committee of the Church and indeed most of the population of the island had been greatly impressed with the funeral service he had conducted for his late Grandmother, Mrs Martha McGillivray some months before.

The Kirk Session and Congregation of the Church of Scotland in the village of Kinlochmhor were unanimously agreed that Colin would be just the right Minister for them. As one of the Elders had said, *"Old Nick himself would be converted by his sublime preaching!"*

However, there was another 'fly in the ointment' (*or should it be - a 'midgie in the hand cream'?*) Colin thought to himself,

His previous trip to Rhua had thrown his future plans into turmoil.

It wasn't so much the journey that had caused his internal turmoil but a certain Miss Lorna MacDonald who he had the great pleasure of meeting while visiting that far off island.

He had fallen for her in a way that he had never experienced before and was sure that she felt the same. Their parting had been both sad and tearful but the letters and the phone calls they shared over the past few months had served to deepen their long distance relationship.

They had agreed that this was no fleeting romance and were planning a long term commitment to each other.

But what to do? Where would they settle down into Parish life? There were two very different options – Glasgow or Rhua, but which one would

God call him to?

He believed that God had a plan for them, he just wished that God would tell him what it was!

But he also knew that it was up to himself and Lorna to arrange the details.

After much thought, numerous cups of tea, a packet of Custard Cream biscuits and time in prayer, he saw the way forward. He would travel up to Rhua and arrange to meet the Church Vacancy Committee as they had requested, while at the same time clearing out and tidying up his grandmother's croft and grounds which had been bequeathed to him on her passing.

It would also be a good opportunity to see Lorna again and talk things through.

Colin felt it was the right time to get things moving. The first thing was to arrange his trip up to Rhua and he knew the very man who could help him – his good friend, Iain McDougall.

Iain had been a fellow Divinity student at Glasgow University with Colin and although he lived in the village of Appin near Oban, he had family spread all over the West Coast of Scotland and could arrange a safe passage to Rhua or anywhere else North of Glasgow and West of Oban.

Colin looked up Iain's phone number in his diary, which was actually the number for the Post Office in Appin where Iain's father was the Post Master, and dialled his good friend.

A loud voice boomed, "Hello, this is the Post Office in Appin here, we're out of three-penny stamps if that is why you are calling." It was Iain McDougall. "It's me, Colin, how are you, you scoundrel, are you still poaching the deer?"
"Och it is yourself!" Iain said with a smile, "I only shoot the deer that are old and infirm, why, are they not getting down on their knees and begging me to put them out of their misery?"

Colin laughed out loud and said, "Iain McDougall, you're an awful man!" shaking his head. "And how is your mother keeping?"
"She is well thank you, as busy as ever with the jam making and the knitting jumpers for the poor

children in Ballachulish. Did I tell you that she has taken up a new hobby?'

"No, you didn't, what is she up to now?"

"It's something called the Ju Jitzu – it's the talk of the village!

Old Mrs McRae from the W.R.I. is running lessons in the village hall every Wednesday afternoon but the Meenister says it is the work of the devil!

Two of the ladies have done their backs in already and Mrs Grant the School mistress accidentally knocked out her husband, old Tommy, when she was practicing a Kung Fu drop kick! The tongues are fair wagging!"

"Goodness me," Colin said, not quite sure what else to say.

"Aye, father is not happy," Iain continued, "He says that no good will come of these new fangled ideas!"

He paused and then asked, "Is there something I can help you with my friend?"

Colin outlined his plan to return to Rhua and Iain

said he would contact his cousin Donald John on Coll to arrange a boat to take him over to Rhua, just as he had done the first time Colin visited the Island.

Now that was arranged, he could phone Lorna that evening as planned and give her the good news that he would soon be heading for the Islands. He felt sure that she would be delighted to see him again, he was certainly excited at the thought of holding her in his arms once more.

Chapter 2

The Rhua Riots

The last time Colin visited Rhua, he made an overnight stop on the island of Coll with Iain MacDougall's cousin, Donald John, and he was looking forward to meeting him and his lovely family again. Never had he seen a more loving, caring and contented family.

Donald John was a likeable rogue who saw poaching as an integral part of Island life. He felt it was part of his birthright and would often quote the old Highland saying –

"A Salmon from the pool
A stick from the wood,
A deer from the hill
Are thefts that no man should be ashamed of."

The first line, *'A salmon from the pool,'* was particularly close to Donald John's heart, for as he was fond of saying, "There's plenty more fish in the sea!"

His longsuffering wife, Rhona, and daughters Kirsty and Mhàiri, were gentle, kind and caring folk, full of innocent fun and still unspoiled by the ways of the outside world.

Uisdean and his wife Donalda were the kind of neighbours that anyone would love to have. Not only were they good neighbours but good friends too.

As Colin daydreamed, the clock on the mantelpiece struck 1pm, it was later than he thought.

"This won't get the baby washed," Colin thought to himself. He still had a number of things to do before he could get away - letters to write, people to see, phone calls to make and a case to pack.

He hadn't got around to returning the family suitcase to his Aunty Bunty after his last trip to the Islands, it was still on the top of the wardrobe in his bedroom. He went through, opened it up and packed it with all the necessities for a few days away, including his 'Ministers tool kit' comprising of a King James Bible, his Prayer book, notebook, a pencil, pencil sharpener and a rubber.

There seemed to be so many things to arrange that the afternoon just flew in and before he knew it, it was 6.30 and it would soon be time to speak to Lorna at their regular 7 o'clock call.

*

Meanwhile, it was a cold, damp, dreich day in the village of Kinlochmhor on the little island of Rhua, and Lorna MacDonald had been kept busy in her fathers' Emporium due to the rush on the 'latest thing from Oban' items of ladies clothing which had come off the Oban ferry that morning.

There had nearly been an uprising when the ladies found out that the traditional whalebone corsets with laces at the back, had been replaced by a new stretch-elastic version. "It's all the rage in Oban," Mr MacDonald had said in the hope of pacifying the irate ladies, but it only inflamed the situation.

Mrs McPhee shouted, "Whalebone corsets were good enough for our grandmothers and our mothers and they are good enough for us!"

Mrs Lamont agreed, "Aye, we can't be doing with these fancy new modernisaashuns – and our husband's will be up in arms too!" which set off the other ladies as general mayhem broke out.

"Oh dear," Lorna's father said. "I hope the Oban Times doesn't get to hear of this! I can just see the headlines – *Corsets cause civil unrest in the world famous 'Harrolds' Emporium!*"

"Don't be worrying father, think of the publicity! Ladies from as far away as Kilmacolm and Kinlochleven might hear of it and we will be overrun with boat loads of fashion conscious ladies making a bee line for the shop."

Mr MacDonald's mind was contemplating the possibilities. "Aye, you have a point Lorna. We might even make the headlines in the London edition of the Oban Times, can you imagine it? *Whalebone riots in world famous Emporium.*" His imagination was racing as he thought of the endless opportunities that such a headline could bring to his modest business.

"They might even write a Sea Shanty about it one day! Can you imagine it Lorna? 'The Rhua riots!' and we would be at the very heart of it!"

"Yes father," Lorna said, realising that she had started something which could very easily get out of hand. "But let's just deal with today. Can we think of an idea which might pacify them?"

"Mmmm, what can we say? – I know!" Mr MacDonald called out for quiet.

"Okay ladies, there is something I have to tell you." The room went quiet. "I wasn't supposed to make this public but as you are my faithful customers, I'll let you in to a secret," all ears were open.

"These fancy new corsets have been banned by the Pornalogical Police Squad. Their very name 'Bodyfirm' is causing demonstrations in Glassgow for being too licensashous! I know that you are all upright members of the Church – so perhaps I had better send them back for fear of mass riots here in Rhua!?"

The ladies looked at each other and then pounced on the counter, "I'll take two," said Mrs McGibbon.
 "And so will I!" said old Mrs Thompson. The rest of the stock was sold out in a matter of minutes.

"You sly old fox," Lorna smiled.
"Aye well, we wouldn't want to be *too* famous would we? The ferry from Oban wouldn't be able to cope with the crowds. Can you imagine the Lochearn sailing up the sound of Mull overloaded with a cargo of fractious women?"
"It doesn't bear thinking about father," said Lorna with a smile.
"Aye, just that," said her father, feeling very proud of himself, "Just that…"

*

At 6.45 that evening, Lorna made her way over to the Kinlochmor Hotel.
She had spoken Colin the day before, but he had seemed agitated and ended their conversation rather suddenly which wasn't like him at all.
She sensed that he had something on his mind, but what?

'I hope he hasn't found someone else,' she couldn't bear the thought of it.

She looked at her watch, 'Oh Mercy, it's nearly 7 o'clock, perhaps now I'll find out what is going on in that head of his,' and she hurried along to the Hotel and waited by the public telephone, she wouldn't want to be late for his call.

Chapter 3

Sharing the Good News

Colin had given Moses a nice piece of fish for his tea and then fed himself with a cheese sandwich and a cup of tea with two custard cream biscuits, before phoning Lorna.

He had slept well the previous night and thanks to the wonderful feeling of calm which had come over him, he now had a plan, and it was a simple one, 'Let go - and let God.'

Feeling a great sense of relief, he picked up the jar of change that he kept on the sideboard, went out into the hallway to the communal phone and dialled the number for the Kinlochmor Hotel public telephone.
As soon as it began to ring Lorna immediately lifted the receiver.
"Hello darling," she said and started to chatter hurriedly, "How are you? Are you alright? Is

everything okay? Do you still love me? Oh, please say you do. You haven't changed your mind, have you?"

"Whoa! Hold up sweetheart, of course I still love you, whatever makes you think I would change my mind?"

"I don't know, you would tell me the truth, wouldn't you?"

"I *do* love you Lorna – it's just…. well, my head was in a bit of a muddle last night – but I've been doing some thinking. But before that, I have some good news – a couple of churches in Glasgow are keen for me to be their Minster." Lorna's heart sank.

"Oh, right," she said. *'Does that mean he won't be coming back to Rhua after all?'* she thought to herself.

Colin heard the disappointment in her voice and said, "But I have some even better news! Do you remember I said that I might apply for the Church in Rhua? Well, a letter came in this morning from the church in Kinlochmhor and asked me to come up for an interview with a view to being their

Minister, and I'm coming up to Rhua to talk it over with them as soon as I can get it arranged, hopefully in the next week or so!"

Lorna squealed with delight, "Oh Colin, that would be a dream come true! But are you sure? What about your plans to work in Glasgow? I know you had your heart set on it."

"Yes, we have a lot to talk about when I come up, but that letter must be a good sign that God is leading us in a certain direction. Lots for us to talk about!"

"Oh Colin, you make me so happy! Thank you."

"You make me happy too sweetheart. I'm looking forward to seeing you soon. Tell me, how is your lovely mother keeping?"

"She is well and asking for you – oh she will be delighted to see you again, and so will I!" Lorna was thrilled that Colin was sounding more settled now and that she would soon be seeing him again.

"I'm also planning to clear out my grandmother's croft while I'm up there, will you help me?"

"Yes, of course I will," Lorna was beyond excited at the thought of the two of them in the croft. She was imaging all sorts of scenario's which included a white fence, smoke coming out of the chimney, two children playing outside and a wee dog called Rannoch, chasing after them.

Lorna's daydream was cut short as she felt the earth rumble beneath her. Suddenly she gave out a loud scream and toppled over, landing on the floor.

"Lorna, Lorna whatever is happening!?" Colin shouted down the phone. *Was there an earthquake on Rhua?*

To Colin's surprise Calum McLeod, the well known Poacher, spoke into the phone, "Hello, Hello, this is Rhua calling, Calum McLeod speaking, and who might you be?"

"Calum, it's me, Colin the Minister – what on earth is going on? What's happened to Lorna?"

"Och it's yourself Meenister, how are you?

The weather is just awful up here, how is it with yourself in Glassgow?"

"Never mind the weather! – what's happened to Lorna?"

"Och, it was myself that was carrying a box into the kitchen and knocked young Lorna off of the stool."

Colin could guess what was in the box – fish, newly poached fish, straight out of the loch and bound for the hotel deep freezer.

"Is she alright? Put her on the phone," Colin was more concerned about Lorna.

"Och she's fine, it was just a wee shock that she got. Here she is now."

"Are you alright sweetheart?" Colin said with concern.

"I'm okay," Lorna replied, "I just got a bit of a shock when I was knocked off of the stool." Lorna sounded a bit shaken.

"Sorry, sorry," Calum shouted as he bumped and

clattered his way along the hallway and into the hotel kitchen with the large box of very fresh fish.

"He's an awful man," said Lorna with an affectionate smile.
Colin knew Calum well from his previous visit to Rhua. He also knew that he was a lovely man – a 'likeable rogue' some might say, however it was not an opinion shared by the local policeman PC John Malcolm who was otherwise known as 'Bookem' because of his motto, *'Book'em first, ask questions later.'*

Colin and Lorna chatted until the money ran out, both agreeing that it would be Lorna's turn to phone tomorrow evening at 7o'clock.
Lorna felt like she was floating on air all the way home.

She ran in to the house excitedly and blurted out, "You'll never guess what, mother, Colin's coming up to Rhua, soon!" and ran into her bedroom.
Her mother followed, "Did you say that Colin is

coming back up to Rhua, sweetheart?"

"Yes, and he's coming to see _me_!" and she gave a squeal of joy as happy tears began to flow down her cheeks.

"Don't you be crying now," said her mother.

"But I'm so happy mother, I wondered if I would ever see him again, but he's coming up to see me!" Lorna buried her head in her pillow.

Her mother smiled, she was pleased that Colin was coming back to Rhua, it meant that he was serious about Lorna. *'He'll make a lovely son-in-Law, and a good Minister too,'* she thought.

There were no secrets in Rhua, and she knew that the Church had written to Colin, but she hadn't heard any more about it. She didn't say anything to Lorna incase it all came to nothing and she would be so disappointed.

 Her mother went over to Lorna's side and put her arms around her, and they shared tears of happiness together – her daughter's future was looking rosy after all. "Thank the Good Lord," she whispered.

*

Colin hung up, went back in to his flat and put the kettle on.

He spent the rest of the evening catching up on his daily Bible readings but found it hard to concentrate as his mind kept wandering up to the lovely island of Rhua, or more specifically, to the lovely Lorna MacDonald.

As he day-dreamed, he became aware of a knocking sound, whatever could it be? It seemed to be coming from the kitchen and he went through to find his scruffy wee cat Moses, looking up at him and then looking down at his bowl.

He was rattling his bowl with his paw!

"Ok Moses, I get the message," Colin laughed, opened a tin of Cat food and emptied half of it into the bowl.

He tidied up the papers which were lying about, made himself a cup of warm milk, let Moses out for the night, and went to bed.

Chapter 4

The long and winding road

Colin was wakened early the next morning by the public telephone persistently ringing in the hallway outside the door of his flat.

He, like most of the other residents, who were Students, waited for someone else to answer, but it just kept ringing.

Reluctantly Colin put on his dressing gown and went out into the hall and picked up the receiver.

"Hello, is it yourself?" It was a voice he recognised well, it was his good friend Iain McDougall from Appin.

"Yes, it's myself, what are you doing up at this hour in the morning?"

"Good Heavens man - it's halfway through the morning, it'll soon be 7.30 !" Iain said, sounding far too cheerful for this time of the morning.

"Yes, but the rest of the world is still sleeping!" Colin replied.

"Not in Appin! The Appin folk are known for being early risers!"

"Good for them," Colin answered, "but why are you calling?"

"That's what I have been trying to tell you. Do you remember the lorry driver who gave you a lift home from Oban on your last visit up North?"

"Oh yes, would that be Harrold with two R's?"

"The very one. He said to tell you that if you should want a lift up to Oban, he will meet you at the Kelvin Bridge on any Monday morning at 8 o'clock. He heads back up to Oban the same time every week. What do you say?"

Colin still had memories (or was it nightmares?) of rattling down Loch Lomond-side through the night, as Harrold had one hand on the steering wheel while rolling a cigarette with the other hand, and singing Gaelic songs at the top of his voice.

"Well, ...um, that's very kind but..." Colin mumbled.

"Ok, that's fixed then, next Monday morning. I'll pass that on, and he will arrange for a boat to be waiting for you at the North Pier in Oban which will take you the rest of the way.

If it's the boat I am thinking, she has a motley crew, so be on your guard! Anyway, I'd better fly, time for my morning medicine." Colin was about to protest when the phone went dead.

He knew that Iain's 'morning medication' would almost certainly be out of a bottle – but not a medicine bottle!

'*Oh well, next Monday it is then,*' he said to himself. It was a bit sooner than he had expected but he still had a few days to get himself organised.

First things first – he had to phone the Church Office in Glasgow to let them know that he would be way for a couple of Sunday's. He had already warned them that he would have to go North on family business soon, so that wouldn't be a problem.

He would also have to call Dr Killmennie, the chairman of the Kinlochmhor Parish Church Vacancy Committee to arrange a meeting with them for some time next week, if that were possible.

The next few days were spent tidying up loose ends and making the necessary phone calls to get the wheels in motion for his impending trip.

Colin and Dr Killmennie had chatted on the phone and his meeting with the Church committee on Rhua was arranged for the following Wednesday at 11am. Things were falling in to place.

Colin felt that he ought to pop up to see Aunty Bunty in Bearsden, to put her in the picture before heading North.

He was very close to his Aunt as she had looked after him after his mother had passed on. He was in his teens then and didn't really need someone to 'look after' him, or so he thought, but his favourite Aunty had been there for him whenever he needed wise advice or moral support.

As he had a few days before leaving to go North, he donned his motorbike helmet and gloves, and rode up to Bearsden, dodging the trams on the way.

He always enjoyed a warm welcome whenever he went up to see her and this visit was no different.

"So, you're away up to the Heelands again are you?" Aunty Bunty said.

"Yes Auntie, I'm going to sort out Grannie Martha's estate, the Croft and so on."

"And see thon lassie Lana too, I imagine? A fancy name if ever there was."

"It's Lorna, not Lana Aunty, *Lorna*, and yes, I'll probably bump into her while I'm there." He crossed his fingers.

"Oh yes, well, it's a good Scottish name anyway. I'd like to meet her one day."

"And you will Aunty, once things are sorted out."

Aunty Bunty thought she heard the faint ringing of distant Wedding bells.

"You're not driving up there on thon motorbike of yours I hope, you'll end up in a loch somewhere!"

She never liked Colin going out on his motorbike,

'*Death traps on wheels,*' she called them.

"No Aunty, don't worry, I'm going up with a lad from the Island who drives a lorry up and down to Oban."

"Oh well, at least you'll be safe."

When Colin thought of Harrold's driving, he wasn't so sure.

Before he left, Auntie Bunty gave him a hug and the usual bag of scones and homebaking, some of which he would eat when he got home and the remainder he would give to his loyal housekeeper Mrs McRae.

"You're a growing lad!" Aunty Bunty said and she added another scone or two into the bag before he fired up his motorbike and took off for home.

With everything in place, Colin felt the butterflies flying around his stomach at the thought of seeing the lovely Lorna again.

 On the following Monday morning Colin stood on

the Kelvin Bridge at 7.45 am waiting for Harrold to pick him up at 8 o'clock as arranged.

It was a wet, misty morning and the Bridge was busy with people cowering under their umbrella's rushing right and left, each with their head down as they bustled past each other.

As he waited, he subconsciously began to sing the words to Psalm 40 *"I waited patiently for the Lord…"* which raised a few eyebrows from passers by. Indeed, a nice elderly gentleman threw a few pennies at his feet as he walked by and tipped his hat in Colin's direction. "It's terrible that Ministers aren't paid enough that they have to resort to singing in the street!" he mumbled. Colin smiled.

Half an hour later, and there was no sign of Harrold. Colin was hoping that the 'communication by jungle-drums' hadn't broken down and Harrold didn't know he was waiting.

As Colin stood under his umbrella with his mind wandering on this and that, he imagined that he might be in some romantic spy film, waiting on the bridge to rendezvous with a Russian contact. All he needed was a copy of the Oban Times under his arm and red carnation in his lapel.

It was now 8.40 and he was sharply wakened from his daydream by a loud rattling noise. People stopped and looked around in alarm, but Colin recognised the clatter and the smell of Harrold's fish lorry.
He stepped forward and hoped the heavy rain wouldn't stop Harrold from seeing him. As the lorry drew closer Colin waved his arms about but it didn't appear to be slowing down.

It had almost passed him when Harrold slammed on the brakes and skidded for a few yards along the road before coming to a halt. A number of vehicles behind had to jam on their brakes to avoid a collision. Colin ran alongside, reached up and climbed into the cab.
"It's yourself Meenister, I was nearly half way to Ballachulish before I saw you there!"

"Yes Harrold, I thought you were going to fly past me."

"Aye, I'm running a bit late today as I had to take a parcel of fish to my wife's cousin in Partick. I'm glad I came by in time, Donald John said you would be wanting a hurl up the road but didn't say which Monday, but never mind, here you are."

"Aye," was all Colin could think to say.

Harrold pulled out without looking in the rear view mirror and Colin heard a screeching of brakes and a number of cars blaring their horns.

"These Glagee drivers! Can they not see me pulling out? I come along this way every week you'd think they would know me by now!" and he put his foot to the floor and accelerated along the Great Western Road. It was another a hair raising drive up to Anniesland Cross, through Dumbarton and up Loch Lomond side, Crainlarach, Tyndrum and on up to Oban.

All through the journey Colin remembered the words in the book of Deuteronomy 31:8,

"The Lord himself goes before you and will be with you. Do not be afraid."

Chapter 5

Uisdean played the Melodeon
both in and out of tune

The scenery was spectacular, but the nerve-racking journey to Oban left Colin feeling shaken and in need of a strong cup of tea. Harrold had other ideas as he parked in the Station Car Park and walked round to the Bothy Bar at the back of the West Coast House Hotel for a 'refreshment.'

Colin thanked Harrold for giving him a lift and his kind offer of a 'wee dram,' but he had a boat to catch.

As he walked around the bay to the North Pier, he looked for the boat that Iain McDougall said would be waiting for him, but although he saw no boat, he could hear a Melodeon playing and voices singing 'Cailin Mo Ruinsa,' voices which seemed vaguely familiar.

He walked over to the quayside and looked down and there was the 'Donalda Dream' with Donald

John and his pal Uisdean singing with great enthusiasm.

"Ahoy there!" Colin shouted, "What are you two rogues doing here?"
The singing stopped, "Ah, it's yourself Meenister! Come aboard."
He could see that the pair had enjoyed the convivial hospitality of the Bothy Bar for some considerable time that morning.

"Climb down the steps – you'll have to jump the last wee bit tho'." Uisdean pointed to the short planks of wood nailed to the side of the Pier which served as a ladder but didn't quite come down as far as the Donalda Dream.
Colin looked down with considerable apprehension.

Donald John shouted, "You'll be alright Meenister, the good Lord will be with you!" Well meant words but they gave little comfort to Colin as he made his way precariously down to the boat.

Once on board he was greeted with firm handshakes and an offer of a 'wee dram to settle yourself,' but Colin felt that it was more that his stomach could take.

"What are you doing here, boys?" Colin asked.

"To take you over to Rhua of course! Did Harrold not tell you?"

"He said there was a boat waiting but I never dreamed it would be you two rascals!"

"Well, you wanted a boat – and here we are – the bonniest boat that ever sailed the Sound of Mull – at your service!" Which caused the two sea farers to stand to attention and salute before laughing loudly.

Colin had to grab Uisdean or he would have been over the side.

'*A motley crew right enough,*' Colin thought to himself. '*It's going to be quite a journey!*'

The words of the Hymn, "*For those in Peril on the sea,*" sprung into his mind as the Donalda Dream got underway. They passed the tip of the beautiful wee Island of Kerrera on her Port side and across the Firth of Lorne, up through the Sound of Mull, past Craignure, Tobermory, round the top of Mull and then through 'Gunna Sound' which passes between Coll and Tiree and up to the lovely Island of Rhua, North West of Tiree.

The 'boys' regaled Colin with Gaelic songs and Uisdean played the Melodeon both in and out of tune while they passed a half bottle of the 'water of life' between them.

Colin smiled to himself and thought, *'Well, I'm back!'* and he hummed along to the tunes which seemed surprisingly familiar.

The crossing was a fairly smooth one, and he remembered his last crossing when he had returned to the mainland after his grandmothers' funeral some months ago. He had seen basking sharks, dolphins and various sea birds – and this short passage did not disappoint either.

The sights, the sounds, the smell of the sea and the songs of long ago being sung in the ancient Gaelic language, heightened his senses and made Colin feel as if he were part of some amazing daydream and yet he felt comfortable with it all – in short, he felt very much at home.

'Is this God's plan for me?' He very much hoped that it was.

A lovely feeling of serenity of mind and body came over him – but his reverie was broken when he heard Uisdean say to Donald John, "Will you look at the Meenister, Donald John, is he not sleeping? It must be our 'heavenly' voices!"

"More like your 'divine' playing of the Melodeon!" Donald John replied, and they both laughed and took another sook of the half bottle which rendered it empty.

"Better destroy the evidence!" said Donald John as he pitched it overboard. After a few moments the bottle filled with water and sank, the evidence was well and truly disposed of.

Colin shook his head and smiled, "You two are not getting any better!"

"Better?" replied Uisdean, "Why, even the good Lord himself can't improve on perfection!" which sent both himself and Donald John into fits of laughter and another shake of the head from Colin.

Uisdean opened a cubby hole which was secreted behind the ship's wheel and brought out another half bottle of whisky and handed it over to Donald John who gave a cheer, took the cap off and threw it into the sea, saying "slainte!" (slanj) and then took an ample swig and passed it back to Uisdean.

And so the sea journey continued – a song, a dram and howls of laughter – all to the amusement of Colin and numerous shakes of his head, which only brought more laughter from 'the boys.'

The scenery and the entertainment made for a quick journey and soon the second half bottle was consigned to the deep before they landed on the shores of the beautiful wee Island of Rhua.

Colin thanked Uisdean and Donald John for the lift and promised to send a telegraph to the Post Office on Coll to let them know when he was ready to leave.

Colin jumped out of the boat and made his way up the jetty. He turned and waved as he watched the 'Donalda Dream' make its way slowly out of sight, on its way back home to Coll with the sounds of "Bonnie Mary of Argyll," floating in the air.

Chapter 6

What's in a name?

Colin made the short walk up to Mrs McLeod's Bed and Breakfast where he had stayed on his last visit to the Island.

He smiled when he saw the sign outside which boasted, *'The best B&B in the whole of Rhua.'* Which was quite true, in fact it was the *only* B&B in the whole of Rhua.

He knocked on the door of the Croft and called, "Is anyone at home?"

"Oh, for mercy's sake, come away in Meenister. It's yourself!" Mrs McLeod was fair excited to see Colin again.

"It's lovely to see you again too, Mrs McLeod, I'm sure you are looking younger than ever!"

"Och, away with you!" Mrs McLeod blushed and plumped up her hair. She was all aflutter.

As she turned, Colin could see that she had left one of her rollers in at the back.

"Your room is all ready for you. Donald John sent a message yesterday to say that you would be here some time today and I have a nice pot of Fish soup and a plate of boiled potatoes waiting for you, you will be hungry after all your journeying."

"Sounds delicious Mrs McLeod. Is Calum about?" The mention of fish reminded him of Mrs McLeod's husband Calum, who was a renowned poacher and all round likeable rogue.

"No Meenister, he is away with Lachie Mhor on business over on Eilan Beg, a wee island off the south end of Rhua. Only the good Lord knows what they are doing, it's a bonnie wee place but there's not much going on over there, it's as quiet as a graveyard at midnight."

'Aye,' Colin thought, *'I can guess what kind of 'business' he is on, he'll probably be selling his 'fresh fish' to the many customers he supplies Salmon, Sea Trout and the occasional Lobster to.'*

"That's a shame, I was looking forward to having a blether with him," Colin said, trying to hide a smile.

"Never mind Meenister, he'll likely be home soon, or maybe in the morning if he gets caught up."

'He'll be getting caught up by 'Bookem' the local Bobby if he's not careful!' thought Colin.

"Does he often get 'caught up'?" Colin asked mischievously.

"Oh aye, he's an awful man for getting caught up."

"Oh well, I'm sure I'll see him soon enough."

"Aye, just that Meenister, just that," replied Mrs McLeod as she gave the fish soup another stir.

*

Meanwhile, in Mr MacDonald's 'world famous' Emporium, the demand for more of the new 'all in one' corsets was bringing in the ladies from all over Rhua as they bought them for themselves and for their friends.

Mrs Lamont had previously bought two for herself and was looking for another two to send to her sister on Scalpay.

"That's the last two we have in stock Mrs Lamont but don't be telling anyone, I don't want the ladies to know that there are no more left, but I just can't get enough of them."

"It's no wonder Mr MacDonald, what comfortable they are! My husband Hector is fair taken with them," she said as she blushed and looked around to make sure no-one was overhearing the 'indelicacy' of their conversation.

"Oh, forgive me for being intimate with you Mr MacDonald, I'm all aflutter to be sure."
"Think nothing of it, Mrs Lamont, you'll be surprised how many of my customers are intimate with me – but my lips are sealed Mrs Lamont, sealed. Your delicacies are safe with me."
Lorna couldn't help smiling. "*It's a good job that mother isn't hearing you,*" she thought, "*or you would be for the high jump!*"

Harrold looked over to Lorna and with a wink and said, "Be sure to wrap them in plain brown paper for Mrs Lamont, Lorna, we don't want Bookem catching her with the contraband corsets do we now?"
"Dear me no Mr MacDonald, we wouldn't want that at all," said Mrs Lamont," looking around the

shop to make sure there was no-one was listening.

Harrold looked left and right and said quietly, "My cousin who is on the fishing boats tells me that they are all the rage in Glassgow! The Barra's is fair heaving with ladies buying them up. He said that there was quite a stramash last week when the Polis raided the market and found lots of 'under the counter' corsets!"
"Oh, good Lord!" said Mrs Lamont.
 "Aye just that Mrs Lamont, just that," said Mr MacDonald shaking his head.
Lorna smiled to herself throughout this surreal conversation wondering what Colin would make of it.

"I'll check outside before you leave, better to be safe," said Mr MacDonald as he opened the shop door and feigned looking up and down the street.
"All clear Mrs Lamont, hurry now," and Mrs Lamont left the shop, looked around and scurried up the road as if being chased by Bookem himself.

"That's a shame father," said Lorna with a smile, "you'll have the ladies seeing the secretive service at every street corner!"

"Aye maybe Lorna, but it's good for business and sure there's no harm in it," her father replied with a wink.

*

Mrs McLeod was adding a pinch of salt to the soup as she asked Colin, "Will you be seeing young Lorna MacDonald while you are here?"

"Oh yes Mrs McLeod, but it will be a surprise as she doesn't know I'm here yet. I wasn't due to arrive so soon but I managed to get a lift up at the last minute. I was thinking I might pop into her see her later on - is Calum away with the car?"

"No, he's away on Lachie Mhor's boat."

"Are they on 'conversational' business Mrs McLeod?" Colin said in a mischievous smile.

"Aye that'll be it Meenister, he has a great passion for the conversation."

Colin smiled as on his previous visit to Rhua, Mrs McLeod had tried to convince Colin that her husband Calum was working for the Conservation

Society or as they called it, the 'Conversational Society'.

An inventive name for poaching!

Colin smiled, and with a serious expression asked, "Would it be alright for me to use the car to go into the village later?"

"Of course, Meenister, I wouldn't want to get in the way of true love. I'll put out your soup and it can be cooling if you want to go out to the garage and check over the car."

Chapter 7

A Surprise Visitor

Colin went out to the garage and got in behind the steering wheel of the 1929 Rolls Royce Barker 2 Door Saloon Coupe and took a few moments to savour the sheer opulence of this wonderful old car. It had been Mrs McLeod's grandfather's who had been the Free Church Minister on the Island many years ago.

As he sat back, he stroked the luxury of the upholstery, closed his eyes and took in the ambience and the smell of leather – but what was that other smell? Of course - fish!
Colin walked round and opened the boot where he saw the source of the smell – some nets, a Lobster pot, a few cork floats, fish scales and a couple of ropes – all evidence that Mrs McLeod's husband Calum was still up to his old tricks, and far from being busy doing 'conversational' work, they were busy supplying the locals with a supply of fresh

fish, straight out of the sea!

He opened all the doors and windows to clear the strong smell just as Mrs McLeod called him in for his soup.

"Mrs McLeod, your soup is as tasty as ever, fit for a King," said Colin as he mopped up the last drop of his fish soup with a chunk of Mrs McLeod's home made soda bread.

"Och, thank you Meenister but you have Calum to thank for that, he brought in the ingredients this morning, fresh from the sea."

"That may be, Mrs McLeod but it's what you _do_ with those ingredients that makes all the difference."

Mrs McLeod blushed, she wasn't in the way of receiving compliments. "Och, it's the flatterer that you are!" she said, blushing.

'Poor man, he has fairly got the bug for me,' she thought, and she looked in the wee mirror hanging above the sink on a piece of string, and tidied her hair.

*

In Harrold's Emporium, Lorna was busy in the small office catching up on some paperwork and her father was humming a Gaelic tune as he tidied up the bed socks and hair nets in the shop. "It's been a grand day Lorna," he called cheerfully.

Lorna looked out and saw that it was raining. "Yes, father," she didn't want to burst his bubble.

Just then, the bell above the shop door tinkled.

"Would you get the shop door Lorna?" called her father, "I'm up to my eyes in hair nets."

Lorna came through from the office and nearly passed out with surprise. She stood, frozen for a few seconds before rushing over to the door. It was Colin.

"Oh Colin, Colin! Is it really you?" and she threw her arms around him and squeezed him tightly just to make sure she wasn't dreaming.

"It's lovely to see you too Lorna, you are just as beautiful as I remember!"

"Och, you're a sweetheart Colin, so you are!" and she buried her head in his chest as he put his arms around her.

"Father, look who's here!" Lorna shouted excitedly.

Her father turned and saw it was his future son in law (he hoped) standing in the doorway.

"Well bless me, if it isn't the Meenister! Lord preserve us! How are you, Colin? It's lovely to see you again, come away in." Mr MacDonald ushered Colin in and closed the shop door.

"Look everyone!" Mr MacDonald said excitedly to the three customers in the shop. "It's the Meenister, here in our famous Emporium," and he steered Colin through the shop and into the office.

"What brings you here? As if I need to ask," he winked at Lorna.

"He's here to sort out his dear grandmothers' croft, father."

"Yes, that's right – and to see you too, of course!" Colin smiled at Lorna who blushed and squeezed his arm.

"I was wondering if you could spare Lorna for a wee while Mr MacDonald, we have a lot to catch up on."

"Yes of course – it'll soon be time to close the shop anyway - take the rest of the afternoon off dear."

"Thank you, you're a sweetie!" Lorna hugged her father. Colin stepped forward and shook Mr MacDonald's' hand saying, "Thank you, sir, I'll take good care of Lorna, you can count on me."

"I know I can, Meenister, thank you." Lorna's father became quite emotional and turned away to compose himself.

"Oh, I am so blessed to have two wonderful men in my life," Lorna said, and before they knew it, the three of them had a tear in their eye and a lump in their throats.

After a few minutes, Mr MacDonald straightened himself and said, "Well, this won't do at all, the three of us sniffling away, I'd better get back to the hair nets!" and he went back into the shop feeling very emotional but not wanting to show it.

Chapter 8

Away with the Fairies

It was getting late in the afternoon and the rain was getting heavier by the minute. Lorna collected her coat as they left the shop and jumped into the car. They leaned across and kissed, but almost instantly both were struck by the strong smell of the contents of the boot.

They looked at each other, sniffed and simultaneously shouted, 'Fish!' and they burst out laughing. "Calum! That old rogue!" said Colin and they held each other tight and giggled together.

"Okay," said Colin, "were shall we go?"

"Can we go to the Fairy Well? It's a special place where I used to go when I was young if I wanted to talk things through."

"Yes, of course." Colin started up the car and Lorna gave directions. They were there in just a few minutes and as they pulled into the layby, the rain stopped and the sun came out, as if on cue.

It was a delightful spot, just as Lorna had said.

Colin was struck by a bank of purple flowers around an old stone well with a circle of what looked like miniature daffodils in the centre swaying in the breeze, except, as Colin noticed, there was no breeze.

"Shall we go for a walk around while the rain's off?" Lorna asked.

Colin was eager to have a look around, "Yes, that would be good."

As they got to the edge of the carpet of flowers, Colin could see that in the centre of the miniature daffodils there was a bare circle of about 3 feet in diameter.

"Come on, be careful where you tread," Lorna said as she took Colin's hand and led him carefully through the tiny flowers into the centre.

They stood silent for a few moments and as Colin was about to speak Lorna said, "Shhhhh - can you hear them?"

Colin listened hard but could hear nothing.

"Don't listen with your ears, listen with your heart."

Colin closed his eyes and listened intently.

After a few minutes Colin opened his eyes suddenly.

"What is it Colin, can you hear them?"

"I can hear the sound of children laughing!"

"That's them, the *sìth (Shee)*, the Fairy folk!" Lorna said excitedly.

"But… but it can't be! It must be the water flowing in the bottom of well." Colin was struggling to understand.

Lorna smiled and said, "I've seen them – and spoken to them – it's them alright – they're waiting for you to say something, they are very cautious – and shy, but they will speak to you - if you believe in them."

Colin suddenly felt awkward. He didn't want to upset Lorna but 'talking to Fairies' was beyond rational for him, yet he had to admit that he did hear and feel something.

The carpet of small yellow flowers seemed to be glowing and shimmering as they swayed from side to side.

Not wanting to offend Lorna he thought he would play along.

"Okay sweetheart but maybe if you spoke to them first," Colin said tactfully.

"Alright, but you have to close your eyes, so you're not distracted." Colin closed his eyes and then, after a few moments, opened one eye to see what Lorna was doing.

She was looking so serene and more beautiful than he had ever seen her. Her face was so peaceful – and then he heard it…. voices engaged in an indistinguishable conversation! He opened both eyes, Lorna's lips were moving but he could hear no words being spoken out loud.

He closed his eyes again and the softly spoken conversation continued. He couldn't understand the language, but he knew it certainly wasn't water babbling in the well. And then it stopped.

As he opened his eyes he saw Lorna lift her head

an open her eyes. She had a lovely warm smile and a calm glow about her.

"Are you okay sweetheart?" Lorna asked.

"Yes, I'm fine, how are you?"

"I am feeling on top of the world Colin, I'm so glad we came here today, my mind is at rest now and I know that everything is going to be alright."

Whatever Lorna had just experienced he could see that it had a good and profound effect on her.

 "We'd better head back to the car, the rain isn't very far away," Lorna said. Colin looked up and saw only blue skies.

Just as they got back into the car and closed the doors, the heavens opened and a heavy shower accompanied by a grey mist swept over them.

Colin felt a shiver run down his spine.

"Gosh, look at the time, it's nearly 5 o'clock, I'd better get you home sweetheart, it's time for you to help your mother make tea for your father coming in from the shop." said Colin.

"How nice of you to remember, yes I suppose I'd

better get home, will you come for your tea? I'm sure mum would be pleased to see you."

"I'd love to but I had better see Mrs McLeod, to see if she has made anything for my tea. Have we time to go round by her croft first?"

"Och yes, we can take the back road and it'll take us round to the village by way of the McLeod's croft."

As they drove back, Lorna felt a lovely warm glow and thought, *'I've never been this happy in my whole life,'* and she reached over and squeezed Colin's arm and kissed him on the cheek.

Colin had been thinking of all that happened at the Fairy Well but didn't want to question Lorna incase it upset her.

Lorna broke the silence and asked, "Colin, can I ask you something?"

Of course you can, what is it?"

"What did you think about the Fairy Well?"

Colin wasn't sure what to say, he didn't want to upset Lorna, so he said, "Well ... er... it was interesting, I'm not sure *what* I feel about it."

"Did you not hear them for yourselves?"

"Well, I certainly heard something," Colin was sure he had heard children's voices but was struggling to make sense of it all.

As they rounded the next bend, they were confronted by a huge stag standing in the middle of the road. Colin braked as hard as he could and only just managed to stop just a few inches in front of it.

The stag stood his ground and made it quite clear that he wasn't going to move, after all, this was *his* territory.

Colin and Lorna felt a sense of intimidation as this beautiful beast stared, snorted and put his head down showing his impressive set of antlers.

It was the biggest Stag Colin had ever seen, not that he had seen many stags close up before, but its sheer size and fierce look was enough to scare the living daylights out of a hairy highland haggis.

"Oh, my goodness!" Lorna shouted. "Be careful

Colin, stags can be very aggressive at this time of year. It might be best to reverse so he doesn't feel threatened."

"Okay," Colin said, glad that Lorna knew what to do. But as Colin reversed the car, the stag moved forward, snorting and glaring at Colin, looking more threatening with every step.

"What next Lorna? He still doesn't look very happy!"

"Well, when dad had the van, I would often go with him around the Island – and if ever a Stag or a deer stood in the way, he would blare the horn and they'd get a fright and run off. I always told dad off for scaring the poor things." Lorna said.

"Well, I would much rather the Stag got a fright than you and I, so, here goes!" At which point Colin blasted the horn and the stag jumped back and ran off across the road and into the trees for safety.

"Awww, poor thing!" said Lorna as she watched the stag disappear into the woods.

"It was him or me!" Colin said, feeling like a white

hunter who had just bagged a particularly large tiger.

"My hero!" said Lorna with a giggle in her voice.

"It was nothing, really," Colin said with mock modesty and a smile as he drove off to Mrs McLeod's croft.

Colin was pleased that the diversion with the Stag meant that there would be no more talk of Fairies, for now anyway.

Chapter 9

The Ladies are a Mystery, right enough

As they pulled up outside Mrs McLeod's croft, they saw that she was in the garden at the side of the house, taking in her washing.

Lorna called out, "Hello Mrs McLeod, it's Lorna and the Meenister!" Mrs McLeod looked round and seemed to go into a panic.

"Oh..er..will you just go in and put the kettle on Lorna – and take the Meenister in too!" She immediately took her newly dried 'Bodyfirm undercover corset' off the line and put it under the towels in her washing basket, out of sight.

'I can't have the Meenister seeing my 'unmentionables', oh mercy no!' she said to herself.

Lorna had noticed the 'offending item' and smiled to herself at the thought of the Minister seeing things a 'man of the cloth' ought not to be seeing.

As Mrs McLeod came into the house Colin asked, "Are you alright Mrs McLeod?" with genuine concern.

"Oh yes, thank you Meenister, just a wee problem, nothing for you to worry about, thank you."

"You know you can speak to me about anything don't you? Anything you say to me is in complete confidence," Colin said in his most comforting pastoral voice.

Mrs McLeod was getting uptight, wishing that Colin would give it a rest and stop badgering her, but she managed to say politely, "Thank you Meenister but I like to keep my confidences to myself – and now I'll go and make us a cup of tea," and she went through to the scullery.

"Oh dear, I think you have upset Mrs M," Lorna said quietly.

Colin was bewildered as he wasn't sure what was going on. "Yes, it seems so but I'm not sure what I said to upset her!" He was genuinely confused.

"Oh Colin, you have lot to learn about women!" Lorna said with a smile. "So it seems. Aye, the ways of women are a mystery, right enough," he added thoughtlessly.

"Hey, be careful now!" Lorna scolded Colin playfully.

Mrs McLeod overheard their conversation, smiled and hid the washing basket in the kitchen cupboard and shouted through, "That's the kettle on, tea won't be a minute."
"Not too strong for me please Mrs McLeod," Colin shouted.
"There's only one way to make a proper cup of tea Meenister and that's one spoonful of tea for each person and one for the pot, so four spoons it is!" Mrs McLeod said firmly.
Lorna looked at Colin and whispered, "That's you told!" and they both smiled.
"That's just fine Mrs McLeod," Colin called.

A few minutes later Mrs McLeod came through with a tray on which were the three of her best china cups and saucers and a tea pot with a tea cosy in the shape of a West Highland Terrier's head.
"Oh, I love your tea cosy Mrs McLeod!" said

Lorna, "Have I not seen it somewhere before?"

"It was a gift from a very special Meenister," she looked bashfully at Colin.

"Of course!" Lorna remembered Colin had given it to Mrs McLeod the last time he was on Rhua.

"You are right there Mrs McLeod, he certainly *is* a very special man," Lorna said giving his arm a squeeze.

Colin blushed and changed the subject. "I've been invited out for my tea at the MacDonald's household this evening, would that be alright Mrs McLeod? I wouldn't want to cause you any inconvenience."

"Mercy no, I haven't got round to thinking about tea yet, I've been so busy with the washing and all, so please don't be worrying yourself."

After a very sociable 20 minutes or so, Colin suggested to Lorna that perhaps they ought to be going. "Yes Meenister, you don't want to be keeping dear Mrs MacDonald waiting," Mrs McLeod said.

As they left the croft, Lorna turned and whispered,

"Don't worry, Mrs McLeod, your secret is safe with me."

Mrs McLeod blushed and said quietly, "Aye, it's good to keep some confidences to yourself isn't it?"
"Yes, of cor-set is," replied Lorna with a smile.
There was a few seconds silence before the penny dropped - "Och, it's terrible that you are Lorna MacDonald!" and they both laughed.

"What's going on in there?" Colin shouted.
"Nothing sweetheart, Mrs McLeod and I are just chatting, you know, women's talk."
"I'd better go," Lorna said to Mrs McLeod and gave her a hug and went out to the car with Colin.
'Aren't they just the loveliest couple?' Mrs McLeod said to herself with a tear in her eye.

"What was that all about?" Colin asked Lorna.
"Never you mind, just ladies blethers," she replied and leant over and kissed him on the cheek.
As Colin drove over to the village, he knew he had missed something but hadn't a clue what it was.

Chapter 10

Uncle Hector proposes a Toast – or two –
or three!

Within 15 minutes they drew up outside of Lorna's front door, just round the corner from Harrold's Emporium.

As they entered the house, Lorna called out, "It's only us mother!"

"Oh, come away in!" Lorna's mother called from the kitchen, "Is the Meenister with you?"

Colin answered, "Yes Mrs MacDonald, like the bad penny!"

"Away with you, you are always very welcome here! Come through, tea is nearly ready.

Lorna, your uncle Hector is over from Tiree to see you."

Hector was her mother's brother and Lorna's favourite uncle, he was always good fun and ready with a joke or two. He had spent most of his life at sea and a had lots of tales to tell, many of which were not repeatable in polite company.

Lorna hurried through to the front room and as Uncle Hector stood up, she wrapped her arms around him and gave him a big hug. "Oh, Uncle Hector it is lovely to see you!" she said, almost in tears. "It seems ages since we last saw you!"

"Steady on!" replied uncle <u>Hector</u> as he steadied himself. "My, but you're as bonny as a picture. You will break a few hearts, that's for sure, just like your dear mother."

Colin walked in and extended his right hand saying, "Uncle Hector I believe."

"I am that – and who might you be?"

Lorna kissed Colin on the cheek and said, "This is Colin, Uncle Hector, he's my – er – boyfriend, no, my…"

Colin came to the rescue, "I am Lorna's 'soon to be' fiancé, if she will have me."

He looked over at Lorna and she almost burst with excitement. "Really? Of course I'll have you, I wouldn't want anyone else in the whole world!" And she burst into tears and hugged Colin tightly.

Lorna's mother came in on her wheelchair and said, "What on earth is going on? Hector, what have you been saying to Lorna?"

"Not guilty this time Peggy!"

Lorna ran over to her mother and put her arms around her shoulders. "Colin just asked if he could be my fiancé!"

"And I hope you said yes."

"Of course! Colin is the most wonderful, loving, caring man in the whole world!" Lorna gushed.

"Oh, that's just wonderful sweetheart! Colin, come over here so I can give you a hug!"

"Of course, Mrs MacDonald."

"It's Peggy! We're all family now, well, almost."

Hector thought it was too good an opportunity to miss so he suggested, "I think perhaps we should be taking a dram, just to celebrate the moment of course," and he went and brought through a bottle of whisky and 4 wee barrel glasses with the image of a kilted piper on the side.

All glasses were charged, and Hector took it upon himself to propose a toast, "To the happy couple!" and they all said, *'Slainte'* together and drunk a toast.

Just at that very moment Lorna's father came in from the shop.

"And what's all this?" he said, "I might have known Hector would be at the centre of it if there was a dram involved!"

"Oh father," Lorna said, "It wasn't Uncle Hector's fault, Colin just proposed to me – and I said yes! Oh, please be happy for us father, please." Lorna looked at her father with appealing eyes.

"Happy? … Happy? I am absolutely over the moon my dear, how could be I cross at a time such as this?"

"Well, you'll be taking a dram then Harrold, for the sake of the happy couple?" Uncle Hector said with a wink to Colin.

"Of course, Hector, how could I *not* raise a glass to my beautiful daughter and the dear Reverend Colin?"

Uncle Hector took out a fifth glass and poured another round of drams, taking a sideways glance to make sure that he wasn't being watched as he poured himself a more than generous measure.

Harrold raised his glass and said, "To Lorna and the Reverend!" and knocked the dram back in one gulp and then shook Colin's hand and welcomed him into the family.

Lorna and her mother looked at Harrold in amazement. They had never seen him drink whisky before, or for that matter be so friendly with Uncle Hector as he had always thought of him to be a bit coarse, and his language a bit too 'colourful' for his liking.

As they all chatted excitedly, Lorna drew Colin aside and asked, "Are you sure Colin? I mean *really* sure you want to marry me?"

"Of course sweetheart, but I'll have to speak with your father first. I just know in my heart that you are the one for me."

"And you are the one for me!" Lorna said as the happy tears began to flow. Colin put his arms around her, and they hugged each other tightly.

Lorna's mother saw them and smiled, saying in a whisper, *"Thank you Lord,"* as she pulled a small handkerchief from the sleeve of her cardigan and dabbed her moist eyes. It was a happy day, to be sure.

In a lull between Uncle Hector's singing and proposing yet another toast, Colin saw his opportunity and drew Lorna's father to one side.

"Mr MacDonald, I am sorry for not speaking to you sooner and ask for your daughter's hand in marriage, but events seem to have overtaken my good intensions."

"Well, I have to say I would have preferred to have been asked in the traditional manner – but as it's yourself may I say that I couldn't be happier with her choice – and you have my permission and full support. Let's have another dram to seal it!" Harrold slapped Colin on the back and called "Hector – two drams over here please!"

Uncle Hector poured out the two drams and handed them to Harrold and Colin, then poured out a large measure to himself and announced, "A toast!" and downed his drink on one go.

Lorna's mother smiled and as she looked around the room and saw the joy and happiness on everyone's face, she couldn't hold the tears back any longer.

Lorna saw her mother and went over and put her arm around her shoulder and before long they were both crying with happiness.

After a few minutes Lorna's mother said, "Och, just look at the two of us bubbling away here, come on through to the kitchen we'll set the table.

"I'll be through in just a minute mother," Lorna said and walked over and took Colin's arm. "Thank you," she said. "You have made me the happiest girl in the world."

Uncle Hector continued to refill the glasses to propose yet another toast to, "The happy couple!"

"What has your father got against uncle Hector, he seems a jolly enough fellow?" Colin whispered to Lorna.

"Hector likes to tell tall tales of his voyages to exotic places, but father thinks he never got past the Falls of Lora."

"Where's that?" Colin asked.

"About 5 miles from Oban!" Lorna laughed.

"But was he not on the ocean-going ships? He certainly has a way with the stories," Colin was puzzled.

"No," said Lorna with a smile, "Father says he was a stoker on the Ballachulish ferry!"

Colin burst out laughing, bringing a silence to the room.

"By jove, that must have been a good one!" Uncle Hector declared. "What's the joke? Come on, share it with us Meenister," Hector insisted.

"Well, er… Lorna was just saying… um..." Colin was stuck for words but Lorna came to the rescue.

"It was myself Uncle Hector, I said that he should be wearing the kilt at the wedding, but Colin said he hasn't the legs for it!"

Uncle Hector didn't think it was much of a joke and said weakly, "Oh well then…" followed by an awkward silence.

Lorna walked through to the kitchen to help her mother set the table.

As the evening wore on, Uncle Hector began to sing some more of his 'songs of the sea' as he called them. They got progressively bawdy and when he started to sing 'The mademoiselle from Arnisdale,' Colin thought it was time to leave, and Lorna walked him to the door. They said their good-nights and Colin drove off leaving her on the doorstep with a tear in her eye. *'Was it all a wonderful dream?'* she thought to herself as she closed the door.

It was late as Colin drove back to Mrs McLeod's croft which was in darkness, except for a candle flickering in the window. He had hoped to share his good news with the McLeod's but that would have to wait until the morning.

Colin felt an overwhelming sense of joy, it was a deep feeling that the hadn't felt before. *'God is good indeed,'* he thought to himself.
He slept well that night, it had been a very long and very tiring day.

Chapter 11

I've even had ladies from as far away as
Melvich and Munlochy

The next morning as Harrold opened his
Emporium, his head was thumping and his
stomach was rumbling. *"I must have had a bad pie*
last night. I'll have to have words with Gordon Fraser,"
(the butcher), he said to himself.

The joy of the engagement of his daughter was
marred by the loud banging in his head. Every
noise seemed to be exaggerated and he was sure
that someone had turned the volume and daylight
settings up to maximum.

He had planned to tell his customers the good
news that Lorna was betrothed to a man of the
cloth – but word had got round that the 'world
famous' Emporium had run out of the racy new
corsets, much to the dismay of many of the local
ladies.

As he opened the shop a crowd soon gathered, and they were far from happy.

"Oh dear," said Mr MacDonald, "Some of the ladies are turning ugly."
"Some of them are *already* ugly!" remarked Murdo the Postie who had just popped in with the post.
"Murdo! Don't be so cruel," Lorna reprimanded Murdo.
"Och, was I not just joking, Lorna?" Murdo smiled and left the shop while it was still safe to do so.

Mrs McPhee, one of the more formidable ladies, stepped forward and asked, "Is it true, Mr MacDonald? Have you really run out of the, well.. you know what's?" in a secretive tone.
 "I'm afraid so, our stockist has had the most fearful call for them. I've even had ladies from as far away as Melvich and Munlochy wanting to buy them. I was thinking of selling lemonade at the door when the queue was so long.
Sure, did we not have the crew of a Puffer from Tarbert Loch Fyne making a diversion on their

way home from Castlebay just to buy some for their good ladies!?"

"That's as may be, but what about us?" shouted Mrs McPhee. "Our husbands are fair taken with them – my Duncan is so disappointed he has gone back to talking to his sheep – I'm sure he thinks more of them than he does of me!"

At this, the ladies became rowdy and shouted in their support of Mrs McPhee.

"Aye, my man spends more time speaking to his dear Lizzy than he speaks to me!" shouted Mrs McVittie.

"That's a lie! I hav'na seen your husband for weeks!" objected young Lizzy Black.

"Not you! It's his prize-winning Heifer, the one who got a 1st at the Rhua Show last summer."

"Imagine naming a cow with a woman's name, the very idea!" someone shouted out.

"Oh, that's nothing," said Mrs McVittie, "he has a Catherine too."

"Hey, that's *my* name!" shouted Mrs Cameron."

"And a Christina," Mrs McVittie continued.

"That's *my* name!" shouted Mrs McLeish.

It wasn't long before it became apparent that Mr McVittie had named his entire herd of cows after most of the ladies of the village!

"Wait 'til I get home!" Mrs McVittie was fuming as she rolled up her sleeves and made for the door.

Lorna was struggling to keep a straight face as it all unfolded. "Is there a Lorna?" she asked with a mischievous smile.

"No, I don't think so," replied Mrs McVittie as she left the shop.

"Thank the good Lord for that!" said Lorna's father.

Deflated and mumbling between themselves, the other ladies left the shop too.

"My, but that was a close shave Lorna, I fair thought we were going to have a revolution on our hands," said Mr MacDonald as he went through to the office and phoned his supplier to double his next order of the 'undercover' corsets.

As he went back through to the shop, he was thinking of the increased profits which this new line of 'racy corsets' had brought him.

'Perhaps the good Lord is smiling upon us since my dear Lorna took up with the Meenister," he thought, and whistled a few bars of Isaac Watts hymn, *"Joy to the world..."*

Lorna couldn't remember the last time she had heard her father whistling. "Are you feeling alright father?" she asked him.

"Never better Lorna, never better," and he gave a little skip as he walked over to 'The latest thing from Oban' section and with a warm smile and a feeling of inner contentment.

He thought, *'am I not just living the dream!'* and he began to sort the new stock of lady's knee length winter Bloomers into three bundles – Large, Extra Large and XX Large.

Then he remembered that he hadn't mentioned Lorna and Colin's engagement to his customers. "Oh dear, with all the furore I forgot to tell the ladies our good news!"

"Don't worry father," Lorna said, "The jungle drums will be going full pelt – they'll all know by eleven o'clock."

"Aye, just that, he replied and hummed a happy tune as he rifled through the bloomers.

"Aye, I'm living the dream, right enough!"

*

Colin had wakened early and in good spirits. He was sitting at the kitchen table reading his Bible as Mrs McLeod came through from her bedroom.

"Goodness me Meenister, it's early that you are this morning, and here is me with my rollers still in!"

"Don't be worrying Mrs McLeod, you look just as bonny as you always do. Is Calum awake yet? I'd very much like to talk to you both – and don't worry it's not bad news, just the very opposite."

"Well, he was still snoring his head off when I came through just now but I'll go through and give him a shake."

"Calum McLeod, get out of that bed right now, ye lazy devil! It's the Meenister that wants to speak to us!" The words rang through the house.

She appeared at the kitchen door with a sickly smile on her face wearing her best pink candlewick dressing gown (the one without the holes) and her hair brushed. "He'll be through in just a minute. I'll put the kettle on."

A few minutes later Calum entered the kitchen, half asleep, scratching his stubbly beard and wearing a faded old pair of striped pyjamas that looked like they were at least two sizes too small for him. It was not a pretty sight.

"Och, Calum!" Mrs McLeod said, "You could at least have put on your dressing gown, the Meenister is here!"

"I canna, the moths got at it last winter, do you not remember?"

Colin tried hard not to smile as the scene played out in front of him. "Don't worry Calum, please take a seat, I've got some good news for you."

Mr and Mrs McLeod sat down, intrigued to hear the good news, although Mrs McLeod had a fair idea of what it might be.

As Calum sat down, a button flew off his tightly stretched pyjama jacket and landed in Colin's cup of tea.

"Good shot!" Calum said with a chuckle.
Colin had to turn his head away for fear of bursting out laughing, however, Mrs McLeod was not amused.

Chapter 12

Sharing the Good News

Colin took a breath and said, "Well, as you both know, Lorna MacDonald and I have been courting for some time now – and, well – last night I proposed to her and she accepted!"

"Oh my! What wonderful news!" said Mrs McLeod.

"Well done òganach (*young man*)," said Calum, vigorously shaking Colin's hand. "You're a lucky man right enough, she's a lovely lass and will make a good wife. If you are half as happy as Mrs McLeod and I have been all these years, then you'll be a very happy couple!"

Mrs McLeod blushed, "Och, Calum you're an old softie, so you are!"

It warmed Colin's heart to see the unexpected affection shared between Mr and Mrs McLeod.

"That's wonderful news Meenister and we wish you both every blessing." Mrs McLeod said, dabbing a tear from her eye with her handkerchief.

"May you both be blessed with long and happy lives together," Calum added. His emotions got the better of him and he coughed, sniffled and hurried out of the room.

"Never you mind him Meenister," said Mrs McLeod. "He is a rascal to be sure, but he has the soft heart."

After breakfast, Colin drove to the village and called into the Emporium to see Lorna.

When he entered the shop Lorna ran over and hugged him tightly and said excitedly, "Oh Colin, is it true or was last night just a dream? You haven't changed your mind, have you?"

 "Whatever makes you think that sweetheart?" Colin replied, "I love you more each day."

Lorna thought she might faint with joy.

Her father spotted Colin and came over to speak to him, "Well, good morning Meenister, how are you this fine morning?"

"On top of the world Harrold – and please call me Colin, we're almost related now!"

"Of course, Colin. You just missed a full scale riot, yes a riot - here in the Emporium!"

Lorna could see that her father was beginning to get worked up. "Now steady father, you know what Dr Livingstone said about getting excited. It's not good for your blood pressure."

"It wasn't a riot," she explained to Colin, "but the ladies aren't very happy with father."

"Well, it isn't my fault," Harrold replied, "Am I not just trying to scrape a living to put a crust on my family's table?"

Lorna looked at Colin and raised her eyebrows, "Now father, don't get carried away."

Colin was finding it difficult to follow the account of what actually happened, "What were they so upset about?" he asked.

Harrold looked at Lorna with a 'don't let on' kind of look and Lorna replied, "Don't ask," which left Colin even more confused than he had already been.

The thought of talking to the Meenister about ladies 'unmentionables' was beyond civilised conversation in good highland society.

"Oh right," was all he could think of saying.

"Can you be spared for an hour or so? We have lots to talk about," Colin asked Lorna.

Lorna looked at her father imploringly. He smiled and said, "Oh alright, I was thinking I might close up early today anyway, I seem to have a bit of a headache, it must be this humid weather."

Colin and Lorna smiled at each other, *"Perhaps it was a dram or two too many last night,"* Lorna whispered to Colin.

"Aye, father, that's what it will be, the weather."

As they got into the car Colin asked Lorna where they might go to talk. "How about the beach on the south side of the Island?" Lorna suggested, "It is miles of white sand and a beautiful view of nan Eilan Beag, across the from the bay. It's a lovely, peaceful spot."

"Sounds perfect, let's go!"

Lorna gave him directions and within 10 minutes they were standing on the edge of the machair looking over miles of pure white sand. Colin's breath was taken away. "Oh my goodness," was all he could find to say as he gazed at the whiteness of the sand and the deep blue water of the Atlantic as it lapped against the shoreline.

About half a mile or so away, he saw a little island with a similar white beach and what seemed to be palm trees swaying gently in the breeze.

"That's nan Eilan Beag which means the small island," Lorna said.

"Are those Palm trees?"

"Oh yes, lots of the islands around here have them. The Gulf stream passes around this coastline bringing warm water."

"Gosh, it really *is* like a paradise island," Colin said in amazement.

"Shall we take a walk?" Lorna suggested. "Let's take our shoes off, the sand is so warm and soft."

So, they left their shoes by the car and stepped onto the soft carpet of white sand. Colin felt like he was walking on a soft cloud made of warm cotton wool. He slipped his hand into Lorna's as they walked and asked, "How are you feeling about things now sweetheart? I hope I didn't pressurise you into saying yes."

"Goodness me, certainly not. I have to admit that I was a bit surprised, but it was a good surprise! Honestly Colin, I really have never been so happy."

"Oh, I am so pleased, but I haven't got a ring to give you, I'll bring one back with the next time I come up from Glasgow, it's all I can do. Oh dear, is that okay?"

"Don't be worrying about that, I have your promise and that is good enough for me – for now…" Lorna smiled, stopped, turned and kissed him. They held each other for several minutes before Colin said, "That's great, now we have some decisions and plans to make, are you okay with that?"

"Just try and stop me!" Lorna laughed and ran ahead calling Colin to chase her. They ran along the beach laughing as if they hadn't a care in the world.

They walked for what seemed like miles, talking and laughing.

Colin stopped and said in a serious voice, "I have the interview at the church in the morning, I suppose we had better not make too many plans just yet, they might not want me as their minister."

Lorna had forgotten about the interview but she knew that everyone wanted him as their minister. "Don't worry about that darling, they all love you, but who wouldn't, you're so loveable!"

Colin blushed and replied, "Well, I don't know about that…"

"Well, I do, that's why I love you so much," Lorna said as she hugged him, and they walked back to the car arm in arm.

Lorna had been busy and produced a flask of tea, and scones with butter and jam wrapped in greaseproof paper and in a metal sandwich box, and they sat on the beach and enjoyed their picnic. It reminded Colin of the picnics that he used to enjoy at Ayr beach with his mother and Aunty Bunty, when he was a boy.

Colin was feeling emotional as he kissed Lorna on the cheek and said a simple, heartfelt, "Thank you," to her.

"What was that for?" Lorna asked.

"Just because……"

They smiled at each other, and they both knew that they had met their soulmate.

Chapter 13

A Trip around the Island

Colin and Lorna drove around Rhua for most of the afternoon with Lorna pointing out a number of places of interest. There was the Witches Cave, the Selkie's grave, the Bay of Sorrows and many more places with interesting sounding names.

"What a lot of fascinating places there are on Rhua," Colin said.

"Aye, Rhua's history goes back for centuries, some say it has been here since before the dawn of time," Lorna said with a hint of pride in her voice. "There have been Bishops, battles and Bards. Fairies, Seals, Mermaids, Banshees and strange happenings which defy any reasonable explanation, all recorded here on Rhua. It is said that there is a book, written in an ancient Gaelic tongue, a tongue long since lost, which tells the early history of Rhua with stories, poems, drawings and magical spells which were all part of our heritage. Some of the old bodachs (old men) can remember many of the stories which were handed down to them but were sworn to secrecy. Old Mrs Black is said to be descended from a witch called Corrag who cast spells on her neighbours cattle if there was any dispute between them. Even yet, most of the islanders keep a safe distance from her."

"Sounds fascinating, can you remember what the book is called?"

"I think it's called, 'The Black Book of Rhua' or something like that, but I'm not sure. Old Mr McLean at CulBaithen Farm would know, he has studied the tongue and traditions of the early Irish Gaelic settlers who brought their mystical ways with them.

There is an ancient site on the West side of the island where there are signs of an early settlement, close to Mr McLean's farm.

St CulBaithen was an early Saint who lived here, or so it is thought. He is the Patron Saint of Rhua and was one of St Columba's monks, sent over from Ireland.

This site has never been searched or excavated so who knows what secrets lie here?"

Colin was intrigued and resolved that one day he would try to find out more about this ancient site and the missing book."

Lorna looked at her watch, "Mercy, look the time! I'll have to get home to help mother with the dinner."

"Mrs McLeod will soon have my tea ready too, I'd better not be late."

As they drove back to the village, Lorna felt a deep sense of happiness. "What a lovely afternoon it's been, hasn't it sweetheart?" she said," Just being in each other's company and chatting non stop."

Colin had a twinkle in his eye as he said, "Aye, you're an awful blether!"

"It's *you* that's the blether!" Lorna answered with a giggle and hit Colin playfully on his arm, causing him to swerve and just miss a sheep that was wandering across the road.

As they drew up outside Lorna's house, she asked, "Will I see you this evening?"

"I've got my interview in the morning, so I'd better do some revision I suppose."

Lorna knew he was right but she couldn't bear the thought of having to wait until tomorrow afternoon to see him again."

"I'll come straight over to the shop after my interview and let you know how I get on," said Colin.

This perked Lorna up, "Okay sweetheart. I'll be thinking of you in the morning, I'll say a wee prayer for you."

"Thank you darling, prayer always helps," and he kissed her on the cheek before she got out and waved goodbye as Colin drove away.

Colin tooted the horn a couple of times which caused Mrs Grant, who was walking by, such a start that she and her wee dog Hamish leapt to one side and fell into a large Rhododendron bush.

He spent the evening in his bedroom reading his bible and contemplating on God's word.

It gave him great comfort and he slept well, knowing that whatever happened at the interview, it would be God's will.

Chapter 14

The Interview with the Kirk Session

It was Wednesday day morning, the day of Colin's interview with the Kirk Session, and he had wakened early, washed, dressed and was sitting on the edge his bed with a bible and a notebook at hand.

Mrs McLeod had heard him moving about and she knocked and opened his bedroom door and asked if he would like a cup of tea.

"That would be great Mrs McLeod, thank you," he laid down his bible and followed her through to the kitchen.

"I have a big day today and wanted to get myself prepared with some words from Scripture."

"Oh yes, of course, I was forgetting that that you have your meeting with the Kirk Session this morning."

"That's right Mrs McLeod, I am looking forward

to meeting them."

"And from what I hear, they are very much looking forward to meeting *you*," Mrs McLeod said, smiling.

"But I must confess to being a wee bit nervous," Colin admitted.

"Ah, Meenister, remember the words of Psalm 37, *"Commit your way unto the Lord; trust in Him, and He will act according to His will,"* Mrs McLeod said as she put the porridge pot on the stove and gave it a good stirring.

"Aye, you're right of course Mrs McLeod, it's in *His* hands."

The meeting had been arranged for 11am in the church hall and Colin arrived in good time.

As he got out of the car, he heard a buzz of excitement as the Elders chatted outside the church.

"Well, he's here anyway," one said.

"Aye that's a good sign, oh, I do hope he likes us and wants to stay!" said another.

The side door of the Church opened and a stern looking lady in brown tweeds said loudly, "Come along now, we don't have all day, we have a meeting to attend, important church business to deal with!"

She reminded Colin of a school head mistress calling the children into class.

It was Mrs Killmennie, the Assistant Clerk to the Kirk Session. She looked over at Colin and raised her eyebrows as if to say, *"Sorry about the noisy children."* Colin smiled and looked out over the machair, the rain wasn't far away.

Dr Eustace Killmennie, the Session Clerk, called the meeting to order and the Rev McCrimmond, the local Free church minister, opened the meeting with a prayer.

Dr Killmennie explained the purpose of the meeting, of which everyone there was already fully aware, and clarified how the meeting would proceed.

Agenda
1. The Minister would be called in and welcomed.
2. Various questions would be put to him by Dr

Killmennie.

3. Other pre-prepared questions would be asked.

4. Members of the committee would be free to ask. questions.

5. Rev Campbell would be asked if he had any questions to the Committee.

6. Rev Campbell would be asked to retire from the meeting.

7. The committee would discuss and then vote on the suitability of Rev. Campbell for the post of Minister of Rhua Parish church.

8. Rev Campbell would be called back into the meeting and informed of the committee's decision.

9. Rev Campbell would then be asked if he wished to respond.

10. Dr Killmennie would sum up and the meeting would be closed with prayer.

Dr Killmennie handed out a number of slips of paper, each piece had a question typed on it, and then he asked the other members to think about any other questions they might have.

It was all very organised, just as Dr Killmennie liked it.

After a few moments, at exactly 11am, Colin was called into the meeting and welcomed.

The meeting was very amicable and went more or less as planned, until that is, it came time for 'any other questions' – item 4 on the agenda. It was as Dr Killmennie had feared.

Mrs Grant's question was, "What are your feelings about putting out the washing on the Sabbath?" and Mr Beattie wanted to know how the Minister felt about feeding the cows on the Lord's day.

Colin was taken aback and elected to take the road of least resistance and answered, "Well, the scriptures tell us that the Sabbath is to be kept holy," which brought a general murmur of approval.

Before Mrs McKenzie could ask about baking scones on the Sabbath day, Dr Killmennie intervened and suggested that was quite enough questions for today and moved on to item 5 and asked Colin if he had any questions for the committee.

"Well, perhaps just one," Colin said, "If you deem me to be suitable, and don't want to be presumptuous, but when do you think I might expect to start?"

Dr Kilmennie said, "From our point of view, as soon as possible!"

"Well, I have a few things to tie up in Glasgow, so perhaps 3 or 4 weeks time, would that suit?"

Everyone nodded and agreed that would be fine.

There being no further questions, Colin was invited to retire to the hall and enjoy a cup of tea and a scone provided by the ladies of the church.

The committee came to a decision in record time and Colin was called back into the Session room before he could finish his cup of tea and taste one of Mrs McMaster's tasty fruit scones.

Dr Killmennie informed Colin that the committee were pleased to recommend him to the congregation for the post of Minister.

All that was left to do was for Colin to preach to the congregation and they would vote for or against him. The Kirk Session saw this as being a mere formality but it had to be done and so it was agreed that he would preach on the following Sunday and that would be everything done and dusted.

This was met with warm applause from the committee as well as the cheers from the ladies out in the hall who had been 'accidentally' listening at the door.

As Colin left the church he was astonished to find a large group giving him a standing ovation. Some slapped his back while others shook his hand.
"How did you all get to know so soon?" he asked, "I only knew myself a few minutes ago!"
"Ah, the jungle drums have been beating Meenister – and right pleased we all are too! You'll be a blessing to us to be sure."
Colin became quite emotional as he struggled to get through the crowd and into the car.

He drove a short distance from the church and pulled off the road to catch his breath.

As he switched off the ignition, he gave a long, deep sigh.

So that was it – his future was rolling out before him. An impending marriage to his dear Lorna and also taking up the post of Parish Minister on a delightful Island with so many lovely people. Life was good and he closed his eyes and said a short prayer, *"Lord, your faithfulness never ceases to amaze me. You watch over me each moment of each day, leading me safely along your path. You guide me and you keep me safe. Thank you for all your goodness to me and thank you for bringing dear Lorna into my life. Thank you for leading me to this wonderful part of your kingdom and may I prove worthy of your calling to this Parish. Amen."*

A feeling of deep calm came over him and he sat for a few minutes to savour the feeling.

He had promised Lorna that he would tell her how the interview had gone, so he drove into the village and parked outside her father's shop.

Lorna must have heard his car pull up as she came

running out and hugged him, "Oh, well done sweetheart, I am so happy for you!"

At first, Colin was surprised but then he remembered that the method of communication on Rhua was faster than any modern system he could think of.
"How on earth did you know already? Of course, the jungle drums!?"
"Yes sweetheart," Lorna said smiling, "Mrs Campbell was accidentally listening at the church window and raced over on her bike to let me know." Colin couldn't help but laugh.

He looked forward to many happy years on this beautiful Island with lovely people and the most beautiful wife. Life was good.
Thanks to God who had planned it all.

Chapter 15

From the Sublime to the ridiculous

As Colin entered the Emporium, the ladies who were browsing in the 'latest thing from Oban' aisle turned and clapped and cheered.

Lorna's father came through from the office to see what the commotion was all about when he saw Colin and Lorna, arm in arm walking down towards him. He smiled and joined in the applause, "Well done your Reverendship! It's a happy day for Rhua – and for our family. It's blessed that we are, aye blessed!"

The clapping began to fade after a few minutes causing Harrold to glower at them and they clapped all the louder with renewed enthusiasm.

"Oh gosh!" was all Colin could say.

"Don't be shy sweetheart," Lorna said as she hugged him even tighter, "They are so pleased that you are going to be our new Meenister. You'll be a breath of fresh air to us all, just what Rhua is needing. Father is right, you are a blessing to us! The good Lord is surely looking down upon us."

Seeing the joy and the enthusiasm all around him Colin began to feel quite emotional. Lorna saw him struggling to keep his composure and led him into the office and took a small, embroidered handkerchief from the sleeve of her cardigan and dabbed his eyes. Her heart went out to him and she knew that she would always love this kind, caring, funny, emotional man of God – and she knew that she was the luckiest girl in all the world.

Sensing the touching moment taking place in the office, a silence had fallen over the customers in the shop. The ladies looked at each other, smiling and feeling quite tearful. "Och is it not just a wonderful day? The Lord is good indeed!" said one lady.
"Aye, he is that!" replied another, "I can't remember the last time my Archie showed me any affection."
"Neither can I!" another lady added.
"My Donald is the very same" said another.

"Huh! I can't remember my Calum *ever* showing me any fondness, well, there was that one time when he came home from the Bothan with a good head of steam on him… but that's another story," said yet another lady.

A warm, mellow feeling spread throughout the shop as old memories came flooding back. Even Lorna's father recalled the first date he and his dear wife had gone on. Happy days.

The atmosphere was suddenly broken when the shop door burst open and in came the Post Mistress shouting, "Oh Mercy me, mercy me. It's a disaster! it's a disaster! The Lochinver's broken down in the Sound of Mull. It'll not be over to Rhua today!"

"You know what that means don't you father?" Lorna said quietly. "What's that Lorna?" he replied with a puzzled expression on his face.

"It means that there will be no delivery of the *'bodyfirm corsets'* this week," she whispered.

Harrold quickly realised the gravity of the situation – takings would be down this week!

He stood looking around with a glazed expression saying, "No corsets this week? No corsets?....but, but....."

"What's that you say?" asked Mrs McAlister, "No corsets this week!?" There was a sudden silence in the shop as the news sank in and then mayhem broke out with customers running this way and that. Some were rifling through the bloomers and others looking under tables and opening large wooden drawers where the surplus stock was kept, all in the forlorn hope that perhaps Mr MacDonald may have missed an 'illicit corset' or two.

Harrold was quite shocked at the mayhem, "Ladies! Ladies! For goodness sake, calm down!" but no one heard his pleas.

Just at that, Lorna got up on to a table, put two fingers in her mouth and gave a loud, shrill whistle.

Everyone stopped and looked at Lorna. They had never heard her whistle in such a way before – neither had Colin, he was quite taken aback.

As silence rang out across the room, Lorna's father was shocked to see his demure daughter whistle in such a loud, course way. "Lorna MacDonald! Where in earth did you learn to whistle like that!?"

"When I was young and used to help uncle Hector round up his cows at the croft. He taught me how to call them in from the hill."
"I might have known thon Hector would have a hand in it!" Lorna's father was not best pleased.
The ladies just stood and stared at Lorna. "Well, I never," said Mrs MacDonell, "You have a fair set of lungs on you young lady, I'll give you that."
 Lorna blushed and bowed her head "I'm sorry father, I just thought it was getting a bit out of hand."
"Ah well, it's right that you are, it certainly got everyone's attention to be sure," said her father, smiling.

One or two of the ladies saw the funny side of things and began to laugh, soon everyone was in good spirits.

"You're certainly full of surprises," Colin said with a chuckle as he helped Lorna down from the table.

"Yes," said Lorna with a cheeky smile, "And if you don't behave when we are married, I'll be whistling at *you* my lad!" She winked at Colin and walked into the office.

Colin was stunned for a moment or two – then burst out laughing. *"What a girl,"* he thought, shaking his head, *"What a girl!"*

Chapter 16

Aye, it's a great thing the discreshancy

It was soon lunch time and Lorna asked her father if she could go out for lunch with Colin. "We'll just go to the hotel for a pot of tea and some sandwiches, is that okay father?"

"Of course, my sweet, but be sure and not be late back after lunch, you know how busy we can be on the last Wednesday afternoon of the month." He whispered under his breath to Colin, "That's when I reduced the prices for those on the Unemployment Benefit - *the Buroo*," and he tapped his nose and winked knowingly.

"But of course, I don't advertise it. Aye, it's a great thing the discreshancy," Mr MacDonald said quietly. If his arms had been longer he would have patted himself on the back.

Lorna and Colin chatted excitedly over lunch in the Kinlochmhor Hotel but Colin noticed that the locals were looking at him and whispering to each other.

"What's going on? Have they not seen a Minister before?" Colin felt quite conspicuous in his clerical collar.

"Oh yes, they've seen a Meenister before but they have never seen a Meenister in the bar before."

"Not even the Reverend McCrimmond?" Colin was surprised to hear that.

"Oh, he never comes in here," Lorna said, "He is regularly seen going in and out of the Bothan, but he insists it's for purely for Pastoral purposes!" Lorna winked knowingly to Colin who took a minute or two before saying, "Pastoral? Oh right!" and they both laughed, causing a few tuts and more whispering.

Colin gave a wry smile as the irony had been completely missed by the onlookers, not seeing that they too were drinking in the bar at lunchtime, the very same offense for which they were condemning Colin. He remembered the saying, "*A hypocrite is someone who conveniently forgets their own faults so they can point out the same faults in others.*"

He looked over at the group standing at the bar, lifted his glass of Iron Brew (which looks like whisky, to the untrained eye) said "Slainte!" and knocked it back in one while the lads looked on in awe and wonder.

Lorna laughed and said, "Colin Campbell, the devil is in you today!"

Colin walked Lorna back to the shop and as they stood at the door he said, "Well, you are going to be busy this afternoon, I think I'll go back to Mrs McLeod's and plan out my service for Sunday. Are you still okay to come up to the croft tomorrow to help me sort things out?"

"Yes, I've arranged the day off with father. What time will you pick me up?"

They agreed to meet at 9.30 in the morning and parted with a hug and a lingering kiss.

Colin spent the rest of the day in his bedroom reading his bible, taking notes and looking for some divine inspiration for his service on Sunday.

Throughout the afternoon Mrs McLeod would pop in with cups of tea and home made treacle scones. "Aye, the brain is fed by the word of God, but the body needs feeding too!" she said as she placed a tray on the small table at his bedside.

"Oh, Mrs McLeod, you are an angel in disguise." Colin was beginning to get a soft spot for her.

"Och away with you! It's the charmer that you are!" she said as she ran her fingers through her hair and blushed.

"It's a nice piece of Sea Trout that you'll be getting for your tea tonight. They say fish is good for the brain."

"That will be just perfect Mrs McLeod, I need all the help I can get!"

"Well, there's a washing to do and a carpet to beat out on the wash-line so I'd better get my sleeves rolled up and get on with it. I'll leave you in peace Meenister, and don't worry, the good Lord will provide you with the words you need, he always has in the past, I'm sure."

"You are quite right Mrs McLeod, '*put your trust in Him,*' the good book tells us," Colin said with growing confidence.

He never used notes when preaching, he had always found that when preaching, the words came to him as he needed them, his 'divine prompter' had never failed him.

Every Sermon, for Colin, was about bringing meaning to those Ancient words found in the bible and explaining their relevance to our everyday lives in the here and now.

However, he felt that this Sermon was also to be one which would bring both comfort and hope to the good people of Rhua.

He deeply believed that God was calling him to the Island to bring a new era of faith and spiritual renewal and he wanted to be sure to convey that clearly to them. There are many passages in that holy book which talk about making a new start – and Colin had the spark of an idea which ones he would use.

He knew that Lorna, her mother and father, as well as a good many other Islanders, of all denominations and none, would be in church on Sunday and he admitted to being more than a touch nervous.

The evening meal was Sea Trout as promised and both Mrs McLeod and Colin enjoyed a good chat about the Island, the Church and some background to the people and their beliefs.
Calum McLeod was 'at work' which Colin had learned meant, 'away poaching.'

"Would I be right in saying that the islanders are very superstitious, Mrs McLeod?" Colin asked.
"Superstitious isn't a word that we would use, Meenister. It's more about tradition and heritage. Many of our 'superstitions,' as you would call them, come down to us from our ancient ancestors, and in turn they would have had them handed down from *their* ancestors from away back before our time began. The Celtic race were a people who were in tune with their surroundings, the trees,

rivers, wells, lochs and the animals which live alongside us. They understood the language of nature, the whispers of the wind, the movements of the moon and how it affects our everyday lives.

We don't dismiss talk of Kelpies – water-horses, or Selkies, *they're Seals who can interchange between seal and human form.* We don't believe that Fairies or Fae folk are a figment of imagination but part of a very real world which co-exists with ours. A world that only the few can see.

It's a matter of respect for things that we don't always understand.

Like those among us who have the 'gift' of 'second sight' or those who have the healing hands.

Many of our beliefs flourished in the old world, but the more 'civilised' we become, the less we understand what is going on all around us..

"Gosh, Mrs McLeod, I hadn't thought of it like that! You put it so convincingly that I feel guilty of my own ignorance of such a world."

"Don't worry Meenister, we'll soon educate you

once you are living here," Mrs McLeod said with a kindly smile. "Anyway, it's time for another cup of tea, don't you think?"

"Absolutely, Mrs McLeod, absolutely." Colin was enjoying his chat with Mrs McLeod and was fascinated with her view of the two worlds co-existing.

"But where is our great God in all of this?" he asked.

Mrs McLeod sat down with the empty teapot in her hand "The good book tells us that "God created the heavens and the earth and all that is in it." He is the great Father of <u>all</u> life, and we assume that means only <u>us</u>, here on this small planet - but our God is greater than we could ever imagine, He is the God of the Universe and the creator of *all* life contained within it. There is nothing He can't do, nothing he can't create, so why is it such a leap of faith for us to imagine that there are other worlds, other life forms which coexist alongside of us, if we have the eyes to see them?"

Colin was astonished at the conviction and wisdom of Mrs McLeod.

"Gosh Mrs McLeod, I have to say that you put up a very convincing case. And you are quite right, of course, that God can make or create anything He likes. Mark's gospel tells us that, *"With God, <u>all</u> things are possible."*

"Exactly my point Meenister!" said Mrs McLeod as she measured 3 spoonful's of tea from the tea caddy into the teapot. "One for each person and one for the pot and stir it three time clockwise and three times anti clockwise, as my dear mother, God rest her soul, used to say."

Why three times each way Mrs McLeod?" Colin was intrigued.

" Three and three - thirty three – the age of our dear Lord Jesus when he passed on to higher glory."

Colin was fascinated, much of Mrs McLeod's words seemed to go against all that he believed, yet it all made complete sense.

He had a good night's sleep despite his head being full of fairies, seals, kelpies and all sorts of strange beings. He had experienced similar dreams before but couldn't make sense of them, but now, perhaps subconsciously, they were trying to give him a new sense of awareness and understanding.

Perhaps.

He still wasn't fully convinced.

Chapter 17

Are ye Dancing? – are ye asking?

The next morning Colin picked up Lorna at 9.30 as arranged and drove over to his Grandparent's croft, which was on the eastern side of the island known as Clochan, so called because of an old stone dwelling which looked like a big beehive, where it is said that one of St Columba's Irish monks, St Baithene, had lived around 570 AD.

As they drove towards his grandparent's croft, Colin could feel his stomach doing somersaults.
It was a beautiful, idyllic scene with the tiny homestead surrounded by a mass of bright purple heather and a small burn running alongside. The heather seemed to be glowing and the burn was like a silver thread running through it as it twisted and turned its way down the hill beside the little croft.
They found the key 'hidden' under a flat stone by the back door and let themselves in.

It was dark as he and Lorna had closed the curtains the last time he was on Rhua, *for the funeral of his dear grandmother*, and the mirror above the fireplace was covered over, as was the custom when someone had passed on.

It gave a warm, tranquil, atmosphere and Colin felt a sense of humility and peace as they stood and took in the sight and smells which greeted them.

'This place, this house, this Island, is where my family originated,' Colin thought to himself. He felt Lorna squeeze his arm. "It's perfect," she said, close to tears.

"Yes, it is," Colin agreed. "I feel that I know this place but how could I? I was born and brought up in Glasgow and have never visited Rhua until recently."

"Aye, maybe your *body* has never been here before but perhaps your *soul* has," Lorna whispered as she looked around the room.

She felt 'something,' something she couldn't quite explain but it told her that this was a special place, a place of peace, calm and more importantly, she felt the presence of God.

"God is here, I can feel it Colin. Your grandmother's neighbour, Mrs McLean, sat with her as she passed on and said that she heard your grandmother talking, asking for God's forgiveness for herself and blessings on her family.

Then she opened her eyes, smiled and held out her hands and said, *"Ah, it's yourself, Lord, you have come for me at last, take my hand and take me with you,"* and she closed her eyes, held out her hand and took her leave of this world.

Mrs McLean said she heard a most beautiful choir singing as your grandmother passed with a contented smile on her face."

Colin and Lorna hugged. "You've come home sweetheart, your roots are here," Lorna said, "This is where you belong."

"Yes, thanks to you Lorna, you really are my soulmate," Colin struggled to hold back the tears, tears of happiness and thanksgiving.

"Not thanks to *me* sweetheart, thanks to God who brought us together and led us to this heavenly place."

They opened the curtains and removed the towel that had been placed over the mirror.

As they walked through the rooms, they both agreed that this was no 'empty cottage' but there was a real sense of peace and serenity in every corner of the home.

"Well, where do we start?" Colin wondered.

"How about we start with a cup of tea?" Lorna said as she sat down, opened a shopping bag and brought out a small bottle of milk, a tartan vacuum flask of tea and a brown paper bag with homemade fruit scones which she had made earlier that morning and were still warm.

Colin smiled, "You think of everything," he said, and he leaned over and kissed her on the cheek.

Lorna was having a lovely day and she was sure that there would be many more such days with this wonderful man.

Lorna began in the bedroom, while Colin looked around the living room, chatting as they tidied up. After a wee while, Lorna noticed that Colin was very quiet, so she went through.

"What have you got there?" she asked, as Colin took the lid off of a large tin box.

"I've come across some more old photos, mostly family I think, how stern they all look," Colin said as he rifled through the sea of faces which looked out at him.

"Aye, life was hard in those days – not a lot to smile about I suppose," replied Lorna. "But they had each other, just like us. We'll be together whatever life throws at us, won't we?"

"We certainly will sweetheart, God is good," said Colin as he leaned over and kissed her on her cheek.

They sat in silence for a few minutes, looking through the photo's, just enjoying each other's company.

They continued to tidy up, stopping here and there as they came across things which caught their attention – and it wasn't long before Colin said, "Well, it must be lunch time, fancy a pot of tea for two and a wee sandwich at the hotel?"

Lorna never said 'no' to a pot of tea, so they drove into the village, not bothering to lock the door, after all who would break in? No-one on the Island ever locked their doors.

Lunch went well, a group of lads were standing at the bar, smiling at Colin and saying, "See you on Sunday Meenister! You've got my vote. Will you take a dram yourself?"

Colin politely refused, saying, "Not today boys, but thanks for the offer!" It seemed that Colin had been accepted by 'the boys.'

In the afternoon Colin and Lorna continued working their way around the wee croft, tidying and putting things aside either for keeping or to be disposed of.

Colin had found a gramophone record player with an image of a dog looking down a large phonograph, along with a number of 78 rpm records in faded sleeves.

As he looked through them, he recognised some old songs that his other grandmother used to play. They brought back happy memories.

After a while he realised that Lorna was very quiet and he went through to find Lorna sitting on the bed with a large jewellery box in her hands.

"Look at this!" she said excitedly.

As she opened the box it played a tune and a tiny ballerina twirled as if doing a pirouette.

Lorna was fascinated as she had never seen anything like it before.

"What's inside?" Colin asked.

"I haven't looked, I didn't like to, without asking you."

As Lorna opened the box fully and lifted out a thin wooden lid, they saw quite a number of items of jewellery, some of which looked a bit dated to Colin, not that he was an expert on women's jewellery. Lorna took out various bracelets, necklaces and rings.

"Oh Colin, they're beautiful," she said as she laid

them out on the pink candlewick bed spread.

As she rummaged through the contents, she opened a small drawer inside the box and saw the most beautiful ring. As she lifted it out she gasped and said, "That's strange, it feels warm."

"How can it be warm, silly?" Colin said as Lorna handed him the ring. "Gosh, you're right sweetheart, sorry, it *is* warm. How peculiar!"

Lorna was transfixed by its beauty, "Oh Colin, it's *so* beautiful and there's something very special about it, I can feel it. It's as if your dear grandmother had just taken it off."

They looked at each other for a few moments – surely it couldn't be – could it? Laura felt a tingle run up her spine.

"Try it on sweetheart." Lorna didn't need to be told twice, and she slipped it on her finger.

How does it fit?" Colin asked.

"Perfectly, it could have been made for me," and she stretched out her hand and turned it left and right until it glinted in the light of the bedside lamp. "Oh, isn't it just beautiful?" Lorna was captivated by its beauty and the wonderful feeling of calm that it gave her.

"Can I see it?" Colin took the ring and felt it's gentle warmth. He got down on one knee, took Lorna's left hand and offered up his grandmother's ring and said, "I know I didn't do things right the first time when I blurted out about being your fiancé without asking you - but now I am going to ask you properly – Lorna MacDonald, will you marry me?"

Lorna felt as if she was floating in a dream, and immediately answered, "Yes, YES! Of course I will." Colin pushed the ring on to her wedding finger and said, "You have made me the happiest man in the world."

They stood and hugged, just savouring the moment. It was just as Lorna had dreamed – a lovely man, a lovely ring and a lovely future to look forward to, *"What more could any girl ask for?"* She admired her new engagement ring and said, "Colin, do you think that your grandmother left this ring just for me?"

"No doubt about it sweetheart. Aunty Bunty once told me that my grannie had 'the gift,' so I am quite sure that she left it there, just for you."

He leaned over to the old gramophone, wound it up and placed the needle onto one of the records. It crackled and then started to play, "There's a wee hoose amang the heather," by Harry Lauder.

Then he asked, "Excuse me Miss, may I have the honour of the next dance?"
Lorna giggled and said, "Of course, kind sir, if you're asking."
"Aye, I'm asking."
"Then I'm dancing," and they slowly danced their way around the living room, as if in some wonderful dream.

Chapter 18

A Surprise Gift from Grannie

They agreed that they were far too excited to carry on tidying up the Croft and headed back into the village to show Lorna's mother her beautiful engagement ring.

"Oh Lorna, it's absolutely beautiful and it fits you perfectly!" Lorna's mother said.

"Yes, it was in Mrs McGillivray's jewellery box," Lorna said excitedly, "It was just sitting there waiting for me to find it!"

"It's blessed that you are, the good Lord is watching over you to be sure." Lorna's mother looked up at Colin and took a hold of his hand.

"Thank you so much, you have made my daughter, and me, very happy indeed. May the Almighty bless you!"

"And may He bless you too Mrs MacDonald."

All three had a tear in their eye when uncle Hector walked in. "What's going on, has the cat died?" He said in his usual misplaced, jovial way.

Lorna couldn't speak but held out her left hand for her uncle to see. "Oh my goodness, what a beautiful ring. Who's the lucky man?" Hector winked at Colin.

"Hector, it's the Meenister!"

"Oh, so it is!" he laughed. "We had better celebrate this suspicious occasion with a dram," and he walked over to the side-board and took out a bottle of whisky which was about half full. Lorna's mother was sure that bottle was full when she went to bed last night.

"Not for me, thank you Hector," Colin said, "I have the car outside."

"I drive better _with_ a good dram in," Hector boasted. "Instead of seeing one white line on the road, I actually see two, and make a bee-line between the two of them!"

"Hector, it's only the middle of the afternoon!" Lorna's mother said.

Hector had never understood what the time of the

day had to do with taking a dram, for him, *any* time was a suitable time for a 'wee sensation.' So he shrugged his shoulders, poured himself a more than generous dram and held it up high and said, "To Lorna and the Meenister on their engagement!" and downed it in one.

He poured himself a second dram and toasted, "May they have many happy years together!"

He was just about to pour a third dram when Lorna's mother said sternly, "Ok Hector, I think that's enough now!"

"Och Peggy, I was just about to put up a great toast about the patter of tiny feet." Hector was in full flight now.

"That's enough Hector. I don't think it's appropriate to be talking about 'the patter of tiny feet' when the Meenister is here, thank you very much!"

Colin looked at Lorna who was blushing and they both burst out laughing, more out of embarrassment than anything else.

"I'll get the kettle on," Lorna's mother said

awkwardly – any one for tea?"

*

Lorna's father was busy in the shop, he had received another consignment of the new 'racy' corsets, among other items such as woollen lingerie, heavy duty stockings and packs of various coloured hairnets.

"These fancy new items should fly off of the shelf," he said to himself, humming a Gaelic tune.

The shop door opened and an old gentleman wandered in off of the street and went over to the counter and asked, "Can I be having a postal order for 5 shillings please Miss MacDonnell?"

Harrold smiled and said in a soft voice, "Good afternoon Fachie, I think you're getting a wee bit mixed up again."

"Is this not the Post Office?" he asked looking around.

"No, this the Emporium, Fachie, the Post Office is next door."

"Are you new here? Where is Miss MacDonnell the Post Mistress?"

144

"She's in the post office. This is the emporium."

"Oh dear, have I done it again?" said the old gentleman realising his mistake.

"Don't you be worrying about it Fachie. If I had a postal order I would give it to you gladly, but I don't think Miss MacDonnell would be too happy with me taking away her business."

"She's never happy, she has a face that would curdle milk!" Fachie said with an impish smile.

Harrold tried not to laugh but he wasn't about to disagree with a customer.

Tactfully changing the subject, Harrold asked, "How is your good lady, Fachie?"

"Och, she's still complaining."

"Just the same then," Harrold said seriously.

"Aye, just the same. Well, I'd better be going, seeing as you have sold out of postal orders," and he wandered out of the shop.

Fachie McLean was a kindly old gentleman, he had been known as, 'The Whistling Postie' or 'Whistler' for many years. Everyone on the Island had a soft spot for him. Since retiring he was prone to walking into the wrong shop or even into the wrong house, sitting down and having a nap. People would come home and find Fachie fast asleep in the armchair, and they would wait until he wakened and give him a cup of tea and a biscuit and walk him home, to make sure he got home safely.

However, his good lady, Mrs McLean, was not so understanding. Perhaps she couldn't cope with the fact that he was no longer the man she had once married – but then, Fachie occasionally thought, *she* wasn't the woman he had married all those years ago either - but they still loved each other in their own way and had supported one another through the many ups and downs that life had thrown at them.

On top of that, Mrs McLean did make the most excellent treacle scones, which endeared her to many on the island.

Clouds and silver linings.

Chapter 19

A B C D

Friday morning saw Colin and Lorna return to the croft. Lorna continued to tidy up the rooms while Colin went out to the shed to see what he could find out there.

Just inside the door, he saw a wooden box of old tools and a neat stack of logs ready for the winter fire. There was an old scythe, a big double handed saw for felling trees, a peat cutter, a large brush (*a Besom*) made from sticks and branches, used for beating out peat or heather fires. Colin smiled as he thought it was just like the type of broomstick you might imagine a witch flying around on. Various other tools were neatly lining the whitewashed interior stone walls of the outbuilding.

Colin was surprised as he was expecting to find a jumble of junk and rusty old implements lying around.

As he looked up to the eaves, he saw a hand made stepladder, and a few planks and two oars lying across the beams. But then, something caught his eye – it was a tiny mouse running across a beam and it disappeared into an old boot, one of a pair, which were hanging by the laces from the wooden beam. As he looked closer he could see that a family of little field mice had made their home in the boots!

As he stood, taking in his surroundings and seeing the hills and the loch through the small window, he felt a deep sense of peace and contentment, happy to a degree that he had never experienced before. He had certainly been blessed beyond anything he could have hoped for, asked for, or deserved.

He sat on a low wooden three legged stool and said a wee prayer of thanks. He had just finished his prayer when he heard a voice saying, "Is that you skyving? I leave you alone for a few minutes and I find you sitting down!" Lorna had come to see how Colin was getting on.

"Oh, it's you sweetheart, I was just giving thanks

for all God's goodness to us."

"Yes," Lorna said, "He has certainly blessed us. Whatever have we done to deserve such happiness?"

"Nothing, that's the beauty of God's love – He loves us, not for anything *we* have done, but because of who *He* is, the God of love."

Colin stood up and they hugged each other tightly for quite a while as they tried to take it all in.

"Hello, is anyone in?" a voice broke the atmosphere.

It was Donnie D. Macdonald, an elderly man who lived in the croft just along the road.

"In here," Colin called, and the jolly red face of a large man looked into the shed.

"Och, it's here that you are. I thought I would just drop in to say hello, seeing as I am your neighbour from across the field. I'm Donnie Macdonald, no relation, we're related to the Macdonald's of Keppoch. They call me Donnie D."

"Well, Donnie D," Colin replied amiably, "It's a

pleasure to meet you. What does the D stand for, if I may ask, is it Daniel, as in the bible?"

"I'm afraid not Meenister, my parents had 4 boys and called them all Donald and I am the youngest of the four of us. To save any confusion at school my older brothers were called Donnie A, Donnie B and Donnie C, and I'm Donnie D!"

Colin couldn't help but laugh out loud, "What a great idea and so easy to remember, but would it not have been easier to call you by different names?"

"Oh no, that would never do Meenister, our father's name is Donald so we are called after him. I have a sister too." Donnie D added.

"And what is her name?" Colin inquired, almost afraid to ask.

"Don-alda!" came the reply.

Colin looked at Lorna to see if he was being serious.

"Oh yes sweetheart, that's not unusual," Lorna replied.

"Well, I never," Colin shook his head and smiled. "I see that I still have a lot to learn about the Islands."

"Don't be worrying about it Meenister, I've been here all my life and I am still trying to figure it all out!" Donnie D said with a deep, hearty laugh.

"There's hope for you yet sweetheart." Lorna said and gave Colin a kiss on the cheek.

"Well, I'll not be holding you back from, er, whatever it was you were doing, I have five little mouths to feed," said Donnie D said.

Colin looked startled at this news. Five children? he thought.

Lorna could read Colin's mind and stepped in, "Yes, Donnie has five new wee lambs to feed."

"Oh yes, lambs, of course," Colin gave a sigh of relief. He was glad that Lorna had intervened before he put his foot in it and said something inappropriate.

"Well, I'll be off, be sure and call in if you need anything, anything at all." Donnie D strode out and across the field singing, *"I'm following in*

Father's footsteps, following my dear old dad…" which had been sung by the music hall star Vesta Tilley. Happy days.

With the croft being tidied up, Colin and Lorna sat down and started to think about their future together. They were both keen to get things moving but knew that there was much to arrange, and it needed careful planning.
Lots to think about.

Colin always carried a notebook and pencil in his pocket and they spent the rest of the day excitedly making notes as they planned their future together.

Chapter 20

David and Goliath

The next morning the sun was shining into Colin's bedroom prompting him to get up early and take a walk along the road from the McLeod's croft, up to the crossroads a mile or so up the narrow single track road.

As he walked, his head was full of so many things, such as leaving his home in Glasgow and moving away to a remote island leaving behind his Aunty Bunty and Mrs McRae his trusty housekeeper, not to mention his friends. Then there was the church service on Sunday – and of course, the wedding and all the planning that would need to be done prior to that. His heart raced as he considered it all, it would be a busy time ahead, would it all work out smoothly?

He turned around intending to walk back to the croft, when the smells of the bog myrtle and the incredible views in all directions forced him to stop and take a deep breath as he looked around this beautiful wee Island.

"Surely, if there is a heaven on earth, this must be it," he thought as he gazed at God's amazing handiwork.

He suddenly heard a cry of distress from a bird above him. He wasn't very well acquainted with the names of the different birds but as he looked up he saw a small brown bird being chased by what he thought was a hawk of some description. He was transfixed by the chase which unfolded before him.

Up and down, left and right, the small bird swerved this way and that in an attempt to save its own life. Then as quickly as it started, it all went quiet. Colin couldn't see either bird and feared that the smaller bird must have drawn its final breath. But then, falling out of the sky, the hawk dropped like a stone, making no sound other than its wings rustling in the wind. The smaller bird flew up and just as the hawk was about to strike, it turned about sharply and the hawk crashed into a clump of bright purple heather. It let out a screech, shook his head and stood for a few moments gathering his wits before flying away, no doubt with a sore head and quite possibly a dented ego too, if birds have ego's, that is.

Colin couldn't help smiling at the quick witted small bird who had outsmarted it's bigger and more hostile attacker.
It reminded him of the biblical account where David, the boy shepherd, overcame the giant Goliath against all the odds.

He thought of all that lay ahead for Lorna and himself, and he knew that with faith, trust and perseverance, all their obstacles, no matter how daunting, would be overcome too.
He stepped out with renewed enthusiasm and he was soon back, sitting at the kitchen table eating a bowl of Mrs McLeod's hot porridge with a cup of cream on the side.
"A sign from God and bowl of porridge, what better way to start the day?" he thought.

Lorna had managed to persuade her father to give her the day off so that she could spend more time with Colin before he went back to Glasgow.

"Of course, sweetheart, I think it's going to be a quiet day in the shop. It's a dull, dreich day, a day for the fireside. Have you done your wee jobs for your mother?"

"Yes, father, the fire is made, the milk is in the cold press, and the tatties and the vegetables are all prepared and steeping in a bowl of water by the sink in the scullery - and the scones for your strupach are all made and in the biscuit tin," Lorna said.

"You're a good girl to be sure, we're going to miss you once you are married and have a home of your own."

"But this will always be home to me, it's where you and mother are, it's where my heart will be." Lorna gave her father a hug, and a tear fell from her eye. "I'll always love you, wherever I may be," and she could feel her father hug her even tighter.

Colin came into the shop to see if Lorna had managed to get the day off. She spotted him coming in the door and ran over to him and put her arms around him and said, "Oh Colin!" and buried her head in his chest and said, "I love you," over and over again.

"Goodness me, whatever brought all this on sweetheart?"

Lorna attempted to compose herself but the tears wouldn't stop running down her cheeks.

"Oh, I don't know, I think it's all just hit me, how blessed I am to have such a wonderful man who loves me and a loving, caring family too. And on top of that you will be going away on Monday and I don't know when I will see you again. You *will* come back won't you? I couldn't bear it if you didn't." Lorna's tears flowed once more.

"Of course I'll be back silly, just as soon as I can wrap things up in Glasgow, I'll be back, I promise."

"Promise?"

"I promise," Colin smiled, "And now, where's that beautiful smile?"

"I'm sorry, I'm just being silly but it all seems too good to be true and I'm afraid that it might all fall apart."

Colin took out his handkerchief and wiped away her tears.

"Thank you sweetheart, what must you think of me?"

"What I think is that you are the loveliest, most kind, caring and beautiful person in the world and I love you so much, that's what I think of you."

Colin put his arms around her and held her close.

After a few minutes they became aware that a small group of ladies were silently standing, each with a tear in their eye, watching as the 'happy couple' declare their undying love for each other.

"Och, is that not just the most beautiful moment you have ever seen?" Mrs Cameron said to her friends. Some of the ladies couldn't speak, others nodded and wiped their eyes as they sniffled and coughed.

Colin and Lorna looked at each other and smiled,

"Aye, we really are blessed!" Colin said, feeling quite emotional himself.

Lorna's father watched it all and said, "Well, we'd better get on," as he wiped his eyes. "Lots to do, these combinations won't fold themselves up and jump onto the shelf you know!"
There was a moment's silence as his words sunk in, they all looked at each other - and then erupted in laughter. "Now, that _would_ be a sight for sore eyes to be sure Mr MacDonald!" Mrs McLean remarked, bringing more laughter from everyone, everyone except Lorna's father who feigned a smile so as not to show his embarrassment.

Colin and Lorna drove up to his grandmother's croft – it seemed the perfect place to talk, its air of peace and tranquillity were just what they needed as they planned their future life together.

Chapter 21

In God we Trust

The croft was unusually warm, considering it was a miserable day outside, and Colin and Lorna chatted excitedly about their future together.

"Things _will_ work out won't they Colin?" Lorna asked anxiously.

"Of course they will sweetpea, Everything will go to plan, there might be one or two hiccups along the way but we _will_ get there, I just know it."

Colin sounded genuinely convinced, so much so that Lorna felt a shiver of excitement run through her body. "Whoever would have thought that your dear grandmother's passing would have led to this? Do you think she knew this would happen? After all she did have 'the gift' of the second sight."

"Yes, I am convinced she knew something," Colin said, "after all, if she had asked Reverend McCrimmond to take her funeral, you and I would never have met. I think she knew exactly what she was doing."

As they sat, taking in the emotional feeling that their meeting was somehow 'meant to be' and not some random kind of lucky encounter, the little musical jewellery box in the bedroom unexpectantly began to play Schubert's Ava Maria. Looking at each other they stood up, held hands and went through to his grandparents bedroom and there on the little table, the music box was playing and the tiny ballerina was dancing to the music.

Coincidence? Lorna and Colin knew that it was much more than that, it was the stamp of approval from Colin's late grandmother, Martha MacGillivray.

"That's Martha letting us know that she approves of our love for each other and our future together," Lorna said with happy tears in her eyes.

They stood and watched the ballerina dance until the music slowed down and finally stopped.

Colin said, "I hate to spoil this special moment but I really will have to get going and finish off my service for the morning."

"Of course sweetheart, it's going to be a big day for you – and don't worry, they will love you and vote for you, you're the best thing that has happened to this Island in many years, everyone says so, especially me! I can't wait for you to be my Minister," Lorna said smiling.

"And husband, I hope!" Colin reminded her with a smile.

"Of course, and husband!" Lorna squeezed Colin tightly and kissed him on the cheek.

Colin dropped Lorna off at her home and went on to Mrs McLeod's croft where he spent the rest of the afternoon and evening running through his Bible readings and Sermon for Sunday morning. Tomorrow was going the be an important day as the congregation made their decision on whether or not to accept him as their Minister.

But what would they do if the church folk *didn't* vote for him? It didn't bear thinking about.

A sudden rush of panic ran through him before he reminded himself that it was all in God's hands. That gave him a profound sense of contentment as he got ready for bed.

He slept right through until Mrs McLeod woke him the next morning with a cup of tea.

"Good morning Meenister, it's a glorious morning, the Lord is looking down on us this Sabbath day. I've have a cup of tea for you – and a wee surprise to get your day off to a good start."

Colin looked over and saw a cup of tea and a plate with two custard creams on it. She knew that he was partial to a custard cream or two and had bought them specially from Mr Ali's shop in the village for him.

He smiled and said, "Oh Mrs McLeod you really are one of God's angels. Who could ask for a better start than with a nice cup of tea and two custard creams?" Colin smiled and said quietly, "Thank you Mrs McLeod, that was a lovely thing to do."

Chapter 22

At Your Service

Well, this was the big day, Sunday, the day he had been planning, preparing and praying for.
After his tea and custard creams, he rose and spent some time reading his Bible. He found that he gained strength and a feeling of calm in God's words.

He reminded himself of the main points of his sermon. Colin had crafted his service to contain three main points and then elaborate on each.
1. Looking back at the past, how things had been.
2. Looking at the present day, how things are, and
3. Looking ahead to the future, at what lies ahead.

He hoped that the ancient texts which he had chosen would strike a chord with the people and encourage them to work together, and with himself, to go forward with optimism and hope. That was the plan, but it's success, or not, would depend on his ability to get those important points over to the congregation. He felt that he was the weak link in the chain but prayed that God would provide him with the strength and the right words to give confidence and assurance to the good people of Rhua.

That was all very well, Colin thought, but that didn't stop the butterflies from taking flight in his stomach.

He arrived at the church in good time and found a large number of islanders had already gathered outside and were chatting. His nerves gave another jangle as he walked from his car to the church.

John McRae the Presenter and Catherine Cameron, the caretaker, were inside getting things ready for the service.

"Come away in Meenister," Catherine said, "The kettle's on, I'll make you a nice cup of tea."

"Not for me thank you Catherine, I'm afraid my stomach is a bit unstable."

"Don't you worry, I'll make you a special cup of tea that will settle your stomach," she said and gave John the presenter a wink.

John McRae smiled at Catherine and had to look away for fear of alerting Colin that Catherine was up to something.

"Everything is ready Meeenister," he said. "I'll take the bible in and then come back out for you, if that's alright."

Colin agreed, even though it wasn't his usual way, but he thought it best to do as John suggested, after all, he didn't want to get off on the wrong foot right from the start.

As he looked around, he remembered that the first time he had been in the church was when he had conducted his grandmother's funeral.

The church had been full, and the people were very kind and compassionate, he hoped they would feel the same after this morning's service!

It was five minutes before the service was due to start and Colin's butterflies were in full flight as they soared around in his stomach.

Catherine said, "Drink this Meenister, it'll settle your stomach," and handed Colin a cup of hot tea with a special ingredient added.

This time he was aware of Catherine's ploy to fire up his sermons with added enthusiasm. He knew she meant well but he felt strongly that if he was to be accepted by the congregation as their Minister, he would have to win their hearts and minds in an honest and sincere way without any enhancement from a glass of Whisky.

"Thank you Catherine, I know you mean well and I thank you for it, but I must do this under my own steam. The only spirit I want inside of me, is the Holy Spirit," Colin said firmly and politely.

John McRae the Presenter came into the kitchen and said to Colin, "Ok, Meenister, are you ready?

Before we go in, let us bow our heads in prayer."
John prayed that God's blessing be given to Colin
as he preached to God's people, in God's house."

Colin was quite taken aback and experienced a
deep feeling of calm, composure and complete
serenity as he entered into the church and up the
steps to the Pulpit.

As he turned to face the congregation, he was
overwhelmed to see that the church was absolutely
jammed packed with islanders. Every seat was
taken, there were people standing at the back too.

He stood in silence for a few moments taking it all
in, there was complete hush from the people too,
you could hear a penny drop.

Someone realised that Colin was lost for words
and started to clap to cover his embarrassment.
Others joined in and soon the whole church was
clapping Colin willing him on.

It took a few moments for him to gather his
thoughts, then he took a deep breath and held up
both of his hands and the clapping slowed then
stopped. Colin said, with a tear in his eye, "You

truly *are* God's chosen people, may He bless you, may He bless you richly and may He bless your families and loved ones too."

There was hardly a dry eye in the church as Colin's genuine emotion flooded through each one present. Everyone felt it, they were moved in a way they had never experienced before. It would be a day they would never forget, a day, a service, which would be spoken of for many years to come. *'He's the one for us!'* John the presenter thought to himself. It was a thought that was felt by everyone there.

Colin composed himself and preached the most moving and inspiring service of his life. And all without a glass of Jura in him.

At the end of the service, he came down the pulpit steps and walked through to the kitchen as the congregation stood and applauded him with great enthusiasm and warmth.

He turned to Catherine, who had followed him out of the church, and said, "I'll take that dram now Catherine."

Lorna was beaming with happiness and pride. Her mother was dabbing her tears of joy, she knew that Colin would be accepted by the people which meant an Island Wedding for her daughter and the lovely Minister who had come into all their lives, would soon to be their Minister. Now it was more than just a dream, it was a reality.

Mrs McLeod was struggling to keep her composure and her husband Calum was wiping his eyes with a rather grubby handkerchief.

"Calum McLeod, could you not have used a clean handkerchief? It's the Sabbath day you know!" Mrs McLeod was mortified, "What will people think? They will be saying that I must have run out of the soap flakes!"

"Och, loosen your stays my sweetness, the Reverend is going to be our Meenister!" Calum was excited at the prospect. He wasn't a regular church goer but with Colin as the Minister he felt sure that from now on he would be attending the church more often, after all, he wouldn't be poaching on the sabbath anyway, so it wouldn't clash with his 'business' activities.

Calum was right, it was a day of celebration, and Mrs McLeod smiled at him, wiped away another tear, then opened her handbag and handed him a clean handkerchief.

She, like everyone else, was feeling very emotional. It has been a very long time since such a moving and inspirational sermon had been preached in their church.

Colin's theme of past, present and future had struck home with the good people of Rhua. It was what they needed to hear – an acknowledgement and acceptance of the past and hope for the future.

Chapter 23

The Anonymous Vote

After the service, Dr Eustace Kilmennie, stood before the congregation and asked all those in favour of asking the Reverend Colin Campbell to take up the post of Minister of their Church, to raise their hand. Hands went up all around the church, some even raised both hands! No-one voted against, so he declared the vote to be unanimous.

Outside the church, the people gathered and there was an optimistic buzz as they chatted excitedly about their new minister.

"Wasn't he great!?" one lady said to her friends. "Aye, his preaching is much better than Mr McCrimmond's gloom and doom!" said another.

Old Donald Cleapach, the bus driver, said in a sombre tone, "Aye, McCrimmond is old fashioned, he preaches the same sermon every Sunday but just uses different words. I know I'm a sinner but I don't want to be reminded of it every week!"

The small group laughed as Donald's remarks rung a loud bell with each of them.

"Aye Donald, you're an awful man, so you are!" said wee Jean Robertson. The other ladies looked at each other and smiled as Jean and old Donald were reputed to be 'doing a line' or as some might say, 'walking out' together. Unfortunately, they were both in their late 80's and were long past walking very far.

Back in the church, Dr Kilmennie went through to the vestry and advised Colin of the congregation's wishes and asked if he was willing to accept their invitation to become the Islands' Parish Minister. As Colin said the words, "Yes, I would be happy to accept their kind invitation," he felt a warm, tingling sensation surge through his body, it was like an electric charge. He knew it was God's approval of his call, and with a future with Lorna to look forward to, he was more than happy to accept.

As if by accident, the church door was inadvertently left open and a group of parishioners just happened to be standing close by as Dr Kilmennie and Colin were talking. Mrs Chisholm had been delegated to stand closest to the open door and it was her role that if, accidentally, she *was* to involuntarily hear something, she would feel obliged to share it with those around her, who would pass it on to others.

So, Colin's acceptance went round the crowd outside like wildfire and a slow, gentle applause started and grew ever louder with each clap.

Dr Kilmennie knew what was going on and invited Colin to come to the door with him. The doctor pulled open the door and stood back, leaving Colin facing the crowd.

The clapping and cheers erupted and Colin was touched by the people's genuine joy. "How... how did you know I had been accepted?" Colin asked Mrs Chisholm.

"It's the second sight that we have Meenister," she replied with a smile and a wink.

Lorna, who was standing behind Mrs Chisholm, couldn't help but smile as she saw that she had both hands behind her back with her fingers firmly crossed!

Mrs Chisholm sensed she was being watched and turned and saw Lorna smiling. She realised she had been overheard and said, "Och well, what's a wee white lie in the whole scheme of things? I'm sure the good Lord would understand on an occasion such as this, don't you think Lorna?"

Lorna nodded saying, "I'm sure he would Mrs Chisholm. He is smiling down upon us today."

"Aye, He certainly is Lorna – and wasn't it great that it was anonymous?"

Lorna laughed, she was sure that Mrs Chisholm had meant to say that the vote had been *unanimous*. The crowd slowly dispersed as the people made their way home, it was a happy day in Rhua – although one or two of the older generation felt that such levity was out of place, it being the Sabbath day.

Colin had been invited back to the MacDonald's home for a 'wee celebration.' Lorna and her mother had prepared a table of sandwiches, scones and nibbles in little dishes and of course there was a bottle or two of 'the water of life' to help the celebrations go smoothly.

Uncle Hector had appointed himself as head barman and made sure that everyone had a charged glass for the toast. Lorna's father stood up and called for silence. "And now ladies and gentlemen, a toast. I give you the Reverend Colin Campbell, our new minister." A cheer went up. "Congratulations on your appointment and long may you be with us. To – the Reverend Colin!!"

All present repeated, "The Reverend Colin!" and downed their dram in one.

Lorna could not have been more proud of Colin, or happier with the way things were turning out for the both of them.

Colin noticed that Mrs McLeod was across the room wiping her eyes and he went straight over and put his arm around her. Her husband Calum slapped him on the back saying, "Well done Meenister, you are one of us now, it's blessed that we are, to be sure!"

Mrs McLeod was flustered and went a bright shade of red as Colin said, "Thank you so much for all you have done for me Mrs McLeod," and gave her a hug.

Uncle Hector began the call - "*Speech, speech!*" which was soon taken up by everyone in the room. Colin wasn't sure what to say and he remembered an old tutor saying, *'when giving a speech, keep it simple.'* He had also noticed that most of the better speakers started with a joke or something humorous, *'Get them on your side right at the start,'* seemed to be their motto, so he began, saying, "As my Irish grandfather used to say *I'd like to say a few words before I speak!*" Which went down well. Heartened by the response, he continued, "Thank you all for your support and good wishes and I look forward to getting started in this most beautiful part of God's creation." Lorna went over, took his arm and kissed him on the cheek.

"I never thought that I would ever have taken up a charge so far away from the central belt," Colin continued, "I had always thought that I would serve in Glasgow - but obviously, God has other ideas!"

"The Lord is good!" shouted Uncle Hector (the whisky was taking a hold of him) and he called, "A toast to the Meenister and Lorna, may God bless them with health and happiness!" To which they all whole-heartedly responded.

The rest of the evening went well with Uncle Hector making sure that all glasses were kept topped up, especially his own.

Chapter 24

Making plans

The next morning Colin woke up in Mrs McLeod's bed and breakfast, feeling decidedly jaded, and he couldn't remember how he got home from the party at Lorna's last night. It was out of character for him which only heightened his feeling of self-reproach.

"Oh dear!" he thought, *"What would Aunty Bunty say?"* Aunty Bunty was an ardent tea-totaller and would not be best pleased if she knew that Colin had 'taken a glass or two to be sociable,' as the locals on Rhua would say.

In actual fact, Colin hadn't drunk very much at all, in Rhua terms, but it was enough to give him a major hangover. His good friend Iain McDougall, who was known for never refusing a dram, would be proud of him.

He wasn't able to eat very much at breakfast prompting Mrs McLeod to ask, "Are you feeling alright Meenister? It's not like you to leave some of your porridge."

Before he could answer, Calum said, "Maybe it's the hangover that you have Meenister, you're looking a wee bit pale, right enough."

Mrs McLeod spoke up in Colin's defence, "Now don't you be embarrassing the Meenister, it'll be all the excitement of yesterday I'm sure, what with the Service and the voting and everything,".

"Yes, that will be it," Colin agreed a little too quickly.

"Aye, I'm sure you are right mo ghràdh *(my love),*" Calum smiled sweetly at his good lady. He wasn't convinced but decided that agreeing with Mrs McLeod was the best course of action.

Colin picked up Lorna later that morning, as agreed, and they drove over to the croft. She was full of excitement and eager for them to draw up plans for their future. "Oh Colin, it's like a wonderful dream that's come true," she said as they entered the croft. It was warm and homely and had a special feel to it. She was sure that

Colin's grandparents had left their gentle and compassionate aura imprinted into the very fabric of every room, it was quite tangible Lorna thought, but then she *was* sensitive to such things.

As she looked around, she pictured how she could make it a lovely home for the two of them - but she was getting ahead of herself, first they had a wedding to plan.

Colin's thoughts were similar to those of Lorna as he looked around his grandparent's croft. He felt the warm sense of peace and tranquillity and saw the potential for a comfortable and contented home for the two of them.

"Now that the church has agreed to call me as their Minister, should we take a while to think about what we do next, sweetheart?" Colin asked.

This was exactly what Lorna had hoped Colin would say but she didn't want to be too forward. "Oh yes, I suppose we could now we're here," she said, trying not to sound too eager.

"We really need a sheet of paper," Colin said as he looked around hoping to find something to write on.

"I've brought a note pad and a pen with me, and some scones," Lorna smiled. They looked at each other and laughed out loud. "We're on the same wave length anyway!" Colin said and put his arms around her.

"Oh Colin, everything is just perfect!" A tear ran down Lorna's face as she spoke.

They spent the next couple of hours speaking about the wedding, and as the day wore on they decided that it should be sooner rather than later. They knew that they loved each other, and marriage was the right thing to do, so why wait? But there was something else to consider, Colin's Induction into the Church.

"But we can set the date once you know when your Induction is going to be, can't we?" Lorna sensed that she was sounding too impatient.

"Good idea sweetpea, I'll have to head south before too long and I'll get in touch with Head Office in Edinburgh and see what they are planning. I'll also have to get in touch with my good friend Iain McDougall to see how his dates are for coming up to be my best man – and I was thinking of asking Mr McCrimmond if he would conduct our wedding, he was a faithful visitor to my grand parents, what do you think?"

"Yes, for all his faults he is a kind and caring man, I think that would be a good choice." Lorna's emotions were all over the place, she was both happy and sad. Happy that the wedding was going ahead but sad as Colin had to return to Glasgow so soon.

"Do you *have* to go back? Can't you just stay here?" Lorna knew that wasn't possible but hated the thought of being apart from Colin, even for a short time.

"Yes, I have to return to Glasgow sweetheart, there's so many things to tie up before I leave, but I'll be back as soon as I can."

"When will you be leaving?" Lorna was hoping he would be able to stay for a while yet.

"Well, I had planned to leave this morning but there are a few things I have to sort out with Dr Killmennie, and I'll have to see Rev McCrimmond before I leave, so as today is Monday, er.. probably on the Thursday ferry to Oban and then take a bus down to Glasgow."

"Oh, so soon, can't you stay a bit longer, pleeeease?" Lorna threw her arms around him and held him tight.

"The sooner I get away, the sooner I'll get back." Colin would be quite happy to never leave the island, but knew it had to be done.

They spent the rest of the day planning their future and enjoyed a lunch of scones on a paper doily with tea from a tartan thermos flask. It was the happiest day they could both remember but then, every day was a happy day when they were together.

Chapter 25

The Official Secrecy Act

The next day was taken up with visiting Lorna's family around the island. Congratulations and a dram was offered on every visit and Colin was glad he was driving or he might not have survived the day intact.

The highlight of Colin's day was their visit to Lorna's aunt Chrissie who was a small lady with a smiley face and a soft, gentle voice.

"Oh Lorna, it's yourself! Come away in," she said excitedly. "And you've brought the Meenister with you! And here's me in my pinny, whatever will he think of me?"

"Don't be worrying Aunty Chrissie, Colin won't mind that, it's *you* we've come to see."

"No, please don't worry, I'm so pleased to meet you, I've heard lots of nice things about you," Colin said.

"Och, you're very kind, Meenister."

"Colin, please call me Colin."

"Oh no, I couldn't possibly call the Meenister by his first name, it wouldn't feel right. Is it okay if I call you 'Meenister,' Meenister?"

"Well, if it makes you feel more comfortable then that's just fine by me," Colin said smiling.

"Och it's a lovely man that you have Lorna, aye a lovely man. Will you pour the Meenister a dram Lorna, you know where the bottle is."

"Not for me thank you, I'm driving. I wouldn't want the two of us to end up the loch now would I?"

"Mercy no, we wouldn't want that Meenister! Lorna, I'll take a wee glass myself, just to be sociable of course."

"Aye Aunty, a wee sherry is it?"

"Oh well alright then, seeing that we have the Meenister in the house, we'll be blessed now."

Colin warmed to Aunty Chrissie, she was so sweet and had a refined elegance about her.

As the three of them chatted away, he was surprised to learn that when she was a young girl,

Aunty Chrissie had once been a handmaid to the Queen.

"Oh yes, I used to lay out her majesty's clothes for the day as well as looking after her daughter Elizabeth when they were up at Glamis castle. She was a lovely girl and will make a good queen one day."

"My goodness, I bet you have lots of tales to tell," said Colin.

Aunty Chrissie tapped her nose and said, "Oh yes Meenister, but I'm sworn to secrecy," with a sweet little smile and a wink.

When Lorna said it was time to go, Colin was reluctant to leave, such was the pleasant and enjoyable company of Aunty Chrissie.

"Your Aunt is quite a character, isn't she?" Colin said as they drove back to the village. "I could sit and listen to her all afternoon."

"Yes, she's lovely, you wouldn't think that she was a hundred just a few months ago, would you?"

Colin was shocked, "A hundred? She looks more a lady in her 70's. Her skin is flawless and her pale blue eyes still have a twinkle of mischief in them!"

"They certainly have," Lorna agreed. "Her late father was from Rhua and she moved here to the family croft and settled down just a few years ago after years of working in the Royal household at G;amis.

"Gosh, she's full of surprises, she certainly has had an interesting life," Colin said as he turned on his windscreen wipers, the rain was back on, no surprises there.

They had a busy day visiting, and Lorna was pleased that Colin had met most of her family. Needless to say, they all thought that Colin was a lovely man and were delighted that he was going to be the island's new Minister.

Colin was amazed at what an interesting array of people were living on the Island. From crofters who had never left the island to others, like Aunty Chrissie, who had amazing and interesting backgrounds with even more interesting stories to tell.

He was beginning to feel more settled on the island and was very much looking forward to life on Rhua with all these lovely people.

Chapter 26

No Tramps, no Hawkers and no Campbells!

The next morning, Colin made a visit to the Rev. McCrimmond.

"Och, it's yourself Colin, come away in, you'll be taking a wee glass of 'something medicinal' to keep out the cold?" Rev. McCrimmond said.

Colin was a wee bit taken aback as it was a glorious day. "The cold…?" Colin said, "but it's a fine day." "Aye, well you can never be too sure. You wouldn't want to be caught off guard!" Rev. McCrimmond replied as he poured two drams. "Not for me thank you," said Colin. "I'm on the motorbike and don't want to take any chances."
Rev. McCrimmond looked puzzled at Colin not wanting a dram. "Och well, if you're sure," and he poured the two drams into one glass and sat down. "Take a seat Colin, please call me Angus. And what do I owe the pleasure of a visit from the Parish Meenister?"

"Well, I was wondering, how long have you been covering for the Church of Scotland Minister on Rhua?"

"It will be about 8 or 9 years now."

"And have you stayed in the Church of Scotland Manse all that time?" Colin asked.

Aye, pretty much."

"So, is it going to be a problem when I move up to Rhua?" Colin asked.

"Oh, I see what you mean Colin, you'll be wanting to move into the Manse."

"I was wondering, do you have anywhere else to go?" Colin asked.

"Well, no. The Free Church manse was falling apart, that's why we were allowed to move into the church of Scotland manse. There are are a few empty houses around the island but they will need doing up and we really don't have the money, so we have left it in the good Lord's hands."

"Well, here's a thought Angus. How about if I approach the Church of Scotland offices and ask if I can live in my grandparent's croft which will leave you and Mrs McCrimmond to stay where you are? It will be a goodwill gesture for 'services rendered' as it were. How does that sound?"

He hoped that Mr McCrimmond would agree as he and Lorna really had their hearts set on living in the croft.

"Well, that would be marvellous Colin, but do you think they will agree to it?"

"We can only try," Colin replied. "I'm going back to Glasgow in the morning and I will pop over to Edinburgh and see what I can do. I think it's only fair after all you have done for our church over the years." Colin had made a friend for life.

"That is very kind of you Colin, we would be in a pickle if we had to move from here, to be sure."

"I can't promise, Angus, but it would suit us both, and the croft is just on the edge of the village so it's still handy for the parishioners if they need to come and see me. "I'm hoping they will reassign the Croft to be the Manse, I can only ask."

Mr McCrimmond called his wife through and told her of Colin's plan.

"Oh, you are a blessing to be sure," she said tearfully. "We would be in a pickle if we had to find somewhere else to live."

"That's *exactly* what I said my love!" Mr McCrimmond added.

'*Aye,*' Colin thought, '*word for word.*'

He was touched to see how in tune they were. They both showed tough and formidable exteriors to the outside world but inside they were as kind and as caring as anyone, a side that many wouldn't see.

"I'll be back up in a few weeks or so and I'll let you know how I get on."

"Oh, that would be grand, thank you so much," Mrs McCrimmond said. "Oh, and by the way, I believe congratulations are in order, Lorna is such a lovely girl, I wish you both every happiness.

And please excuse my husband's manners – we were never introduced, my name is Zena."

"Zena? That's an unusual name," Colin hadn't heard of that before.

"Well, it's short for Angusina, after my late grandfather Angus from Lewis. It's quite common in the Western islands for a girl to be called after her father or grandfather – it keeps his name alive even after he has passed. My sister is called Murdina, after our own father, Murdo," Zena explained.

"What a lovely idea!" Colin was quite taken with the tradition of keeping the family names alive.

After another cup of tea, Colin said his farewells to the McCrimmonds, donned his motorbike helmet and gloves and rode across the island to the Mrs McLeod's croft.

He wondered if, in time, his own name might be kept alive in the same way as Angusina. He pondered a few possibilities and all he could come up with was Co-leena. No, he thought, sounds too much like Semo-leena.

That evening Colin packed a few essentials in his small suitcase for his trip down to Glasgow, then drove into the village to see Lorna.

Lorna was tearful but knew that his stay would be short.

"I'll be as quick as I can sweetheart, but I have quite a few things to tie up in Glasgow before I head back home." Lorna was pleased to hear him call Rhua, 'home'.

"I know, it's just that I'll miss you so much," she said.

"I'll miss you too, but it won't be for long, and then we will be together forever," Colin said affectionately.

"You know how to say all the right things. I love you so much Colin Campbell."

"I love you too Lorna MacDonald, I can't wait to be back and for us to be settled in our own wee place as a happily married couple. Imagine, 'Mr & Mrs Campbell', sounds good doesn't it?"

"It sounds wonderful!" Lorna said, "but I'm not sure how Father's family will feel - a MacDonald becoming a Campbell!"

Colin found it hard to understand the MacDonald/Campbell animosity thing, especially after so many years. It was over 300 years since the Massacre of Glencoe had taken place.

It was, for the most part, good humoured banter, but deep down there had been a long standing undertone of mistrust for anyone with the name of Campbell – or as Donald John *(McDonald)* would say in jest (?) "Aye. it's the long memories that we have up here."

On one of his climbing trips to Glencoe, Colin remembered seeing a sign on the door of a local hotel which said, "NO TRAMPS, NO HAWKERS AND NO CAMPBELLS!"
(Note : On my last visit to that hostelry – purely for research purposes - the sign was still there).

Colin told Lorna about his meeting with Mr and Mrs McCrimmond.
"Hopefully I can talk the Church of Scotland into allowing us to stay in the croft, wouldn't that be great?"
"It would be just perfect!" Lorna replied excitedly.
"Well, I'll certainly do my best to persuade them sweetheart, and when I get back from Glasgow, we can get cracking and get it cleaned and spruced

up."

"Yes, of course dear," Lorna smiled. Little did he know that a number of ladies in the village had already arranged with Lorna to go in and clean the croft from top to bottom while Colin was away in Glasgow.

"It's better to get the men folk out of the road when there is serious cleaning to be done!" one of the ladies had said.

"Yes," said another, "I always put my Hector out into the byre when I am doing the housework! He keeps asking daft question like, *"Why are you hoovering again? It was only two weeks since you hoovered the croft!'* Do you know what he said a couple of weeks ago?" Before anyone could answer she said, "He had the cheek to say, *'mercy, the dust doesn't get a chance to settle when you're around!"*

"Men!" said Mags McKenzie, with an exasperated tone which was met with nods and general agreement that men were better kept well away when serious housework was taking place.

Little did they know that it suited the men just fine.

Chapter 27

We're not happy, Mr MacDonald,
not happy at all

The next morning Lorna waved Colin off as he boarded the ferry to Oban.
They were both sad, but they knew it was only a temporary parting.

Colin's journey was fairly uneventful, except, that was, for the American lady on the bus to Glasgow, who, although there were plenty of seats available, chose to sit next to him and relate her whole life story to him.

He kept a polite demeanour as Mrs Betsy Crockett regaled him with details of her family tree, right back to the famous American woodsman, Davy Crockett.
"Yeah, I'm from Tennessee but I'm a quarter Scottish," she informed Colin. He wondered which quarter of her was Scottish, was it an arm? Maybe

a leg?

"How fascinating," he said, trying to sound interested. The truth was that he was thinking of Lorna.

Betsy continued with a story about visiting a long lost cousin in Edinburgh (Edinburg as she called it), who she had been corresponding with for the last 3 years, but Colin had zoned out at that point and simply smiled and nodded every minute or so until they reached Glasgow.

As he got off the bus he waved goodbye to his new friend Betsy, and as they parted their ways, Colin breathed a sigh of relief.

He walked down to his flat in Kelvingrove, and as he opened the door, he was met by his wee pal Moses who rubbed against his leg as Colin tried to get in and close the door behind him.

"Goodness me Moses what a welcome, at least let me get in!" Colin picked him up and stroked his head as Moses purred and snuggled in. Moses was as pleased to see Colin as Colin was to see him.

It was good to be home with all his own bits and pieces around him, but he missed his dear Lorna and the lovely people of Rhua very much.

'The sooner I get things tied up here, the sooner I'll be able to get back up to Rhua,' he thought to himself. So he decided to get cracking. But first things first, he must make a list!

'It's the only way to keep tabs on everything that needs to be done,' he said to himself – and he had much to do. People to see – things to arrange – loose ends to tie up, so much so that he felt it necessary to make three lists!

His priority was to tell family and friends that he had been accepted by the Church in Rhua and would be moving up there before too long – and, of course, tell them that he and Lorna were engaged to be married.

Then he would have to give the Barony Church, where he was the Assistant Minister, notice that he was leaving to take up a Parish of his own. They would be pleased for him and it would be hard saying goodbye to the many friends he had made while working there. It was very much a University Church and as such, was largely attended by students and Professors of Divinity, many he had known for years.

Over the following few weeks Colin ticked off the various items on his several lists – each tick gave him great satisfaction.

Every evening at 7pm, he and Lorna spent time chatting on the phone as he updated her with his progress. "It shouldn't be too long before I can finish up here and move to Rhua permanently," he told Lorna.
"Oh, I can't wait! It's all like a wonderful dream," she said, and they ended their calls promising their undying love for each other.

Correspondence between Colin and Dr Killmennie had resulted in the date for Colin's Induction being arranged for three weeks ahead.

Most of the items on his lists were ticked, and the next week or so would give him time to say his final goodbyes to family and friends and make his way up to Rhua – and to Lorna.

The thought of what lay ahead for him – a life with Lorna and a Parish of his own in a remote Island Parish, gave him a feeling of joy and thankfulness. Yet the thought of leaving Glasgow behind, and all that he knew and cherished, gave him an element of sadness too.

It was a big step, was he doing the right thing? Was this what God really wanted him to do? He had a momentary blip of doubt before pulling himself up sharply and settling himself in the sure and certain knowledge that this *was* what his faithful God was leading him to do.

*

A few days later, Lorna was sitting in the office of her fathers' drapery shop, daydreaming of her wedding day.

They hadn't fixed a date yet, but she hoped it would be soon.

Traditionally, the wedding would be a year after the announcement of the engagement, which was far too long for her liking.

The more she thought about Colin, the more she missed him.

Lorna's daydreaming was interrupted when the door of the office opened and her father walked in.

"Did you manage to get those invoices finished Lorna?" he asked.

Lorna jumped, "Oh! Sorry father, no, I was just thinking… but I'll get on to them just now."

"Oh Lorna, what a day dreamer you are. I can guess who you were thinking about – Colin, am I right?"

"Yes, but how did you…"

"Because you have been in a daydream ever since he left a few weeks ago."

"I'm sorry father, it's just that I miss him so much. He *will* come back, won't he?"

"Of course he'll come back sweetheart, how could he ever stay away from such a pretty face?" her father said, and he walked over to the desk and gave her a hug.

"Now, let's dry those tears and get busy, time passes much quicker when we occupy ourselves."

"Yes father," Lorna knew her father was right, and she picked up the invoice book, opened it and began to check the figures, but within a few minutes her mind had drifted back to Colin and their wedding plans.

Her father shook his head, *'Poor lassie, she's fairly got the bug.'* He was pleased that she had a promise of marriage from such a lovely man as Colin – *'Aye, and it'll be good for business too!''*

He hummed a wee tune and went out into the shop where a group of ladies from the village had gathered.

There was a murmur of chatter which stopped when Harrold came through from the office.

"Oh Mr MacDonald, the very man!" said Mrs Chisholm.

"Yes ladies, how can I help?"

Mrs Chisholm, who was the self appointed ringleader of the group, stepped forward.

"Well, it's just…… well, you see…" she stuttered, suddenly losing her confidence.

"Go on Isabel, tell him!" Betty McLeod encouraged her friend.

"Yes, tell him Isabel, tell him!" the other ladies called out.

"Well, Mr MacDonald, it's er…"

"Get on with it!" shouted Mrs Cameron.

"Yes, of course. Well, it is the new style corsets, Mr MacDonald." Mrs Chisholm felt her confidence draining away but she steeled herself, took a deep breath and said, "We're not happy, not happy at all Mr MacDonald!"

Cries of, "That's right," and, "Aye, we're not happy!" came from the group.

Mr MacDonald was fair taken aback, "Goodness me ladies, whatever is the problem? Surely it can't be *that* serious, can it? Will I need to be calling in PC Bookem or Sergeant Galbraith from Oban to investigate?" Harrold said, hoping to lighten the mood.

"There's no need for that Mr McDonald, but it's serious alright," Mrs Grant called out from the back of the band of disgruntled ladies.

Lorna heard the shouting and came through to the shop to see what was going on.

Mrs Chisholm was on a roll. "Yes, it *is* serious. You see, Mrs McAulay was down in Glasgow seeing her son Donald, the one with the squint, and his wife Senga, the one with the glass eye – and she said the 'bodyfirm' corsets are in all the shops and at half of the price that you are selling them for!"

Mrs Chisholm gave nod as if to say, *'There, I've said it!'*

Mr MacDonald stood for a few moments in stunned silence. What would he say? What *could* he say? After all, it was the truth. As his mind was racing, thinking of a story that would satisfy the ladies.

In a moment of inspiration, Mr MacDonald said, *"It will be the transportation costs. Think of those brave sailors braving the elements, and their wives and children at home, trying to make ends meet - we wouldn't want to drive them further into poverty now would we? Those poor wee urchins! Is it not enough that they have to live in destitution in the slums of the city – without us God fearing people taking the very food out of the poor wee souls' mouth's..."* he continued, giving a slight sob for effect.

"I'll phone my Glasgow agent in the morning and see what I can do about getting the price down, if that's what you want." Harrold said, dabbing the corner of his eye.

The ladies looked at each other, and silence fell over the shop. After a few awkward moments, Mrs Chisholm said grudgingly, "Aye, well then…"
The wind had been taken out of her sails.

Mr MacDonald struck an indignant pose, lifted his head and went through to the office, closing the door behind him.

"Goodness me Lorna," he said. "Whatever can we do to get out of this mess? It was only a bit of harmless fun."

"Yes father, that's how it all started but it's got a bit out of control, is all it is," Lorna said trying to calm her father down. "I've just had a thought father, you can't phone Glasgow in the morning."

"Why ever not?"

"Because tomorrow is Sunday."

"Oh, so it is," he said with a wee smile, "So it is.'

Lorna was quite sure that her father knew exactly what day it was, "There's no flies on you, father!"

"Aye, maybe that," he replied and sat at his desk and lifted last weeks' Sunday Post and turned to the centre pages to read the latest escapades of the Dundee schoolboy, Oor Wullie.

"Oor Wullie, he's some lad, eh Lorna?"

"Aye father, he is that," replied Lorna, shaking her head. Her father never ceased to amaze her.

Chapter 28

I'll need to see about getting a new hat!

Back in Glasgow, Colin had packed up most of his belongings, and his good friend Iain McDougall knew someone with a big van who would come down to Glasgow and pick up his belongings and take them up to Oban. Donald John would arrange to get his neighbour's boat, the Donalda Dream, to transport it all over to Rhua where it would be picked up at the jetty and taken up his grandparent's croft. Lorna had arranged for a group of big lads to carry it all into the croft and she and Colin would sort it all out.

It was like a military operation, thanks to Iain McDougall's organisational skills. Colin hoped and prayed that it would all work out as planned on the day of the move.
His housekeeper, Mrs McRae, was in tears when Colin told her that he was moving so far away from

Glasgow. "It's wild country up there – and wild people too!" she had said to him.

Colin smiled to himself. It always amused him that many in the Central belt of Scotland thought that anyone north of Perth had heather growing out of their ears!

Aunty Bunty was not surprised with Colin's news. "I thought there was something going on with thon Lana lassie," she said.

"It's Lorna, aunty, *Lorna*."

"Oh well, whatever her name is, I hope you will be very happy together," and a tear ran down her cheek.

"Don't be sad, we'll see you at the wedding!"

A big smile came across Aunty Bunty's face, "You mean… there's going to be a wedding?"

"Of course!" Colin replied.

"When is the big day going to be? I'll need to see about getting a new hat!" She was feeling a lot brighter now.

"We haven't arranged the date yet but when we do – you'll be the first to know."

"Och, you always were a good boy, your mother would have been proud of you." The tears began to flow as she thought of Colin's late mother and what a dear soul she was.

"When are you moving up there?" she asked Colin.

"In a week or so."

"So soon? I was hoping you would be staying down here for a while yet."

"Well, my induction into the church is in a few weeks, so I want to get settled in before then."

"Oh, I see," Aunt Bunty looked sad.

"Don't worry Aunty, God is watching over me, he'll keep me safe. He will love me just as much up there as he does down here."

Aunty Bunty knew that to be true, but she also knew that she would miss him terribly.

After a hug and a kiss on the cheek, he left Aunty Bunty's with another hug – and a bag full of home baking tied to his handlebars.

As he criss-crossed through the Glasgow traffic on his way back to his flat in Kelvingrove, he felt a real sense of sadness. He didn't like to see his favourite Aunt in tears, she had been good to him over the years, especially after his dear mother had passed on, and now she would be on her own.

Her husband Billy had passed a few years ago and now Colin was going to be leaving her too.

'Once I'm settled in, I'll bring her up to Rhua for a wee holiday, she'll like that,' he thought to himself.

It was getting dark by the time he got home but he felt a sense of satisfaction that he had done pretty much all he had to do before leaving for Rhua.

Their 7pm phone call was a short one, Colin was weary with all the packing, and running around over the past few weeks, but hearing Lorna's voice once more gave him great comfort.

"I'll be heading home in a day or so, that's me just about ready to go." He told Lorna.

"Oh, I can't wait!" she was so excited at the thought of it.

"I just have to let Iain McDougall know when I am ready and he'll come down and pick me up. I'll phone him shortly and that will give him time to sort out his pal Keith and make their way down to Glasgow with the van. I'm so looking forward to being with you again, I've missed you so much."

"Oh Colin, please hurry home,"Lorna's mind was racing with all the thoughts and plans which were constantly flying around in her head.

"I will sweetheart, but I'd better go now and call Iain and get the ball rolling. Take care my love, see you soon."

They were both excited at being together again.

He phoned his friend Iain and arrangements were made. Colin would get the last bits and pieces done tomorrow and Iain would come down for him at 8am the following morning. Now it was becoming scarily real. He wished that those butterflies would take a rest.

A feeling of tiredness came over him and he decided to have an early night. He fed his wee pal Moses, let him out, and turned in for the night.

As he lay in bed, he thought about all that the future held for him. There was the journey North, moving into the croft, his Induction Service at the Church and of course, the Wedding, whenever that might be. If he had *his* way that would be soon, but he knew that the locals would think it unseemly if it were to be rushed, tongues would wag.

But Lorna wasn't worried about the gossips, she would be happy to marry Colin the minute he stepped off the ferry – if she could.

Chapter 29

Farewell to the dear Green Place

After a restless night's sleep, Colin woke early the next morning, he had today to make his final preparations before setting off on his journey up to Rhua.

He had organised all the important things, with just a few loose ends to tie up and soon he would close the door of his flat and 'head for the hills.'
*

Lorna was getting excited as she knew that she would be seeing Colin soon. She was always thrilled to see him but this time, it would be for good. He was going to be taking over as Minister on the Island and, more importantly, he was going to be her husband!

She had the wedding all planned out in her head. Every detail was thought out and written down in her diary, the one that no-one else gets to see.

All her deepest thoughts, dreams, plans and hopes for the future were written there, and were strictly for her eyes only.

She had been planning her wedding since she was 12 years old, who her bridesmaids were going to be, the colour of their dresses and the style of her hair were all noted down, just waiting for her Prince Charming to come and sweep her off her feet.

Colin was her Prince, and she couldn't be happier. *'God is good,'* she thought to herself, and a deep sense of peace and contentment came over her.

*

The 'man with the van' was coming in the morning and Colin wanted to be sure to get away on time.

The flat that he was renting was fully furnished when he had moved in, so there wasn't too much to take with him, just his desk, his captain's chair, some clothes, and books, lots of books.

He would phone Lorna at 7pm as usual and tell her that he had spoken to head office in Edinburgh who had okayed the Croft to be designated as the

Manse (the Minister's home). It would be their home too, once they were married. He knew Lorna would be excited about that, *he* certainly was. He would also confirm that he was coming up to Rhua tomorrow.

His housekeeper, Mrs McRae, would look in on Moses each day until Colin got settled on Rhua, then he would come down and collect him and take him up to his new 'forever home.'
It was all falling into place.

He spent the day tidying up the last minute bits and pieces, making phone calls, writing a few letters and making sure that nothing would be left behind.

It had been a busy day, and it was 7pm before he knew it. Lorna would be waiting for his phone call, he had better get moving.

Lifting the jar of coins, he went out into the hallway and called Lorna.

It had rang only once when Lorna answered it saying, "Hello sweetheart, when are you coming home?"

Colin smiled, "I'll see you tomorrow!" and he heard a squeal of delight from Lorna.
" Tomorrow!? Oh Colin that's wonderful!" and they chatted excitedly until the money ran out. "I've no more coins sweetpea, so I'll have to go now – see you tomorrow!"

"Yes, Colin. I can't wait to..." and the phone went dead.
She had so much more to say to him but that would have to wait until tomorrow, then they would have a lifetime together to talk as much as they wanted.

Lorna had lots to do before Colin arrived.

The group of ladies who had offered to clean and tidy up the croft, had already spent a few busy days there – so it just needed a final once over.

They were now on standby, just awaiting Lorna's 'call into action.'

She would arrange that for tomorrow morning, and it would be clean and fresh for Colin's arrival. Now, she was *really* excited!

*

Before he knew it, it was 7am and Colin's alarm clock burst into life. "Oh my goodness, I can't believe the time!" He only had an hour before the boys were due to arrive with the van to take his things up to Oban!

By the time he had washed, dressed, fed himself and Moses it was 7.45 and his housekeeper, Mrs McRae had arrived to help Colin get away on time. "Aye, it's a sad day," she said tearfully. "I'm going to miss you – oh dear…" words failed her, and she started to cry.

"Don't be upset Mrs McRae, it's a new start for me, I'm really looking forward to it, and I'll miss you too, you've been so kind to me."

"Well, I promised your dear mother that I would take care of you after she passed on…"

"Well, you have certainly done that, thank you so much," Colin was becoming tearful too. "Anyway, I'll be back before too long to collect Moses – and if you can make it, I'd be happy if you would come up for the Wedding, what do you say?"

"Oh, my goodness – a Wedding! – and you want *me* to be there?"

"Yes, and Mr McRae too. We haven't set the date yet but I'll let you know in good time for you to get a new hat."

"Well, I'm not sure about Mr McRae – what with his 'problem' and everything – and I wouldn't want to travel all that way on my own, but I'd love to come up, thank you so much for asking me."

"Well, my Aunty Bunty will be coming up, perhaps you two ladies could travel together?"

"Oh, that would be great! Two girls together, all alone in a strange land, you never know what could happen, we might get taken away by a sailor! Safety in numbers, as they say."

Colin thought it was some years since either of the ladies had been 'girls' but took the kinder option and said, "Don't worry, you'll be fine."

Mrs McRae was warming to the idea of getting away from Mr McRae and his 'problem' for a few days and she cheered up significantly.

It was 8.15 before Colin's old friend, Iain MacDougall, arrived with his 'partner in crime', Keith Campbell from Kinlochleven, with his van.

"Well, òganach (*young man*), this is my good friend Keith, he's a Campbell too. Bad buggers, the Campbell's!" Iain laughed, "but you two are alright!" he teased, and laughed even louder.

"Well, we can't stand about all day blethering, we'd better get the van loaded and up the road to Oban, Donald John and Uisdean will be waiting for us at the North Pier," said Iain, and he lifted up a huge box of books and put it in the van.

Once they had loaded up the van, the three of them jumped in, waved goodbye to a tearful Mrs McRae, who was holding Moses in her arms, and they took off at great speed.

Colin had a heavy heart as they left his home town of Glasgow. It was all he had ever known, until he was introduced to the Highlands and Islands.

He had been born and bred in Glasgow, went to school and then on to Glasgow University. He had graduated, was ordained and laid his dear mother to rest there.

He never knew much about his father except that he was from a wee village in the highlands and had been in the Royal Navy, serving on the Russian convoys during the war, when he was killed and buried at sea.

It was quite a wrench, but he knew that his future lay in a charming, remote Scottish Island with a beautiful young lady called Lorna McDonald.

As difficult as it was to leave Glasgow behind him, Colin absolutely knew that he was following the path that God had set out for him.

Chapter 30

I know exactly where they will be – the Bothy Bar!

As the 'boys' headed north, Keith and Iain were in fine voice as they sang a selection of Gaelic songs. Colin always felt that these songs invoked a certain sadness in him. He didn't understand the words but loved the haunting tunes which conjoured up images of the beautiful islands with their magnificent scenery which he was coming to love so much. He always thought that the music reflected the hills and the sea as those mournful songs gently rose and fell so beautifully.

They had just passed Luss when Iain rummaged behind the passenger seat and lifted out a carrier bag. "Here, Meenister, take one of these and pass one over to Keith."

Colin looked in the bag, there were six tins of 'Wee Heavy' beer.

"It's a bit early for me Iain, but thanks all the same," said Colin handing a tin to Keith.

"It's never too early for a wee refreshment, Meenister," Keith said as he took the can and expertly opened it with one hand, while holding on to the steering wheel with the other.

Colin was sure they were going to knock a cyclist off his bike as Keith pulled out to overtake at the same time as performing the 'opening a can of beer with one hand' trick.

Colin heard a stream of unsavoury language as they went past the cyclist and saw him shaking his fist in anger at Keith's dangerous manoeuvre.

"That was a close one!" said Iain looking out of the passenger's side window.
"Don't worry, I'll get him on the way back!" Keith said and laughed as he put his foot down on the accelerator.
"You're an awful man, Campbell!" Iain said shaking his head.

Colin was shaken at the near miss and what could have happened if their van had been just a few inches further over to the left. He closed his eyes and said a wee prayer for a safe journey, for themselves and for anyone else they might encounter on their way.

They finally arrived at Oban in one piece and pulled up at the North pier. It was high tide and the Donalda Dream was tied up just a few feet below the level of the Pier.

"It's God's hand that's in it," Iain said. "It'll make it easier for us to transfer the Meenister's cargo onboard, to be sure."

"What can I say?" Colin smiled, "God looks after his own."

Donald John and Uisdean were nowhere to be seen.

"Where could they be? They can't be too far away," Colin said to no-one in particular.

It was no mystery to Iain. "I know *exactly* where they will be – the Bothy Bar!"

"Will I go and get them?" Keith kindly offered."

"I'd better come with you, just in case," Iain wasn't going to miss the opportunity to take a wee refreshment to relieve the stress after the long journey from Glasgow.

Colin thought that the four of them meeting up in the Bothy bar was a recipe for trouble – would he get over to Rhua today? He wasn't so sure.

As Iain and Keith started to walk round to the Both Bar, Colin thought that he should go with them rather than wait in the van, he might be able to encourage them not to stay too long – or at least he could try.

An answered prayer ~

They had just got halfway around the bay when, to their surprise, they saw two 'worthies' singing a 'Gaol ise gaol I' (*my love is she*), making their way to the North Pier.

It can't be… can it? Not while the bar is still open? Yes, it was Donald John and his good friend Uisdean heading back to the Donalda Dream!

Iain McDougall shook his head and said, "Man, I've seen some strange things in my life, but never have I seen such a sight! Donald John and Uisden leaving a bar before they were put out!"

The boys laughed as Donald John and Uisden sang a final chorus *'Hu ri ri o hu o'* before meeting the 'search party.'

"Are you feeling alright boys?" Keith said cheekily.

"Aye, we're fine, we were just wanting to use the 'facilities' and it would be bad form not to buy something, so we had a wee dram, just to be sociable."

It looked like it had been more than just a 'wee dram' as both of them were taking a wee 'list to starboard' (*leaning to one side*) as they were talking.

"Well, we'd better get going if we are to get the Meenister to Rhua before nightfall, any later and we'll miss the tide," Donald John said as he lurched forward. The others looked at each other, shrugged and followed on.

Colin whispered, "Thank you Lord, thank you."

The plan was for Iain and Keith to lift the furniture and boxes from the van over to Donald John and Uisdean on the boat.
All was going well, they had been unloading the van for about 15 minutes or so when Iain lifted a heavy chest of drawers out of the van and handed it over to Uisdean who slipped. He managed to hold onto the chest, but all the empty drawers slid out and fell down into the sea.

"Oh no!" shouted, "The Meenister's drawers have fallen into the water!"

For a few moments there was a stunned silence… then they all burst out laughing at Uisdean's innocent comment – everyone except Colin, that was.

After a minute or so, they realised that Colin wasn't laughing and there was an awkward silence – until Colin said, "Hey, leave my drawers out of this!" and smiled. The laughter erupted once more.

"Aye, you'll do Meenister, you'll do," said Uisdean as he fished out various items of Colin's clothes with a oar.

Before too long, Colin's belongings were lashed securely, and a refreshment was the order of the day.

Colin gave Iain and Keith a £5 note saying, "Here's a wee 'thank you', see and spend it wisely now."

'Oh, we will Meenister, don't you be worrying," Keith said. "We're away to the Bothy bar to think about how we can spend it."

They shook hands and hurried away like two wee boys heading to the sweetie shop.

The Donalda Dream cast off and slowly made its way out past Kerrera and on to the sound of Mull – destination Rhua.

They were just passing Torosay Castle when, out of the blue, Uisdean remarked, "I was just thinking, is it not desperate how thon two couldn't wait to head for the bar? It must be terrible to have the drink on your mind all the time."
Colin couldn't believe his ears! It often seemed like Donald John and Uisdean thought of nothing else!

"Aye, it's a fair shame," said Donald John. "It must be terrible for the wives!"
As he was speaking, he took a half bottle of whisky from a wee cubby hole in the helm, beside the ship's wheel, and handed it to Uisdean.
Colin laughed out loud, he couldn't help himself, the bizarre conversation he was witnessing was just so – well, bizarre.
"What is it Meenister, are you alright?" Donald John asked.

"Oh, it's nothing, nothing at all, I just thought of something."

Donald John and Uisdean looked at each other and shook their heads, "Poor Meenister," Uisdean whispered as he tapped the side of his head. "Too much sun!"

"Aye, just that, "Donald John agreed, and took another swig from the half bottle.

They made their way up the sound of Mull with a song and a dram, all Colin could do was smile and think to himself, *'Aye, they're awful lads but salt of the earth,'* and he hummed along to the Gaelic songs, picking up the odd word here and there, much to the appreciation of the boys.

"Aye Meenister, we'll have you speaking in God's own tongue before you know it," said Uisdean.

"That would be great – could you teach me to say my wedding vows in Gaelic? That would surprise Lorna, what do you say?"

"We could easily manage that couldn't we, Uisdean?"

"Aye, no bother, we'll have him speaking like Highland Mary by the time of the wedding." Uisdean took a final swig of whisky, said "Slanj!" and tossed the empty bottle overboard.

Chapter 31

What's wrong with making a Profit?
The Bible is fair hoaching with them!

"Rhua on the Starboard side!" Donald John shouted. Colin looked over to the right hand side of the boat and was relieved to see the coast of Rhua appear through the mist. *'Nearly there,'* he thought to himself as Uisdean steered the Donalda Dream towards land.

Butterflies started to take flight in his stomach as he knew that it wouldn't be long before he would be seeing Lorna again.

"Aye Meenister," Donald John said. "You'll be seeing herself soon."

'How did he know that was exactly what I was thinking?' Colin was surprised at his friend's remark - but it was no supernatural prediction, Colin was glowing with excitement for all to see.

Before long, they secured the Donalda Dream to the Pier, where a group of lads were waiting to offload Colin's belongings.

"You made good time Uisdean," Fred Fraser, *who was in charge of 'the lads,'* remarked, "We weren't expecting you for a while yet, what happened, was the bothy Bar closed?"

"Not at all, there was a man of the cloth needing to get home, show some respect!
And besides, Henry MacInnes, you know Henry, he's an awful lad, well, he had thrown a cigarette end into a bin and set fire to the curtains. There was flames everywhere, so they had to evacuate the bar."

The boys on the pier laughed as one of them said, "What a couple of chancers!"
Colin shook his head as he realised that was the *real* reason that Donald John and Uisdean had left the Bothy Bar early!

"Hurry now lads!" Donald John shouted, in the hope of changing the subject. "The rain's no' far away and we wouldn't want the Meenister's paraphernalia to get wet, now would we?"

Uisdean couldn't remember loading a paraffin heater but shrugged and lifted up a box of books and passed it over to Fred who was standing on the pier.

"And don't be dropping any of the Meenister's belongings into the loch, he's already got his drawers wet and we had to fish them out of the water," Uisden said loudly, which brought a few strange looks and a couple of smiles.

A tractor and trailer had been reversed onto the pier and it wasn't long before all of Colin's belongings were offloaded from the boat, stacked on the trailer and secured tightly with rope.

Colin smiled as he imagined what the good people of Kelvingrove would make of such a 'flitting.'

*

Meanwhile, in the 'Emporium' the ladies of the village were harassing Harrold once more about the price he was charging for his new line of the 'Bodyfirm' corsets.

"You said you would get in touch with your man in Glasgow and ask why he was charging us so much, that was the last we heard of it, what's going on!?" The ringleader was Mrs Chisholm.

Harrold had crossed swords with her on a number of occasions and come off second best on every encounter.

"Oh aye, yes, um, my Glasgow connection, that's right. He, er, wasn't in when I phoned him, he's a busy man, always in a business meeting. I'll need to try again, I've..er.. just been so busy."

Harrold was flustered, he had hoped that the ladies might have forgotten about it all, but Mrs Chisholm wasn't going to be fobbed off so easily.

The truth was, he *had* made contact with 'his man in the Barras' a few weeks ago but got short change from him. "That's the price, take it or leave it, ya Teuchter!" he had said to Harrold.

Harrold's Glasgow 'business associate' was an ex boxer called 'Big Mental Malky' from Maryhill, who was well known for not taking any prisoners, so in the interest of self preservation, Harrold had agreed that on reflection, perhaps it *was* a fair price after all.

Harrold said to the ladies, "If I take down the price anymore, I'll be cutting my own throat, but if that's what you want…"

He knew that he had been putting a hefty percentage on to the items in the *'Latest Lingerie line from Oban'* collection, but surely it wasn't a crime to make a profit? "After all," he said to Lorna, "The Good Book itself is fair hoaching with talk of great Prophets on every page. If it's good enough for them, then it's good enough for my humble self!" and he gave a slight bow of respect to 'the good Book.'

Lorna just rolled her eyes and said, "Yes, father," and continued typing. Harrold was grasping at straws.

But then, an idea sprung into his head - "Okay ladies, I'll tell you what I'll do, out of the goodness of my heart, I'll take a shilling off the price of each corset."

"A shilling!?" Mrs Chisholm exploded, "Half a crown would be more like the thing!"

"Oh Mrs Chisholm, would you take the very shirt off my back? I could agree to one and sixpence, and I will be making a loss at that."

"Two shillings and not a penny less! Or we will withdraw our custom. In your own hands be it." The ladies cheered in support of the tenacious Mrs Chisholm.

"Oh mercy, is it my very livelihood that you would take from me? Alright, I'll agree to two shillings on one condition – that each of you buy two corsets, and you will give you a discount on each one, that's two discounts! I can't say fairer than that. I'm being a martyr to myself but that's what I'll do, as it is yourselves."

The ladies thought for a minute or two and they agreed that it was a good deal and within a few minutes they had bought every Bodyfirm corset in the shop.

The ladies left the shop feeling quite sure that they had got a good bargain – two corsets with a double discount!

Harrold knew that he had just made a week's takings in the last ten minutes. He would have to phone big Mental Malky in the morning to order another bundle of the corsets – after all, it's the very least he could do for his lovely ladies.

Chapter 32

*Fred's idea of the 'Spirit World' is
the Bothy Bar in Oban!*

Back at the Croft, the lads were offloading the
trailer and Lorna was directing them where to put
the various bits and pieces.

Once the trailer was unloaded, Lorna made them
all tea and scones. The 'boys' looked at each other
a raised eyebrow and a slight shrug indicated that
they had hoped for something a bit stronger.
Colin picked up on the signals and said, "Well,
thanks lads, you've done a great job – you'll get
your reward in heaven!"
"Thanks Meenister, and you too Lorna, we are glad
to help, but we're hoping that we still have a few
years to go before we are in the *'spirit world'* and
get our reward!" Fred said as he picked up another
scone.

"Fred's idea of the 'Spirit World' is the Bothy Bar in Oban!" Henry added with his usual mischievous smile.

Lorna and Colin spent the rest of the afternoon getting things unpacked and the furniture put in place. It felt good being together again and they both looked forward to the day when they would be husband and wife and able to live in the beautiful croft, as Mr & Mrs Campbell.

"Oh Colin, I wish we were married, it would be just perfect, wouldn't it? Do we *have* to wait a year? I can't wait to be your wife.
Imagine *me*, a Minister's wife! Whoever would have thought it?" Lorna said with growing excitement.
"Well, I suppose the date is up to us, but you know what the gossips will say. If it was up to me, I would marry you right now!"
"Oh Colin, if only we could. I don't care about the gossips, but I think mum would be disappointed,

she has so many things to arrange, it'll be a big day for her too.'

"Perhaps we could have a talk with her and your father and see what we can arrange with them, maybe we can agree on a compromise."

"A good idea, but they are both quite traditional so don't expect too much. Maybe you could work your charm on them!" Lorna said and kissed him on the cheek.

"I don't know about that," Colin said," but it won't do any harm to talk things over with them. We should talk it through ourselves first, what do you think?"

"I think I would marry you today if I could, but I don't suppose mum and dad would agree to that!" Another quiver of excitement ran through her body at the thought of marrying Colin and settling down with him.

Lorna's head was full of, '*How many children will we have? What will we call them? What colour shall we paint the living room? What breed of dog will we have? What will we call it?'*

But Colin was more practical, he was thinking, *'How soon can I get my motorbike up from Glasgow? Where will I get petrol for my bike on Rhua?* and, *The twisty roads here are perfect for the motorbike'.*

"What are you thinking, sweetheart?" Lorna asked. Colin was caught completely off-guard and after a nifty bit of quick thinking, he crossed his fingers and replied," I was just thinking, um, how lovely it will be when we're living here as husband and wife."

"Aww, you're so sweet," Lorna gave Colin a hug and snuggled into him.

Colin simply said, "Och well, that's me, ever the romantic."

"I love you, Colin Campbell," she said dreamily.

"And I love you too sweetpea."

They sat in a comfortable silence, each with their own daydreams.

Chapter 33

Lorna was thrilled to be asked
to sit at the top table

The next few weeks were taken up with getting settled into the croft and preparing for his Ordination and Induction as Minister of the Parish. There was great excitement as the Islanders looked forward to their new Minister taking up his post. He had visited Mr & Mrs McCrimmon and given them the good news that the Church of Scotland Head Office had agreed that 'The Croft' would be designated as 'The Church of Scotland Manse,' and the McCrimmond's could stay where they are for a token sum per year of £5, in perpetuity *(for life).*

A tearful Mrs McCrimmond thanked Colin for arranging this agreement which ensured that they would have a place to live for the rest of their natural lives. It was the start of what would turn out to be a deep and lasting friendship.

Three weeks after returning to the island, the evening of the Service of Colin's Ordination and Induction had arrived.

There was an excited buzz as a large number of islanders filled the church.

Prayers were put up, Psalms were sung and speeches were made. Lorna and many others were close to tears. Colin felt quite emotional too as he was quite sure that Rhua was exactly where God wanted him to be.

A social evening was laid on in the church hall after the service, which consisted of home baking, sandwiches and biscuits (including Custard Creams, which were at the special request of Lorna).

It was a great night, albeit a bit muted by Rhua standards, only tea and the occasional cup of Camp coffee were served. Anything stronger was taken from a hip flask or a half bottle round the back of the church hall.

Lorna was thrilled to be asked to sit at the top table beside Colin. *'If only this was our Wedding day,'* she thought to herself, *'I really hope that mum and dad will agree to us having our Wedding sooner than the traditional year.'*

It was a pleasant social evening, filled with good wishes and warm congratulations. Lorna felt like she was walking on air in a wonderful dream. Colin rounded off the evening with the words – "I look forward to seeing you all in Church on Sunday – but until then, take care and keep safe. And may God go with you until we meet again."
The people applauded and spontaneously burst into song, singing the 19th Century Hymn by Jeremiah Rankin ~

"God be with you 'til we meet again,
Loving counsels guide and uphold you.
May the Shepherd's care enfold you.
God be with you 'til we meet again."

It was a lovely end, to a lovely evening.

Chapter 34

You're a sneaky beesom Colin Campbell,
but I love you!

It was Sunday morning and the church was full for Colin's first Service as Parish Minister.

People from all over the island filled the pews and quite a few had to stand at the back.

"I wish it was like this every Sunday," Mr Brown said.

"Aye Andy, there are some here I haven't seen in church for years," his wife agreed.

"Oh mercy!" said Mrs MacArthur, "There's that scoundrel Calum McLeod! It's a wonder the walls of the Kirk don't fall around our ears!" The others who were close by agreed and shook their heads.

Colin peeked in from the kitchen and couldn't believe his eyes. "Oh my goodness, where are they all coming from? I didn't realise there were this many people living on Rhua!" He suddenly felt a tremor of nerves as he closed the kitchen door.

"Don't you be worrying, they are all here to support you – and don't forget, the good Lord is with you, "Catherine said, "I've got the very thing, a nice cup of tea."

"With no 'added ingredients' I hope, Catherine?"

"No Meenister, just tea. Oh, there is one thing more," Catherine said with a cheeky smile,"

"Oh yes, and what might that be?"

"A custard cream! Look…" she opened a kitchen cupboard door and there were at least a dozen packets of custard creams with a notice saying, *'For the Meenister only!'* "It's your own personal stock!"

Colin was over the moon. "Aww, Catherine, that is so kind of you, thank you so much, you are a lovely, dear soul. Does anyone else know about this?"

"Just you and me, Meenister."

"Then it's *our* secret," Colin said as he tapped his nose and winked.

Catherine was thrilled that she and the new Meenister shared a secret that nobody else knew about.

After a short prayer, the Beadle led Colin up to the pulpit – and the Service began.

He looked down and saw Lorna and her mother in the front, both giving him the thumbs up.

Colin's message was one of 'new beginnings,' reminding everyone that no matter what had gone before, we must look forward to God's great plan for what is to come.

"He forgives your past and promises you a bright future.

He loves you and wants only the best for you," were his parting words.

It struck a chord with just about everyone there, including himself.

At the end of the Service the congregation stood and applauded as Colin came down from the pulpit and walked up the isle to the front door where he spoke to each one as they left church.

Many shook his hand while others hugged him. Colin was becoming quite emotional with all the kind remarks and expressions of gratitude for such a meaningful sermon.

"Oh Meenister, you have given me comfort and hope that God himself has forgiven my past and has a bright future waiting for me," Mrs Carmichael said with tears running down her cheeks.

Lorna was beyond proud, *'That's my future husband!'* she thought to herself, *'what a kind and caring man he is.'*

Lorna's mother had invited Colin round for his Sunday lunch after the Service, and Lorna's favourite Uncle, her mother's brother Hector from Tiree, was also there.

Hector came over and shook Colin's hand, "My, but the service was sublime Meenister. The very thing we needed to hear. I admit that my attendance at church has slipped a bit…"

"Slipped <u>a lot</u>!" Lorna's mother said.

Hector continued, "Well, yes, quite a bit, but that's due to… um… my many travels to the Far East…"

Lorna looked at Colin and mouthed, "B.a.l.l.a.c.h.u.l.i.s.h F.e.r.r.y!" and giggled. Colin had to put his hand over his mouth to hide a smile.

"…but your sermon has fair made me think about things." Hector continued.

Colin smiled at Hector kindly, "We all have our crosses to bear Hector, but the good Lord knows what's in our hearts."

"I thoroughly agree Meenister, did I not say the same thing to the crew just the other day on our way through the Strait of Gibraltar!?"

It appeared that Uncle Hector had 'seen the light,' for now at least.

"Come through everyone, dinner is ready," Lorna's mother called from the front room.

Harrold asked Colin to say grace and they held hands around the table as Colin gave thanks.

Uncle Hector then lifted his glass and said, "A toast! – To the Meenister!" which was echoed by all.

"How's life in the Manse, Colin?" Harrold asked as they ate.

"It's so peaceful and it feels like my grandparents are just in the next room. Sometimes I'm sure I can hear them talking to each other in their lovely gentle Island voices! And that lovely smell of sweetpea's fills the house."

"That's your grandmothers' scent Colin," Lorna said. "You could always tell when she was in the shop, for the aroma of sweetpea's was in the air."

"Sounds like your lovely grandmother is still with you Colin," Lorna's mother said, "How lovely."

"Yes, I feel her presence every day. It's comforting to know that she is watching over me." Colin felt quite emotional.

Lorna leaned over and held his hand, "I think you are sensing things now that you are living up here, *'nearer my God to thee,'* as the old hymn says.

Now the *air* is clearer, your *mind* is clearer, away from the noise of the big city, free to hear and see things you never realised were all around you."

"It's like I've been wearing blinkers all these years and now I've taken them off! I'm seeing, hearing and feeling things I've never felt before!" replied Colin.

"I'm the same, Meenister, I see and hear things that no-one else can." Uncle Hector said with an air of mystery.

"That'll be the drink!" Lorna's mother said.

Colin and Lorna couldn't help but laugh out loud.

"Oh, sis, that's harsh! You know I only take a refreshment to be sociable and on special occasions."

"*Every* day seems to be a 'special occasion' for you, big brother."

Hector looked hurt, "Och, there's no need for that, so there's not."

Lorna went round and gave him a hug. "Never mind, uncle Hector, you're still my favourite uncle," and kissed him on the cheek.

Hector cheered up and a broad smile lit up his face. He looked around the table, "Anyone need a top up?" he said as he made for the bottle of Whisky on the sideboard.

Before long, Uncle Hector was sleeping in the armchair, much to the annoyance of Harrold.

The afternoon was taken up with pleasant conversation and the topic of the wedding was brought up by Lorna's mother.

"Have you two set a date yet?" she asked.

Lorna looked over to Colin. They hadn't had a chance to talk it through but they both agreed that they didn't want to wait a year as was the local custom.

Colin spoke first, "Not yet, it's been a bit of a busy time with moving into the croft and my

Ordination, but from my own point of view, I know just how stressful life as a Minister can be, especially for a Minister without a wife by his side. The very thought of having to live alone in the Manse with all the stressful issues, which many don't realise, for a year or more, doesn't bear thinking about."

'Good for you Colin,' Lorna thought to herself, *'but don't lay it on too thick!'*

Harrold joined the conversation, "Oh well, yes, we hadn't thought of that. Lorna's mother and I were hoping you would wait for the usual twelve months like other young couples on the Island, it's our tradition you know."

"Yes, and I whole heartedly agree with you, of course, but these other couples don't have the stresses and strains that a Minister and his wife have to deal with. I'm quite sure that my parishioners would want what's best for their Minister and his good lady of the Manse, don't you think Harrold?"

"Oh, well, um, yes of course but...." Harrold found it hard to dispute Colin's reasoning.

"I'm so pleased that you agree, and I thank you for being so understanding – shall we say six months then?"

"That's a bit hasty, you know how the gossips love to talk, shall we split the difference and say nine months?" Harrold suggested.

Lorna's mother spoke up, "Nine months! The gossips would have a field day!"

"Oh yes, of course, no, that wouldn't do at all," Harrold agreed.

"So, it seems like we are left with the six months option, shall we agree to that? It seems for the best all round." Colin could be very persuasive when he has a mind to be.

"Well, I suppose if you put it like that, we .. er..." Harrold said with a slight feeling of being rail roaded. He looked at his wife and said, "Well, yes, it's ..er.. what do you say mother?"

"If that's what they want, then I agree," Lorna's mother said, "but I'm going to have to get cracking, there's lots to do, not least of which, we have a wedding dress to design and make!"

"Oh, thank you both *so* much!" Lorna said, and she went over and gave them both a hug.

She bent down and kissed Colin on the cheek and whispered in his ear,

"You're a sneaky beesom, Colin Campbell, but I love you!"

Uncle Hector woke up and said, "Sorry folks, it must the heat in here, "have I missed anything?"

"Nothing much Hector, nothing much at all," replied Harrold.

"Well, nothing much – other than chatting about a date for the wedding," Lorna's mother said.

Hector stood up, raised his glass and said, "A toast, The Wedding!" and promptly fell backwards into the armchair without spilling a single drop of his dram.

Chapter 35

Preparing for the big day

The wedding 'production line' was now in full swing around the island.

Betty Martin was baking and decorating the wedding cake. Peggy Morrison was making the bridesmaids dresses. Murdina MacKenzie had offered to supply the bridesmaids and the flower girl's bouquets – and Charlie Campbell was getting his 'band' together for a major comeback gig in the village hall, for the evening ceilidh.

Although the band was only himself on the squeeze box (accordion) and old Kenny McIsaac who played the moothie (mouth organ) and if he got really got swinging, Kenny would often break out the Jews Harp (or Trump) and then the spoons to 'jazz things up a bit' - and sometimes he would even take his jacket off.

Colin had asked the Reverend McCrimmond to conduct the wedding, and his best friend Iain McDougall, to be his best man. Both were delighted to be asked.

Wedding presents were arriving at the McDonald's house and the usual 'viewing' of the gifts were arranged in the evenings.
The many gifts had been neatly arranged in the spare bedroom and neighbours would bring in home baking saying, *'Here's a wee scone for your visitors, no, I'll not stop thank you. You'll be busy enough without me getting in the way.'*

Lorna's father had opened a Wedding list in the shop, offering discounts on any item bought as a gift.
There were special offers on toasters, kettles, crystal glasses, bedding, irons, crockery and canteens of cutlery in a box.
Sales were going well and Harrold could be heard to whistle or hum a jaunty tune as he moved around the shop guiding customers to the best

deals, but Harrold's deals were not always what they seemed.

Lorna and Colin were in the croft, making up the wedding guest list.

"I'm afraid there won't be many on my side, except my Aunty Bunty and Mrs MacRae. I don't really have any family. Of course, there'll be my best man Iain from Appin and also Donald John, Rhona and the girls. Oh, and Uisdean and Donalda – and that's about it," said Colin.

Lorna pouted and said with a smile, "Aww, what a shame – but I've got lots of aunties, uncles and cousins - you can borrow some of mine!"

"I wouldn't like it to be too one sided in the church with all those MacDonald's glowering over at the Campbells."

Lorna laughed and said, "Och, it'll be fine, I'll warn my lot to be on their best behaviour. "

A top table seating plan was made up – and it was everyone for themselves after that.

Lorna had a few meetings with the bridesmaids and between the nerves and the giggles, it seemed that everyone knew what they were to do on the 'big day.'

It was all coming together.

The weeks flew past and before they knew it, the day of the wedding was only a week away!

"Oh my goodness! I can't believe that this time next week, we will be getting married!" Lorna was excited and nervous at the same time.

"We've been given lots of lovely gifts from so many people," Lorna continued, "and we're alright for kettles, toasters and candlewick bed spreads for the next 50 years!" They both laughed.

"Oh well, that'll save us a fortune! People are so kind, aren't they?" Colin said.

"Aye, they're lovely, well most of them anyway," Lorna replied with a smile.

Colin looked at Lorna and the beautiful island scenery which surrounded them, and said, "If ever there was a Heaven on earth, this must surely be it."

They sat in silence for a few minutes before Lorna noticed the time. "Mercy, will you look at the time! The girls are taking me out tonight, I've still got my hair to wash. You'll need to get going too, what time are you meeting the boys?"

"They said 7pm in the Kinlochmhor hotel. I could do without it to be honest." Colin would have been happier having a night in, just like every other night.

"Oh, you'll *have* to go, it's tradition. That's where *we're* going, I'll see you there!" Lorna was better pleased that she would be seeing Colin, later.

"Now I'll have to be on my best behaviour," she laughed.

"Aye, me too!" said Colin.

As the Kinlochmhor hotel was the only licensed premises on the island, it was inevitable that any parties or celebrations were held there. Of course, there was the highly illicit bothan out on the machair but it was hardly a place for a Meenister and his 'financier' to celebrate their up and coming nuptials.

The girls gathered in the Lounge Bar while the boys headed for the Public Bar.
Colin was like a fish out of water and as there were only three other lads there, it wasn't exactly 'the wild bunch.'
After an hour so Colin feigned a fierce headache and had to go home.
Word soon got through to the girls, and Lorna went up to the croft to see if he was alright, leaving both groups joining together and celebrating in style, albeit without the bride and groom to be.

Lorna and Colin were pleased to be away from the partying and spent the next few hours making plans and just enjoying each other's company, laughing, drinking tea and eating custard creams.

He walked Lorna home and was back in the croft by midnight.

He missed his wee pal Moses who was always there to greet him when he got home late. He would have to go down to Glasgow and collect him before too long, at least Mrs McRae was taking good care of him meantime.

Chapter 36

It was the 'Big Day'!

It was a lovely morning as Lorna looked out of her bedroom window, she was excited and nervous in equal measure. It was the day of her Wedding to the man of her dreams.

She had always dreamed of marrying a kind, caring man with a good sense of humour, and if he was good looking then all the better, Colin ticked all her boxes and more.

He was admired and well respected across the island of Rhua and beyond, as well as being a firm favourite with the ladies of the church.

As she day-dreamed about Colin, a shout came through the house, "Lorna, are you not up yet? Mrs McQueen is coming to do your hair in half an hour!" It was her mother who had been up since first light getting things ready for her daughter's big day.

She had contracted Polio many years ago and was now in a wheelchair, which made everyday chores about the house more difficult and time consuming - and today there was lots to do!

She had her dress to lay out, as well as organising her husband Harrold who had insisted on going into the shop for a few hours just incase someone was wanting to buy something. "I can't be letting my people down," Harrold said rather piously. "It's a public service that I provide and a man in my position has a duty to provide for the community." His wife, however, thought he was just afraid of missing a sale!

And then there was Lorna who would need help with her dress and all the many other important things that a bride has to do on her wedding day.

So, it was a busy morning in the MacDonald household. Lorna's father was under strict instructions to be home no later than 12 o'clock. Everyone was told to be in the church by 1.30 for the service at 2 o'clock.

It was now 9 am and Colin's good friend and best man Iain McDougal hadn't arrived on Rhua yet. Colin was in a spin as Iain was to be bringing Colin's kilt with him – but where on earth *was* he? Iain was staying with his cousin, Donald John and his family on Coll, they were all coming over for the wedding and were due to arrive on Rhua last night – but they hadn't appeared – what had happened? Where were they? What will he do if they don't turn up in time? Colin was getting anxious, it was only a few hours until the wedding was due to start! What to do?

Mrs McLeod had offered Colin the use of the Rolls Royce for his wedding day, so he drove down to the Emporium to see Lorna's father, to put him in the picture.

As he entered the Emporium he saw that Harrold was busy with a group of ladies at the 'latest thing from Oban' counter. Word had got out that he had received another order of the new elasticated 'Bodyfirm' corsets which he assured the ladies were banned around the world for being too 'li-cen-sacious', but he was able to get undercover orders sent out to Rhua, wrapped in plain brown paper from his 'business associate' in Glasgow, Big Mental Malky from Maryhill.

The ladies were taking it all in until they saw that Colin had entered the shop whereupon they dropped the 'illicit' corsets and flocked around him. "Oh Meenister, today is the big day!" said Mrs Fraser.

"Are you not nervous? What a lovely couple you will make. "Mrs McKinnon added.

As they fussed around Colin, Harrold picked up a number of corsets from the floor and made his way over to join the small gathering. "Now, now, ladies, don't be overwhelming the Meenister. Stand back, stand back, he has a wedding to go to! Come through the shop with me Colin where we can talk in private. Is everything alright?" Harrold could see that Colin looked harassed and hoped he wasn't getting cold feet at the last minute.

Colin explained his dilemma. "What if something is wrong? What if Donald John's boat has broken down? What if they don't turn up in time? What will I wear?" Colin was nearing panic mode.

Relieved that Colin was not about to call off the wedding, Harrold said, "Now don't you be worrying, I have the very thing. I have been keeping it for a special occasion and what could be more special than that of my own daughter's wedding, eh? I'll just give it a dust off and it will be ideal for a gentleman such as yourself."

'Dust off?' Whatever could he mean?' Alarm bells began to ring in Colin's head.

Harrold came out of the back shop carrying a grey suit. "This is just the thing Colin, slip it on and I'm sure it'll fit like a glove."

He tried on the suit and to be fair it wasn't a bad fit. "Are the lapels supposed to be so wide?" Colin asked. "And the trousers are very baggy."

"That's the latest style Meenister, it's all the fashion these days. You'll be all the rage, so you will." Harrold tried to calm Colin and just when he thought he was going to agree that it was indeed the latest thing, Colin put his hand into the jacket pocket and pulled out a number of strong smelling white pellets the size of a child's marble. "What's this!? Mothballs!? Is this one of your old stock of de-mob suits Harrold!?"

"Well, um, good styles never go out of fashion Meenister, I mean… I thought you…"

"You thought that I would want to get married in a de-mob suit?" Colin was not best pleased. "I can't turn up at church smelling of moth-balls, whatever will Lorna say? She thinks I am wearing a kilt. I only have a few hours, oh dear, what am I to do?"

Harrold looked around the store and suddenly had an idea. "Don't be worrying yourself Colin, I think I have the answer, you'll be a proper Highland gentleman."

Colin followed Harrold into the part of the shop which was kept for the 'more discerning shopper' as Harrold had once told him.

By this time the ladies had followed him through and saw what Colin was wearing.

One of the ladies said, "Oh for mercy's sake, it's one of Mr MacDonald's de-mob suits! Imagine giving the Meenister a demob suit for his wedding?" The other ladies tutted and shook their heads. "Poor Meenister, he looks like thon James Cagney in one of the gangster films, and him on his wedding day too!" said another.

As they walked through the shop, Colin saw where Harrold was heading, "Don't even think about it!" he said loudly as Harrold stopped beside two mannequins which had a sign saying, 'Highland Gentleman with Lady in Tartan.'
"Now, don't be hasty Colin, you must admit that the gentleman is about your size and build - and the kilt is good quality. Why not try it on, what harm can it do?"

Colin was at the stage where he would try anything, there were only a few hours before the wedding!
"Okay Harrold, I suppose I have no choice, anything is better than walking down the aisle

looking like an American gangster on my wedding day."

Colin changed into the Kilt and tweed jacket which nearly fitted him. As he walked out of the office in his tartan rig out, the ladies were fair excited. "Oh Meenister, how handsome you look, a proper highland gentleman!" One of the ladies remarked. "Aye, so he does," said Mrs Macneill, "and it's my own tartan too!"
"What tartan is it?" Colin asked as he inspected the fabric. "Do you not recognise the bonniest tartan in all the Islands? It's the 'Ancient Macneill of Barra' tartan!"

Mrs McLean covered her mouth and whispered under her breath, "Aye its ancient, just like herself!" much to the amusement of those around her.

Chapter 37

Never fear – MacDougall is here!

All of a sudden, the shop door burst open and to Colin's relief, his friend and best man, Iain MacDougal, made a grand entrance. "Never fear – MacDougall is here!" he shouted for the whole village to hear.

"Oh, thank the good Lord!" Colin said, mightily relieved that Iain, and his Kilt, had arrived in good time. "I was beginning to worry something had happened."

"Och no, Donald John and myself did a wee bit of fishing last night and we had a few boxes to deliver to the hotel - and we couldn't leave without taking a dram, it would be very bad form!"

"I might have known a dram would be involved somewhere along the line! Never mind, you're here now, have you got my kilt?"

"Aye, Donald John has it outside, I'll bring it in and maybe Mr MacDonald will find you a safe place to change into it."

As he turned to go outside, Donald John entered the shop holding Colin's kilt, jacket, brogues and all the other bits and pieces needed to complete the outfit.

"Oh, it's yourself Meenister, how are you today?" said Donald John.

"All the better for seeing you!" Colin breathed a sigh of relief to see his Wedding outfit in the flesh, so to speak, and he hastily changed in the ladies changing room.

As he emerged from the changing room all the ladies were in a flutter. "Oh, it's handsome that you are Meenister," said Mrs Macneill.

"Aye, it's Lorna that is the lucky one!" called Mrs McLean.

Colin's embarrassment greatly amused Iain and Donald John.

"Och, he's a bonnie boy right enough. Just a pity about the legs!" his friend Iain said. Donald John called in his wife Rhona and girls Kirsty and Mháiri to see Colin in all his highland glory. Uisdean and Donalda, Donald John's neighbours, were there too and they all agreed that he was indeed the finest highland gentleman in all the Islands.

If only to stop the hilarity at his expense, Colin said, "Well we can't stand around all day gassing, there's a wedding to go to!"
"Lead on MacDuff!" Iain MacDougall shouted and ushered the family and friends out of the shop.

Harrold noticed the time, he was under strict instructions not be home any later than 12 o'clock and it was now 11.55!
"Ok Ladies it's time to go, I have to close up and get ready for the church.
It's alright for you. You're all dressed up and ready to go – but I have my kilt to put on and maybe get a cup of tea, so come away now." He opened the shop door and ushered the ladies out.
Cathy McIvor said cheekily, "Oooh Mr McDonald, I've never seen your legs before, that'll be a treat for us ladies!"

The others giggled, causing Harrold to turn a bright shade of red.

"Now, now, that's enough of that kind of lewdatious talk Mrs McIvor. Remember, it's to the Lord's house that you will be going." Which only served to set the ladies off again.

Outside, Kirsty and Mhàiri kept looking admiringly at Colin and nudging each other. "He's a smasher isn't he?" said Kirsty.

"Aye he is that!" replied her sister Mhàiri and they both giggled.

"Now stop that giggling you two!" said their mother Rhona sternly. Then she lowered her head and whispered, "But you are right, he *is* dishy isn't he?"

All three of them went into a fit of laughter bringing a glower from Donald John. "Don't be calling the Meenister 'dishy', that's blastfeemious. The good Lord will be taking notes on you three!" They looked at each other and that started them off again.

Aunty Bunty and Mrs McRae were completely bewildered with all that was going on and they looked at each other wondering what sort of place they had found themselves in, it seemed like an alien country and culture like nothing they had ever known. Little did they know that things were going to be even more 'alien' in the next few days!

Round the corner, in the MacDonald household, Lorna was getting the rollers taken out of her hair by Mrs McQueen, and then the finishing touches were completed by applying a few skooshes of hair lacquer to keep it all in place.

Ailsa the Flower girl, the Maid of honour and two bridesmaids were next.

Lorna's mother was keeping them supplied with scones, pancakes and cups of tea as they all chatted excitedly.

One of the bridesmaids said to Lorna, "I hope you have 'something old and something new, something borrowed and something blue,' Lorna, it's tradition you know."

Another bridesmaid added, "Oh, and a garter, you must have a garter!" and all the girls giggled.

Lorna's mum chastised them saying, "Now there's no need for that kind of talk girls! It's the Meenister Lorna is marrying, not one of the local boys just down from the hills."

"Yes, Mrs MacDonald," they said in unison as they looked at each other and smiled.

Chapter 38

The Wedding

Colin went to the croft for the final preparations. On the way, he dropped Aunty Bunty and Mrs McRae off at Mr & Mrs McLeod's croft. Uisdean and Donalda were lodging with Chrissie Logan, and Donald John and the girls were staying with Rhona's cousin, Ina.

Colin made himself a cup of tea and a sandwich, not forgetting a custard cream. He sat, taking a few moments to calm himself and say a short prayer.

Then he stood up, took a deep breath, picked up his speech and left for the church.

*

Lorna and Colin had sent an open invitation around the island inviting everyone who fancied a 'good day out', to come the Wedding. A large number turned out in their best 'bib and tucker,' with hats, frocks, kilts and the men were wearing a sprig of white heather in their lapel.

There was an air of excitement as the church filled up.

"Oh my, what a turn out!" said Mrs Cochrane looking round as the people flocked in.

"Aye, Pat they're just a lovely couple – and the good Lord has sent a good day for it too!" her friend Jan, said.

The Reverend McCrimmond was mingling and chatting to the people as they arrived. He was wearing his usual black cassock, with a black Geneva gown and black shirt, which was why he was known affectionately as 'the man in black.'

He knew just about everyone there and was liked and respected by them for his many years of faithful service to the islanders.

Colin and his best man, Iain MacDougall, were looking like proper highland gentlemen, resplendent in their kilts and Argyll jackets, as they waited for Lorna to arrive.

Iain was soon a favourite of the people, with his cracks and banter with the guests. Colin joked that Iain was his 'warm up act,' which added to the happy atmosphere.

Everyone was relaxed and enjoying themselves as they waited for the bride to arrive.

Lorna was fashionably late which gave poor Colin a few nervous minutes as he wondered if Lorna had changed her mind at the last minute.

Finally, someone at the door nodded to Reverend McCrimmond that the bridal party had arrived.

Reverend McCrimmond called all present to be upstanding, the door was opened and Lorna and her father entered and walked slowly down the aisle to, 'Here comes the Bride.'

Harrold was every inch the proud father, resplendent in his 'Macdonald Lord of the Isles' tartan kilt, looking around as if to say, "Am I not just the proudest father in all the world?"

Lorna looked stunning in her Bridal gown and veil. So much so that some of the ladies in the church gasped saying, "Oh my, how beautiful she is!" and, "Oh, she is *so* bonny, like a princess, so beautiful and serene."

Little did they know that Lorna's heart was beating nineteen to the dozen.

Colin and his best man stood transfixed – it was as if Lorna was shimmering in slow motion, gliding regally down the aisle.

Colin felt that his tears weren't far away – never before had he seen anyone quite so beautiful.

Lorna's dress was of the whitest white, with intricate lacework over the bodice, cascading into a full length dress which swayed gently as she moved.

Her hair was pinned up with sparkling clips, and loose strands of hair fell gently under her veil.

She carried a bouquet of summer flowers, peony roses and hydrangeas bound with a strip of lace which was taken from her grandmother's wedding dress.

Ailsa, the little flower girl, who was Lorna's God daughter, came next, looking so sweet in her off white lace dress with a lilac ribbon around her waist.
She wore a headband of flowers in her flaming red hair, and in her hand she carried a little posy of Peony roses which were tied with a lilac ribbon. Her freckled face and beaming smile was enough to melt the hearts of everyone there.
If Lorna hadn't been quite so beautiful, Ailsa might well have stolen the limelight.

The Bridesmaids were led by the Maid of honour, Josephine Ireland. Lorna and Josephine were actually cousins but they had also been best pals since their early school days. They looked so beautiful with their full length lilac chiffon dresses, hair pinned up with small lilac flowers and carrying bouquets of summer flowers tied with lilac ribbons – they completed the stunning bridal party.

Everyone was spellbound, it was like a fairy tale procession and Lorna was the beautiful Princess.

Everyone was seated and the service began.

Reverend McCrimmond said, "Who gives this woman?"

To which Harrold proudly answered, "I do," and he gave Lorna's hand to Colin. Lorna stood beside her husband to be and they smiled at each other as Lorna squeezed Colin's hand.

Harrold sat down and Lorna's mother took a handkerchief out of her handbag and handed it to him as the tears ran down his face.

"Thank you, Peggy. Isn't she bonny?"

"Aye Harrold, we've done a good job, don't you think?"

"We have that," Harrold agreed, "I'm the luckiest man in the world, having two beautiful women in my life!"

She slipped her arm under his and they both shed tears of happiness as they watched their beautiful daughter marry the man of her dreams.

Reverend McCrimmond gave a lovely ceremony, it was a good balance between the old traditions and the modern ways, which was much appreciated by the young as well as the older folk.

The highlight of the service was when they were taking their vows and Colin took a deep breath and made his vow to Lorna in Gaelic.

When he had finished, Lorna leaned over and kissed him and said, "It's the dark horse that you are, Colin Campbell!" and the congregation clapped and cheered in appreciation.

Donald John looked over at his friend Uisdean, winked and gave the thumbs up sign.

With the help of Calum McLeod, their clandestine coaching had paid off.

Mrs McRae was so enthralled by it all that she called out, "Oh, he's saying his vows in Garlic!" Much to the amusement of all.

Everyone agreed that it was the most moving and beautiful Wedding they had ever seen.

Chapter 39

The Ceilidh

As Mr & Mrs Campbell walked down the aisle and out of the church, there was the usual cheering, clapping and confetti throwing.

Miss Grant, Lorna's old school teacher, was so pleased to see her former student looking so happy. "Oh, what a lovely couple they make," she said. "Surely a marriage made in heaven if ever there was," as she dabbed emotional tears of joy from her eyes.

Colin had planned to drive off in the McLeod's Rolls Royce but it was nowhere to be seen. Just at that very moment he heard the chug-chug of a tractor as it came round the corner and stopped outside the church.
It was decorated with garlands of flowers and two wooden chairs were fixed in the trailer.

Calum McLeod jumped out of the cab and said, "Mr & Mrs Campbell, your carriage awaits!" to which there was a loud cheer.

Colin and Lorna were helped up into the trailer, and the sound of tin cans tied to the back could be heard throughout the island as they were escorted down to the village hall.

Outside of the church, a group of children were eagerly anticipating the bride's father carrying out his traditional duty which was known simply as – 'the scramble.'

Harrold dutifully obliged by opening the car window as they left the car park and threw out a handful of pennies, thruppenny bits and sixpences. The children were delighted and made an excited 'scramble' for as many coins as they could each gather.

It was traditional for the Minister to be invited to the Wedding Reception and to be seated at the top table to give the Grace before the meal.

Quite often there would be a swift bit of 'slight of hand' as place names were swapped around to avoid sitting next to the Minister. But on this occasion the dubious honour fell to the best man, Iain MacDougall, who was more than happy to keep the 'Meenister' company.

The Reverend McCrimmond said Grace which lasted nearly five minutes and closed by saying, *'and may we never forget the needs of those who are not so blessed as ourselves. Amen.'*

The 'Wedding Breakfast,' as it was called, consisted of chicken soup, chicken or Salmon, (*poached, of course*), potatoes and veg, followed by trifle and cream.
It was enjoyed by all and there was a lovely warm buzz as the guests chatted away.

After the meal, the speeches were given, with Harrold becoming quite emotional. But he lightened the proceedings by saying, "We might have lost a McDonald but we welcome a Campbell into the family – and don't worry Reverend, you're quite safe!"

As might be expected, Iain MacDougall's toast was both humorous and emotional as he remembered happy days in University, hillwalking in Glencoe, and some scrapes in the Glencoe Inn, where Colin took his first ever dram.

Iain also remembered Colin's mother and father and said how proud they would have been of their son.

Once the meal and the speeches were over, the serious business of the Ceilidh, began.

Two '40 ouncers' of whisky were brought out and placed on the top table as the 'Band' struck up.

'Charlie Campbell and his band' played a waltz for the first dance. After Colin and Lorna had been around the floor a couple of times, others joined in and soon the dance floor was full.

As the evening progressed the music became faster with old Kenny McIsaac jazzing things up by breaking out the spoons and showing his dexterity by tapping out the beat on his elbows, knees, fingers, chest, and to the horror of some of the elderly ladies, on his rear-end.

It was a great atmosphere as grannies and children danced and laughed together.

Particularly good fun was had during the eightsome reels, the Gay Gordons, Canadian Barn dance and the Strip the Willow dances, where there was much laughing and barracking if someone went the wrong way.

Throughout the evening, Colin and Lorna circulated round the tables, chatting and thanking guests for coming along to their wedding.

The Raffle was drawn and everyone sat in anticipation as the winning numbers were called out.

There was great cheer when Colin and Lorna won the 10 pound Salmon (kindly donated by Calum McLeod).

Lorna's mother won the bottle of Sherry, Mrs McLeod won the pair of silk stockings and her husband Calum, won the bottle of bubble bath.

Old Mrs Cameron, who was a staunch teetotaller, won the bottle of whisky and Calum was quick off the mark to ask her if she'd like to swap the bottle for the bubble bath, and was highly delighted when she agreed! Calum never missed a trick, especially if there was a dram involved!

The highlight of the evening for most of the guests was having a small wager on who would drink who under the table, as they watched Reverend McCrimmond and Iain MacDougall taking dram for dram.
Most of the money was on Iain due to his substantial bulk, but as the night wore on, Reverend McCrimmond began to slowly pull ahead and Iain seemed to be struggling, *'I shouldn't have had that last double helping of trifle,'* he said to himself.

But Iain got his second wind and pulled ahead in the final hour of the evening.

"Aye, it was a near thing," Iain admitted later, "but I got him on the home straight!"

Throughout the evening, two elderly brothers, Sandy and Danny McGillivray took a shine to Aunty Bunty and Mrs McRae and got them up for just about every dance.

"Don't be getting any ideas!" Mrs McRae said to Sandy, "I've got a husband waiting at home!"

But Aunty Bunty was quick to make it clear to Danny that she was a free agent!

They hit it off and Danny manged to get Aunty Bunty's address and promised to keep in touch.

"Can I see you home Bunty? I have the tractor outside,' Danny said with a wink. *(Not a line you often hear at the dancing these days).*

"What, to Bearsden?" Bunty said with a cheeky smile.

Sandy said to his brother, "It's the smooth tongue that you have. You always had a way with the ladies!"

"What can I say? I can't help it if I am the spitting image of thon Gary Cooper," Danny teased.

"Gary Cooper? More like Tommy Cooper!" Sandy gave as good as he got.

Everyone agreed it was a great day all together.

It was almost midnight when Colin and Lorna made their weary way back to the Croft, hand in hand, Lorna and Colin were on cloud nine.

It was a lovely starlit night and Colin seemed to be daydreaming. "What are you thinking about sweetheart?" Lorna asked.

"I was thinking about how blessed we are and what a lovely wee croft we have – our *forever home.*"

"Yes, God certainly is good," Lorna agreed.

"I was thinking about a name for it.

Calum McLeod said a good name would be 'Marag Dhubh', it sounds very 'Gaelic' doesn't it?

Apparently, it means 'peace and happiness', at least, that's what Calum said.

"Oh, did he now?" Lorna smiled and said under her breath, *"Wait 'till I see that rascal Calum McLeod!"*

It was the end of a perfect day –
but not the end of their exploits –
they were only just beginning………….

To be continued……

If you would like to follow the continued exploits of Colin and Lorna, plus a lot more Highland High Jinks – keep your eyes open for **Book 3** - 'Even more Tales of a Highland Minister' which will be coming out in the not too distant future…

It is a collection of short stories including ~

The Minister and the Tinkers Curse

The Minister and the Bothan

The Minister and the Black book of Rhua

The Minister and the Whisky Olympics

The Minister and the Selkies grave

The Minister and the Haunted Croft

The Minister goes Fishing

The Minister and the Witches Cat

*

A Taster of Book 3 ~

The Minister and the Whisky Olympics

It was the day of the Rhua and District Gaelic Mod where all thing Gaelic were celebrated. There would be competitions for songs, poems, recitations, Highland Dancing and much more. It was a hub for all things Gaelic, and people would travel from near and far to compete, support or simply experience the atmosphere.

Last year there was a Gaelic skiffle band from the small Island of Eigg who called themselves, 'Eigg and Chips,' which nearly caused a riot as the lead singers trousers fell down while hitting a particularly high note during their own version of, "A dram's a dram for a' that and a' that!"

This year there was a record number of contestants in attendance and Rhua was awash with campers and travellers. Tents covered the Machair and just about every home had taken in a lodger for the week of the Mod.

"My goodness, what a swarm of incomers," observed Mrs McKinnon.

"Aye Zena, sure they're like the midgies, there's clouds of them everywhere!" replied her husband Fred. "I was in Mr Ali's shop this morning and by the time I got to the front of the que, there were no rolls left and not a tea bag in sight!" Zena was not amused. *The locals silently (and sometimes not so silently) tolerated the cultural tourists.*

"Och, but they're harmless tho', didn't my brother Norrie not say the same thing."

"Harmless!? Have you tried to get a half bottle of uisge *(whisky)* while the Mod is on? My cousin Murdo stocks up a few weeks before they come, just to be safe."

"But it's only for a week, Fred."

"Aye, but a week is a fair sentence when there's no' a dram in the house!"

"Aye Zena, just that," Fred had to agree.

It was Day 2, the Mod was now in full swing and already there had been controversy in the under 9's children's singing competition.

8 year old twins Jimmy and Jeannie Fraser has to be stopped mid verse as they innocently sung alternate

verses of the old ballad, 'The Ball of Kirriemuir', in Gaelic.

At first they appeared as sweet little angels – until they got into their routine.

The judges sat with mouths open and horror-struck as the two little cherubs sang the song and added a little dance for effect.

"Where did you learn that song?" one of the Judges asked them. "Oh, it's a song that daddy sings when he comes home from the pub," said wee Jeanie. "Would you like us to sing the other verses for you?"

"No, no!.... that will be all for now, thank you."

Little Jimmy and Jeannie came down from the stage in tears for not being allowed to sing the rest of their father's favourite song.

Their father, who was in the audience, and was fortified by strong drink, stood up and harassed the judges so much that had to be escorted from the premises...

...and there's more.... in Book 3

Gabh cùram agus Dia beannaich.

'Take care and God bless'

I hope you enjoyed reading
my book and it gave you
a few smiles along the way.
Slainte!
Iain

The Tale of *Quisquis*

Reading the Rule of
St Benedict as Story

The Tale of *Quisquis*

Reading the Rule of
St Benedict as Story

Hugh Gilbert, OSB

G<small>RACEWING</small>

First published in 2014

Gracewing
2 Southern Avenue
Leominster
Herefordshire HR6 0QF

ISBN 978 0 85244 754 3

Typeset by Action Publishing Technology Ltd
Gloucester GL1 5SR

Contents

Preface

Like St Benedict proposing the measure of his monks' wine, it is 'with some misgiving' that I publish these monastic conferences; I am all too aware of their limitations. Further, since becoming a bishop, even while remaining a monk, I no longer live in a monastery and in that sense am removed from the Rule on which these conferences turn.

However, here they are. There is no call for misgivings about the Rule of St Benedict. It is not always as cuddly as some contemporary advocacy of it suggests. It is far more. It is a reading of the Gospel given us by one of the great Spirit-filled saints of Christian history, one in whom was the spirit of all the just and of Christ himself, as St Gregory the Great perceived. Those individuals and communities that take it to heart find the Gospel taking flesh in and among and around them. If western monasticism slips this anchor, it will drift aimlessly and, mixing metaphors, bear no fruit on the vine of Christ. And only with a flourishing religious life and a goodly number of monasteries is the Church truly herself. At the same time indeed, the Rule must be constantly rediscovered, its deepest intentions explored and re-expressed. It is this living validity of the Rule these pages would like to serve.

This book is a collection of monastic conferences. The monastic conference is a genre of its own. Not quite homily, not lecture, not scholarly exegesis, and notoriously capable of inducing sleep in the listeners. The conferences that follow were originally given either to my own community of Pluscarden or to other communities of monks or nuns, often in the context of annual retreats. They may begin from a particular setting, be it in the liturgy or in life, or simultaneously in both. They are, in that sense, occasional. They presuppose a certain biblical and patristic culture. The Prologue of the Rule, Chapter 7 on Humility and, more briefly, Chapter 72 on Good Zeal seem to me specimens, transposed within the Rule itself, of what a conference is. It aims to be a bridge between the word of God and the minds and hearts of the listeners. Given that the monastic life endeavours simply to live out the demands of our faith and baptism, and indeed the primordial human longing for God, the things that concern monks are hopefully of concern to all Christians. Happily, contemporary monasticism is aware of how much it receives from those lay men and women who cherish the wisdom of the Rule. These pages are at least as much for them.

I dedicate this book to all those monks and nuns from many lands, 'serving under the Rule of our holy Father Benedict', whom it has been and is such a privilege to know and to have as brothers and sisters. And I ask the prayers of all those who read it.

+ Hugh Gilbert, OSB
Bishop of Aberdeen

Explanation

A word is in order to explain not simply the title, but the general approach to the Rule adopted in these conferences. It is based on a distinction.

The Rule has been called either *Regula monasteriorum* (a Rule for *monasteries*) or *Regula monachorum* (a Rule for *monks*). It is both. As a Rule for monasteries, it outlines the way in which the 'house of God' (31.19; 53.22; 64.5) is to be built up. As a Rule for monks, it shows the individual the way to 'return' to God (Prol. 2). The Rule is therefore an 'instrument' (cf. 73.6) at the simultaneous service of social and personal charity, and it can be read from either or both perspectives.

A Rule for Monasteries

As a *Rule for Monasteries*, it offers a kind of architecture. If St Thomas Aquinas, a genius in the speculative order, constructed a theological house of God in his *summae*, St Benedict, a genius in the practical order, provided in his Rule for the building of a cenobitic house of God. From this perspective, the Rule unfolds as follows:

By the end of the Prologue, St Benedict is ready to launch his cenobitic enterprise: 'we must therefore establish a school of the Lord's service' (v. 45). Thereafter, like the divine Wisdom of Proverbs, he sets up seven pillars (Prov. 9:1) which create the space for this school, this house, to take shape.

These seven pillars are:

- a Rule and an abbot (chs 1 – 3), that is, both a law, an agreed pattern for life in common, and a head, leader, father, shepherd and teacher who is believed to hold the place of Christ;
- a spiritual teaching (chs 4 – 7), received from Scripture, the catechetical tradition of the Church and the teaching of the monastic fathers, to be imparted by the abbot for the nourishment and guidance and common commitment of the brethren;
- a pattern of common prayer (chs 8 – 20), creating and expressing a climate and habit of prayer, having the form of the Divine Office or Work of God, distributed over day and night and of which the major ingredient is psalmody, the Eucharist being taken for granted;
- a programme of pastoral care (chs 21 – 30) for the spiritually and morally weaker brethren, offering a disciplinary process drawn from the Gospel and St Paul and the early Church, enabling the community to address errant behaviour and creating possibilities of reintegration for the delinquent and self-isolating;
- guidance for work and the communal economy (chs 31 – 57), aimed at a provision for the community's physical and material well-being permeated by a spectrum of Christian values;
- structures for continuance (chs 58 – 66), enabling a future for the community through processes both for the initiation of new members and for the appointment of members to office;
- infusion of spirit (chs 67–72/73), a restatement of the spiritual teaching given earlier but in a more openly cenobitic key, aimed at inspiring the 'body' of the community with a 'spirit' / ethic / ethos of pure intentions, generous obedience, non-possessiveness and non-aggression, good zeal and a desire to progress beyond the initial.

Thank God, there is a healthy true-to-life untidiness to the Rule and not every chapter fits neatly into the proposed scheme. But the patterns summarized above are not purely subjective. There is a quasi-orderly unfolding of the essential elements that build community. This perspective has a further potential. It enables superiors and communities to be faithful to the Rule in changing circumstances. It helps name the essential requirements while leaving freedom to adapt to circumstances of time and place. This perspective therefore serves the programme proposed by the Second Vatican Council in *Perfectae Caritatis*. In my own monastic lifetime, for example, I have witnessed a passage from the almost complete neglect of chapters 23 to 30 to a painful rediscovery of their relevance provoked by the scandal of child abuse. In other words, sin and human weakness remain alive in monasteries and are not a purely private matter, but require some kind of corporate response, an assumption of responsibility on the part of the whole. This is precisely the essential St Benedict envisages in those chapters.

A Rule for Monks

As a Rule *for monks*, St Benedict's masterpiece can be read as a guide for the individual on his journey to eternal life.

It is this perspective that the following conferences largely adopt. Here the Rule is more than an architect's plan. It is a signpost indicating a path. It offers a horizon and a direction for one 'truly seeking God'. It enables an individual life to become a story.

The great biblical image of the 'way' underlies and unites the whole Rule, most visibly in the Prologue (vv. 2, 7, 13, 20, 21, 22, 24, 25, 42, 44, 48, 49) and the Epilogue which is chapter 73 (vv. 2, 4, 8, 9).

A focus on the individual also suffuses the whole and is captured in the simple pronoun *quisquis* – 'anyone', 'whoever you are'. This neatly brackets the Rule by appearing in v. 3 of the Prologue and v. 8 of the Epilogue. So this is a way of life for 'plain Jane', for any Tom, Dick or Harry. Echoes of Tolkien! Even more, echoes of St Paul: 'Consider your own call, my brothers: not many of you were wise by human standards, not many were powerful, not many were of noble birth.

But God chose what is foolish in the world to shame the wise; God chose what is weak in the world to shame the strong; God chose what is low and despised in the world, things that are not, to reduce to nothing things that are, so that no one might boast in the presence of God. He is the source of your life in Christ Jesus . . .' (1 Cor. 1:26–30).

A next step is to uncover in the Rule a *narrative* of such an individual's return to God as it unfolds in his inner and outer life. As the chapters follow their at times disorderly order, it seems possible to discern a hidden 'story of a soul'. Hence the title and sub-title of this book, *The Tale of Quisquis: Reading the Rule of St Benedict as Story*.

A pedagogical conceit in the seventeenth-century sense? Undoubtedly! Eisegesis? Often enough! Yet I can't quite shrug off this impression of a story being told, a biography being written, a journey narrated. So here it is. The intention is not to irritate or, for that matter, make a contribution to scholarship. The hope is rather that readers find points of contact with their own Christian experience, and sometimes smile. A Benedictine friend recently pointed out how ch. 66 on the Porters of the Monastery, often thought to be the Rule's original ending, paints a beautiful picture of a 'wise old man', and therefore of a monk nearing the end of his life's journey. There he is, an embodiment of the spirit of the Rule, hospitable, gentle, with a fervour of love born of fear of the Lord, mature, that is, ready to give himself, available for others and not given to wandering about, grateful, perhaps hearing in every knock on the door and poor man's cry the coming of the Lord for whom he now longs in a heart purified by the grace of God and 'long probation in the monastery'. It is *Quisquis* nearing his goal.

The Plot

Here is an outline:

In the Prologue, *Quisquis* is led by the word of God to a captivating encounter with Christ himself, who calls him to follow him along his way. At the end of the Prologue, it becomes clear that this following takes place in the company of others – the *schola*. So, in chs 1 to 3, *Quisquis* finds himself becoming a disciple with others in a structured and regularized community – *sub regula vel abbate*. In chs 4 to 7, as he assimilates the teaching given in this *schola*, he is drawn ever more deeply into the following of Christ, and especially into the paschal virtues of obedience, silence and humility. Pursuing this way with his whole heart, he finds himself 'reduced to nothing', 'humbled completely', that is, conformed to the cross-bearing Christ, and at the same time paradoxically raised up into a life of the perfect love that casts out fear and makes him a bearer of the Spirit. He knows the Cross, the Resurrection and Pentecost from within. This resurrection of the inner man expresses itself, first, in chs 8 to 20, in a God-ward direction, in psalmody and prayer, praise and intercession, and then, in chs 21 to 72, in constant service of his brethren. This service, offered in awareness of personal sinfulness (23 to 30, applied to self) and physical limitation (22), is directed to the brethren in both their spiritual frailty (23 to 30) and their physical needs (31 to 57). It flowers in a spiritual fatherhood which forwards the life of the community (58 to 66), and leads to an ever fuller experience of brotherhood, the 'I' taken up into the 'we' (67 to 72). In ch. 73, *Quisquis* is pointed further still: into the deepest life of the Church, to the *doctrina* of the holy Fathers and the *virtus* of the Holy Spirit.

Of course this is not, in reality or experience, a rectilinear process. Just as the Rule is to be read often in community (66), so the different stages of this journey are to be traversed repeatedly. Nor is it a triumph of the will. It is a work of God. At its heart, it is a story of an ever-fuller immersion in the Paschal Mystery of Christ, and an ever-fuller expression of that in the twofold commandment of love.

> As we progress in our monastic life and faith, our hearts shall be enlarged, and we shall run with unspeakable sweetness in the way of God's commands (Prol. 49).

Put more briefly still, the *Tale of Quisquis* tells how someone who has fallen in love with Christ (Prologue) and entered a fellowship of brothers (1 to 3) is led through the humility of obedience (4 to 7) to a love of God expressed in constant prayer and a love of neighbour expressed in assiduous service (8 to 72).

Corroborations

The same trajectory underlies, I think, this paragraph of John Paul II's *Vita Consecrata*:

> From the first centuries of the Church, men and women have felt called to imitate the Incarnate Word who took on the condition of a servant. They have sought to follow him by living in a particularly radical way, through monastic profession, the demands flowing from baptismal participation in the Paschal Mystery of his Death and Resurrection. In this way, by becoming bearers of the Cross (*staurophoroi*), they have striven to become bearers of the Spirit (*pneumatophoroi*), authentically spiritual men and women, capable of endowing history with hidden fruitfulness by unceasing praise and intercession, by spiritual counsels and works of charity (*Vita Consecrata*, 6).

There is a tacit story-line here too. It begins with a 'feeling called' to imitate the Incarnate Word. This leads to participation in the Paschal Mystery, which in turn bears Spirit-inspired fruit in Godward 'praise and intercession' and manward 'spiritual counsel and works of charity'.

From this it is an easy further step to parallel the way opened up by the Rule with that traversed by the first disciples according to the New Testament. There Peter and Andrew, James and John, Mary of Magdala and the others, are first captivated by an encounter with Christ and drawn into each other's company in his *schola* where his teaching is the Rule and he himself the Abbot. His beauty and their love draw them to follow him to Jerusalem where they too, in another mode than their Master, die and rise. In the Acts of the Apostles, gifted now by the Holy Spirit, the disciples live a 'risen' life in constant prayer and praise, in mutual service and mission to others. The same is implied in the Apostolic Letters.

Under the Guidance of the Gospel

If these insights are valid, then the New Testament, the monastic wisdom of the Rule and the teaching of the contemporary Church conspire together. They indicate the one same path. It is not a rigid progression of achievements but a natural unfolding of the Christian life. It is a tale that grace writes over and over again in our lives, and that we rediscover again and again in the light of the Holy Spirit. It is made of demanding and beautiful things: the encounter with Christ, the engagement in Christian community, progressive initiation into the Paschal Mystery, a fruitfulness to the glory of God and the salvation of souls.

What other story could the Rule tell?

The Essential Rule

'Simon, son of John, do you love me?' (Jn 21:16)

'To prefer nothing to the love of Christ' (4.21) is the central call of the Rule of St Benedict. It is repeated twice more: '. . . those who hold nothing dearer to themselves than Christ' (5.2); 'let them prefer absolutely nothing to Christ' (72.11).

The final formulation, with its *omnino* ('absolutely'), is the most decisive. It is followed by the clause, 'and may he lead us all together to everlasting life' (72.11). So there is both a vertical intensification of the call to love Christ and a horizontal extension of it. Doesn't this suggest the Cross?

In any case, the call to preferential love of Christ sounds three times. Whatever is said three times is said intentionally and emphatically. 'Holy, holy, holy' is not a slip of the tongue. The triple 'nothing' also anticipates the famous 'Nada, nada, nada' of St John of the Cross.

St Benedict's call 'to prefer nothing to the love of Christ' echoes that of Jesus in the Gospel – the call to follow him wholeheartedly, putting him even over the claims of family.

> Whoever loves father or mother more than me is not worthy of me; and whoever loves son or daughter more than me is not worthy of me; and whoever does not take up the cross and follow me is not worthy of me. He who finds his life will lose it, and he who loses his life for my sake will find it (Mt. 10:37–39).

This is the 'apostolic Rule' followed by Mary, the apostles, the first disciples. It is a call to an 'undivided devotion to the Lord' (1 Cor. 7:35). Celibacy arises here. This call implies the divinity of Christ, for who can require such love unless one who shares the Godhead? It embodies the devotion of the early Church to the person of Christ, 'the true King', against the claims of Caesar to absolute allegiance.

It recalls the spirituality of the Church of the martyrs, deriving as it does from formulae of St Cyprian, martyred himself.[1] One of the ways we live the prayer, 'Thy will be done', says St Cyprian, is 'to prefer altogether nothing to Christ *because he preferred nothing to us.*' Our love of Christ is rooted in Christ's love of us (cf. Gal. 2:20; Rev. 1:5).

It was part of the advice St Anthony, the 'first monk', gave to all Christians as he emerged momentously from his twenty years of solitude and struggle: 'to prefer nothing in the world above the love of Christ'.[2]

By putting the preferential love of Christ at the heart of the Rule, St Benedict makes the monastic life a *lived profession* of the divinity of Christ, a parallel to the *doctrinal profession* of the early Ecumenical Councils. One can sense in the Rule his own passion for the person of the Lord. Within the Rule itself, this preferential love of Christ translates in practice into:

- 'obedience without delay' (5.1; cf. 71.3);
- 'care of the sick before all and above all' (36.1);
- 'let them prefer nothing to the work of God' (43.3).

Thus the three great spiritual strands of the Rule – obedience, service of the brethren, and prayer – are all expressions of the love of Christ. These three 'preferences' verify the great preference for Christ. And this love unifies our life.

It is a love awakened by the Holy Spirit and grown into over the years. It both arouses and orders all other loves. It is nourished by the encounter with Christ, especially in word and sacrament, the Gospels and the Eucharist.

It is also possible to take the phrase 'the love of Christ' not as an objective genitive, but as a *subjective* one denoting the love Christ himself has and lives. Read thus it becomes a call to live the monastic life as a share in Christ's loving, especially his spousal *love for the Church* (Eph. 5:2; 5:25).

The more we love Christ, the more his loving enters our hearts and takes over our lives. Once again, we are brought to the Cross.

Notes

1. St Cyprian, *On the Lord's Prayer,* 15; *To Fortunatus*, Preface 5, 6, and elsewhere.
2. St Athanasius, *Life of Anthony,* 14.

1

Catching the Ball

Forgive me opening, not with Scripture, but with some lines of an Austrian poet who once described himself as 'almost rabidly anti-Christian', Rainer Maria Rilke:

> Catch only what you've thrown yourself, all is
> Mere skill and little gain;
> But when you're suddenly the catcher of a ball
> Thrown by an eternal partner
> With accurate and measured swing
> Towards you, to your centre, in an arch
> From the great bridge-building of God:
> Why, catching then becomes a power –
> Not yours, a world's.

Marvellous lines! Are they not a contemporary equivalent of Ps. 1, and its two ways, the way of the just and the way of the wicked? They cut to the root. They 'image' the two contrasting stances we can take. Personally, they remind me of solitary childhood hours playing cricket (a great English game) throwing a ball against a wall and hitting it with a bat, all by myself. 'Catch only what you've thrown yourself, all is / Mere skill and little gain.' How much better when the older boy two houses away would condescend to play. Then it was for real. He could bowl! One thing to swim in a swimming pool, another to plunge into the living water of the river or the sea. One thing to think philosophically as an idealist, within a world essentially all of one's own mind's making, another to think as a realist, exposed to the terrors and joys of a world greater than oneself. Is not this the fundamental choice that faces us? To close ourselves or open ourselves. To clutch our own ball, play our own game, live solipsistically, be it alone or with others, or open our hearts and minds to the mysterious gift that comes through the air, silently maybe, from 'an eternal partner / with accurate and measured swing / Towards [us], to [our] centre, in an arch.' 'Why, catching then becomes a power – Not yours, a world's.' In other words (I take it): enter this game, accept the Eternal Partner, and be enlarged, become a world, a creation which answers to Him, gives back His glory.

There is indeed a secular humanism, there is a self-centred way of living, there is a spirituality which, however gilded, come to nothing more than catching what we've thrown ourselves. 'Buddhism is a coherence without God', I read recently; it lacks the Other. 'I wanted to be virtuous but not religious,' said John Henry Newman of himself as an adolescent.

But polemics are not the point. Rilke begins with catching what we've thrown ourselves, talking to ourselves, living for ourselves, but he goes on to the ball that comes swinging through the air from elsewhere, 'from the great bridge-building of God'. And mercifully it does. Early in Cardinal Newman's *Apologia pro Vita Sua* come two sentences (in exquisite English). 'When I was fifteen (in the autumn of 1816) a great change of thought came over me. I fell under the influences of a definite Creed and received into my mind impressions of dogma which, through God's mercy, have never been effaced or obscured.'[1] Mercifully, the Eternal Partner makes himself known. 'The Lord said to Abram ...' 'God called to him out of the bush, "Moses, Moses!"' ... 'Jesus said to her, "Mary!"' ... 'And he fell to the ground and heard a voice saying, "Saul, Saul, why do you persecute me?"'

'But when you're suddenly the catcher of a ball / Thrown by an eternal partner.' The imagery may bring to mind the great New Testament theme of *paradosis* (*traditio*, handing-over, handing-on). The Father hands over the Son; the Son hands over himself, and, exalted, hands over the Spirit he has received from the Father. The apostles in turn hand on what they receive from the Lord, the Church hands on what she receives from them. She hands the catechumen the Creed and the Lord's Prayer: the Lenten *traditio,* to be answered by a *redditio.* The ball both bounces down the centuries and comes straight, again and again, from the great bridge-building of God, towards us, to our centre, in an arch. And generation after generation, hands are raised to receive it. 'I believe', 'Our Father'. 'Why, catching then becomes a power – not yours, a world's'.

We have been opened up by this approach of God's, mercifully, each of us, just as human history as a whole has been opened up by the approach of God, in creation and in the story of salvation. Opened up above all by the empty tomb, that great wound in humanity's flank.

I only hope it's not too shattering an anti-climax to introduce here the Rule of St Benedict. It has its place, though. Monastic initiation, like Christian initiation, makes use of *traditiones.* Very concrete and most expressive. At solemn profession (in our rite), the cowl (symbol of the new man) and the psalter or antiphonal (the symbol of prayer). For a nun, a veil, a ring, a crown. There is also the Rule, given *chez nous* at first profession and then just prior to final profession. 'My son,' says the Abbot, 'behold the Law in the light of which you wish to fight for Christ.' An abbot is also handed the Rule when he is blessed. He is handed it now for the third time in his life. He's handed it, not just for himself, but for others. 'Take this Rule,' says the Bishop, 'which contains the tradition of holiness received from our fathers. As God gives you strength and human frailty allows, use it to guide and sustain your brothers whom God has placed in your care.' How often, as we know, the iconography of St Benedict features this *traditio.* What a suggestive and eloquent gesture it is!

'Catch only what you've thrown yourself . . .' The Rule is not something we have thrown ourselves. It is not a fruit of our *voluntas propria*; so we are safe. The monastic life, of which it is a concrete symbol, is not something we have thrown ourselves. It comes from the Eternal Partner, 'with accurate and measured swing'. The *Rule* has been put into my hands, literally and metaphorically. Christ himself has put it there. It is part of the bridge-building; it is part of His mercy. He has handed me this humble, awkward, rugged, sometimes distasteful thing, the Rule of St Benedict: *Ecce lex!* And, so doing, he has thrown me, not without a smile perhaps, this way of life in the Church, this 'tradition of holiness received from our fathers'. It comes 'with accurate and measured swing / To [my] centre, in an arch / From the great bridge-building of God.' It is precisely what prevents me playing my own game, living in my own world only. It is precisely what cracks me open, enlarges my hands and my heart, enables me to enter into the real game, makes me a world – someone who corresponds, answers to the Lord, is capable of a *redditio,* as Mary was *par excellence. Ecce ancilla Domini.* 'Standing before God, I promise . . .'

So yes, I am taking the Rule as my text. Not as an absolute, but as a physical, verbal, literary symbol of the great bridge-building of God in our lives; as something to which we open our hands; as a sacramental of our vocation, our way of life in the Church. Just as the gifts to the catechumen of the Creed and the Our Father symbolize God's gifts of faith and prayer, so the gift of the Rule symbolizes the Spirit's gift of our monastic life.

So, one can put together two sayings of the Rule:

- *Ecce lex sub qua militare vis,* 'Behold the law under which you wish to fight' (58.10).

- *Ecce pietate sua demonstrat nobis Dominus viam vitae,* 'Behold in his loving-kindness the Lord shows us the way of life' (Prol. 20).

But when you're suddenly the catcher of a ball . . .

For now, some simple reflections on this gift of a way of life, our monastic vocation in the objective sense. It is not the first gift. 'In the beginning God created the heavens and the earth' (Gen. 1:1). The first gift is our existence, our human life. This life received immediately from our father and mother and ultimately, radically from God, from the Father. This life to be developed, from within, in human society, in the world.

This life comes from love (the *creative* love of God) and is for love (the twofold commandment in our conscience). In English, as in German, there is this close link between the two words, *life* and *love, Leben* and *Liebe*. To be alive is to be loved and to be called to love. How easy to say! But that is the first gift.

Nor is vocation precisely the second gift. 'In the beginning was the Word . . . and the Word became flesh and dwelt among us' (Jn 1:1, 14). The second gift is life in Christ, the gift of grace. Life received through faith and baptism, springing from the womb of the font. Life to be developed, from within, in the Church, the Body of Christ. A life that comes from the *saving* love of God revealed in Christ and unfolded in loving as Christ loved us (cf. Eph. 5:2). The second gift.

But if a young person, let us imagine, has at least in some sense recognized these two gifts, and the task they imply, if he has seen that his humanity will be fulfilled in following Christ, there remains the question, the practical question: what shall I do with my life? How will I love? There is a fine translation of the Rule in English, dating from the 1950s. The translator ends his *Preface* with words from Plato's *Republic*: 'It is no chance topic that engages us, for our subject is: How shall a man order his life?' This is the question. How be a Christian? How live by the guidance of the Gospel? How live love in the Church? How give back – and give on – what I have received? There is this fire within me, but where is the fuel to feed it? What should I do 'while there is still time, while we are in this body and can fulfil all these things by the light of this life' (Prol. 43)? In this instant between two eternities? 'Lord, teach us to pray, as John taught his disciples' (Lk. 11:1).

Ecce pietate sua demonstrat nobis Dominus viam vitae! It is at this point, in answer to this question, this desire, that this way of life is shown me by the Lord, that this ball comes towards me 'to my centre, in an arch, from the great bridge-building of God'. And this gift, this way of life is what completes, implements, actualizes, fulfils the earlier gifts. It is what brings them to a point, for their verifying in action. It gives love a body. It is therefore what enables me to 'await our blessed hope, the appearing of the glory of our great God and

Saviour, Jesus Christ' (Titus 2:13), that final gift to which all others are ordered, the gift of eternal life. It is my way of 'waiting for and hastening the coming of the day of God' (2 Pet. 3:12). It is what opens my small hands towards the gift of eternal redemption.

Newman once made an acute remark about logic: 'It is a chain loose at both ends.' One can say the same of the Rule and of our way of life. It both presupposes something behind itself and beyond itself. 'Whoever you are, renouncing your own will ...' (Prol. 3). 'Whoever therefore you are hastening to the heavenly fatherland, fulfil first of all by the help of Christ this little Rule written for beginners. And then ...' (73.8–9). In our Sunday Creed, we profess 'one baptism for the forgiveness of sins', and then immediately 'the life of the world to come'. It is in that brief gap, that mysterious space between these two that we are handed the Rule and shown this way of life, this way to life. 'Teacher, what good deed must I do, to have eternal life?' (Mt. 19:16), asked the young man. *Ecce pietate sua ...*

Our vocation, very simply, is this way: from baptism to eternal life.

Another simple thought: 'The Lord God took the man and put him in the garden of Eden to till it and keep it' (Gen. 2:15). 'Man', says the Psalmist, 'goes forth to his work and to his labour until the evening' (Ps. 103:23). 'That you may return to him by the labour of obedience ...' (Prol. 2). 'The Lord seeks his workman ...' (Prol. 14). 'Let nothing be preferred to the work of God' (43.3). 'Behold these are the tools of the spiritual craft', *Ecce haec sunt instrumenta artis spiritalis* (4.75). I am a man. I must work. Christ has called me to be His workman. Our vocation is this 'work of the Lord' (1 Cor. 15:58). To plough our hearts with the word of the Gospel. In giving us the Rule, the Lord is giving us, putting into our hands, the tools with which to work – this unique work which only He can do in us.

In giving us the Rule too, is not St Benedict giving us a sword? I am a man, and I must go to war. I will not be a man if I do not. My father, all my uncles, even my aunt took part, did military or naval service in the Second World War. Et moi? 'To thee are my words now addressed, whoever (*Quisquis*) you are who, renouncing your own will to fight for the true King, Christ the Lord, are taking up the strong and glorious weapons of obedience' (Prol. 3).

A journey, a work, a war: these are the simple, wholesome images we find in our Rule. It would not be right to regard ourselves as beyond them, superior to them. Of course, they need deepening. In Christ they will all be paradoxes, but they will not be less themselves for that. They can steady us and feed us.

To conclude, though, one step more. None of this is a private venture. It calls for the death of what St Benedict calls *propria voluntas* and its resurrection as what St Bernard calls *voluntas communis*. It belongs to more than myself, my vocation. 'I am under obligation both to Greeks and to barbarians, both to the wise and the foolish' (Rom. 1:14), says St Paul. 'Why catching then becomes a power – not yours, a world's', says Rilke. What is God's will for humanity, the world, creation? God's plan is God's kingdom, the establishment of His Rule. We are allowed to see 'in a mirror', to taste in a foretaste this Kingdom at every celebration of the Eucharist. 'Blessed are those who are called to the Supper of the Lamb!' Here already is the gathering of humanity, from east and west, north and south, around the slain and risen Lamb. Here is humanity being hosted and fed by the Father. Here is 'Mount Zion and the city of the living God, the heavenly Jerusalem, [the] innumerable angels in festal gathering' (Heb. 10:22). Through the window of the Eucharist, then, we can glimpse the culmination of God's Kingdom: that to which Creation, the Promise of salvation and the Covenant with Noah, the choice of Israel, the sending of the Son, the mission of the Church all lead. These things are God's pathway through human history, the 'way of life', for the redemption of man and the fulfilment of creation. And our way of life – our work, our warfare – is lived in, is part of this divine way, part, more specifically, of the mission of the Church. If the Church is at once the beginning, the presence of the Kingdom and the means by which it comes in human history, then our lives, our monasteries are called to be both signs of this Kingdom and its instruments, the means by which it is spread, creation fulfilled, the world reconciled. 'Why catching, then, becomes a power – not yours, a world's.' It is not a private venture, my search for God, my militia. It is working with God, a convergence of wills. It is in function of the Kingdom of God. 'I am under obligation both to Greeks and barbarians, the wise and the foolish.' And so, 'Necessity is laid upon me. Woe to me if I do not evangelize', says St Paul (1 Cor. 9:16). *Obsculta, o fili,* praecepta *magistri.* We are asked to open our small hands to something immense.

I began with Rilke. May I end with Dostoevsky. It is Fr Zosima speaking:

> Love one another, Fathers. Love God's people. Because we have come here and shut ourselves within these walls, we are no holier than those outside, but on the contrary from the very fact of coming here, each of us has confessed to himself that he is worse than others, than all men on earth... And the longer the monk lives in his seclusion, the more keenly he must recognize that. When he realizes that he is responsible to all men for all and everything, for all human sins, national and individual, only then the aim of our seclusion is attained... only through that knowledge, our heart grows soft with infinite, universal, inexhaustible love. Then every one of you will have the power to win over the whole world and to wash away the sins of the world with your tears...[2]

Notes

1. John Henry Newman, *Apologia pro Vita Sua* (London: Dent, 1993), p. 89.
2. Fyodor Dostoevsky, *The Brothers Karamazov*, Pt. IV, Ch. 1.

2

The Prologue:
A Word of Exhortation

During the dark days of the year we hear some strangely bright pages. I'm thinking of chapter 1 of the Gospel of St John which comes between Christmas and Epiphany: those radiant first meetings with Christ. Or of chapter 1 of the Gospel of Mark which we hear after the Baptism of the Lord: so full of energy and urgency, flashes of light in Galilee. You know perhaps R. S. Thomas's *The Bright Field*. For us, the field can be a page, heard or read.

Another page we hear at the beginning of the year, not Scripture but certainly inspired, is surely the page of the Prologue, read from 1–7 January.

> Listen, my son, to the precepts of the master, and incline the ear of your heart: willingly receive and faithfully fulfil the admonition of your loving father; that you may return by the labour of obedience to him from whom you had departed through the laziness of disobedience. To you, therefore, my words are now addressed, whoever you are, that through renouncing your own will you may fight for the Lord Christ, the true King, by taking up the strong and bright weapons of obedience.

The Prologue is full of energy and urgency, too. And it's a radiant meeting. Probably everything I want to say I've said before, but it can't be wrong to suggest, at the beginning of the year, that we turn aside to this little patch of brightness.

The Prologue is like nothing else in the Rule. The reason is that it's not regulation but exhortation. It's what Scripture calls a 'word of exhortation'. It's an exhortatory homily. It's a preacher – master, father – addressing a young man, a group of young men, who are, in modern terms, wondering what to do with their lives. It could be set in the guesthouse on a 'monastic experience weekend'. It could be what St Benedict would have said to a group of youngsters as he sat outside the front door of Monte Cassino with a codex of the Bible on his lap. It belongs to the spring or morning. It's Christ walking by the Sea of Galilee or rising to life in human hearts. It's Antony or Francis hearing the Gospel. It's the deliberate, intended echo of the call of God to the individual soul. And this, paradoxically, is what makes the Prologue so enduringly effective. It's like the 'brightness/that seemed as transitory as your youth/once, but is the eternity that awaits you', This 'word of exhortation' has the power to re-actualize over and over again the call of God – because this call is not something that happened once only but something always there, resounding. The Prologue is a sacramental of this call.

And this in two ways. It reminds us that we are called and to what we are called. The two are inseparable anyway. It's aimed at commitment; it appeals to the will, to personal choice, but it makes its appeal by way of the mind. It fires by enlightening.

It is, of course, simpler to talk about the second. So I will. That's to retrace the Prologue's own path. What is it, then, we are called to? It's the great gift of the Prologue to take us back to first principles. Even its omissions are a help. It doesn't compare different vocations. It doesn't try to define religious life over against lay life. The great bulk of it could be read to any Christian audience. It comes to the monastery at the end, but only as a consequence of things more fundamental. It reminds me of something my paradox-loving Novice Master used to say: 'It's my job to form Christians, not monks.' Abbot Bernardo Olivera spoke of the 're-evangelisation of the contemplative life'. That's precisely the function of the Prologue.

According to the Prologue then, what is it we are called to? The answer is all in images, and all images of ourselves in relation to Christ. 'It is only in the mystery of the Word made flesh that the mystery of man truly becomes clear,' *Gaudium et Spes* famously said (22), and that's St Benedict's anthropology too. And the images are biblical – which can be a snag. So familiar that we never put them on our knees and get to know them better. Four images stand out: all found in those first verses and then recurring. And I think there's a kind of pattern. *Obsculta, o fili* . . . In one sense, this is just the teacher clapping her hands and saying, listen, children, please . . . The listening is to the preacher and his homily. But, of course, it moves on and, as it moves, it yields image number 1, the image of the *disciple* (albeit without explicit use of the word). Not a disciple of the preacher, but of Christ and the Christ who teaches through Scripture. 'Let us open our eyes to the deifying light; let us attune our ears to what the divine voice admonishes us . . .' And what does he say? 'Come my sons listen to me, I will teach you the fear of the Lord.' Seeking his workman, the Lord cries out in the words of the psalm, 'and if you, hearing him, respond, "I am the one!"' God speaks to you again, giving still more instruction. 'What could be sweeter to us, dearest brethren, than this voice of the Lord inviting us?' And when the instruction is completed, the Gospel is quoted: 'He who hears these words of mine and does them . . .' Yes, the first call is to listen, to be a listener, to be a disciple. And so it's natural that the first presentation of the monastery should be as a 'school', and that this monastery be conceived of as a place where 'never departing from his [Christ's] guidance (*Magisterium*), [we] persevere in his teaching (*doctrina*) until death'. What was first for the apostles is first for us too: discipleship. *Obscultare, aurem inclinare, audire* . . . And listen to what? To the precepts of the master, yes, but through and beyond them to Scripture (v. 8), the divine voice (v. 9), the voice of the Lord (v. 19), the Spirit speaking to the churches (v. 11), the Lord speaking through the psalms (vv. 14ff.), the Lord in the Gospel (v. 33), his words (v. 33), his *Magisterium*, his 'doctrine' (v. 50). See how abbot Benedict eclipses himself before the teaching Christ, just as he tells the abbot in chapter 2 that he is 'not to teach or enact or command anything outside the precepts of the

Lord' (2.4). 'Call no man your father on earth, for you have one Father, who is in heaven. Neither be called masters (teacher), for you have one master, the Christ' (Mt. 23:9-10). The monk/the Christian the Prologue is so anxious to father and form is, then, first of all, a disciple, a disciple of Jesus, the one true Rabbi. He's someone who's a pupil in the school of the Word, a student of Scripture, a lover of revealed Truth. 'Hear, O Israel . . .' 'This is my beloved Son, with whom I am well pleased; listen to Him!' (Mt. 17:5). In and through all the particular monastic practices that serve this call to discipleship, it is Christ we're trying to hear. It is Christ who is speaking to us.

Immediately, though, lest we go all gooey, another image rises up. Image number 1 is only in function of image number 2. 'Listen, my son . . . so that you may *return to him* . . . Come, my sons, listen to me; I will teach you the *fear of the Lord* . . . What could be sweeter to us, dearest brethren, than this voice of the Lord inviting us? Behold, in his loving kindness the Lord shows us *the way of life* . . .' We listen to learn what to *do*. We listen in order to act. We listen in order to follow. In one sense, the Prologue is not in the slightest contemplative. Vision and rest belong to the end. Now is the time for a journey. Scripture 'rouses' us and the light of life is for 'running' by. We must gird our limbs with faith and the observance of good works, following Christ's paths under the guidance of the Gospel, walking without stain and doing righteousness, building a house of good works, amending our evil ways, running and doing now what will profit us for all eternity. The imagery of action and movement is constant. The Prologue is a call to be up and doing. In a real sense, for the Prologue, for St Benedict, sloth – *desidia* – is the original sin; it's certainly the first sin to be mentioned. Let there be no passivity, then, no reluctance, no ambiguities in the follower of Christ, just as in the obedience of chapter 5 there's to be nothing timid, tardy or tepid. This follower is fully awake, fully doing, completely mobilized, wholly actuated. All his energy, his every faculty is now enlisted. His eyes are bright. He's alive. Not in the way of torrenting feet and slamming doors, of Br Frenetic or Fr Compulsive, but as someone to whom life's purpose has been revealed, who has been shown this way of life, way to the Tent, way of salvation, way of God's commandments and doesn't want to be doing anything else. It's a matter of hearing and obeying the 'upward summons'. It's deserving, by one's life, to see him who has called us into his kingdom: 'the eternity that awaits you'. It's Christianity lived to the hilt. Who is the man who wants life? Yes please. So, here's a first threefold rule: keep your tongue from evil and your lips from deceit; turn away from evil and do good; seek peace and pursue it. The following is not a pleasant amble round a sunlit Galilee admiring the Master's miracles, emotional tourism. It is living ethically in every domain. And so we ask the Lord again, because we really want to get this right: Lord, who will dwell in your tent or rest on your holy mountain? This time the following is spelt out in a sevenfold rule: he who walks without stain and works justice; he who speaks truth in his heart and doesn't lie with his tongue; he who has done no evil against his neighbour nor believed false accusations; he who has crushed the thoughts the devil puts into his heart; he who isn't elated by his own goodness but acknowledges the work of the Lord; he who hears and does. The whole of the rest of the Rule is anticipated in these ten (three plus seven) commandments of the Prologue: the seventy-four good works of chapter 4, the three virtues of chapters 5 to 7, the twelve steps of humility, the eight injunctions of chapter 72. The following of the Prologue becomes the *conversatio morum* of profession.

So after the disciple comes the follower. Christ the Truth becomes Christ the Way; the Teacher becomes the Leader and Guide. We want to follow him to glory, to share by patience in the passion of Christ, that we may deserve also to be partakers of his kingdom. Once again, we seem to be repeating the pattern of the apostles: first hearing, then doing; first disciples, then actual followers.

And so to image 3. Here it's a little cluster of images, or a father and two daughters. What is it we are called to? To be disciples, yes, and therefore followers. But this following, in turn, has other names. Service, work, combat. We are called, says the Prologue, to be servants of Christ, workmen of the

Lord, soldiers of the King. Christ the Teacher, Christ the Guide on the way, is also – precisely – Christ the Lord, Christ the King. Having taught his disciples and opened for them the way to heaven, he's seated now at the Father's right with all things under his feet, and we are proud to call ourselves his slaves, to work in his vineyard and he enlisted as a soldier. The parent image, here, if we take the Rule as a whole, is certainly that of *servus*, but work and soldiering are present too and naturally connected, adding their own nuances.

Anyway, the Prologue has them: obedience is 'toil', the work of a slave; it's also a taking up of strong, bright weaponry. The Lord is 'always to be served with the good things he has given us'. Should we fail in this, there is the terrible punishment that awaits 'most wicked servants'. The Lord, indeed, is seeking his own workman in the multitude of the people to whom he cries out. 'Therefore our hearts and bodies must be prepared to fight in holy obedience to his commands' and we find ourselves joining a 'school of the Lord's *service*'. No need to trace these images through the rest of the Rule. It's clear how they lead into the 'service and work' of the work of God and the service and struggle of obedience. To the image of the follower, they add a little stability perhaps. They do suggest, too, a form of consecration and with that a mission, something more than merely getting to heaven and saving my soul. The fighting of the monk, for example, is always principally directed at the vices of his own flesh and thoughts, but this is a fight against evil as such. It is a struggle to establish the good and the peace of God in the world. Again the apostles come to mind. They became disciples first and found themselves following, caught up in the Passion and Resurrection. And then the mission began. They were sent out: to serve, to work and to fight. All these images occur in Paul, the most apostolic of all the apostles.

All I'm trying to do with these images is point to their presence. Each of them – disciple, follower, servant (and the fourth to come) – is sitting there like a nip of brandy waiting to be taken, and then to fill the inner man with its warmth. It's up to us individually to lift the glass and empty it, in other words to let these images in, to make them an object of our *meditatio*. But I am pointing too to their biblical character, and to the fact that they are the transposition to us of imagery applicable, first of all, to the twelve, to the apostles. They connect, one could say too, to those bright pages that begin the year: John 1:19ff., Mark 1:14ff. The 'word' of the Prologue is really the emergence of Jesus, the beginning of his public life in the heart of the young men St Benedict is preaching to. And we are, to the day of our death, young men wondering what to do with our lives too. The images, as I say, are too familiar. But it's in the Bible that we find the meaning of our lives. These images answer that constant human search to know who we are and what we're about. And the transposition – apostles to us – suggests something wonderful. Namely, that so far as we carry these names of disciple, follower, servant – worker – soldier (and the fourth still to come), so far is the Gospel history, salvation history, God's work in the world going forward in us. I can be peeling vegetables or bringing sinners to repentance in the parlour, singing a psalm or biting my tongue, but I am disciple, follower, *servus Dei*.

And so to image 4: son. *Obsculta, o fili*. Again, it's first of all 'son' of the speaker, son of abbot Benedict. But again, in no time, it's sonship of Christ, of him who has deigned to count us among the number of his sons – who in the context, as in the famous *Abba, Pater* of chapter 2, is certainly Christ. To be a son, in the context of the Rule, brings us back to image 1. It means – compare the Wisdom literature – being a pupil, being a disciple. 'Come, sons, listen to me. I will *teach you*.' But it needn't be held there. What is it we are called to be? To be sons, in every sense. And what is it Jesus says when he's speaking to sons, speaking as father? 'He said to the paralytic, "My son, your sins are forgiven"' (Mk 2:5). 'Little children, yet a little while I am with you. You will seek me; and as I said to the Jews so now 1 say to you, Where I am going you cannot come. A new commandment I give you, that you love one another; even as I have loved you, that you also love one another' (Jn 13:33–34). And still at the table, after Communion as it were, 'I will not leave you orphans; I will come to you' (Jn 14:18). 'Just as day was breaking, Jesus stood on the beach; yet the disciples did not know it was Jesus.

Jesus said to them, "Children, have you any fish?" ... Jesus said to them, "Come and have breakfast" ... They knew it was the Lord' (Jn 21:4–5; 12). I'm not meaning to be sentimental, just to suggest that the image of Christ the father and we the children, we the sons, brings us into something very tender – and is, I think, a final image, completing the pattern. It looks forward to the brotherhood of the monastery and beyond, to the inheritance of heaven. If sons, then heirs. It's the fullness of sonship we can imagine the apostles entering into by way of their service. 'And when you have done these things, my eyes will be upon you and my ears to your prayers, and before you call on me, I will say to you: Look, I am here!' 'Thou my true Father, and I thy true son.' And, of course, there's no need to stop at sonship of Christ. The Son of God became the Son of man so that the sons of men might become sons of God, of the Father. This is the heart of the Gospel, of Paul and John, and everything in the Rule too calls to this sonship.

So there we are. The Prologue leads us to prayer in the end. It is a meeting. There's a passage in Søren Kierkegaard where he says something like this: the baby talks about 'me', the voting man talks about 'I', but the mature man thinks of himself as 'thou': 'thou shalt or shalt not'. The mature man, one could say, lets himself be addressed by another. In the Gospels that begin the year, in the Prologue, this is Christ. He comes to us over these bright fields, and says: You are my disciple, you are my follower, you are my servant, you are my son. And it's in the light of this word that the mystery of me becomes clear.

3

The Entrance of *Quisquis*

And the Lord seeking his workman among the crowd of people to
whom he cries these things, goes on to say, 'Who is the man who
wants life and longs to see good days?' (Prol. 14–15)

I

The Prologue is surely a text which speaks to the heart of
the monk in a quite special way. One hears of a dying monk
asking to have it read to him. In the old days, one was
expected to learn it by heart. A monk once remarked, 'You
could let the rest of the Rule go, but the Prologue, ah! That's
something.'

If the Rule as a whole is a sacramental of our vocation in
the objective sense of the word, our way of life in the Church,
then the Prologue is a sacramental of our vocation in the
subjective sense. It is a sacramental of the act of being called,
of the original inspiration of our monastic life. And the
'grace', dare we say, of every re-reading (re-hearing) of the
Prologue is the grace of hearing that original call again, of
having that first inspiration reawakened. As the Prologue prefaces and is part of the Rule, so our lives are prefaced and
sustained by a 'Prologue-grace'. It's that I'd like to dwell on,
the *res* so to speak of this *sacramentum*; this presence in our
life and memory, of a grace of awakening. As Charles Péguy
said, 'it is memory which makes the whole depth of man.'
There is much ordering in the Rule, there is much ordering

required in our lives (*ordinavit in me caritatem*), but first of all comes *jaillissement*, the springing up, the gushing forth, the mystery of life; in the words of Dylan Thomas, 'the force that through the green fuse drives the flower'. We are, as Benedictines, experts at plodding on, eloquent on monastic life as long march, not glorious cavalry charge. Patience! It is our gift perhaps. But our *Rule* also begins with this lively, leaping Prologue and ends with a chapter on good zeal and fervent charity, with boiling and burning. *Gloria Dei vivens homo!* 'The glory of God is man fully alive!' (St Irenaeus)

What is the Prologue? It is, clearly, unlike anything else in the Rule. It has its own literary form. It is an exhortatory homily. It is a homily by Abba Benedict to an individual, indeed to several, interested in the monastic way. It is a homily exhorting them to embrace this way and culminating in the assertion, 'Let us therefore establish a school of the Lord's service' (v. 45), that is, let us take this way together.

Thinking of it as St Benedict's exhortatory, initiatory homily, we can glimpse certain figures in the background, certain predecessors: i) The Jewish sage we meet in the first chapters of Proverbs canvassing for pupils to enter the school of Lady Wisdom: 'Hear, my son, your father's instruction' (Prov. 1:8). 'Wisdom cries aloud in the street; in the markets she raises her voice' (Prov. 1:20). ii) The Greco-Roman philosopher calling on a young audience through a *logos protreptikos* to take up the pursuit of philosophy, the search for the 'happy life', and enter his academy. Aristotle wrote a book-length version of such an introductory exhortation and so did Cicero (his lost *Hortensius*). iii) The Christian bishop giving catechesis to the newly-baptized, showing them how to live in the school of Christ, the Church. St Benedict stands in this tradition, but in a monastic context, in a line of *abbas*.

As a Christian homily, it is impregnated with Scripture. It is almost nothing more than an echo of the Bible. St Benedict subordinates himself to Scripture. It is Scripture, the Word of God itself, which addresses us.

And whom does this homily address? Clearly, as I say, those considering the monastic way. And that means the young ('my son'). When is it spoken? It isn't fanciful, I think, to set it in the morning, or at least to acknowledge that it uses the imagery of the morning.

> Up with us then, at last, for Scripture rouses us, saying, 'Now is the time for us to rise from sleep.' Let us open our eyes to the divine light and let us listen with attentive ears to the warning the divine voice cries to us daily, 'Today, if you would hear his voice, harden not your hearts' (vv. 8–10).

Where is it spoken? Well, there is the respectable thesis that this is a 'Clothing Discourse' set in the chapter house of the monastery. But I prefer to imagine St Benedict sitting one morning after Lauds outside the front door of Monte Cassino, as the Dialogues portray him. Out of the bushes rolls a drowsy young man, a student from Rome perhaps, sent by his chaplain. He arrived too late the night before; the guesthouse was closed. St Benedict intuits his motives, seizes the moment, and begins, 'Listen, my son ...' As he speaks, the sun rises higher, and others appear too, stumbling out of sleeping bags hidden by the morning mist, or young Goths in black leather who've slept by their bikes. So he moves from singular to plural: 'Let us open our eyes to the divine light ...' And so on. At least such a setting confers coherence on what seems otherwise a random clutter of imagery. The Prologue is a summons to a young man / young men on the threshold of the monastery to wake up, to open eyes and ears, to get up, to dress ('let us gird our loins'), and to set out on a journey – the journey back to God. *Ecce pietate sua demonstrat nobis Dominus viam vitae!* 'See how the Lord in his love shows us the way of life' (v. 20).

It is a homily carefully constructed. Its central section is a commentary, as we know, on verses from Pss. 33 and 14. And this central section is preceded by an introduction and followed by a conclusion. So it is possible to see a chiastic structure in the Prologue. Vv. 1–7 are a general introduction, A; vv. 8–13 an introduction to the commentary on Ps. 33, B; vv. 14–21 the commentary on Ps. 33, C; vv. 22–34 the commentary on Ps. 14, C.1; vv. 35–39 (or 38) the conclusion to the commentary on Ps. 14, B. 1; vv. 40–50 the conclusion to the whole, A.1.

This means that the beginning, the conclusion, and the central body each have their own weight. From the introduction, one might highlight, not only the famous *Obsculta,* but v. 3 and its taking up the weapons of obedience to fight for Christ; from the conclusion, v. 45: 'Therefore we must establish a school for the Lord's service.' And from the centre, according to the above analysis, one might underline the centre of the centre, so to speak, vv. 21 & 22: 'Let us, therefore, gird our loins with faith and the observance of good works, and following the guidance of the Gospel walk in his paths, so that we may merit to see him who has called us into his kingdom. And if we wish to dwell in the tabernacle of his kingdom, unless we run there with good deeds we will not arrive.' At the centre, then, is this resounding call to walk towards the vision of the risen and ascended Christ in his Kingdom under the guidance of the Gospel.

As a homily impregnated with Scripture, it not surprisingly has as its central image the Way: 'the way of life' (v. 20), 'the way to the tabernacle' (v. 24), 'the way of salvation' (v. 48), 'the way of God's commands' (v. 49). All the other imagery is tributary to this – even that of 'the school *of* the Lord's service' (v. 45).

So, in this *Prologue,* on the threshold of the monastic life, on the threshold *of* a decision, we are addressed by the Word of life. There is a shining of the divine light and a sounding forth of the divine voice, opening our ears (cf. v. 9) – as there was for Moses at the burning bush, as for the three apostles on the Mount of Transfiguration, as for the young man called Saul outside Damascus. There is an encounter with Christ. 'Who is the man who wants life?'(v. 15)

II

Personally, I find it is the commentary in vv. 14–21 on the fragment of Ps. 33 which most moves me. This is the moment when Christ himself enters into dialogue with us. What goes before leads to this. 'Listen, my son' (v. 1). The Rule begins with St Benedict, teacher and father, talking to *Quisquis,*

addressing a prospective postulant, opening his ear. Then – in
v. 8 – St Benedict yields to Scripture: 'Scripture arouses us,
saying . . .' (v. 8). Scripture speaks; the divine light shines, the
divine voice cries out. The quotations multiply, and the single
Quisquis has also multiplied, and become a silent, plural gathering. But what is Scripture? 'Let us listen to what the Spirit
is saying to the churches' (v. 11). It is the voice of the Spirit,
and the Spirit is the risen Christ. We have moved from St
Benedict to Scripture to the One who speaks in and through
Scripture. And so: 'the *Lord* seeking his worker in the multitude of the people to whom he cries out, says again . . .' (v.
14). We have come to the moment of encounter. A vocation is
a new presence in our life. Christ speaks. Christ puts the question. 'Who is the man who wants life and yearns to see good
days' (v. 15). And the response springs up: 'I do, *Ego!*' (v.
16). This is the 'annunciation to the monk', and his fiat in
return. It's the moment, 'early in the morning', when the
landowner goes out to hire labourers for his vineyard (Mt.
20:1), and they agree to work. It's the moment when the Lord
looks at the rich young man and loves him (Mk 10:21). Christ
calls *Quisquis* to life, and he responds with a 'yes', springing
up from within: *Ego*. So, *dicit tibi Deus*. God – Christ in the
context – shows the way to life, to 'true and everlasting life'
(v. 17), that is to say, the Christ-life, the life that is stronger
than death. Three summary maxims: 'keep your tongue from
evil and your lips from speaking deceit; turn away from evil
and do good; seek peace and pursue it' (v. 17). Speech, action,
relationships – probably all to be understood with reference to
the other, the neighbour. A vocation always involves this
reordering of our whole life. Then the mystical promise to
those who 'do these things': 'my eyes will be upon you and
my ears open to your prayers; and before you call on me, I
will say to you: See, here I am, *Ecce adsum*' (v. 18). This new
presence, once it has been accepted, is always ready to reveal
more of itself. Now St Benedict who, all along, has been
discreetly stage-managing this dialogue, can't resist an intervention: 'What could be sweeter to us, dearest brethren, than
this voice of the Lord inviting us? Look, in his loving kindness, the Lord shows us the way of life!' (vv. 19–20). And so,

like a bugle, there rings out the call to action: 'Our loins girt then with faith and the performance of good works, let us follow his paths by the guidance of the Gospel, so that we may deserve to see him who has called us to his kingdom' (v. 21). Let us set out! Let us turn our inner and outer selves to this wonderful goal: the vision of the risen Christ! Let us follow Him, His paths, under the guidance of the Gospel!

Quis est homo qui vult vitam? 'Who is the man who wants life?' Here we see what vocation is, the *res*. A vocation is a call to live.

To develop this a little. We emerge from the womb, and from our first cry we are wanting life. But we are born into a world gone grey, under the shadow of death, and we need to be put this question again – indeed, again and again: do I want to live? The life St Benedict has immediately in mind is what he calls 'true and everlasting life', the Christ-life stronger than death. But there is just plain, first-level life too. Here too, there comes a moment of awakening. I mentioned Cicero's *Hortensius*. In the second half of the fourth century an eighteen-year-old North African, too famous to need naming, read it. Later he described its effect.

> The book changed my feelings. It altered my prayers, Lord, to be towards You yourself. It gave me different values and priorities. Suddenly every vain hope became empty to me, and I longed for the immortality of wisdom with an incredible ardour in my heart. I began to rise up to return to You.[1]

Surgere coeperam, ut ad te redirem. Language very close to that of the Prologue. It is the teenage Augustine discovering Cicero, discovering wisdom, beginning to 'rise up to return to You', finding a reason to live.

What a mysterious thing this awakening to 'real life' is! I was woken up in my teens by the discovery of classical music, especially that of Beethoven. What was conveyed to me with the force of a revelation was that being human is wonderful, that life – however full of suffering – was truly worth living, the game worth playing. No one had actually said that to me! A Prologue, or at least pre-Prologue, grace. It can be the most surprising things that mediate this. 'One of the most impressive and thrilling experiences of my life' is how an Englishman, William Barlow, in a droll autobiography *Intent only on Life* describes seeing the Coldstream Guards do drill.[2] He knew instantly he had to become a Guardsman too. He had had a vision of the human that nothing before had ever given him, and it started a journey which eventually took him out of English religious nothingness into the Orthodox Church. Or take the vision that comes, in a short story of the American writer Flannery O'Connor, to a very simple fourteen-year-old boy from Alabama. He's at a fair, and there he sees a man

> tattooed from head to foot ... a single intricate design of brilliant colour ... mov[ing] about on the platform, flexing his muscles so that the arabesque of men and beasts and flowers on his skin appeared to have a subtle motion of its own. Parker [the boy] had never before felt the least motion of wonder in himself. Until he saw the man at the fair, it did not enter his head that there was anything out of the ordinary about the fact that he existed. Even then it did not enter his head, but a peculiar unease settled in him. It was as if a blind boy had been turned so gently in a different direction that he did not know his destination had been changed.[3]

Strangely, the same awakening can occur by way of its opposite, by the suicide of someone near and dear perhaps. This is not uncommon. 'Whatever life is, it is for living fully without fear or doubt' was the conviction that one of those held hostage in Lebanon in the 1980s, Brian Keenan, spoke of when he emerged. The more common-or-garden of boy meets girl and vice versa can run the same way. By way of all these things, whether they come in power and glory or creep up on us like the dawn, a raison d'être comes our way, a purpose, a value to the enterprise. Suddenly, it's good to be alive. There's a glimpse of the glory of existing, 'standing out'. We want to live.

Something got us going in the first place. We were 'touched'. And that something is still there – a source, a well-spring – just as the Prologue is always part of the Rule. We need to keep in touch with it. It lives on after all, it grows with us. It shouldn't be relegated to our past, or our embarrassing adolescence. If the art of life is to become an adult without ceasing to be a child, it's also, I suppose, to become an adult without ceasing to be an adolescent. The Fathers of the Church remained an inspiration for Newman from his teens to his 80s, and his conversion as a schoolboy was the wellspring of his whole life. And the Prologue, it seems to me, is a symbol of this first awakening to life, of what provoked it, of the God who gives joy to our youth and does not repent of his gifts.

Another aspect: the word, the Word of God. How full of Scripture the Prologue is! St Benedict's call is mediated by Scripture, by passages from the two psalms especially, but also from much else, and that much else not only Old Testament but New. St Benedict effaces himself before Scripture, because Scripture – all of it – is the voice of Christ. 'The Lord said to Abraham, "Go from your country and your kindred and your father's house to the land that I will show you."' There's the ancient idea, beloved of Syrian Christianity, that Mary conceived by way of her ear. She conceived the Word of God by the word of the angel: *attonitis auribus*, her ears thunderstruck. And as in the Prologue, as in the Bible, so in vocation, the call often comes by way of a word, the Word. A word. There's that episode in the life of St Thérèse when her father simply remarks on her childishness, and she's changed. An army chaplain in Burma said to a young soldier, 'You could do something with your life, young man.' And the result was Fr Fabian Binyon of Prinknash! The word of a life perhaps. Edith Stein read St Teresa's autobiography through the night, and closed it saying, 'This is the truth.' These are words which open up the way to 'true and everlasting life'. And no words do this like the biblical Word.

> With these things in his mind, he went into the church. It happened that the gospel was then being read, and he heard what the Lord had said to the rich young man, 'If you would be perfect, go, sell what you possess and give to the poor, and you will have treasure in heaven; and come follow me.' As though this reminder of the saints had been sent to him by God, and as though that passage had been read specially for his sake, Antony went out immediately, and gave to the villagers the possessions he had inherited from his ancestors.[4]

It seems such words of the Lord, heard in the liturgy, encountered in *lectio*, mercifully punctuate our lives. 'Morning by morning he wakens, he wakens my ear, to hear as those who are taught' (Is. 50:4). Perhaps one thing we can do during a retreat is recall them deliberately – 'lest we forget'. The words of life in our life . . .

A final aspect: how full the Prologue is of Christ! The figure of Christ holds sway from beginning to end of the Prologue – even when this may not be immediately obvious to us. It is probable that the 'him', *eum*, to whom we are bidden to return by the toil of obedience in v. 2 is not God the Father, or God 'in general', fine theology though that be, but actually Christ – the Lord and King about to be mentioned. Things could hardly be more explicit at the end of the Prologue: 'sharing by patience in the sufferings of Christ, so that we may deserve to be sharers of his kingdom' (v. 50). But the Father, Master, Spirit, Lord (especially), and even the God who features in between is also – in serious exegesis – one and the same throughout: Christ, the Second Person of the Trinity in his glorified humanity, the *Kyrios* of St Paul and the Liturgy. Over the tympanum above this west door of the Rule there stands the figure of Christ – in at once severe and loving patristic majesty. For what the Prologue is essentially about, what it evokes, it seems to me, is what the late Holy Father said the Jubilee Year was essentially about: an encounter with Christ, a personal encounter. A vocation is a Christophany and therefore, if you can bear the language, a falling-in-love. Every time we hear the Prologue, we are invited back to that first love.

Being Christian is not the result of an ethical choice or a lofty idea, but the encounter with an event, a person, which gives life a new horizon and a decisive direction.[5]

The Christian faith is this: encounter with Christ, the living Person who gives life a new horizon and a definite direction. And when the heart of a young person opens up to his divine plans, it is not difficult to recognize and follow his voice. The Lord calls each of us by name, and entrusts to us a specific mission in the Church and in society.[6]

How to revive our drooping spirits? How avoid the seemingly inevitable coarsening of the spirit, the clogging of the wells that come with the passing years? How keep our hands open to that ball thrown by the Eternal Partner, with accurate and measured swing, towards us, to our centre, in an arch? How start afresh from Christ? By remembering, the Prologue seems to suggest, what first spurred us into really living and still does so; by returning again and again to the Word of God; by lifting our eyes to the face of Christ where shines the beauty of God. *Ecce adsum!*

Notes

1. St Augustine, *Confessions,* 111, 7.
2. William Barlow, *Intent only on Life* (London: Fount, 1990), p. 74.
3. Flannery O'Connor, 'Parker's Back' in *The Complete Stories* (London: Faber, 1990), pp. 512–13.
4. St Athanasius, *Life of Antony*.
5. Benedict XVI, *Deus Caritas Est,* 1.
6. Benedict XVI, *Address to Youth in the Czech Republic,* 28 Sept 2009.

4

Community, Rule and Abbot

It is clear that there are four kinds of monks. First are the cenobites: that is those who live in monasteries and serve under a rule and an abbot... *hoc est monasteriale, militans Sub regula vel abbate* (RB 1,1–2).

Our hero *Quisquis* has responded to the call, the Lord seeking his workman. He wants to live his Christianity to the full, in heart and body as the Prologue expresses it. And this general resolve now takes, at the bidding of the Holy Spirit, the specific form of joining this *schola*, of assuming the yoke of a Rule, of submitting in all obedience to a superior.

From the perspective of the *Regula monasteriorum,* as I've mentioned already, the first three chapters outline the constitution of the *schola.* Other, later, chapters will further enrich this: chapters 21, 63, 64, 65 for example. St Benedict never loses his interest in this aspect of things. It is never simply something that can be taken for granted. The walls need rebuilding now and then. *Quis est homo qui vult vitam?* That question was answered with an *Ego.* And now St Benedict provides an environment for the grounding and growth of that life, that 'true and everlasting life', the Christ-life. Coming back to the *Regula monachorum,* one might imagine *Quisquis* as a plant. The community is his soil, the Rule that supporting stick which guarantees a straight and upward growth, or that trellis which keeps the rose from wasting its fragrance in a chthonic sprawl, the abbot the gardener. Stability would be the vow that roots, *conversatio* the vow which guarantees that straight course upwards, obedience the vow which brings to flower and fruit. 'You did not choose me but I chose you, and placed *you* (*ethéka/posui*; by *stability*) that you should go (by *conversatio*) and bear fruit (by *obedience*), and that your fruit should abide (in the Church to eternal life)' (Jn 15:16).

What is the 'grace' of these opening chapters? Objectively, the 'grace' of community, Rule and abbot. This is one of the many triads in the Rule. As I've said already, it's a very natural one. Any society, any association – even a yachting club – needs these three components: people, members; a law of some sort; an authority of some sort. The simplicities of the sixth century have undergone many subsequent elaborations. The *community* forms part of a Congregation of communities, more or less bound to one another. Our Congregations are now united in a Confederation. Our monastic institutes are understood as one species of religious institute, the latter in turn understood as a species of institute of consecrated life. The Rule has been supplemented by Constitutions, Declarations, Ordinances, Customaries and other such documents, and our proper law been more and more circumscribed, completed, permeated by the general Canon Law of the Latin Church. The role of the *Superior* has been more closely defined. Externally, there is now a super-structure of General Chapters, Abbot Presidents or Generals, Visitations, not to mention the relevant Congregation of the Apostolic See. Internally, the roles of Chapter and Council have been clarified, and the consultative and deliberative distinguished. It's best, no doubt, to take all these things in good part, even, in the language of scholasticism, to look on them as 'external graces' – each and all, be it said, at the service of the welfare of individual communities and individual members thereof.

For simplicity's sake, though, I will restrict myself to St Benedict's original triad. 'A threefold cord is not easily broken', and there is a treasure in this triplet. In his way, St Benedict is to the constitutional solidity of monastic life something of what Moses was (is) to Israel, or Lycurgus to Sparta or George Washington to the U. S. Or, what St Basil is to the theory of cenobitic life, St Benedict is to its practice. 'There were those,' says Sirach, who ruled in their kingdoms, and made a name for themselves by their valour; those who gave counsel because they were intelligent; those who spoke in prophetic oracles; those who led the people by their counsels and by their knowledge of the people's lore; they were wise in their words of instruction; ... rich men endowed with resources, living peacefully in their homes (Sir. 44:3–4, 6).

Like many such, St Benedict disappears behind his work. Remembering St Benedict's *romanitas,* one might add the poetry of Virgil to the wisdom of Ecclesiasticus.

Others will cast more tenderly in bronze
Their breathing figures, I can well believe,
And bring more lifelike portraits out of marble;
Argue more eloquently, use the pointer
To trace the paths of heaven accurately
And accurately foretell the rising stars.
Roman, remember by your strength to rule
Earth's peoples – for your arts are to be these:
To pacify, to impose the rule of law,
To spare the conquered, battle down the proud (*Aeneid,* VI).

It has become unfashionable in scholarly circles to make anything of Benedict the Roman, but Roman he was. And what this particular Roman has done is (generally) simple, natural, wholesome. It makes for strength: *fortissimum genus.* It works. In the ancient world, Sparta was admired for her *eunomia,* her 'state of being well-lawed'. It would be good to think our communities might be similarly admirable. Of course, more is required, but it is something not to be sneered at, part of our patrimony, something for which each of us can feel responsible.

How, then, do these elements of the *Regula monasteriorum* relate to the *Regula monachorum*? What does this triad mean for *Quisquis,* for his *militia*? *Dei Verbum* famously envisaged Tradition, Scripture and Magisterium happily conspiring in their functions of transmitting God's Word and saving souls. How does St Benedict envisage Community, Rule and Abbot doing likewise? An abbot of my own Congregation once remarked that, when it comes to their spiritual lives, all contemporary monks are sarabites. Clearly, St Benedict's hope would be that as Community, Rule and Abbot impinge upon us (confuse our life, if you like), we all become true cenobites, 'sons of obedience', therefore, and ultimately – as I said earlier – disciples of Christ in the school of His service.

Later in the Rule the implicit question is, what does *Quisquis give* to the Community? Here it is rather, what does he *receive*?

Let me reflect on the gift of Community first. When Abbot Thierry was elected Abbot President of our Congregation in 1996, he remarked in an interview, *C'est grâce à En-Calcat que je suis ce que je suis.* 'It is thanks to En-Calcat [monastery] that I am what I am.' That's it essentially. One great weakness in our society, undoubtedly one source of the yob culture, is surely the lack of local, middle-sized communities. There is so little between the fragile, nuclear family, on the one hand, and, on the other, the nation or simply the alien, unmanageable great 'out-there' of giant corporations, impersonal institutions, remote bureaucracies, unfathomable economic forces. Of what, of where, of whom can I say, it is thanks to them that I am what I am? 'Collections of solitudes' is one recent characterisation of our world. Hence the ravaging loneliness of so many. A sense of the individual is a fruit of civilisation, and of Christianity. Aren't St Paul and St Augustine, for example, the greatest 'individuals' of the ancient world? But it is a fruit long severed, gone bad. The results appear in strange, stray details: 25% of Parisians live alone, 40% of houses in the U.K. have only one occupant, 'inability to live in community' has become a ground for dispensation. And so on. Something has slipped. In Africa, by contrast, 'it is impossible for anyone to be alone'. For St Benedict certainly, the cenobitic way is the norm. The hermit is the post-cenobite, the sarabite the pseudo-cenobite, the gyrovague the sub-cenobite. The way is clear.

The painful question is, of course, are we following it? I heard it said of one monastery recently: 'It used to be a community; now it's just a collection of individuals.' Would it be fair to say that in each community (each monk?) there is a play of the centripetal and the centrifugal? Once the latter prevails, one has merely 'a collection of individuals', and it becomes a matter, sooner or later, of *sauve qui peut*. Certainly each community has its own way of being such – moulded by its tradition, its work, but also by other things: money (wealth tells against community, broadly speaking, and poverty for it); the buildings; numbers (an abbot once remarked that a real change comes when a community falls below thirty; again I suspect, somewhere between fifteen and ten); distribution of age. Ideally, our communities would have three generations: the young men dreaming dreams, the old men seeing visions, and the middle-aged doing all the work! Often now we have only one and a half. All these factors affect how we 'live community'. But live it we must. External changes call for internal ones. They call for the inventiveness of charity. We cannot live in a community of forty as we did in a community of ninety. Always, I think, this is part of our work: the conversion of 'a collection of individuals' into community, or of community into a cenobium. 'Monasteries close for lack of love,' said an Abbot Primate. With love, they open, they open up.

Perhaps, for all its risks, we need to re-instate the analogy of motherhood. *Mater et Magistra*, those are names for the Church and for our communities. The late Henri de Lubac once wrote the following – very nobly considering his own experience. For 'Church' one may read 'monastery':

> The motherhood of the Church, as I have said from the beginning ... is not connected with any sensible experience. It is, nevertheless, a reality which engenders an experience. It would be most unjust if, because we have met with some indifference or lack of understanding in our relations within the Church or because we have been able to verify some abuse here or there, we were not willing to recognize so many facts, so many attitudes, so many institutions, so many emotions, so many initiatives of all kinds which have created over the centuries, and which so often continue to maintain under difficult circumstances, a spiritual climate unknown to one who is not Christian or who has not really drawn near the Church. Does not the very scandal provoked when this climate is, on occasions, absent testify to this fact? Besides,

it is not the satisfaction of a certain sentimentality nor encouragement for an easy life which we are to expect from the Church. A truly loving mother, she saves our personal life, not by flattering our instincts, but by calling us back both to the gentleness and the strictness of the Gospel. We must place ourselves, not on the psychological level, but on the spiritual ('pneumatic') level in order to judge this. It is at the moment when her countenance seems perhaps austere to us that she is fulfilling her maternal function.[1]

One's community is, in God's providence, in the Lord's shepherding, the place thanks to which one is what one is. It is, 'pneumatically', one's home. A place where one can wear one's slippers. A place where one receives a name and that name is respected (cf. RB 63). A place for experiencing what St Benedict calls in two lovely phrases, the *multorum solacium, consolatio alterius* (the solace of many, the consolation of others) (1.4, 5). A place where, instead of what literary critics call a 'hermeneutic of suspicion', an *a priori* adversarial approach to a text, there holds sway a 'hermeneutic of sympathy'. A place where each has his 'place'. ['Suddenly I realized these blokes were my brothers.'] Unrealistic? God help us if it is! These are simply 'maternal' things without which the human being cannot live. And, however self-contained we are, however reliant on the Lord, if we cannot find them within we will look for them without. Without is part of my Providence, certainly, but it's not my community.

Most of all, in St Benedict's perspective, it is through the Community that *Quisquis* receives the Word of God, is called back to the Gospel again and again, is enabled to live in the truth. It is thanks to the Community that we become disciples, or in St Peter's phrase, 'sons of obedience'. In Community, I learn myself, I learn others, I learn prayer, I learn the mercy of God. I learn patience, in other words, and I have somewhere to die. 'Stay in your cell and your cell will teach you everything': the wisdom of the hermit. 'Stay in your community, and your community will teach you everything': the wisdom of the cenobite.

What, next, of the Rule and Abbot? It is they, objectively, which make a monk a cenobite. St Benedict returns to this dyad again and again. The sarabite lives *nulla regula . . . sine pastore* (1.6b, 8). In ch. 7, on the eighth step, we meet 'the common rule of the monastery . . . the example of the seniors' (7.55). The wayward monk of chapters 23ff. is defined as one who 'in any way has contempt for the holy Rule and the precepts of his seniors' (23.1). In chapter 58, the novice, prior to his profession, promises 'to keep everything' (i.e. in the Rule) and 'to observe all the commands given him' (that is, by the Abbot and seniors) (58.14). In ch. 62, the priest is exhorted 'not to presume to do anything he has not been commanded by the abbot, knowing that he will be even more subject to the discipline of the Rule' (62.3). And finally the poor prior 'is to perform with reverence what the abbot demands of him, doing nothing contrary to the abbot's will or arrangement, for the more he is elevated above the rest, the more solicitously he ought to observe the precepts of the Rule' (65.16–17).

The Rule is an objective presence, the Abbot a personal one. The Rule is written, the Abbot is flesh and blood. The Rule is ancient, the Abbot is now. Clearly, for St Benedict, they are complementary opposites. A freshly-blessed abbot once asked his long-toothed President for a word. 'Keep the Constitutions' was the answer. The abbot had hoped for something more, but as the years went by he saw the wisdom of his senior. Experience might also lead one to suggest that, in women's communities, it is especially necessary to uphold the objective authority of the Rule. That of the superior tends to look after itself!

I realize a particular nettle hasn't been grasped. The Rule we actually live by is not the Rule of St Benedict. We are in twenty-first century Britain, not sixth century Italy. Indeed. But, please God, it is the Rule we live by in some real sense, and our actual Rule both hangs upon it and refers to it. The Rule of St Benedict is at once a collation of wisdom and a set of structures and observances. The two intertwine. I don't think the spirit and letter distinction quite does. Rather, the structures and observances remain, at least in substantial part, in a modified way. We still have a Divine Office, even if not St Benedict's. We still have not just an ideal, but an actual discipline of personal poverty, of eating and sleeping, of receiving guests and forming novices, and so on. The 'enclosure of the monastery' means something. We still have abbots and a Rule, Chapter and Deans. And in those modified but persisting structures and observances, the original charism lives on.

What of the Superior? An endless subject ... Thinking of *Quisquis*, it's perhaps enough just to say this. We elect someone an abbot. In other words, we call forth one of our own to this office. And that calling forth must continue. Even if we didn't vote for this man, nonetheless we accepted the community's choice. And so we too must continue to ratify it. There is a real sense in which the Community gets the Abbot it *asked* for and asks for. It is very hard to be an abbot in a grudging community, delightful to be one in a generous one. There is, in chapter 5, that phrase, 'they *desire* to have an abbot over them'. That's the key that unlocks the 'external grace' of a superior.

Community, Rule and Abbot. Again, surely it must be a New Testament and ecclesial pattern. Local Church *militans* according to the apostolic Gospel handed down, under the guidance of the elders and eventually the monarchic Bishop who hold the place of Christ. The People of God living its life in Christ according the traditional Rule of faith embodied in the Creed, under the college of Bishops and their head, the Pope. Could one even think of the Church at prayer, the Eucharistic assembly? There is a *congregatio* coming together to remember the Lord, according to a tradition of praxis embodied in the Missal, with a bishop or priest who is believed to act *vices Christi*. It is an intriguing fact that the emergence of the sacramentary coincides more or less with that of the Rule. In his *A History of Liturgical Books*, Eric Palazzo remarks: '... the advent of the liturgical book demonstrates an increasing codification of usages between the fifth and sixth centuries; it is part of a whole trend of that period: the setting down in writing of tradition and knowledge in many other areas than liturgy, law for instance' (p. 37). He's thinking of Justinian presumably. One might also think of Cassiodorus in the realm of education. And, very much, of our Rule. It is contemporary, more or less, with the first surviving Roman sacramentary, the so-called Verona Sacramentary, some of the material in which alludes directly to the circumstances of the Gothic Wars. One could develop the analogies. Both Missal and Rule are there as humble guides to a personal and corporate activity which quite transcends them, as the growth and fragrance of the rose transcends the structure of the trellis, as the movement of the vehicle is of a different order than the tarmac which sustains it. And yet, in this present order, they have their indispensable place.

Community, Rule and Abbot. They are part, the skin perhaps, of this mysterious ball thrown by an eternal partner, towards you, to your centre, in an arch, from the great bridge-building of God. And received with open hands, they confer their power. *Fortissimum genus.* Through the acceptance, the right use of these things, *Quisquis* becomes a cenobite, becomes a 'son of obedience', and, more deeply, a disciple of Christ in the school of Christ. Through sacraments and liturgy Christ manifests himself to us. Through the Bible, through prayer, He manifests himself to us. Through our work. And also through this triad of ours. There is a sort of lived *lectio* being offered here. In our experience of Community, Rule and Abbot, we learn Christ.

One thing. There are in communities those who have been hurt – by the Community, by the Observance perhaps or at least by its presentation, by Superiors. There are monks and nuns who 'retire hurt'. There are certainly experiences in this domain I would very much hope not to have to undergo. There are misjudgements made. There are acts of institutional violence, even. There is always reason for sympathy. On the other hand – hard saying – it does often appear that outward circumstances have merely triggered an exaggerated reaction, have brought to light some inner unresolved issues which are then projected on the outside. But then that too calls for still more sympathy. I think that in those cases the Community and Abbot have to wait on God's time.

To end positively, thinking of *Quisquis en route.* I wonder if chapter 3 doesn't mark a point of arrival, or a sound test. As a chapter, it beautifully balances Community and Abbot,

Abbot and Rule, initiative and obedience, young and old, the unexpected and good order, man and God. It has been compared to a dance, a *quadrille* with v. 7 at the centre: 'In all things, therefore, let all follow the Rule as mistress.' God forgive our so often dysfunctional Chapters and Councils! But lived by an individual, would it not imply his mature integration into the community, that he has become a true cenobite? That he has now received so well that he can give back? When someone can contribute wisely in a community discussion, not relapsing into either shy or sullen silence nor trying to dominate, surely a threshold has been crossed, a wisdom is in place. The grace of Community, Rule and Abbot is bearing fruit.

Note

1. Henri de Lubac, *The Motherhood of the Church* (San Francisco: Ignatius Press, 1982), pp. 158-59.

5

Summoning the Brethren

I'd like to consider the 'personages' of the Rule, or, if you prefer, the social and economic life of the monastery. My first port of call is chapter 3, *On Summoning the Brethren to Council*. Most of that chapter is about what we now call the Conventual Chapter, and it's that I want to talk about.

It's a chapter with two sides to it. A constitutional side, of great historical significance, without as well as within monasticism. But there's also something broader and deeper, to do with community and abbot, life together and the joint pursuit of the common good.

The section of our Constitutions dealing with 'the Conventual Chapter and the Council of Deans' (chapter 2, Article 2) begins as follows, number 35: 'According to the teaching of the Rule, the Abbot should willingly listen to the brethren, not only when they are gathered in Chapter or Council, but also by other suitable means, as the nature of the business and the norms of law may require; so that the participation and concern of everyone for the good of the community may be better expressed.'

Both abbot and monks are being called to wisdom here. 'Let the house of God be administered wisely by wise men.' And chapter 3 itself is a little lesson in wisdom, in how to seek counsel, in how to give it. For the sake of the 'good of the community' as the Constitutions put it; for the sake of 'what is more useful (*utilius*) . . . better (*melius*) . . . more healthy (*salubrius*)' as the Rule puts it. To discern these things is the business of wisdom. Both the Rule and our Constitutions are talking about co-responsibility.

From the monk's point of view, the facts are: by his solemn profession he has become a full member of the chapter of his monastery, with the rights and duties that flow from that. The community has certain obligations towards him, and he towards it. By virtue of his profession, he is co-responsible for the good of the community. He exercises that co-responsibility formally in a chapter meeting, but as he is always a member of the community, so is he always co-responsible for its welfare. To exercise that co-responsibility, he needs the gift of wisdom. And this wisdom has a name (I think). In this domain, there is an art, there is a wisdom to be acquired. Roll of drums ... anticlimax ... a word used already, used in Constitutions, liable to make one yawn, but vital: PARTICIPATION. From *pars* and *capere*. Therefore, taking part. That's the wisdom, that's the art.

By grace, we're called to 'participate' in the divine nature. Participation is a big word in theology. My concern here is humbler – though it all connects: by being here, by being a member of this community, each of us is called to participate in building it up as a little house of God. Each of us is called, we can say, not to 'dominate' others, not to 'isolate' ourselves 'from' others, but to 'participate with' others. Participation is the royal highway between those two opposite extremes.

In chapter 3, one observes, St Benedict expects a monk, even the most junior, to have something to say, to have an opinion to offer. He certainly expects him to come to the meeting when called. Participation, not isolation. On the other hand, he expects the monk to give his opinion humbly, not to insist on it, to accept whatever is finally decided. Participation, not domination.

'Presumption' is a word much used in the Rule, a vice to be shunned. It means taking responsibility when one doesn't have it. That's on the 'domination' side. On the 'isolation' side, there's murmuring, the refuge of the lazy and cowardly.

What an art it all is! It needs prayer, and it needs common sense. It has never been easy. On the one hand, St Paul has to tell the Thessalonians not to be busybodies (2 Thess. 3:11), to aspire to live quietly, to mind your own affairs, and to work with your hands (1 Thess. 4:11). One of the great monastic skills is knowing how to mind one's own business, to fight the demon of *curiositas*, and its attendants of distraction, rash judgement etc. It's by seeking the Lord in prayer and by doing one's allotted work that one best contributes to the common weal. On the other hand, the author of Hebrews has to tell his flock: 'Let us consider how to provoke one another to love and good deeds, not neglecting to meet together, as is the habit of some, but encouraging one another' (Heb. 10:24–25). *Schola caritatis* ('school of love') must mean something. Don't some secular communities often show higher standards of caring and concern than we? Can't there be instances of real inhumanity in religious houses?

Often, *Quisquis* as monastic beginner is very preoccupied with his own spiritual life and tends to regard community issues as peripheral or beneath his notice. Then, there's a later stage: he's given some fairly responsible job, and he thinks to himself, my work is my contribution to the community (which is quite true), therefore I can leave the others to get on with their own lives (which is a false inference). In neither case, be it for spiritual reasons or because of preoccupation with work, is the monk really 'participating'. He needs to care. It's not an easy rope to walk, the way of humble love – which is what it is. Participation, then ... Let me now take another run at it.

We are on a journey to God, to purity of heart, and as cenobites we make that journey in company with others. And this being-with-others is to help us on the journey: to bring us to human and Christian maturity. Generalizations about the past are always risky, but it does seem that in religious life nowadays much more attention is given to the theme of – much overused word – Community. Much more is expected of community than was so in the past. St John of the Cross said this in one of his counsels:

> You should understand that those who are in the monastery are craftsmen placed there by God to mortify you by working and chiselling at you. Some will chisel with words, telling you what you would rather not hear; others by deed, doing against you what you would rather not endure; others by their temperament, being in their person and in their actions a bother and annoyance to you;

and others by their thoughts, neither esteeming nor feeling love for you. You ought to suffer these mortifications and annoyances with inner patience, being silent for love of God and understanding that you did not enter religious life for any other reason than that others work you in this way, and that you become worthy of heaven.[1]

There is a great truth there, and there are times in one's life ... But our Benedictine tradition and modern need would hope to find more than chisels in community! We read the 1994 document, *Fraternal Life in Community*, produced by the Congregation for Consecrated Life. It has been very well-received (something not true of every Vatican document!). It speaks of 'community as a place for becoming brothers and sisters', of 'personal freedom and the building of fraternity', 'communicating in order to grow together', 'religious community and personal growth', 'from Me to Us', etc. This is the new tone, the new language.

> Because religious community is a *schola amoris* which helps one grow in love for God and for one's brothers and sisters, it is also a place for human growth. The path is a demanding one, since it requires the renunciation of goods that are certainly highly valued, but it is not impossible ... The path towards human maturity, which is a prerequisite of a radiant evangelical life, is a process which knows no limits, since it involves continuous enrichment not only of spiritual values but also of values in the psychological, cultural and social order ... Religious community is the place where the daily and patient passage from 'me' to 'us' takes place, from my commitment to a commitment entrusted to the community, from seeking 'my things' to seeking 'the things of Christ'.[2]

Both the present human situation and the Church herself, then, are calling for the full development of the positive potential of community living. So much is clear.

Hopefully, then, a monastic community constitutes a healthy environment which enables each member of it to grow, even if that growth passes by way of the Cross (or chisel). God is good, and how many opportunities to 'mature' He gives us daily! And how often, instead, we allow our day to fill with little evasions and indulgences, so small or so habitual that we hardly notice them. But, then again, every day, the Community's still there, and we are called, for example, to live with people of different backgrounds, with the elderly (or with the young, if we're old), with authority, with people whose temperaments don't gel with our own. We're called to adjust to the changes that take place within ourselves and our outward life. Every day, the Community's there as *schola maturitatis*, 'the prerequisite of a radiant evangelical life'. And more than a *schola*. We have all already had experience of community, the family first of all, the neighbourhood, school, work, etc. And we have all been more or less 'wounded' in these communities, as Jean Vanier would say. And in order to live community life in a healthy way, in order to give of our best to the community, we have to unlearn, or rather be healed of, deeply-rooted difficulties, maladjustments. So, a monastery is not only a *schola* of maturity, but an infirmary, a hospital thereof.

It is very beautiful too to see this happen, as it does. To see defences come down and confidence grow, or mysterious resentments mysteriously disappear. It's a process both human and divine. Both grace and people contribute to it. For most monks most of the time, community life – assuming the community is essentially healthy – is adequate therapy.

Therapy, too, for our intellectual attitudes towards community and authority. These may be of the 'them and us' kind, or of the 'no such thing as society kind'. 'The Common Good' was an inspired choice as theme and title for the English and Welsh Bishops' recent statement. In practice, one observes that the young monk – and partly because of the intellectual environment – is most preoccupied with what the community will give him: in the process of formation, for example, in study, in work. The older monk, who has come to the quietening of desires, seems to attain a greater objectivity. He's happy to do the work that's needed. Jean Vanier speaks of passing from 'the community for me' to 'me for the community'. This is more healing.

Another approach would be via celibacy. Let me quote from an essay on it:

Most people emerge from childhood and adolescence with many inner wounds, feelings of insecurity, and some lack of confidence. They may feel unwanted and uncertain of their own worth; they may be secretly unconvinced that they are lovable, and therefore afraid of any close, sustained involvement because others may find nothing acceptable in them. Unless the experience of steady, accepting love reduces these fears, the person will spend much of his or her psychic energy on merely staving off personal disintegration. Mature chastity in the celibate life, as in any other, demands a firm inner conviction that one is a lovable, valuable person, capable of faithful and responsible relationships. The predictability and faithfulness of one's own community which flow from vowed stability have therefore a special supportive role to play in the growth of monastic celibacy, by building up a person's sense of being loved, trusted, and needed, and so freeing him to love others.[3]

This is all familiar enough stuff, and in some circles it's the only talk one ever hears. All I really want to say is that 'the path of human maturity, that prerequisite of radiant evangelical life' passes by way of our living together. And it's a process that never ends. And if then we ask, what does this mean in practice? What is maturity? We can answer: participation. The mature man knows how to 'take part'. He doesn't dominate others, nor isolate himself. He's not a conformist. He doesn't cultivate eccentricities or singularities. He's fully himself, and he's fully a member. As the English and Welsh bishops said:

Human beings are made in the image of God, and within the one God is a divine society of three Persons, Father, Son and Holy Spirit. Communities are brought into being by the participation of individual men and women, responding to this divine impulse towards social relationships – essentially, the impulse to love and be loved – which was implanted by the God who created them.[4]

So, a monk needs to question himself as to the quality of his 'participation'. This is a requirement of his profession, one of the meanings of which is 'incorporation into an institute' as Canon Law ungainly puts it. It's a requirement of the vow of *conversatio*, which includes a commitment 'to live the cenobitic life' as the Constitutions say.

Our life is a whole, a seamless garment. And just as my life of prayer should be integrated with the liturgy, so my inner effort towards goodness and responsiveness to God must integrate with my 'social' monastic life and daily work. The more of a sense of being a participator I can have, the better. I think Aelred of Rievaulx knew that: 'Do not, brother, do not kill the soul for which Christ died, do not drive away our glory from this house. Remember that . . . it is the singular and supreme glory of the house of Rievaulx that above all else it teaches tolerance of the infirm and compassion for needs.'[5] That to separate squabbling brothers. An appeal to co-responsibility, to the common good, to participation: in building God's house.

Notes

1. St John of the Cross, *Counsels to a Religious on how to reach Perfection*, 3.
2. Congregation for Consecrated Life, *Fraternal Life in Community*, 35, 39.
3. Daniel Rees, EBC, *Consider Your Call: Theology of Monastic Life Today* (London: SPCK, 1978), p. 180.
4. English and Welsh Bishops' Conference (1996), *The Common Good*, 18.
5. Quoted in Walter Daniel, *Life of Aelred of Rievaulx* (London: Nelson), 1963.

6

The Tools for Good Works

Only then, listening to the disapproving comments of her sister-in-law, did I see an image of Matryona which I had never perceived before, even while living under her roof.

It was true – every other cottage had its pig, yet she had had none. What could be easier than to fatten up a greedy pig whose sole object in life was food? Boil it a bucketful of swill three times a day, make it the centre of one's existence, then slaughter it for lard and bacon. Yet Matryona never wanted one...

She was a poor housekeeper. In other words she refused to strain herself to buy gadgets and possessions and then to guard them and care for them more than for her own life.

She never cared for smart clothes, the garments that embellish the ugly and disguise the wicked.

Misunderstood and rejected by her husband, a stranger to her own family despite her happy, amiable temperament, comical, so foolish that she worked for others for no reward, this woman who had buried all her six children, had stored up no earthly goods. Nothing but a dirty white goat, a lame cat and a row of fig-plants.

None of us who lived close to her perceived that she was that one righteous person without whom, as the saying goes, no city can stand.

Nor the world. [1]

So Alexander Solzhenitsyn ends his short story 'Matryona's House', set in 1953, published in 1963. It is only thanks to the Gospel that such a page is possible; thanks to the Gospel and, as so often in Russian literature, thanks to the monastic tradition. I'll come back to it.

* * *

To continue the *Tale of Quisquis*. He has been seized by the Lord, by the Christian thing. He has entered a community and put himself under a Rule and an Abbot. Chapters 4 to 7 then offer him the teaching of Christ, the way of life. 'See, in his loving kindness the Lord shows us the way of life!' He studies this teaching and tries to practise it. He is in process of becoming a disciple.

In chapter 4, we have, under the rubric of 'tools of good works', a summary of biblical morality as mediated by the Church. It is only slightly 'monasticized'. It is essential Christianity, one could say. It incorporates the two great commandments, the Decalogue, the Sermon on the Mount, elements of the apostolic *parenesis*. It reflects the baptismal (and the martyr) spirituality of the early Church. It has patristic roots in the *Didache*, the *Letter of Barnabas*, the *Apostolic Constitutions*. It echoes more especially Cyprian, Jerome, Ambrose, and Augustine, and sometimes the Desert Fathers and Cassian. The maxims number 74, like the chapters of the Rule. This chapter, in a sense, is the Rule in a nutshell. It follows on from the three maxims of Ps. 33 and the seven of Ps. 14; it looks forward to the twelve steps of chapter 7, and the final eight expressions of good zeal. Most of the 'tools' are short. This is pedagogy; they are to be learned by heart. First, they are all to be memorized by the monk, that is, to be taken into his *heart*; then, to be 'fulfilled' (*adimpleta,* a strong word) by him 'day and night, unceasingly', that is, to be expressed in his *body*; and finally 'handed back' (*reconsignata*) on the day of judgement in the hope of reward (4.76). Perhaps St Benedict has in his mind the passage from Ephesians: 'For we are his workmanship (*poiema*), created in Christ Jesus for good works, which God prepared beforehand that we should walk in them' (Eph. 2:10). By practising these good works, we are fulfilling God's eternal purpose for us and becoming *his* 'good work', his poem, his creation.

The language of 'work' is very prominent in the Rule, beginning with the 'toil of obedience' and ending with one last scolding of the 'negligent' in chapter 73.7. It is the second great image of the monastic life after that of the 'way' or 'journey'.

The monk is the Lord's workman. He is to work diligently at the spiritual craft within the workshop of the monastery (4). He is to prefer nothing to the work of God, the Divine Office (43). Prayer itself is a work (52.5). He is always to be occupied, be it in *lectio divina* or manual labour, because 'idleness is the enemy of the soul' (48). It is important, I think, to remember this global sense of work in the Benedictine Rule. It questions our natural understanding of the matter. It could be our contribution to contemporary discussions on work and leisure. It means that, when a monk is not able to 'work' in the usual sense, when he becomes old for example, or when he is absorbed by the problems of his psychology, he does not become useless, does not cease to be the Lord's workman. Even simply to refuse despair is a 'good work' (4.74), in other words simply to keep hoping. Again, we think of St Paul, writing to the Thessalonians, remembering before God 'your *work* (*ergon*) of faith and *labour* (*kopos*) of love and *steadfastness* (*hupomone*) of hope'. Above all, the monk need never cease to be a place, a workshop, where the Lord is steadily at work, working salvation (28.5) however mysteriously.

From our side the work, the *kopos*, is, above all, love. St Benedict places the two great commandments at the beginning of the chapter and ends with the promise of 'what God has prepared for those who love him' (4.77). So every 'tool' that falls between is for this *ars amandi*. 'The aim of our charge,' says St Paul to Timothy, 'is love that issues from a pure heart and a good conscience and sincere faith' (1 Tim. 1:5). We are already looking to the end of ch. 7. In other words, *Quisquis* is – even in this chapter – being drawn into the paradoxes of the Beatitudes (or of Solzhenitsyn's *babushka* Matryona). There is, in these chapters 4 to 7, an anthropology – not a philosophical one, but a lived one. There is a vision of man living in Christ. And as these chapters unfold, this vision becomes ever clearer, most clear in the last nine verses of chapter 7.

Let us imagine *Quisquis* devoting himself to the wisdom of this chapter, employing these tools of the spiritual craft unceasingly. What might be happening to him? What will he be discovering? First perhaps just how much love asks. The chapter opens with the two great commandments and ends with

the unimaginable reward prepared 'for those who love him'.
And yet how much there is in between! How much there is to
the 'art of loving'! How much vocabulary to learn of this
strange language! Clothing the naked, fearing hell, not loving
immoderate laughter, loving chastity, etc., etc. And yet how
wonderful it should be so. How rich a life of love can be. Bl.
Columba used to quote in his letters 1 Cor. 16:14, 'Let all that
you do be done in love.' Chapter 4 is a gloss on that 'all'.

Then, one more thing. I remember de Vogüé remarking
once that modern, post-Cartesian pedagogy begins with clear
ideas and then proceeds to action, whereas monastic pedagogy
begins from the other end, begins with external actions, with
good works, and from that direction purifies the springs of the
heart. Speaking in a different context, in what I think was his
first Anglican sermon, 'Holiness necessary for future Blessed-
ness', Newman says the same. Heaven requires holiness. Holiness is 'a certain state of the heart and affections'. And good
works are what foster this state of the heart.

> Good works (as they are called) [he says] are required, not as if
> they had anything of merit in them, not as if they could of them-
> selves turn away God's anger for our sins, or purchase heaven for
> us, but because they are the means, under God's grace, of
> strengthening and showing forth that holy principle which God
> implants in the heart, and without which... we cannot see Him.
> The more numerous are our acts of charity, self-denial and
> forbearance, of course the more will our minds be schooled into
> a charitable and self-denying, and forbearing temper. The more
> frequent are our prayers, the more humble, patient, and religious
> are our daily deeds, this communion with God, these holy works,
> will be the means of making our hearts holy, and of preparing us
> for the future presence of God. Outward acts, done on principle,
> create inward habits. I repeat, the separate acts of obedience to the
> will of God, good works as they are called, are of service to us,
> as gradually severing us from the world of sense, and impressing
> our hearts with a heavenly character.[2]

In other words, *Quisquis*, simply by the daily effort to do good
and be good, is already preparing in himself the heart of a
Matryona.

Notes

1. Aleksander Solzhenitsyn, 'Matryona's House', in *Stories and Prose Poems* (London: Bodley Head, 1971), p. 54.
2. John Henry Newman, *Parochial and Plain Sermons*, Vol. I, pp. 8–9.

7

Seeking Eternal Life

One of the tools of good works is 'to keep death daily before one's eyes', *mortem cotidie ante oculos suspectam habere.* And being abbot to the last, as is right, Abbot Alfred is doing that, just now, for all of us (September, 2001). A long life is coming to an end, and it has been a life completely given, from his late teens, to the religious life, to the *sequela Christi* in the path of the vows, given to prayer. And through all the seasons of his life, in England, Wales and Scotland, how adamantinely faithful he has been to that path. What has been striking me over the last few months is that there isn't another person there. He's himself, and he's one, and he's that: this stubborn, rather dour, often grumbly, but un-divertible follower of Christ. So we do our best to accompany him, to carry him on the last lap, over the threshold into something infinitely better than the third millennium will ever be! I'd be surprised if he wasn't actually, or hasn't been, consciously carrying us. There's more of St Aelred and more of the father's heart in him than he could ever publicize. But one little sign. When Fr Bede was here in June, he had a talk with Abbot Alfred, and they were chatting jocularly about some members of the community, when Abbot Alfred suddenly remarked, 'Oh, they're a good lot.'

Another tool of good works which comes to mind is that found in the verse before: 'to desire eternal life with all spiritual longing', *vitam aeternam omni concupiscentia spiritali desiderare.* It was because St Scholastica desired eternal life with all spiritual longing that she wanted to spend the whole night talking about the joys of heaven with her brother. And when he in turn dies, it is with 'his hands raised to heaven'. 'My desire is to depart and to be with Christ,' says St Paul, 'for that is far better' (Phil. 1:23).

We are made in the image of God. This is the most important thing our faith has to say about ourselves, about man. And because of our imageness, we naturally desire God: to know him and be united with him. Such a prospect is certainly terrifying to the creature and even repugnant to us so far as we are sinners, but it always remains and beckons and even sin cannot entirely silence it. In the first half of the twentieth century there was quite a controversy about all this among Catholic theologians. Does the human being *naturally*, that is, prescinding from the presence of grace in his heart, does he naturally desire to see God? Does he naturally desire the beatific vision, even though he could never attain it by his own powers alone, without the help of grace? Does St Thomas teach a natural desire for a supernatural end? The answer appears to be an emphatic yes. 'The desire for God,' says the Catechism, 'is written in the human heart, because man is created by God and for God' (27). And 'for God' here means 'for eternal life with God', even though without faith and grace this desire may well not be conscious and cannot lead us to deduce with certainty that there is such a thing as the vision of God awaiting us. In practice, it will translate into consciousness as desire for ultimate happiness, and into experience as a lack, a void, a restlessness, an unhappiness. But there it is, it is inscribed in our nature and runs like a hidden underground stream through every life. And it's this desire of our nature which Christ and the Holy Spirit enlighten and enkindle, divinize, so that in the Christian, who's carried by faith, hope and love, it becomes an explicit desire for the kingdom of heaven.

The human heart tends to God by its natural inclination without properly knowing who he is; but when it finds him at the well-spring of faith, and sees him so good, so beautiful, so gentle and so kind to all, and so disposed to give himself as sovereign good to all who want him, then, what joys and holy movements there are in the mind, to be united forever to that supremely lovable goodness! I have at last found, says the soul thus moved, I have found what I longed for.[1]

The whole Prologue of the Rule addresses this desire: 'so that you may return to him . . . if you wish to have true and everlasting life . . . so that we may deserve to see him who has called us to his kingdom . . . if we want to live in the tabernacle of his kingdom . . . if, fleeing the pains of hell, we want to reach eternal life . . . so that we may deserve to share in his kingdom.' And when this desire is formally addressed again in the epilogue of the Rule, chapter 73, 6 – 'so that we may come to our Creator by a straight course . . . whoever is hastening to heavenly homeland' – then we realize that this desire, like a hidden stream, must run through and energize the whole life and activity of the monk. What explicit form or forms this desire takes in our minds is a secondary matter, as long as any form is in accord with the faith. St Benedict speaks of desiring 'eternal life'. Well, in John 14:6, Jesus calls himself 'the life', and in 1 John 1:1-2 the phrases 'the word of life', 'the life', 'the eternal life' are all synonyms for Jesus himself. The desire for eternal life may be simply the desire 'to depart and to be with Christ'. It may be the desire to see God face to face, to see the Father, or to be in the Trinity, or to be embraced finally by God. Or it may be rather formless. It's often said that modern Christians are not as eschatologically minded as their ancestors. And yet, in any true Christian, in the measure of his faith, hope and charity, there will be a desire for heaven. It is his share in the desire of the Holy Spirit for the Father and the Son. And everything in our lives, the bad and the good, the good and the bad, is grist to this desire. Life deepens the bed of the stream so that more and more of the water of the Holy Spirit runs through it, until finally it carries us into the ocean of Infinite Being. The weaknesses of old age certainly deepen the desire.
St Gregory is a great encourager here.

To this end [heaven] let us move with all our love, for it is there that we shall be gladdened forever. In that place is the holy community of the heavenly citizens, there is certain festivity and unendangered rest; there true peace is no longer 'left' for us, but 'given' to us.[2]

Why is life so difficult? Why is the path so rough? 'The present life,' says St Gregory,

> is but a road by which we advance to our homeland. Because of this, by a secret judgement, we are subjected to frequent disturbance so that we do not have more love for the journey than for the destination. Some travellers, whenever they see pleasant fields by the road, contrive to linger there and thus deviate from the course undertaken in the journey. As long as they are charmed by the beauty of the journey, their steps are slowed. It is for this reason that the Lord makes the path through this world rough for his chosen ones who are on their way toward him. This is so that none may take pleasure in this world's rest or find refreshment in the beauty of the journey and thus prefer to continue the journey for a long time rather than to arrive quickly. It is also to prevent one who finds delight in the journey from forgetting what he had desired in his homeland.[3]

On the other hand, prayer and contemplation give a taste of what is to come and wean us from the pleasures of this world. It is a datum of experience that physical pleasure is more intense in anticipation than in realization. And it results in 'satiety'. Hence the expression, I suppose, 'being fed up' and hence the Roman axiom: *post coitum omne animal triste*. Spiritual pleasure, on the other hand, is weak on anticipation, strong on possession. 'The more a person experiences its taste, the more he recognizes what it is he loves so strongly.' Hence the need for foretastes in this life, aperitifs, trailers of the glory to come. 'You cannot know his sweetness if you have never tasted it. Rather, touch the food of life with the palate of the heart so that having made trial of his sweetness you may be empowered to love.'

Michael Casey sums up this teaching:

> For St Gregory the Great, desire is an ontological force inserted into man's nature to give him a permanent yearning for heaven.

To the extent that he refuses to be dominated by lesser desires, a person comes under the sway of this fundamental movement of his being. He is led to regret the power sin holds over him and to desire salvation with great ardour. As such love grows in his heart, it begins to find expression in the way he lives, in the priorities he establishes, in the way he acts and in the manner in which he resists temptation. It becomes a shaping force in his life, ordering everything towards heaven and towards the God who draws him to himself.[4]

Western monks of the Middle Ages were faithful disciples of St Gregory. It was said of Blessed David of Himmerod, an early Cistercian, who was always smiling: 'He had, like the saints, a face shining with joy; he had the face of one going toward Jerusalem.'[5]

To desire Heaven is to want God and to love Him with a love the monks sometimes call impatient. The greater the desire becomes, the more the soul rests in God. Possession increases in the same proportion as desire. But just as death is the condition upon which full satisfaction depends, so this pretaste demands that we must die to the world. There is no contemplation without mystical death, without mortification.[6]

But let's go back to a child: 'By definition,' writes his mother, 'heaven cannot be boring. If our picture of heaven is boring, then the fault lies with the picture and not with heaven; it simply means that we have not yet tasted the herb that would allow us to see.'[7] C. S. Lewis famously disparaged the idea of heaven as liturgy, but it is in the book of Revelation and in Hebrews. And what human experience is there that can give us more of a foretaste of heaven, of the union of the theocentric and anthropocentric, than a beautiful Mass? I'm not saying that because theology says it. I'm saying that out of my experience here. And there's Easter too. When St Remigius led Clovis into his cathedral to be baptized, the King turned to the Bishop and asked, 'Is this the heaven you promised me?'

So let us desire, or desire to desire, eternal life with all spiritual longing. Let us ask for the desire. Not because we don't want this life, but because we do want true life. And the

Liturgy – in this second half of the year – is a ready-made Jacob's Ladder. It has been lifting us heavenwards at least since the Ascension – of which one of the graces is desire for heaven. In the Prayer over the Gifts on that day, the Church prays *ut his commerciis sacrosanctis ad caelestia consurgamus*, 'that, through this most holy exchange we, too, may rise up to the heavenly realms'; and after communion *ut illuc tendat christianae devotionis affectus, qua tecum est nostra substantia*, 'that Christian hope may draw us onward to where our nature is united with you'. St Bernard preached more sermons on the Ascension than on the Passion. 'Men of Galilee, why do you stand looking up into heaven?' It sounds like a rebuke and an angelic shove back to the reality of the mission. But monks *are* allowed to remain standing looking up into heaven. That's their position, their station. 'This Jesus, who has been taken up from you into heaven, will come in the same way as you saw him go into heaven' (Acts 1:11). They remain standing there, not in regretful nostalgia, but waiting for the Lord Jesus to come from heaven, ready to alert the rest of humanity that he is on his way. Then, after Pentecost, come the feasts of so many saints, most commonly on the day of their birthday into heaven. Then in August the Assumption of our Lady, when we pray to be *ad superna semper intenti*, 'always attentive to the things that are above'. Then All Saints. Then Christ the King. This is the liturgical time when the final articles of the Apostles' Creed are made flesh before our eyes: 'I believe ... in the communion of saints, the forgiveness of sins, the resurrection of the body and life everlasting.' 'To desire everlasting life with all spiritual longing.' In the Lent of this life we look forward with the joy of spiritual desire to the holy Easter of eternal life: our share in the resurrection.

'On that day,' wrote a Benedictine of the twelfth century,

God will manifest Himself to us and to all our friends, He will wipe away every tear from the eyes of the saints. He will give back great things in return for small, for perishable things, bliss. Then all will become clear to us, everything will belong to everyone; then, visibly, we shall see how God is three and one, all in all, and above all. Then our hearts will rejoice with the fullness of joy, and our joy no one shall take from us, for what we are now in expectation we shall be then in reality: sons of the kingdom, united to the angels, eternal inheritors of God, co-heirs with Christ, through the same Christ our Lord who lives and reigns with the Father and the Spirit, world without end. Amen.[8]

Notes

1. St Francis de Sales, *Treatise on the Love of God,* II, 15.
2. St Gregory the Great, Homilies, 30, 10.
3. St Gregory the Great, *Moralia,* 23, 47.
4. Michael Casey, 'Spiritual Desire in the Gospel Homilies of St Gregory the Great', *Cistercian Studies*, vol. 16 (1981), pp. 297–314.
5. Quoted by Jean Leclercq, *The Love of Learning and the Desire for God* (London: SPCK, 1978), p. 69.
6. Leclercq, *op. cit.*, p. 85.
7. Carol Zaleski, 'When I get to Heaven: Picturing Paradise', in *The Christian Century,* April 5, 2003, pp. 22–31.
8. Quoted in Leclercq, *op. cit.,* p. 83.

8

Keeping the Way of Obedience Open

To obey the commands of the abbot in all things, even though... (RB 4.61)

Introduction

The Rule of St Benedict famously opens with the words, *Obsculta, o fili.* It opens with an abbot, a father and master, speaking to a 'son', a disciple, a would-be monk. It opens, in other words, with a *relationship.* At the other end of the Rule, in chapter 72, v. 10, we find, as the penultimate expression of 'good zeal', the phrase, *abbatem suum sincera et humili caritate diligant,* 'let [the monks] love their abbot with a sincere and humble charity.' We find the same relationship. At the beginning the call is to a single individual, at the end to several; at the beginning the call is to listen, at the end to love. But the same relationship is in play, that of son to father, of monks to abbot.

A few verses later in the Prologue, St Benedict uses the word 'son' again, but in relation to God, to Christ. In chapter 72, the verse following that quoted above speaks of 'preferring absolutely nothing to Christ.' In both passages then, there is a movement from a relationship with a fellow human being to one with God. There is a movement from 'sonship' or love of an abbot to 'sonship' of God and love of Christ.

This brings us, I think, to the essential question before us.

What is the link between this first relationship and the second? How does this first relationship, which is so constitutive of the Benedictine monastic life, serve, lead to, deepen, enhance the second relationship, which is the goal of the monastic life and the very heart of the Christian life itself? There was once a T-shirt with the logo, 'I've swallowed an abbot.' How does 'swallowing' an abbot, we may ask, help us eat the Bread of Life? How today, when obedience is so often problematic, does living in relationship to an abbot help us live in relationship with God?

This is, surely, one 'categorical' instance of a 'transcendent' question which can surface in other ways: namely the link between the specifically monastic and the generically Christian.

Chapter 4, v. 61 begins, 'To obey the commands of the abbot in everything' (*praecepta abbatis in omnibus oboedire*). This is St Benedict's version of the equivalent text in the *Rule of the Master* which reads, 'to give obedience to the instruction of the abbot' (*oboedientiam ad monitionem abbatis parare*, RM 3.67). St Benedict however has added, 'in everything, *in omnibus*.' And then he adds more, a long subordinate clause, beginning 'even if ...' So we have, 'To obey the commands of the abbot in everything, even if he (which God forbid) should act otherwise, remembering the command of the Lord, "Do what they say, but do not do what they do"' (Mt. 23:3).

The result is something richer and more dramatic. First, there is a call to obey, and, St Benedict specifies, to obey 'in all things'. Then, there is the acknowledgment of a difficulty, a ground of objection, a *videtur quod non*. This is the abbot's own conduct (or misconduct); he may 'act otherwise'. Finally though, this is mentioned only so as to be set aside or overcome. The abbot's failure to practise what he preaches should not prevent the monk from obeying him. And there is a play on words here. The reluctance to obey a *praeceptum*, a command, of the abbot is overcome with reference to a *dominicum praeceptum*, a command of the Lord, 'Do what they say, but not what they do.' It is a command of the Lord, of Scripture, which enables the monk to continue to obey the command of his deficient superior.

This surely goes back to real life, reflecting experience. St Benedict must have met this kind of objection from monks: 'Why should I obey this man when he ...?' And, in this tool of good works, he responds to it. One might say, he is enabling the monk to move beyond it. He offers the monk the refreshment of a word of the Lord, thanks to which he can still obey 'even if ...', despite the 'otherness' of the abbot. St Benedict is trying to keep the path of obedience open. We too, in our historical turn – either we ourselves during our professed life or postulants and novices considering joining us – have our objections. They may concern the defects of our superiors, or they may arise from other sources. But they are there. And so for us too the question arises, Can we still follow this way of obedience 'even if ...'? Even in the light of the difficulties, objections, the *videtur quod nons* that we are today aware of? In 1978, the book *Consider Your Call* addressed this question, among others. For example, its chapter on The Abbot begins:

> Many questions arise today about the place of the abbot. Can true Benedictine life exist without an abbot? Is his office one of the historically conditioned items of the Rule or is it essential to monasticism?, etc.[1]

The answer both that chapter and the later one on Obedience give amounts to a re-affirmation. It is a re-affirmation, sensitive to the contemporary certainly but also strong and clear, of the essential role of the abbot and of the enduring value of obedience. *Consider Your Call* also keeps the path open. This is what I would like to try to do also.

At the same time, this tool of good works gives this talk a structure. I'd like to look first at what the Rule and monastic (and post-monastic) tradition have said about obedience – about this relationship of abbot and monk / monks; then at the difficulties this teaching or its implementation may cause us today; and finally at the responses that may be given to these difficulties, enabling us to continue, even with more conviction, along the way.

I

All of us here, I think, are followers of Christ 'according to the Rule of St Benedict', though all of us are heirs also of secondary traditions giving a particular edge to our reading of the Rule. In any case, the Rule is for us a primary point of reference. Let me, then, try to say something about the role of the abbot and of obedience in the Rule. It is, of course, familiar territory.

The Abbot

'There can be little question about the absolute priority that St Benedict gives in his Rule to the place of the abbot,' says *Consider Your Call* (p. 76).

Let one monastic historian speak for many: 'Every reader of [the] Rule,' wrote Dom David Knowles,

> receives the impression that the sovereign authority in the monastery is the abbot. Once elected, he is supreme. He can appoint, promote, command, punish and dismiss his monks of his own initiative and power. He must ask advice, but he need not take it. He orders the daily life of the monastery in general and particular. For the monks he takes the place of Christ, and must be so regarded. He is in office for life, and is answerable to no disciplinary machinery save in the case mentioned, but hardly imagined, of utter unworthiness. As has been well remarked, the Rule is an abbot's Rule. . . Indeed the authority of the abbot is so immediate and so universal that the reader inevitably supposes that the Rule must have been written for a community of moderate size with an ever-present abbot.[2]

Two subsequent developments might be added as endorsement of such a 'high' view of abbatial authority: the general trend of the nineteenth and twentieth centuries monastic revival has been to underscore the position of the abbot as a major religious superior within an autonomous community (for example, within the English Benedictine Congregation at the end of the nineteenth century), and even now, an Abbot, or Abbess, is the sole religious superior who receives a liturgical blessing at the hands of a Bishop, and who, if an abbot, may wear pontificalia.

There then is one pole of the relationship. It seems little short of omnipotent, leaving the other pole – the listening son of the Prologue – little else than unconditional submission. 'And let him be punished likewise who shall presume to leave the enclosure of the monastery, or to go anywhere, or to do anything however trifling, without the permission of the abbot' (67.7).

And yet, 'Regarded more closely,' continued David Knowles, 'the monks are seen to be protected, so far as a rule can give protection, by several safeguards from the dangers of absolute government.'[3]

Michael Casey, not without a twinkle in his eye, once listed the following 'restraints' under which an abbot acts: fidelity to the Rule, free community election, due process, threat of deposition, prospect of hell, community inertia.

Yes, the relationship with which we are concerned does not stand in splendid isolation. The abbot himself only lives and functions within a network of other relationships. Four stand out. He is related, first of all, to Christ. He is not identified with Christ ('I'm not Jesus Christ, I'm only the Pope,' as John XXIII would say), but 'he is believed to act on behalf of Christ, *vices Christi agere*' (2.2; 63.13). Is this to send a surge of elation through his body? No, it is rather to propel his soul in the direction of humility. One of the earliest uses of the phrase 'to act in the place of Christ' (*vice Christi fungi*) occurs in St Cyprian's *Letter* 63. There it is applied to a bishop, and to a bishop in the act of celebrating the Eucharist. It functions as a summons to him to celebrate the Eucharist precisely as Christ celebrated it:

> That bishop truly acts in the place of Christ *who imitates what Christ did*, and he will offer in the Church a true and full sacrifice to God the Father, if he is careful to offer it in the way Christ himself was seen to offer it (*Ep.* 63, 14).

To be believed to hold the place of Christ, therefore, is a call on the abbot to imitate and conform himself to Christ. 'Let him reflect [on this], says St Benedict, and so behave as to be worthy of such an honour' (63.14). It is as much a restriction of his authority as its ultimate endorsement. 'Therefore the abbot ought not to teach, or ordain, or command anything which is against the law of the Lord' (2.4). Such contrary teaching or command, it is implied, would have no claim to obedience. Put positively, the abbot's relationship to Christ involves him in a relationship to the Word of God. It submits him to Scripture.

Secondly, the Abbot is related and essentially subordinated to the Rule. Cenobites, says St Benedict, are 'those who live in monasteries and serve under a rule and an abbot' (1.2). Not only are rule and abbot paired here, but priority is given the former. If the abbot is a *magister* (Prol. 1, etc.), the Rule is also a *magistra* (3.7) which all are to follow. If the abbot has *potestas* (39.6, etc., six times in all), only the Rule, like Scripture, has *auctoritas* (37.1). So, the abbot is to 'do all things with the fear of God and observance of the Rule' (3.11), and the last injunction given him in ch. 64, as prelude to the promise of heavenly reward, is simply, 'Above all, let him keep the present rule in all matters' (64.20).

Thirdly, there is of course the relationship of the abbot to the community. He is himself, no small point, elected by the brethren (64), and is bidden to seek their advice (3). More deeply, he exists for the sake of his monks and not vice versa. All the terms used of the abbot – Father, Teacher, Shepherd, etc. – are relational. He is a servant. At the end of chapter 2, we find the verb *subministrare*; at the end of ch. 64 the verb *ministrare*. In ch. 27 comes the great line, 'Let him know that what he has undertaken is the care of sick souls, not a tyranny over healthy ones' (27.6), and hardly less powerfully in chapter 63: 'Yet the abbot must not disturb the flock committed to him, nor by an exercise of arbitrary authority ordain anything unjustly' (63.2). Rather, 'let him so arrange and ordain all things that souls may be saved and that the brethren may do their work without justifiable murmuring' (41.5). Justice and, still more, charity are to shape his relationships with the brethren. And he has this *potestas* for no other reason than to help them reach the goal of salvation. His fatherhood is in relation to their sonship – their sonship not of him (hardly a prominent idea in the Rule), but of Christ, of the Father. St Benedict would not have been disturbed by the statement in *Perfectae Caritatis*' article on obedience: '[Superiors] are to rule their subjects as sons of God and with respect for the human person' (14).

Fourthly, if the Rule of St Benedict, with that of the Master, gives the abbot an awesome prominence, this does not have the effect of diminishing other 'players' in the cenobium. On the contrary. The Rule brings on to the stage of the monastery's life a large cast of colourful *dramatis personae*: deans, *senpectae*, spiritual seniors, the cellarer, his assistants, the various 'hebdomadaries', the infirmarian, the guestmaster, craftsmen, the novice master (at least incipiently), priests and deacons, the porter and, however reluctantly, the prior. There is no doubt, certainly, of the subordination of all these agents to the central authority of the abbot, but simultaneously the specific integrity of their own tasks and their personal responsibility shines out. If St Benedict gave us two unprecedentedly strong chapters on the Abbot, he also left a memorable one on the Cellarer. There is a symbolic significance to all this.

So, if on one reading of the Rule, the abbot appears to fill the screen of the life of the individual monk and of the whole monastery, on another it is not hard to click 'minimize' and set him in context. If, on the one hand, the abbot stands at the centre, on the other he is de-centred, and is taken up with his brethren into a common relationship to Christ, to Scripture and to the Rule. And in so far as the abbot himself lives in the relationships mentioned, so far will he be able to lead his brethren into them. The relationship abbot-monk is itself in relationship.

Obedience

Let me turn now to the other pole, to the obedience of the monk.

That 'obedience' is a key ingredient of monastic life and, more generally, of the religious life, is an uncontroversial given. As one of the three evangelical counsels, it remains a distinguishing mark of the consecrated life in Vatican II (*LG,*

VI, *PC,* 14), in Paul VI's 1971 *Evangelica Testificatio* (nn. 23–28), in the 1983 Code of Canon Law (e.g. cc. 573, 601), in the *Catechism of the Catholic Church* (in its paragraphs on the Consecrated Life, 914ff.), in John Paul II's 1996 *Vita Consecrata* (cf. ch. I *passim*, also nn. 43, 92 among others). Yet for certain monastic and religious traditions it comes across as more, as *in some sense* **the** distinguishing mark of their life. There are some sayings of the Desert Fathers that tend that way (e.g. of Abba Rufus). It has been claimed, for example, of Pachomian monasticism, in another way of Cassian, who in Book IV of the Institutes, for example, speaks of 'the good of obedience, which holds the first place among the other virtues' (*Institutes* IV, 30, 1); again of the monasticism of Lérins. In a sermon of one representative of the latter, we find the suggestive phrase, '*Nihil oboedientiae praeferat*' (Let [the monk] prefer nothing to obedience) (Eusebius Gallicanus, *Hom.* 38, 170). There is no doubt that the Master stands in the same line, providing, de Vogüé maintains, the most thorough theory of obedience in the whole literature of ancient monasticism.[4] Leaping forward, the Dominican and Thomist tradition would seem to give a particular weight to obedience. It is indeed the only explicit vow a Dominican makes and, in the mind of St Thomas, 'the principal one among the vows of religion' (*Summa Theologiae*, 2-2, 186, 8), offering to God what is most central to the human person (his own will), embracing the other vows, and bringing us, of all the vows, closest to the 'end' of religious life. It features prominently in the *Dialogues* of St Catherine of Siena. Later, in his famous *Letter on Obedience* to the Province of Portugal (1553), St Ignatius Loyola would write:

> Of course, I wish you to be perfect in all spiritual gifts and adornments. But it is especially in the virtue of obedience, as you have heard from me on other occasions, that I am anxious to see you stand out... We may the more readily allow other religious orders to surpass us in the matter of fasting, vigils and other austerities in their manner of living... But in the purity and perfection of obedience and the surrender of our will and judgement, it is my warmest wish, beloved brethren, to see those who serve God in this Society stand out.[5]

What of St Benedict in all this? How important is obedience to him? Is he an 'a' man or a 'the' man? Paradoxical as it may sound, I think he is both. On the one hand, the overwhelming impression that emerges from the Rule is of the centrality of obedience to the whole cenobitic monastic enterprise. '[W]hat he has kept of [the Master's] chapter "On Obedience", together with the first four steps of humility,' writes de Vogüé,

> are enough to range him with the Master among those who attribute to obedience a primordial importance...The same impression stands out, he continues, at the beginning of the Prologue... The word 'obedience' is pronounced there twice and contrasted with 'disobedience' and 'self-will'. It would be difficult to make the theme of obedience more conspicuous in the exordium of a monastic rule. This virtue appears both as the road by which one returns to God and as the 'powerful and glorious weapon' of the soldier enrolling in Christ's service. A unique road and a unique weapon.[6]

It is surely revealing that the last positive adjective attributed to the monk in the Rule, in ch. 73, v. 6, is 'obedient'. For St Benedict most certainly, it is 'by this way of obedience that [we] go to God' (71.2), that is, realize the aspiration of the monastic heart. At the same time, ch. 7 remains the great programmatic chapter of the Rule, and there obedience is integrated into a ladder of humility the issue of which is the perfect love of God which casts out fear, or in Cassian's thought, purity of heart. Obedience, like the abbot, is both central and centred in something else.

'In the doctrine of obedience St Benedict was heir to a complex tradition,' we read in *Consider Your Call* (p. 189). Indeed, and St Benedict at once synthesized much of it and enriched it. His concept of obedience is, I think, less monophonic than polyphonic, corresponding somewhat to what was said of the abbot earlier. We may distinguish:

i)   the notion of obedience to Scripture, to the commandments of God (e.g. Prol. 40), an idea strong in the monastic writings of St Basil.

ii) an obedience to the Rule (e.g. 3.7; 7.55; 62.4, 11).

iii) an obedience to the abbot, itself woven of several strands. Helpful here is a remark of de Vogüé's:

> an abbot [i.e. the abbot in the Rule] is the synthesis of three persons: the father of the desert, the head of the Christian community, and the *paterfamilias*.[7]

a) St Benedict was certainly an heir to the Desert idea of the abbot as spiritual father (49.9), bearer of 'the medicine of the Holy Scriptures' (28.3), healer of the hidden wounds of the soul (cf. 46.5–6), teacher of a disciple (cf. ch. 6), intercessor (28.4; 49.8). Obedience to an abbot emerges here as, to use a Buddhist phrase, a 'taking of refuge', or to use another 'finding sanctuary', as something pedagogical, educational, needed especially (though not exclusively) in the earlier stages of the monastic life, making possible a liberation from the entanglements of self-will (*voluntas propria*), taking us on the narrow way of discipleship, as an imitation of Christ who was obedient unto death (Phil. 2:8).

b) At the same time, though, St Benedict's abbot undeniably takes on some of the features of the head of a Christian community, a pastor, a hierarch. This emerges in the use of the phrase 'believed to hold the place of Christ' in the appeal to Lk. 10:16 ('He who hears you hears me'), in the references to the abbot as 'doctor' and 'pastor', in the role he plays in the liturgy and as moderator of the 'regular discipline', and, implicitly, in the ecclesial language freely used of the community itself. In the monastery, the obedience required of every Christian towards his pastors (e.g. Heb. 13:17) is found again in a more complete and intense form.

c) At the same time again, the abbot is head of the household, the one who has the ultimate management of its officials and activities (65.11–12) and ultimate responsibility for all its members, and who therefore has a claim to be obeyed so that what needs doing is done and done in harmony. The theology of 'Honour your father and mother' (Ex. 20:12) could be invoked here.

In practice of course, these different kinds of obedience merge into each other. But it is worth being aware that just as obedience itself, within the Rule, has more than one face, so does obedience to an abbot. It is complex. It is at once something spiritual, ecclesial, familial. It can call on many motives: fear of hell (5.3), fear of the Lord (5.9), desire for eternal life (5.3, 9), the holy service professed (5.3), the preference for Christ (5.2), love of God (7.34). It is at once, as de Vogüé has often said, obedience *to* Christ, with the appeal to Lk. 10:16, and obedience *after the pattern of* Christ, with appeal to Jn 6:38 and Phil. 2:8. If it is to be authentic, it requires not just prompt external compliance, but an overcoming of inner fear and hesitation, a giving of the heart, an offering to God and a certain élan (5.14ff). It does not exclude the expression of difficulties when an obedience seems beyond the monk's powers (ch. 68). It is, at its deepest level, an opening of the ear of the heart (Prol. 1), a daily listening to the voice of the Lord (Prol. 9–11), a readiness to follow (5.8).

iv) In chapters 71 and 72, St Benedict extends the 'good of obedience' in a horizontal direction. The brethren are to obey one another. It is the attitude, he seems to imply, of love.

The Rule's doctrine of obedience, then, is rich. There is nothing reductionist or monochrome about it. Nor surely should it reduce those who understand and practise it in its richness. Obedience for St Benedict certainly is central, primordial, or whatever such adjective best fits. And yet it never displaces the primacy of charity. Obedience to an abbot is also clearly central, and yet it does not exclude other forms, all of them grounded in Scripture. Dare I say that we need not be apologetic about St Benedict's presentation of obedience? Among the many traditions of religious life in the Church, it has a claim to be at once the broadest and the richest. It is a choice part of our patrimony as Benedictines.

II

All that has been to rehearse the familiar. It is time for the 'even though . . .' Even St Benedict, in chapter 4, recognizes that a monk may find the behaviour of his abbot a stumbling-block. In chapter 68, he recognizes that a monk may find a particular command a stumbling-block. In ch. 5, he warns against the danger of a merely external obedience. Since the sixth century, the roll-call of difficulties has not got shorter. In the long entry *Obbedienza (Voto)* in Vol. VI of the *Dizionario degli Istituti di Perfezione (DIP,* 1980), there is a section baldly entitled *L'Obbedienza Distruttiva* ('Destructive Obedience').

Historically, one might distinguish two waves of objection to the monastic, religious life, and therefore to lifelong obedience to another human person. The first wave coincided with the sixteenth-century Reformation, the second with the rise of the various humanisms. I will focus on the difficulties arising from the second.

The question may be put thus: what more or less conscious theoretical and practical difficulties, what fears, what potential for misunderstanding and misuse, might an 'ordinary', 'Western', young person, newly coming to monastic life and formed within contemporary culture, carry within his or her self? What difficulties might still linger or indeed arise after profession?

First of all perhaps, and at the root of much else, there lies the notion of the free, autonomous individual – the subject, the person. How and when this character came to birth has long teased historians. 'It is impossible to date the beginning of this long and complex process, writes Rabbi Jonathan Sacks,

but we can identify significant moments: when Shakespeare has Polonius say to Laertes: 'This above all – to thine own self be true'; when Descartes sits down to discover certainty on the basis of personal reflection alone; when Rembrandt starts painting his long series of self-portraits; when authors embark on the new literary genre of autobiography; when couples begin to marry because of personal affection rather than social or parental expectation. Each of these testifies to a new and liberating sense of self-awareness. The world within has begun to resonate no less powerfully than the world outside. Reality's centre of gravity has begun its long journey inward to the self.[8]

Romano Guardini too had already vividly evoked both the genesis and the ethos of this modern person:

> Conceived as that which most expressed the human, as flowering from roots intrinsic to itself, as shaped in its destiny through its own initiative, personality became...something primary and absolute which could not be questioned or doubted. The great personality was looked upon as a man who had to be taken inevitably upon his own terms. Only in the light of his own unique 'personality' might one dare to justify the actions of a man. Ethical standards seemed relative when compared with those which genius deserved. This new measure for judging the human act in terms of 'personality' was first applied to the extraordinary man; it soon applied for humanity at large. An ethos based upon objective goodness and truth was discarded for an ethos based in the subjective where nobility and truthfulness to one's own self prevailed... A bearer of the only valid act, the subject became a uniting principle for all categories of activity; in turn the subject determined its own validity... Autonomous and self-existent, the subject became the very ground for meaning in spiritual experience.[9]

'People, serfs and conquerors are with us always,' said Goethe in a poem; 'Personality alone is the highest happiness / Of the children of the earth.' 'I am the master of my fate, I am the captain of my soul.' The central figure, tragic or heroic or even comic, of so much literature and art is precisely such a figure. He is ubiquitous. He's in a log cabin in the North American forests or in the Australian outback, or most likely alone at the wheel of a car – the perfect outward expression of his selfhood. He can never forget himself. He cannot conceive of himself in any other way. To quote Jonathan Sacks again:

> The individual is no longer born into and subordinate to a set of defining roles established by custom and community. Instead roles must be chosen, and the self that chooses is defined precisely by its independence from all non-voluntary ties. Alasdair MacIntyre describes the 'specifically modern self' as one that 'finds no limits set to that on which it may pass judgement'. To be a moral agent in this new dispensation is 'precisely to be able to stand back from any and every situation in which one is involved, from any and

every characteristic that one may possess, and to pass judgement on it from a purely universal and abstract point of view that is detached from all social particularity' (*After Virtue*).

This surely is the heart of the revolution. It is not that before a certain date there were no such things as individuals who were conscious of themselves as such. Throughout history there have been heroic or tragic figures who set themselves against the idols of their age. But at a certain point, what had once been exceptional became the norm. The individual is no longer defined in and through society, but over and against it. Roles become masks, hiding rather than revealing the true self beneath. Conventions become inhibitions, no longer the precondition of individuality but rather of its suppression. Slowly – the process takes several centuries – the biblical narrative becomes reversed. Instead of its being 'not good for man to be alone' it becomes his essential dignity.[10]

The use of the word 'conscience' here is strangely revealing. It means literally 'knowing-with'. Yet the concept of 'following one's conscience' is almost always used in an adversarial sense. 'Here I stand, I can do no other.' We talk of 'conscientious objectors', not of 'conscientious obey-ers'. Obligation is identified with objection, conscience with contradiction. And specifically with objection to, contradiction of human authority. The hero is, so often, the dissident.

From all this will likely arise the conviction, or at least the fear, that a monastic obedience will sooner or later involve one in confrontation or in the temptation to abdicate personal responsibility. Obedience would then seem at least to run the risk of being an invitation to compliance, surrender of personality, immaturity, infantilism. It would seem a negation of precisely this modern sense of the individual/person/subject, of freedom and responsibility. And doesn't this after all have Christian roots? Hasn't it been resonantly, if tardily, endorsed by such Christian authorities as Vatican II and John Paul II?

There are other strands too. Do not both the twentieth-century experience of totalitarianism and the more recent rise of Islamic fundamentalism function as warning lights against anything that seems to imply renunciation of personal identity and freedom? Over any theology of obedience hangs the dark cloud of Adolf Eichmann's terrible reply to the question at his trial, 'Why did you do it?' 'It was obedience, obedience, obedience.' Isn't there a whole historiography which has argued that it was the (originally Lutheran) insistence on whole-hearted obedience to the State which induced that fatal proclivity to compliance which the Nazis could exploit? Didn't Erich Fromm, in this context, write a book called *The Fear of Freedom*?

Then psychology, sophisticated and popular, has insinuated its voice too. We have all acquired certain reflexes. We have all been taught to flee, not so much forgetfulness of God's commandments, as unhealthy self-suppression, low self-esteem, the search for security, the failure to 'be ourselves', the refusal of responsibility, passivity, immaturity. We have all been told and sold the value of authenticity, of self-expression, of following our gut-instincts, and so forth. How then can a contemporary monk or nun not ask themselves: Am I simply in search of the security of a system, of an institution, of a father or mother who will relieve me of the burden of decision? Is my obedience an evasion of responsibility? Have I actually matured because of my monastic life and obedience, or in spite of them? Have I claimed a patina of piety for what was simply moral cowardice? Have I, in moments of community decision, trusted overmuch in the wisdom of authority or of the consensus? Is my obedience just a fear of being 'me', of being 'who I really am'?

There are, too, some more immediately contemporary trends which tend the same way. There is the indifference, cynicism, towards politics, signalled in the low turn-outs for voting. There is, not just a suspicion of the institutional, but a deep inability to realize its significance and role; the same as regards authority. There can be, for personal reasons of the most understandable kind, problems of trust in relation to any human being, community, authority. Certainly, there is no social culture of obedience; rather, a growing 'culture' of confrontation and litigation. There is a philosophy of education averse to the idea of being initiated into a coherent inheritance, and focussed instead on a 'child-centred approach' which, at one level anyway, simply seems to leave the child the arbiter of the content and value of its education. Meanwhile in daily life, people can find themselves in two worlds, living schizophrenically almost. On the one hand, the world of work is ever more legally regimented, full of 'obedience', leaving very little freedom, whereas the world of private life has lost much of the form given it by stable families and traditional values and become all but anarchic. There have been discussions about the 'fatherless society', and doubtless any survey like this should at least ask the adjective 'post-modern' to come on stage! It's revealing that those of a conservative bent, drawn to the monastic life by its focus, seriousness and counter-cultural stance, will often be passionate advocates of strong authority and unquestioning obedience, and yet when actually called upon to move beyond a cherished attitude will find themselves unable to do so. One sign among many that it is not easy for people to make the transition from the current environment into the very different one of the monastery.

There is also the inner history of monastic life and of the Church as a whole. It is revealing, for example, where Marmion's *Christ the Ideal of the Monk* situates its chapter on the abbot: immediately after the opening chapters on the search for God and the following of Christ and *before* the chapter on the 'cenobitical society'. That the teaching of Vatican I on the Pope is an influence here is clear. As late as 1927, a retreat-giver at Mont-César could say:

> The Abbot or his delegate has, as it were, received the power of trans-substantiating all his commands into the will of God. The will of the superior is infallibly that of God. Obedience consists in the abandonment one makes to a legitimate superior of everything human and voluntary in our actions. It is someone else who acts and wills through us.[11]

Historians speak of a certain 'sacralization' of the abbot and his role. A reaction was inevitable. It was the generation who had experienced the full force of the First World War who often led it. We find it, for example, in the breakaway at Maredsous which led to the foundation of Le Bouveret or in the attitudes of a pioneer like Lambert Beauduin who, when superior of Amay (later Chevetogne), was always intent on encouraging his brethren's sense of responsibility, stimulating and developing the gifts of each, and expecting a sincere expression of their views, rather than mere compliance, when their advice was sought. Some fifty years later, *Consider Your Call* will set its chapter on the Abbot under the general heading of 'Community' and after treatment of such themes as 'the understanding of human community today', 'the communal structure of salvation', 'communication and responsibility', with, clearly Vatican II in the background. Yes, within the Church itself has there not been a move away from an ecclesiology which one-sidedly emphasized the role and rights of the hierarchy to one centred on the People of God and communion, privileging our essential Christian equality, the recognition of charisms, freedom and maturity, and insisting on the essentially ministerial character of any authority? Where in all this, we may wonder, does obedience belong? Certainly, many who exited the religious life in the 60s and 70s of the last century did so because they were no longer convinced of the value of obedience. We who stick it out may, in turn, find ourselves wondering if we do not share something of the same inability to see, and even our superiors too. Many apostolic religious seem to have relieved themselves of personal superiors altogether, even officially. We may have kept them, but are our abbots nowadays really such? Is obedience an actual reality in our communities?

Meanwhile, too, the old stumbling-blocks remain. 'Both the danger of an authoritarianism which extinguishes the sense of humanity, the quality and hence the joy of personality, and the danger of an uncritical obedience, are not illusory,' says the *DIP* (*loc. cit.*, col. 546). There are, for example, superiors who abuse their authority and may even destroy their communities. The spectre of the sect of Jonesville can rise from the ground. In ch. 64, St Benedict envisages an unhealthy symbiosis between a community and its superior, for which the only remedy is intervention from outside. He is speaking from experience and the experience is not limited to the past. It's as if a viral pathology infects the whole organism. The replacement of the objectivity of the Rule with the subjectivity of personality will be a primary symptom, as will the narrowing of the lines of communion: no salvation outside the superior. 'Obedience' is all too likely to be invoked. Yet, as Michael Casey sagely remarks, a 'bad' abbot will usually indicate something wrong in the body corporate.

'Destructive obedience': that is just one possible monastic example. Still, there is such a thing, both in society and in the Church, and it is good to be aware of it. And there are, as I've suggested, many cultural, historical, psychological sensibilities which may make us hesitant. How then can we move beyond the hesitation? How can we be sure that the obedience we espouse does not destroy us and our communities, but builds, gives life? To this we turn.

III

Here I'd like both to agree and disagree with *Consider Your Call*. The title of its first part is, 'The World and the Church', with the sub-title, 'The Wider Context', and it treats first of the 'Contemporary World'. Vatican II was in the background here. One could say that *Consider Your Call* began its reflections on the monastic life from the portrait of the contemporary world outlined in the conciliar Constitution *Gaudium et Spes*. I would like to agree in taking direction from Vatican II, but disagree by starting instead from *Dei Verbum*, the Constitution on Divine Revelation. Isn't its very opening uncannily close to that of the Rule? 'Hearing the Word of God with reverence ...' (*DV*, 1). The primary 'wider context' of our Christian monastic life is not the contemporary world. It's the Word of God, divine Revelation, faith. If not, we will cease to be salt, cease to be a sign of contradiction, cease to be a word of God ourselves! It is above all from there – from listening reverence, from *obsculta o fili* – that we must begin and always begin again. It is to acknowledge that our monastic life, as the Prologue constantly implies, flows from the Word of God, from 'the guidance of the Gospel', is wholly based on faith, is something received, including in a special way the mystery of obedience. This is not to be 'fundamentalist', 'fideist', 'integrist', 'traditionalist', or whatever. For in chapter II of *Dei Verbum*, on the Transmission of Divine Revelation, we find the notion of a development of doctrine:

> The Tradition that comes from the Apostles makes progress in the Church, with the help of the Holy Spirit. There is a growth in insight into the realities and words that are being passed on (*DV*, 8).

Isn't it this we are after: a 'development of doctrine' as regards monastic obedience? A development – or at least a re-statement – occasioned by the difficulties which our own culture provides and which we carry within us, occasioned by an honest and critical dialogue with these difficulties, not closing the ancient paths to us but helping us take the ever-new path of obedience with greater awareness, even greater alacrity.

The rich and balanced doctrines on religious obedience of Vatican II and of Paul VI were already instances of this 'development'.

It must be said too that the element of 'scandal', of 'folly', of the Cross cannot be excised either from the religious life as a whole or from obedience in particular. The latter will always have its ingredient of 'even though'. It will always require a conversion of mind and heart. It is at the service of self-transcendence.

At the level of practice first, just a few random observations.

There seems to be a difference, real but elusive, in the exercise of authority and the practice of obedience between communities of men and those of women. (One of the participants usefully remarked that when obedience is practised as it should be, that practice will be much the same in communities of either sex, but that when there is aberration, it will manifest itself divergently according to gender.)

There are also different emphases in the same realms between communities of a contemplative and those of a more pastoral orientation.

The 'brethren' tend to loom larger in a superior's mind than vice versa. There is an asymmetry in the relationship. The same would hold presumably for parents and children. An abbot's emotional attitude towards his monks (his *affectus*, 2.24) means more to the latter than they usually avow.

There is a common spectrum of attitudes towards a superior, and modes of relating to him. At one extreme there can be an unhealthy emotional dependence, often manipulative and self-protective. At the other extreme, we find the *longe a superioribus salus* school or the devotees of a hermeneutic of suspicion; they too are protecting themselves. Between there is a range of more or less healthy attitudes. The best would surely combine both the outlook of faith and a sympathetic human realism. Each relationship will be unique, from both sides.

There are many questions relating to maturity/immaturity. I have heard of one abbot who maintains that 'infantilism' is a major reality in our monasteries. Is this fair? Is there more 'immaturity' in monastic than, say, in married life? I doubt it. If the immaturity becomes especially visible in the relationship with the superior, may it not be possible for this to be addressed? May it not be an opportunity rather than a problem? And if so how? If the relationship with human authority (fatherhood/motherhood) moves in the direction of maturity, is that not likely to have a positive effect on the person's relationship with God and with others?

As to some of the difficulties relating to the practice of obedience, pp. 194–196 of *Consider Your Call* remain worth reading.

At the level of theory, what might at least be the elements of a re-stated theology of monastic obedience? I can only suggest some.

1) It must surely be seen as an extension, a continuing realization in the Church and in personal life, of the obedience to which Scripture witnesses. The theology of the Covenant, the whole Deuteronomic and much of the prophetic tradition would come in here, the Abrahamic and Pauline idea of the 'obedience of faith', the classic theme of the obedience of Christ in its Johannine as well as Pauline expression, the apostolic encouragement of relations of mutual respect, obedience and service within the Christian community would all be pillars of a biblical theology of obedience.

2) It must also take account of the different aspects of religious obedience found in the tradition, and especially of the multi-faceted presentation of obedience found within the Rule itself. Picking up from what was said earlier, obedience to an abbot (and to the officials appointed by him) belongs on a continuum which begins with obedience to the commandments, passes through obedience to the Rule and in some sense flowers in the mutual obedience urged by chapters 71 and 72. Another side of this would be the giving of more thought to the delicate subject of the spiritual fatherhood of the abbot and the ways in which it may express itself in contemporary monastic life.

3) Then an adequate theology of monastic obedience would have to continue the dialogue with contemporary 'anthropology'. It could ask the latter whether it isn't in its way a 'myth', whether the icon of the wholly mature, self-motivated individual really corresponds to the full reality of the human being, whether it does not perhaps create its own shadow and its own unreal sense of guilt, while leaving much of human nature in the shade. But that said, such a theology does need to be resolutely personalist. Vatican II surely points a way when it speaks of 'freedom strengthened by obedience' (*LG,* 43). It must emphatically be said that obedience is not only *not* an instrument of oppression or diminishment, is not only simply a practical requirement for getting 'jobs' done or even for guaranteeing social harmony, but is rather at the service of the full flowering of the person. It can indeed call for the relinquishing of enthusiasms or projects that 'may stem from pride, idiosyncrasy, or want of judgement' (*Consider Your Call*, p. 92), but of itself it does not feed on passivity. Rather, it requires the full mobilization of the individual's inner resources. It does not discourage initiative and responsibility, but re-locates them. It situates them, as it were, after a 'command', not in the void preceding it (which, in turn, is not to discourage proposals, suggestions prior to any directions from authority). There is more too. Often, obedience is precisely what takes us beyond the bounds of our own narrow self-definitions. This is perhaps the meaning of St Benedict's 'self-will' (*voluntas propria*). The modern awareness of the

complexity of our psyches could come in here as endorsement of the traditional wisdom, rather than its contradiction. In any case, obedience often asks of us more than we would ask ourselves. I remember two images: one from Dom Daniel Rees of obedience as raising the bar for the high jump just those few inches beyond our comfort or competence, the other from Dom Aldhelm Cameron-Brown of obedience taking us out of our private swimming-pool into the river of life. But even this is not to say enough.

4) Above all, it is a matter of situating obedience not simply within one's own personal development, one's own desire for fulfilment, but within the journey to God, to purity of heart, within the dynamics of faith, hope and charity, within love of the Father and of the brethren; within, in other words, a fully Christian anthropology, within the Paschal Mystery. I offer two quotations which point this way.

The first is from Pope Benedict XVI talking to religious in Austria last year:

> Romano Guardini relates in his autobiography how, at a critical moment on his journey, when the faith of his childhood was shaken, the fundamental decision of his whole life – his conversion – came to him through an encounter with the saying of Jesus that only the one who loses himself finds himself (cf. Mk 8:34ff; Jn 12:25); without self-surrender, without self-loss, there can be no self-discovery or self-realization.
>
> But then the question arose: to what extent is it proper to lose myself? To whom can I give myself? It became clear to him that we can surrender ourselves completely only if by doing so we fall into the hands of God. Only in him, in the end, can we lose ourselves and only in him can we find ourselves.
>
> But then the question arose: Who is God? Where is God? Then he came to understand that the God to whom we can surrender ourselves is alone the God who became tangible and close to us in Jesus Christ.
>
> But once more the question arose: Where do I find Jesus Christ? How can I truly give myself to him? The answer Guardini found after much searching was this: Jesus is concretely present to us only in his Body, the Church. As a result, obedience to God's will, obedience to Jesus Christ, must be, really and practically, humble obedience to the Church. I think that this too is

something calling us to a constant and deep examination of conscience.[12]

The second is from *Consider Your Call*, and as it were takes the above on into the monastic life:

> Thus the heart of monastic obedience is the monk's personal, free, humble and love-impelled surrender to the will of God. He is invited to *listen* and incline the ear of his heart; through obedience he offers himself to God without reservation. He sees this attitude as 'suitable' or 'becoming' for one who holds nothing dearer than Christ, and knows obedience to be his 'good' because it is his road to God. This will to obey is possible only because 'the Spirit we have in common' enables us to 'have this mind among ourselves which was in Christ Jesus'; monastic obedience is not merely an imitation of the obedience of Christ but a participation in it through the gift of the Spirit of sonship.
>
> In practice, therefore, obedience becomes for the monk an effective expression of love, and a means of gaining freedom to follow the will of God by directing his own will towards God and away from self-deception. As St Benedict points out, obedience is also closely related to prayer. The heart of prayer is the loving act of wanting God's will, and since monks are dedicated to the single-minded love of God in purity of prayer the connection between their prayer and the simplicity of heart fostered by obedience is inescapable.[13]

Both these quotations locate obedience within a dynamic of *self-surrendering love*, within the losing and finding of self to which the Gospel calls, and which finds its final paradigm in the death and resurrection of Christ.

On the second step of humility, there emerges a deep desire to put one's own will or way behind one, to imitate Christ in his missionary obedience to the Father's will, to be under such a liberating 'necessity'. These desires find their concrete realization on the third step, where 'a man submits to his superior in all obedience for the love of God' (7.34). Monastic obedience is, as it were, the sacrament of the gift of self to the salvific purposes of God.

Along such lines, among others, it may be possible to articulate an adequate and energising apologia for obedience, and so keep open this way by which 'we go to God' (71.2).

Conclusion

Two last thoughts:
1) I began with the question of the link between two relationships. If we stand within the monastic and Benedictine tradition, we can affirm that the relationship of monk to abbot is normally, with and beyond the many difficulties that may arise, a 'sacrament' at the service of the two deeper relationships that are at the heart of our monastic and Christian life: the relationship of son to the heavenly Father and of brother to our brothers in Christ and humanity. One can speak of it as a preliminary ascesis, as a purification of heart; one can speak of it in many ways, from the mundane to the mystical; one must locate it within the mystery of love. But in the end the mystery of the 'how' and 'why' of the link will remain.

One sign of when obedience is alive and well can be offered though, I think. It is the obedient one himself becoming a father (or mother). It is when Abraham has shown the ultimate obedience on Mt Moriah that he receives the most lavish promises of progeny. Obedience is in view of fruitfulness. The obedience of the 'son' of the Prologue is a door into sonship of the Father and into universal brotherhood, and the sign he has passed through that door will be a blossoming of his own spiritual fatherhood.

2) Despite what I said above about the reinstatement of the abbot in the nineteenth and twentieth centuries' monastic revival, it remains in general true that the modern abbot or abbess is something of a shadow in comparison with his or her ancestors. Congregations, Visitations, Canon Law and the Constitutions, the requirement of consent for the validity of certain decisions, the limitations on an abbot's hearing of the confessions of his monks, the whole post-conciliar atmosphere of the Church, the current ethos in our society, and other factors besides such as the complexity of modern knowledge, all conspire to clip the wings of Superiors. In any case, it always and everywhere remains the case that a superior only

has as much authority as the members of his community allow him. I am not implying that all this is a 'bad thing'. Might it not all mean that a far more informed, clear-eyed, mature, deliberate appreciation and choice of obedience is now required of the contemporary monk or nun? That the ball is in our court? As *Consider Your Call* well put it:

> And so, St Benedict explains, men whom God calls to this way of life, who 'hold nothing dearer than Christ', see obedience as their 'good'; they deliberately choose the 'narrow way' and live in monasteries, not merely enduring authority but 'wanting to have an abbot over them'. A man with this vision and this vocation *needs* an abbot, because of God, because of Christ.[14]

Notes

1. Daniel Rees, EBC, *Consider Your Call, Theology of Monastic Life Today* (London: SPCK, 1978), p. 76.
2. David Knowles, *From Pachomius to Ignatius* (Oxford University Press, 1966), p. 73.
3. Ibid.
4. cf. Adalbert de Vogüé, *The Rule of St Benedict: A Doctrinal and Historical Commentary*, (Kalamazoo: Cistercian Publications, 1983), p. 103.
5. St Ignatius Loyola, Letter 2, 3.
6. de Vogüé, p. 106.
7. de Vogüé, *Community and Abbot in the Rule of St. Benedict*, Vol. I (Kalamazoo: Cistercian Publications, 1979), p. 137.
8. Jonathan Sacks, *The Politics of Hope* (London: Vintage, 2000), p. 82.
9. Romano Guardini, *The End of the Modern World* (London: Sheed & Ward, 1957), pp. 56–57.
10. Sacks, pp. 84–85.
11. Quoted in J. Mortiau & R. Loonbeek, *Dom Lambert Beauduin, Visionnaire et Précurseur* (1873–1960) (Paris: Eds. du Cerf, 2005), p. 119.
12. Pope Benedict XVI, Homily to priests, religious, deacons and seminarians, at Mariazell, Austria, 8 September 2007.
13. *Consider Your Call*, p. 194.
14. Ibid., pp. 87–88.

9

Unhesitating Obedience

The first step of humility is unhesitating obedience (RB 5.1)

Let me, with some trepidation, say a further word about obedience. What follows is just an attempt to offer some help. I think the least threatening thing to do is 'share' some thoughts prompted by 1 Peter, one of the seven books of the New Testament we read during Eastertide. Living by the Benedictine Rule can perhaps make one sensitive to the things Peter says there, and on the other hand the things Peter says light up the Rule. And this not least in the matter of obedience. Three times in chapter 1, Peter uses the word 'obedience'. However, I'll come to that later. Let me begin somewhere else.

I'll start by simply tossing off one thought. For the Christian, obedience is a mystery. I don't mean monastic obedience merely, but obedience in its full scope. Obedience is part of, even a name for, the mystery of our faith. 'Christ became obedient unto death, even death on a cross.' Think how that statement runs like a refrain through the last days of Holy Week. Yet, for the twentieth-century Western Christian, and certainly for twentieth-century Western man, obedience is very often a mystery that has become a problem. To analyse why would be beyond me. There are reasons peculiar to the twentieth century, and there are reasons that transcend it. Ever since Adam, obedience is a mystery that has become a problem. Obedience is opaque to the fallen: 'In pain you shall bring forth children, yet your desire shall be for your husband, and he shall rule over you' (Gen. 3:16).

As for the twentieth century, here are just some illustrations:

> Good morning; good morning! the General said
> When we met him last week on our way to the Line.
> Now the soldiers he smiled at are most of 'em dead,
> And we're cursing his staff for incompetent swine.
>   'He's a cheery old card,' grunted Harry to Jack
> As they slogged up to Arras with rifle and pack.
>   • • • • •
> But he did for them both with his plan of attack.[1]

That's Siegfried Sassoon in 1917. How could 'obedience' not become problematic after the Western Front? Then there's Eichmann on trial in the early Sixties. 'Why did you do it?' 'It was obedience, obedience, obedience.' How could obedience not become problematic after the totalitarian monsters? Then, again, more topically, there are the sects and the cults, always demanding total obedience. And we see what happens. If thirty-nine people 'obediently' commit suicide so as to join a spacecraft, how could obedience not appear problematic to people who've 'kept their marbles'? In a milder form, similar difficulties arise, similar questions are asked about the new movements within the Church. Are there abuses of authority and obedience within these movements? It's not impossible. Is there among their antagonists, former members frequently enough, a preoccupation with the problem that has become a blindness to the mystery?

And then I think this: as Benedictines, we hold obedience to be central to what we are about. As Benedictines, we are cenobitic monks. If the word 'monk' evokes prayer, the word 'cenobite' evokes obedience. Obedience to a rule and to an abbot, a twofold obedience, a 'regular' obedience and a 'personal' obedience. This is central to our life, to the enterprise. How could it not be, given the opening verses of the Prologue, given the definition of cenobites at the beginning of chapter 1, given chapter 5 and rungs 2 to 4 of the ladder of humility? How could it not be given, the four seals, the pre-profession promise and the formula of profession itself from chapter 58? How could it not be when St Benedict extends obedience beyond the abbot to the brethren as a whole in chapters 71 and 72? Why, even the last adjective to be applied to the last use of the word 'monk' in the Rule is 'obedient' (73.6)! If the monastic life is a returning to God, a seeking of God, a going to God, then, says St Benedict, it is by obedience that we return, seek, go. If it's holding nothing dearer than Christ, then prompt obedience is what proves that. If it's the narrow way that leads to life, it is such by reason of obedience. If it is a following of Christ in the path of humility, then the prime step in humility is obedience without delay. If it's love of the brethren, then obedience, once again, is its paramount expression. So much is clear. And granted this, on the one hand, and the contemporary 'crisis' on the other, may it not be true that as Benedictines we are called to resolve the problem by a return to the mystery? May not the Lord be asking this of us? To live obedience in greater truth and freedom, in greater depth, with greater maturity (or whatever)? If we are called to penetrate the mystery of prayer, not just for ourselves but for everyone in the world, can't it be true that we are called in the same way to penetrate the mystery of obedience? To resolve the problem by a return to the mystery?[2]

One way to do this is certainly to explore the New Testament roots of what the Rule and our tradition say about obedience; to re-read that in the light of the Gospels and Epistles. And I'll get there in a second. But first, to follow through a little more what I've just been saying.

If it's true that Benedictines, or all Christians, are being called on the threshold of the new millennium to go more deeply into the mystery of obedience, it is also true that every monk is called to grow/mature in his own understanding and living of obedience. Just as we collectively, as late twentieth-century people, have problems with obedience, so does each of us individually, on account of his own personal experience: difficulties situated at the level of the emotional and psychological. And, by God's grace, we can move through these. The obedience of a senior is not the same as the obedience of a novice. Superficially, it may appear less impressive. In reality (all being well!), it will be truer and deeper. The obedience of a senior professed for thirty years is not the same as that of one professed for three years. Every monk needs to ask himself: is obedience as central to my life as it is central to the Rule? But, at different stages in one's monastic life, the form or meaning of that centrality will appear in very different lights. I wish I were deep enough into all this to say in what the growth consists. At the most I have the odd glimpse. It is a growth, surely, both human and divine, natural as well as supernatural. Br Duthac once said to me, when I was a novice or a junior, that 'obedience needs common sense', and we all know that the obedience of novices and juniors is generally ablaze with a lack of such common sense. And it is a relief when it returns.

Every monk, *Quisquis*, has to learn how to 'disobey'. (Often one sees them disobeying so clumsily!) That is, we have to learn to – I loathe the word – prioritize, as does anyone in practically any walk of life. The Rule on the one hand, the abbot and the officials on the other, people outside too some-times, are all laying claim to us, and we have to discern; we have to decide what comes first, what comes second, what comes third. We have to take responsibility for our obeying, as Vatican II said. We have to know when actually to do what St Benedict says and drop what we have in hand, and when to say, 'Well, in due time'. We have to know when to take our superiors literally and when to use the salt-cellar. There's a very human art to be learned, in other words, and that is certainly part of our maturing. I think the senior will talk about obedience less, even think about it less, but live it more. He'll be in it, rather than entering into it. And that points to the other side: there is to be a divine maturing as well, a super-natural growth. Probably a kind of inner silence and simplic-ity are its clearest signs. Poverty of spirit, which, at the end of the day, is the only thing the monk 'has' to offer, and is the most beautiful thing a person can have. 'The just man lives by faith.' Gradually, we become Christians. Gradually, we move from the psychic level to the spiritual. Gradually, the patterns, conscious and unconscious, positive and negative, established in our family relationships and at school are transformed into authentically Christian patterns of obedience and responsibil-ity. Gradually, I cease to project. Gradually, rule and author-ity cease to be threats against which I protect myself by being immaculate or kicking convulsively, and become, in their place and with all their limits, sacraments of the shepherding of Christ. Gradually my obedience becomes Christian.

There are two kinds of obedience. First, the daily. Obedience to the bell, to the timetable, to the succession of duties, to the regularities and disruptions, to whatever needs doing here and now. I'm washing up today, or the carrots have to be weeded, or I'm the shopper, or there's a letter to be answered or a guest to be received. It's a daily, emptying out to let the Spirit and reality in. Growth here is growth in faithfulness and in faith, doing these things with the Lord in one's eye. And then there's another obedience: more dramatic perhaps, going deeper, deciding the particular shape of one's life. At a moment, perhaps unexpectedly, one is asked to take on a certain position, work in the monastery, and that position and work will affect the kind of person one becomes. Or one will be asked to help in a foundation. One is changed by the obedience. Again, there's an emptying out to let the Spirit and reality in, but going deeper.

To 1 Peter at last:

1. Verse 2 is part of the opening address and greeting. Peter, 'an apostle of Jesus Christ', is writing to the Christian communities in North-west Asia Minor, and he hails them as 'chosen ... according to the foreknowledge of God the Father by the sanctifying action of the Holy Spirit for *obedience to Jesus Christ* and for sprinkling with his blood'. This is striking. Here we have the Father, the Spirit, Jesus Christ; here we have the Trinity. And Christians are those chosen according to the Father's predestining which is put into effect by the Holy Spirit *for*, in view of, obedience to Jesus Christ. The Christian, therefore, is one who has been brought to obey Christ by the Spirit of the Father. This is the goal of the action of the Trinity.

Behind this text lies one of the crucial moments of the Old Testament: the making of the covenant at the foot of Mt Sinai, described in Exodus 24:3-8. There Moses reads to the Israelites the book of the covenant, the Law, the Torah, and they respond: 'All that the Lord has spoken we will do, and we will be obedient.' Then Moses takes the ox-blood, half of which he has already thrown on the altar (standing for God), and throws the other half on the people, ratifying the covenant. Hence Peter's reference to the 'sprinkling of the blood' of Jesus Christ.

Christians, then, are those who have entered into the new covenant. They have heard the Gospel and professed obedience to it, and been 'sprinkled with Christ's blood', that is, been baptized, been initiated sacramentally. Those are the concrete realities St Peter has in mind. And just as obedience is central to Israel, so it is to Christians. But, for the former, it is obedience to 'the book of the covenant', the Law, the Torah; for the latter, obedience to a Person, Jesus Christ.

2. Verse 14: 'As obedient children, do not be conformed to the desires that you formerly had in ignorance.' Literally: 'as children of obedience', meaning obedient children. It's again a recalling of baptism when these former pagans were reborn through their profession of faith, that is, their promise of obedience to the Gospel, to Christ. The former life of ignorance and slavery to desires/lusts has given way to a new life of obedience. So, once again, the Christian, the baptized believer, is 'defined' in terms of obedience. And, once again, one is reminded of the Rule: 'not living by their own will, and obeying their own desires and passions, but walking by another's judgement and orders, they dwell in monasteries, etc.' (RB 5.12).

3. Verse 22: 'Now that you have purified your souls by your obedience to the truth, so that you have a sincere love for the brethren, love one another fervently from the heart.' We have had 'obedience to Jesus Christ', 'obedience' simply; now we have 'obedience to the truth' (that is, the Gospel message). Again, there's baptism here: a purification going with 'your obedience to the truth', which is first manifested in the profession of faith. Again, obedience is the definition of the Christian, of the baptized believer. What is new here is where this leads: to sincere love of the brethren. 'You have been purified through obedience so that you can love like brothers . . .' This is chapter 72 stuff.

So, we have these three references. They're weighty. Christians are people destined and consecrated for obedience to Christ. They are 'obedient children', who have broken with an ignorant and disordered past. They are, from the very beginning of their Christian existence, people 'obedient to the truth', and this obedience issues in the love of the brethren, their fellow-Christians.

Isn't this the best starting-point for reading the Rule, for understanding all that has been said over the centuries about monastic and religious obedience? Obedience to Christ, obedience to the Gospel, child-like obedience is of the essence of the Christian. And the practice of monastic obedience is nothing else than an exaggeration, an excess, a going beyond what is strictly required, but in view of this primordial, universal Christian obedience. Again, one can think of the analogy with prayer. 'To pray constantly' is, for the New Testament, of the essence of the Christian, just as 'to obey' is. The monastic practices of withdrawal and recollection, *lectio divina* and, above all, *opus Dei* seven times a day and once in the night are simply exaggerations, excesses, goings-beyond IN VIEW OF, once again, the primordial Christian vocation of praying without ceasing.

The starting-point and the goal, the beginning and the end, is the nature and vocation of the baptized person: a child of obedience. It is that which our monastic obedience seeks to protect, to develop, to bring to maturity.

Let's stay with the New Testament a little longer. From this baptismal centre, the New Testament's message about obedience extends in two major directions. The first, if you like, is backwards: to the obedience of Christ. Peter's teaching on the obedient Christian points to Paul and John's teaching on the obedient Christ. We know the classic texts: In Paul, Romans 5, where Christ's obedience is seen as reversing the disobedience of Adam, and Philippians 2 where the humility and obedience shown in the Incarnation and death on a cross, again reversing Adam, leading to exaltation, glory and lordship at the Father's right. In John, there are Jesus' constant references to his Father, whose will, whose teaching, whose presence are at the source of everything Jesus does. And we know how much Christian thought, Christian spirituality, monastic spirituality have drawn from contemplation of the obedient Christ. That, then, is one direction. The obedience of the Christian to Christ and his truth finds its source and model in the obedience of Christ to his Father and the mission the Father gives him.

The other direction in which this teaching runs is into the life of the Christian community, into the Church, into the mutual relations between the members. In the *Catechism* we read: 'Having become a member of the Church, the person baptized belongs no longer to himself, but to him who died and rose for us. From now on, he is called to be subject to others, to serve them in the communion of the Church, and to "obey and submit" (Heb. 13:17) to the Church's leaders, holding them in respect and affection' (1269). And so, in the New Testament, we find exhortations to mutual subjection, obedience, service. A classic and beautiful text is Ephesians 5:21: 'Be subject to one another out of reverence for Christ.' 'Out of reverence for Christ': so the obedience to Christ that identifies the Christian is extended, out of reverence for him, to a mutual subjection. In 1 Peter we find: 'And all of you must clothe yourselves with humility in your dealings with one another, for "God opposes the proud, but gives grace to the humble."' (5:5). This is saying the same in other words, and once again a 'theological', God-centred justification is provided.

Then, within this general summons to be obedient one to another, there sounds more particularly the call – as the Catechism says – to 'obey and submit' to those in charge of the community. In Hebrews 13:17 we read: 'Obey your leaders and submit to them, for they are keeping watch over your souls and will give an account. Let them do this with joy and not with sighing [or: groaning] – for that would be harmful to you.' And in 1 Thessalonians 5:12: 'But we appeal to you, brothers, to respect those who labour among you, and have charge of you in the Lord and admonish you; esteem them very highly in love because of their work.' In 1 Corinthians 16:15–16, with reference to a prominent Christian household: 'Now, brethren, you know that the household of Stephanas were the first converts of Achaia, and they have devoted themselves to the service of the saints. I urge you to be subject to such people and to every fellow worker and labourer.' Returning to 1 Peter (5:5): 'You that are younger be subject to the elders.'

Here, then, we find the baptismal obedience of the Christian propelling him, as it were, to 'pastoral' obedience, that is obedience to the Church's pastors. And this, too, is obedience to Christ, in accordance with the Lord's words apropos the seventy-two in Luke: 'He who hears you hears me, and he who rejects you rejects me, and he who rejects me rejects him who sent me' (Lk. 10:16).

This – all this – surely sheds light on the Rule and the monastic teaching on obedience. The elements are the same, if differently arranged, differently orchestrated. St Benedict, one could say, first teaches obedience to an abbot. He begins where the New Testament ends. For St Benedict, the abbot holds within the monastic community the position held by the leaders and elders (even the apostles) within the Christian communities, the 'local churches', of the New Testament. Obedience to him, it follows, is obedience to Christ. And so he twice quotes Luke 10:16. At the same time, he roots this obedience in the example of Christ, as clarified by Paul and John. Our obedience is at once to Christ, and like Christ, after the pattern of his obedience to the Father. Later in the Rule, he extends this obedience beyond the abbot merely: 'let all the juniors obey their seniors with all love and diligence' (71.4); 'let them vie in paying obedience one to another' (72.6). And so he connects with all those New Testament exhortations to obey, to submit to, to serve one another – within the single body. 'We are all one in Christ', and authority itself is nothing but a service and a submission.

One could connect too St Benedict's concern for obedience to the Rule with the New Testament's notion of obedience to the Gospel. The Rule is, as it were, an extension, an application, an embodying of the Gospel. We obey it so as to be obedient to the Gospel.

Every element, it seems to me, of the Benedictine ideal of obedience has these New Testament connections. And therefore, it is to be read in the light of the Petrine (also Pauline) understanding of what baptism means, or rather of what being a Christian, being a baptized believer, means: viz. a child of obedience, viz. someone destined and consecrated to obedience, viz. someone who has become obedient to the truth and so capable of brotherly love. And always and only is this obedience, obedience to Christ.

'You're washing up on Wednesday ... Go and weed the leeks, will you ... Can I have permission to ring my sister on her golden wedding? ... Would you be able to go to Eritrea and found a monastery, please (I've no idea if and when you'll be coming back)? Take over the novitiate, if you'd be so good ... No, please continue with that job you find so boring': all this, which is excess, exaggeration, folly, and to which – more folly – we bind ourselves under pain of sin; all this has only one purpose, the purpose called by the blessed Peter: 'obedience to Jesus Christ', the purpose he attributes to no less than God the Father and the Spirit.

Notes

1. Siegfried Sassoon, 'The General' in *Collected Poems* (London: Faber, 1968), p. 75.
2. John Paul II, *Vita Consecrata*, 91.

10

Restraint in Speech

Revere speech ... Speech makes [the hymns of the ancients]
known and the ancient collections of stories. It makes known
heaven and earth, wind and space, water and fire, gods and men,
beasts and birds, grasses and trees, animals right down to worms,
moths and ants, right and wrong, truth and falsehood, good and
evil, pleasant and unpleasant. Were it indeed not for speech, there
would be no knowledge of right and wrong, truth and falsehood,
good and evil, pleasant and unpleasant: for it is speech that makes
all this known. Revere speech.[1]

We remember, as children, being taught not to interrupt other
people speaking, not to shout unnecessarily or, more seriously,
not to tell lies. Part of being 'brought up' is being brought up
to the right use of speech. Every culture there has ever been
has had a preoccupation with speech, with an ethic of speech.
It's part of the great deposit of human wisdom. My opening
quote was from the Hindu Scriptures. The Old Testament
Wisdom literature, too, is full of reflections and advice on the
subject: 'Like an arrow stuck in a person's thigh, so is gossip
inside a fool ... A person may make a slip without intending
it. Who has not sinned with his tongue? ... The lips of
babblers speak of what is not their concern, but the words of
the prudent are weighed in the balance' (Sir. 19:12, 16;
21:25). One can quote endlessly. And the New Testament too
has its say on the subject: 'I tell you, on the day of judgement
you will have to give an account for every careless word you
utter; for by your words you will be justified, and by your
words you will be condemned' (Mt. 12:36–37). Most

pungently there is the Letter of James: 'Anyone who makes no mistakes in speaking is perfect, able to keep the whole body in check with a bridle ... How great a forest is set ablaze by a small fire! And the tongue is a fire ... No one can tame the tongue – a restless evil, full of deadly poison ... From the same mouth come blessing and cursing. My brothers, this ought not to be so' (James 3:2, 5–6, 8, 10).

Every time we say the Confiteor, we confess we've sinned in word. I don't think a clear conscience is possible for anyone in this area. Sins of speech are the commonest. Live as a hermit for a while, and it's amazing how one's conscience 'picks up'. One understands the Desert Father who, hearing the words 'I will guard my ways that I may not sin with my tongue' (Ps. 39:1), kept a stone in his mouth for several years. But can't the tongue be turned to good, too?

The preoccupation with speech is one of the preoccupations of the Rule. The Rule, after all, is 'wisdom literature'. It has many of the concerns of the Wisdom literatures of many ages and cultures. But it is too, we can hardly forget, Christian wisdom. So, let me try and collate some of what the Rule says.

One shouldn't give the Rule a bad name. One shouldn't turn it into a cartload of imperatives: an unbearable burden. That's true generally. It's true in this domain of an ethic of the word in particular. One can begin with the Prologue and its bright icon of the Lord seeking his workman, and seeking him with the words: 'Who is the man who wants life?', the answer being 'I do!' The Prologue is about vocation. And vocation is the meeting with Christ, the risen Lord, who calls to life. And we respond: *Ego!* And then there follow the Lord's next words: If you want true and everlasting life, keep your tongue from evil and your lips from speaking deceit. Isn't it remarkable that the Lord's first injunction concerns speech – a concern that recurs, over and over again, as the Rule progresses? But at the same time this little passage gives us a way of reading, hearing what the Rule has to say. The postulant, *Quisquis*, has met the Lord. In Sixties language, there has been a 'transforming encounter', and the first domain transformed is the domain of speech. What happens to a person's tongue; what happens to our talking when we come to know Christ? That is the concern of

the Rule, and that is the way to read its injunctions. The same
point emerges from the first step of humility. That again is
about a transforming encounter with the Lord: how knowing
the Lord will repercuss in us, affect us, penetrate us, change
us. The 'fear of the Lord'. Its first effect will be flight from
sin, in every area of our lives. St Benedict mentions six, and
the second of them, after 'thoughts', is 'tongue' (RB 7.12).

The concern of the Rule is man's transformation in Christ.
And transformation in Christ means transformation of one's
talking. A third nugget is found in chapter 6, verse 5: 'Death
and life are in the power of the tongue' (Prov. 18:21). 'By
your words you will be justified and by your words you will
be condemned.'

'Who is the man who wants life?' was the original question.
'Keep your tongue from evil', if you do want life. The tongue
can bring death. But the tongue can also bring life. Man, as he
is progressively transformed in Christ, will progressively
mortify, do to death, all that is death-dealing in his tongue, so
that his tongue can recover its life-giving power. The tongue,
our talking, must be touched by the burning coal of the Paschal
Mystery. It must have its death and its resurrection. And
perhaps it's in between those two that silence has its place, the
place of Holy Saturday. In silence – good silence – bad words
die and good words come to birth.

> Speech and silence are not in opposition. They are complemen-
> tary. One can only practise the virtue of silence if he knows the
> meaning of speech and how to speak properly. One can speak
> properly only if one knows the meaning and value of silence and
> how to keep silence.[2]

A Community that reveres speech will revere silence, and a
Community that reveres silence will revere speech. I
digress . . .

Says St Paul: 'Just as you once presented your members as
slaves to impurity and to greater and greater iniquity, so now
present your members as slaves to righteousness for sanctification' (Rom. 6:19).

What will die in the new man, according to the Rule, is, first of all, evil talk. 'To keep one's mouth from evil and depraved talk' (4.51). 'We should, with more reason still, for fear of sin's punishment, eschew all evil talk' (6.2). Specifically, dirty (smutty) talk, murmuring and detraction should fall away from us (6.8; 4.39–40; 40.9, etc.). I suppose detraction is the hardest of all to shrug off: the gratuitous disparagement of others, the irresistible jibe, the itch to criticize, the passion for amateur psychologizing. Br X irritates me. I know he irritates Br Y too. So, when with Br Y, what joy it is to bring up the topic of Br X. I'm gratifying myself in so doing, I'm gratifying Br Y, the bonding between us verges on the ecstatic! But how sad it is when shared antipathies are what make for 'friendship'. How sad it is when I can only guarantee my own self-esteem by denying esteem to others. One counsel: begin any reference to another, even when criticism is required, with something positive. It's good advice as long as the practice doesn't degenerate into formality. Another counsel I heard from a Methodist: before you speak, ask yourself: Is it true, is it necessary, is it kind? Going more deeply, we can make our own a statement of the Catechism: 'To avoid rash judgement, everyone should be careful to interpret insofar as is possible his neighbour's thoughts, words, and deeds in a favourable way' (2478). Most deeply, it is of course a matter of the heart, 'for it is out of the abundance of the heart that the mouth speaks' (Lk. 6:45). When humility is in the heart rather than pride, contentment rather than disturbance, love rather than fear, reverence rather than distrust, how could detraction come out of it?

What will die in the new man, says the Rule secondly, is 'much speaking' (6.4). The proverb, 'When words are many, transgression is not lacking' (10.19), is quoted twice (6.4; 7.57). 'Not to love much speaking' is one of the tools of good works (4.52), and the same *multiloquium* is even banned from prayer (20.3). The word *taciturnitas*, which heads chapter 6, should not be translated as 'taciturnity', should probably not be translated as simply 'silence' either, but rather as 'reserve or restraint in speech'.[3] According to Ambrose Wathen, the word refers to the virtue of silence, the capacity to refrain from words, especially an excess of good words. 'The wise man (after all) is known by the fewness of his words' – a pagan maxim (7.61), echoed round the world. 'Someone having observed of Yen Yung that he was good-natured towards others, but that he lacked the gift of ready speech, the Master said, "What need of that gift? To stand up before men and pour forth a stream of glib words is generally to make yourself obnoxious to them." '[4] And so it is. The Bible says it too: 'Whoever talks too much is detested, and whoever pretends to expertise is hated' (Sir. 20:8). Br Manywords is lurking in the library: one makes a detour. Br Manywords stands up to speak in Chapter: hearts sink, heads are lowered, teeth are gritted. 'A fool takes no pleasure in understanding, but only in expressing personal opinion' (Prov. 18:2). Ambrose Wathen has written this:

> Granted there is not an absolute silence in RB, neither is there an absolute approval of speech. Speaking is always guarded and conditioned. A monk never speaks without control and a deep sense of the gravity with which he must use his voice. Speaking is a serious matter, and the use of the tongue must always be with restraint and qualified by virtue.[5]

And here we touch on what comes to life in the new man. Another content, another style, another effect. Death and life are in the power of the tongue. It's possible for the human tongue to carry the word of life. And the Rule knows this. It would be so most manifestly when the word of God is read (for example, by the liturgical lectors, by the refectory reader, by the guest master to the guest) or preached (by the abbot). Or when the Rule is read (and presumably explained) to the novice by the novice master. Or again, one can think of the *senpectae* sent to console the wavering brother or the spiritual seniors who 'know how to cure both their own wounds and those of others without disclosing and making them public' (27.3; 46.5–6): a ministry of the word one to one. Deans are to be chosen for their 'wise teaching' (21.4). No monk is to associate or speak with guests unless he has been 'commanded' (*praecipitur*) to do so (53.23) – but that implies that he may be so, that there may be 'colloquy' with guests. Similarly no monk is to receive or give letters, etc. without the abbot's command (*praeceptum*) – but that implies that such a command may be given, that there may be communication with those outside the cloister. Striking too is the teaching of chapter 31 on the cellarer's speech:

> Should any brother chance to make an unreasonable request, he is not to upset him by snubbing him. Instead, he should refuse the unreasonable request in the proper way, with humility ... Above all, he should possess humility; and when he lacks the wherewithal to meet a request, he should give a good word in answer, as it is written, 'A good word is above the best gift' (31.7, 13–14).

We are in a different world here: not the world of spiritual teaching or pastoral comfort, but in the give and take of ordinary living. 'During work,' it has been written,

> the will and Word of God are mediated differently than during the *opus Dei* and holy reading. During work the Word of God comes to a monk through the interaction of brothers. It is especially during work that brothers may be mutually obedient, submitting to one another by the help they give to each other and by the demands made upon them by a mutual task. In order to accomplish their work monks must be able to communicate. . .[6]

The Rule foresees the monks having requests of the cellarer. The request may be unreasonable, but the cellarer should avoid the wounding word in response. Or the request may be reasonable but impossible ('we have no bananas'): the cellarer should give a 'good word'. That phrase – *sermo bonus* – brings us full circle from the original 'keep your tongue from evil'. Christ himself is 'the good Word of the good Father'. We are godlike when we utter a 'good word'. St Benedict seems to love the idea of a word, a response, that is humble and gentle, reasonable and reverent, prompt and loving, serious and cheering. That is – globally – what he expects of the cellarer speaking to his brethren, of the porter responding to a knock at the door, of the monk *simpliciter* (eleventh step of humility). He piles up qualifying adjectives and adverbs, each of them worth mulling over. What he delivers is a sixth-century profile of

Christian speaking. Whether our words are about God or about others or about mundane matters, they can be words of life, or, better perhaps, words of blessing – *bene-dicere*, speaking well, speaking as new men, yielding our members to right-eousness. Blessing in the last resort is what speech is for: the blessing of God in the liturgy ('O Lord, open my lips') and blessing one of another. 'Revere speech.'

> The Word of God was silent as he was led to sacrifice (St Cyprian).

> The devil looks for noise, Christ for silence (St Ambrose).

To end with some twentieth-century words, from Jean Vanier:

> We must, by our voice, by what we say, bring the Spirit to people. We must bring them the peace of Jesus by the way we talk, and by the way we act. When we say to people, 'The peace of Jesus to you', we must give them peace, we must become instruments of his peace. This is what we sing about; this is what Jesus talks to us about; but this must become a reality. We must be able to communicate the peace of Jesus ... By [our] very presence, [we] should create peace, not just harmonising different people and preventing dissension, but much more than that, bringing the peace of Jesus which is a plenitude of silence.[7]

Notes

1. *Chandgoya Upanishad,* VII, ii.
2. Ambrose Wathen, *Silence* (Washington: Cistercian Publications, 1973), p. 227.
3. D. Catherine, Placid Murray.
4. *Confucian Analects,* V, 4.
5. Wathen, p. 223.
6. Wathen, p. 231.
7. Jean Vanier, *Followers of Jesus* (Dublin: Gill & Macmillan, 1993), p. 73.

11

The Ladder of Humility

Quisquis has been grabbed by the Lord, by the Christian thing. He has entered a community and submitted himself to a Rule and an Abbot. He is becoming a disciple. And he comes to the Ladder, chapter 7 – the longest chapter of the *Rule* and, in its way, a *summa* of all the spiritual doctrine found in the preceding chapters. It recapitulates much of what has gone before.

Clamat nobis divina Scriptura, fratres ... 'Divine Scripture calls to us, brothers' So begins chapter 7, *On Humility*. At Pluscarden recently, some of us had instruction in the Alexander Technique (for posture). 'Humility comes into this,' said our teacher. 'Oh, that's our forte!' replied one of the brethren. *Clamat nobis* ... It is a powerful opening. After a chapter on *taciturnitas*, comes *clamat*! If there's to be shouting in monasteries, it should be 'divine Scripture' that does it. *Fratres* is in the vocative. Only in the Prologue and here is its vocative form used. From the point of view of the *Regula monasteriorum*, what we have here is another, a second conference, a second call, from Abba Benedict. It is, as we know, an elaboration of one section (39) of the Conference at the Clothing of a Novice (32–43) by Abba Pinufius which forms the climax of Book IV of Cassian's *Institutes*. St Benedict's second conference, unlike his first, is not addressed to potential candidates outside the monastery door, 'before' the constitution of the *schola*, but addressed to those now on its roll, delivered in the chapter house, so to speak. At the same time, it is not any old conference. It is solemn and thorough. First, the Gospel text is announced: 'Everyone who exalts himself will be humbled,

and he who humbles himself will be exalted.' This is a text in
two parts. The first, negative half is commented upon by
means of Ps. 130, 'Lord, my heart is not lifted up, etc.' Then
the extended commentary on the second, positive half is introduced by reference to Jacob's dream at Bethel and its famous
ladder. Jewish tradition had already identified the ladder with
the Law. Following John 1:51, Christian tradition has identified it with Scripture, with the person of Christ and more especially with his Cross. 'Jacob's Ladder is the mystery of Christ,
which allows the just to rise to the heights, and also that of the
Cross which is raised up like a ladder, at the top of which the
Lord stands.'[1] For Zeno of Verona, the Ladder is the two
Testaments, that is, the Bible, but, in the end, its

> proper name is the Cross, because by means of the Cross, the
> Lord Jesus Christ completed and concluded all the mysteries
> [found in Scripture], carried Adam back to the Father and opened
> the road to heaven for all who follow him.[2]

The twelve steps follow, and the brisk conclusion. Twelve is a
number of completeness. Everything structural suggests a
certain solemnity. And so does the content. It outlines a
'journey of the mind to God', from pride to humility, from
fear to the perfect love that casts out fear. The central image
– the ladder and its steps – is one of the great universal images
of human striving. Clearly we're at the heart of the Rule.

Yet, to be honest, chapter 7 is a problem. There's much
that's alien in it, or that we can only redeem by qualifying out
of existence, or that may seem to encourage the pathological.
There's the strange prominence St Benedict allots humility.
Would we, writing today? Don't we all prefer ch. 72? Some
kind of apologia seems called for, or at least some hard thinking. As Michael Casey has put it, 'it is necessary for us as
readers to come to grips with our latent resistance' [to ch. 7].
For, he observes, 'The texts that at first appear unattractive are
often the ones that will most repay the effort to understand
them.'[3]

How can we be reconciled to humility, I wonder? The
answer lies, I think, in Scripture and in life, that is, people.

First, there is a missing text in chapter 7. It is the first beatitude: 'Blessed are the poor in spirit.' Consult almost any patristic commentary on that logion, and you will find it taken for granted that its subject is humility. Isn't that in itself a clarification? Doesn't it open up a vista? This is a chapter on poverty of spirit. It is about entering into that beatitude, into the Kingdom of heaven. It is possible, thinking back to Cassian, to say it is about interiorizing the first external renunciation that the listeners will have made: the renunciation of material possessions and the social status and security they confer. It is about how we interiorly join, associate ourselves with the poor – to whom salvation is given.

Another thought. The Gospel text St Benedict uses could come from one of three places: one in Matthew, two in Luke. Surely it comes from the story of the Pharisee and the tax collector, the correct reference being Lk. 18:14. 'Two men went up to the Temple to pray etc' (Lk. 18:10). The reference, on the twelfth step, to the prayer of *publicanus ille evangelicus*, 'the publican in the Gospel' (7.65) thus forms an inclusion with it. 'God, be merciful to me, a sinner!' (Lk. 18:13), prays that tax-collector. He was perhaps a rich man, by dubious means, but he was crying out for mercy. Chapter 7 describes the journey from Pharisee to tax-collector, that is, the journey from talking to (and praising) oneself to begging mercy of another, the journey to the prayer of the poor in spirit.

Again, by its reference to the 'weaned child' of Ps. 130, evokes another Gospel figure: the child.

What is humility? It is what happens in us when we accept Reality, are humbled by the truth. It is also a code-word for 'the following of Christ by the paschal virtue of self-abasement' as Dom André Louf well said. The ladder is the way of the Cross. It is also always the intrinsic counterpoint, underwear (!), of love, of charity. Each of those three aspects one could develop. Each could serve as an apologia. But surely the best apologia for the truth of this chapter comes from life. Think of the unobtrusively holy people we have been blessed to know, old monks and nuns in our communities, souls in families, parishes and so on. In his autobiographical *Milestones*, Joseph Ratzinger says this of his mother:

[T]he radiance of her goodness has remained, and for me it has become more and more a confirmation of the faith by which she had allowed herself to be formed. I know of no more convincing proof for the faith than precisely the pure and unalloyed humanity that the faith allowed to mature in my parents and in so many other persons I have had the privilege to encounter.[4]

This is where the truth of chapter 7 is revealed. 'Pure and unalloyed humanity.' Humanity, humility, humour: the three words are connected. St Benedict has seen not into the monk precisely so much as into the Christian (even if dressed as a monk). This is a Christian anthropology. This is Mary, if you like. Because when we meet the poor in spirit, when we meet those who have been formed by faith, who have accepted Reality, surely the least inadequate concepts for what we're meeting are, indeed, humility and charity – the twin concepts of chapter 7, just as for St Augustine they are the least inadequate concepts for describing Jesus. Sometimes there's just gentle goodness, quiet kindness, wonderful eyes; or just an emptied-outness, a readiness to receive. Sometimes a flame of charity and zeal, but with simplicity, approachableness, childlikeness. Sometimes radiance, manifest prayer and joy, but with heart-brokenness, a sense of sinfulness. Always a broken heart and an enlarged heart. Always humble love, loving humility. Always, combined, humility and the love that casts out fear, the soul burned and kindled by the cross and the resurrection. What chapter 7 is about, at the end of the day, is the most beautiful thing on earth: the humble, loving human person. Humanity restored by the touch of God. When we meet such a person, when we meet someone really, deeply, wholly such, when we *really* meet them, we can only be grateful. We may cry. And we find rest for our souls. 'For I am gentle and humble in heart, and you will find rest for your souls' (Mt. 11:29). Here is the weakest thing on earth, and the strongest. This is what St Benedict is on about.

And this gentleness towards men is grounded in the humility of the incarnate Son towards his Father and the mission he gave him:

'For I have come down from heaven, not to do my own will, but the will of him who sent me' (Jn 6:38). 'I can do nothing on my own authority' (Jn 5:30).

Humility introduces us into this relationship.

Another approach is to see humility as the presupposition and consequence of true love. The proud man loves himself too much to love others or God except in reference to himself, except as 'serving' him. The humble man, free of inordinate self-love, loves others as they are, sees himself in reference to them, and so is inwardly free to affirm their goodness and put himself at its and their service. The German word for humility, *Demut*, literally means 'the spirit of service'. And the humility learned in chapter 7 translates into the persevering liturgical service of God and the patient, practical service of the brethren.

Chapter 7 offers the way of humble love.

It's also what Solzhenitsyn is about in his *Matryona's House*. The narrator, a teacher, has just been released from ten years in the camps – it's 1953, the year of Stalin's death. He goes, by choice, to an obscure village in central Russia and lodges with an older widow, Matryona. Her in-laws, taking advantage of her generosity, demolish an outhouse for the sake of the timber. Taking it across a railway line, the sledge collapses, Matryona tries to help, a train comes unexpectedly, its noise drowned out by the tractor. Several are killed, including her. It's only listening to the stories that come out after her death, that the lodger fully realizes what she was – poor in reality, poor in spirit, one of the overlooked righteous who uphold the world. I remember once, in the early 1970s, visiting the Russian War Memorial in what was then East Berlin. What remains in the mind are the friezes of the Soviet soldiers, supermen, all muscles, guns, and faces turned unflinchingly to the glorious future. Soviet man! Think of the ideal of Soviet woman too, heroines of the Union, throwing discuses and all that. 'Loving humility though is a terrible force ... the strongest thing there is.' *Matryona's House is* Russia, of course, Mother Russia, and Matryona the complete and deliberate antithesis of Soviet (and indeed Capitalist) Man. She is not a fervent believer exactly. She just asks God's blessing before she does anything. She is not fussy about cleanliness. She lets herself be ripped off, since it might help someone else. She's killed by a train, but not for the reasons Anna Karenina was. Solzhenitsyn's whole point is that she's indestructible, she's the truth of humanity, she is a Christian. The story is a twentieth-century phenomenology of someone humbled in the truth. And it had a big impact. It punctured the lie. It was a step towards the end of that oppression. 'Loving humility is a terrible force ... the strongest thing there is.' One thinks of Jesus watching the people putting money in the Temple treasury. 'That widow ...' (Lk. 23:3).

What St Benedict is trying to articulate here, what he is portraying in a succession of sketches, cartoons, is a phenomenology – albeit a remote sixth-century phenomenology – of the poor in spirit, of the child in the kingdom, of the tax-collector. Chapter 7 is a phenomenology of humble love. It is more descriptive than prescriptive. It's a series of cartoons. And, I believe, it does describe a progress; it tells a story. The story of *Quisquis* naturally. In a sense, it retells it. It is the story within the story. Or, the heart of the story, the turning point. Our hero has heard the call, has joined the community and is learning its wisdom. He is now *living* the life, the Christ-life. And this will take him to Jerusalem.

Let me try and tell it, simply and briefly.

Step 1, in terms of the story, is almost a replay of the Prologue, and yet different. It has a rather Old Testament air to it. It is man before God: Abraham, Isaac and Jacob before their theophanies, like Moses and the people before Sinai. 'Moses said to the people, "Do not be afraid; for God has come only to test you and to put the fear of him upon you so that you do not sin"' (Ex. 20:20). There is the eruption of the Other into one's life; there is an awakening ('let him always be mindful'); there is a conversion, above all of patterns of thinking and willing and of one's bodily, relational living (vv. 14–25). There is this sense of the gaze, the *expectation* (v. 30), of God. It is the awakening of the fear of God in the soul. It's not a passing experience which leaves us unchanged. *Quisquis* henceforth flees all forgetfulness, is always mindful *(semper sit memor* – a beautiful phrase). This is the memory of God St Basil speaks about. *Quisquis* now lives out, in his thinking, speaking, doing, moving, willing, in his flesh (the six areas mentioned in v. 12), the Church's Eucharistic memorial of all the Lord has said and done on our behalf. Much of what Newman says on natural religion, conscience, and the realization of God's presence is almost like an echo of what St Benedict describes here. The ancient Fathers will say that the first effect of *faith* taking root in the soul is *fear* of God. The Thomist tradition will say that the first gift of the Holy Spirit is the gift of fear, and that one of its effects is a horror of sin. The first step of humility, always and everywhere, is keeping oneself from sin. There really is something primary on this first step – something that can never be left behind, but that goes down deeper into the soul however high it may climb.

And yet *Quisquis* will soon feel himself called further. **Step 2** can be read this way. On step 1, it is a question of not *doing* one's own will (vv. 19, 21), of not *going after* one's desires (v. 25). On step 2, there is something deeper at work. It is a question of 'not *loving*' one's desires, of not '*delighting*' to fulfil them (v. 31). And the person of Christ – the example of Christ, the way of Christ – now comes before the eyes of the soul: this Christ who didn't do his own will, but his Father's, the One who sent him (v. 32). *Quisquis* is being drawn into the Christ-life, the Christ-pattern. 'Did you not know that I *must* be about my Father's business?' (Lk. 2:49) – the famous *must/dei* of Jesus' life, of Paul too: '. . . an obligation is laid upon me, and woe to me if I do not proclaim the gospel!' (1 Cor. 9:16). *Quisquis* wants to be under the same yoke: 'Gratification deserves punishment, but necessity wins a crown' (v. 33).

How though? This becomes the question. And **Step 3** answers it. 'The third step of humility is that for the love of God [fear is already becoming love!] one submits himself in all obedience to his superior, imitating the Lord of whom the apostle says, "He was made obedient even unto death"' (v. 34). Obedience has been called the 'free sacrifice of freedom' (Pius XII), though even that needs understanding rightly. It is a sacrifice of superficial freedoms for the sake of a deep freedom, which in the end can only be the freedom always and everywhere to do the Father's will. 'I always do what is pleasing to him.' What is possessing *Quisquis* at this point is the inner need to surrender, and to give flesh to the Word inside him: to do something definite and irrevocable. St Benedict uses the verb *se subdare*: to give or place oneself under; to be a no. 2 rather than a no. 1. It is the logic of love, of course. One doesn't want a 'private life' apart from the Lord. This is, like the end of the Prologue, a moment when *Quisquis* crosses the threshold of the monastery. Says St Bernard: 'the first two steps will have been climbed before entering the community ... The reason why is found in the Rule which says, "The third step etc." This submission to a superior takes place when the novice enters the monastery, so he must have already climbed the first two steps' (*On the Steps of Humility and Pride,* 49).

Man can give nothing greater to God than subjecting his will to another man's for God's sake (St Thomas).

I became a monk because God revealed to me the greatness and beauty of obedience (Bl. Columba Marmion).

It was something I had to do [be received into the Church in December 1927] ... [I had] reached the point where I wanted to obey ... I was tired of following the devices of my own heart, of doing what I wanted to do, what my desires told me to do, which always seemed to lead me astray ... I wanted to be poor, chaste, obedient. I wanted to die in order to live, to put off the old man and put on Christ ... I loved the Church for Christ made visible (Dorothy Day).

You will not serve; you will be taken into service (H. Urs von Balthasar).

In chapter 5, St Benedict speaks of those 'living in communities/*coenobia*, [who] *desire* to have an abbot over them' (5.12). This is the key.

When I was a young man I read a fair amount of Russian literature and of twentieth-century prison literature, of the kind that came out from behind the Iron Curtain. And I could see how people could (sometimes) emerge from the crucible of these terrible experiences as deeper, freer, truer people. And I used to think, Well, here I am with three meals a day, persecuted by no one, suffering nothing. What chance is there for me? Then it came to me: 'Obedience'. To be honest, I've had an easy time of it . . . But still, after the third step comes the fourth. After the surrender comes the test. 'The **4th Step** of humility is, if *in this very obedience* . . .' 'When you were young, you girded yourself and walked where you would, but when you are old, you will stretch out your hands and another will gird you and carry you where you do not wish to go' (Jn 21:18). Obedience grows into patience. Michael Casey once remarked, 'No one should be professed who doesn't know the 4th step of humility by heart.' The structure is simple. It is situation and response. And it seems graded. The situation is dramatic. This is the Rule's 'Little Apocalypse'. 'Naught for your comfort, naught for your desire, save that the sky grows darker yet and the sea rises higher.' St Benedict speaks of hard and contrary things, injustices, *all* contrary things, facing death and slaughter, testing by fire, snares, backs bowed by tribulation, men over our heads, strikings, strippings, coercions, false brethren, persecution, malediction – an ordinary day in the monastery! This is all drawn, of course, from the Bible: from the sufferings of Israel under Assyrian or Babylonian invasion and Seleucid persecution to the sufferings of the first generations of Christians. The scenario is that of martyrdom. The difficulty, of course, is in connecting our petty, often self-inflicted torments with these lofty historical experiences. Well, there are the monks of Mt Atlas . . . But even in our rural retreats, it is not uncommon for monks and nuns to reach points in their lives which feel like dead-ends. It's not uncommon to find oneself the prey of circumstances to which the natural response is resentment.

The structure is simple. It is *situation and response*. *Quisquis* who has 'given himself under' on Step 3 must now 'hold on under'. And it is the response which is St Benedict's concern. He offers almost a litany: the quiet mind, the embracing of patience/suffering, enduring, being secure in hope, following on rejoicing, offering the other cheek, giving up garments, going the extra mile and finally blessing. There seem to me to be three key verbs: first, *sustinere*. *Se subdare* becomes *sustinere*, with all its biblical echoes of perseverance, endurance. Then at the centre, v. 39, comes the quotation of Romans 8:37: 'But in all these things we conquer (*superamus*) because of him who has loved us.' In the Greek, St Paul is coining a new verb: 'We super-conquer.' We are not to be victims but victors. How? St Thomas in his commentary on *Romans* says, *illibata caritate*, 'by unflecked, unstained, undented charity'. Finally, there's the last word in the Latin text: *benedicere*. At this point, *Quisquis* becomes a Benedictine. The victory can only be love, can only be blessing – 'because of him who has loved us'. So there's no true Christian martyr who doesn't forgive the persecutor, return the curse with a blessing, demonstrate love of an enemy. There are many stories of this, thank God. There are the simple stories monks and nuns can tell too.

Having climbed this step, *Quisquis* will naturally find himself at home on the **5th Step**. The confession of sins will come easily, because he now knows in a new way his need for mercy. 'Make known your way to the Lord and *hope* in him.' 'Confess to the Lord ... for his *mercy* is for all ages.' 'I will accuse myself of my unjust deeds before the Lord, and you have *forgiven* the disloyalty of my heart.' Hope, mercy, forgiveness: these are the realities *Quisquis* moves among now. He is 'coming to a deep heart' – the word occurs in the first and last verses of this step.

So to **Step 6**. It is the hinge, I feel, the moment of breakdown and breakthrough. 'Every breakthrough is a breakthrough in humility.' Someone who really had within him the attitudes sketched on this step would really have entered into the first Beatitude, would have come very close to the crucified Christ and so to the resurrection. He'd be very free, I think. Is this why this is the first step to use the word 'monk'?

What is said of our man here? First (v. 49), that he is 'content with the meanest and the worst'. St Paul is in that word 'content'. 'I have learned in whatever state I am, to be content' (Phil. 4:11). *Quisquis* is content with any circumstances, because his real life, his centre of gravity, is elsewhere. As Nietzsche put it, 'A man can put up with almost any *how* if he has a why.' And the circumstances the Rule has in mind here are not simply material, I think. The next phrase talks about 'all the things enjoined upon him'. He is content with, even judges himself unfit for any of these. But one can take these phrases further. Content with 'the meanest and worst'. *Vilitas* can be understood as the condition of being unappreciated, unloved even (*vilis* means 'cheap'; it is the antonym of *carus*, 'dear'). *Extremitas* could be rendered 'marginalized'. This is freedom from slavish dependence on the love and esteem of others, and from those things which comport esteem: jobs, position, manifest usefulness. All these are good things, normal things, things to be grateful for, objects of reasonable expectation, gifts of God at their level. But they no longer equal our identity. That is somewhere else now, and safe.

Our man is freed now from slavish dependence on the love and esteem of others, and from those things which comport esteem: jobs, position, manifest usefulness. All these are good things, normal things, things to be grateful for, objects of reasonable expectation, gifts of God at their level. But the point is, he no longer rests his identity therein. That is somewhere else, 'hidden with Christ in God' ideally. There has been an entry into *apatheia* – through consent to the experiences of life and the grace of God within them. There's a rather charming picture of this kind of contentment in the last pages of *The Hobbit*, describing Bilbo's return after his great adventure. He finds that much of what had been his had been expropriated by others, and his reputation has gone as well. 'I am sorry to say,' says the author, 'he did not mind. He was quite content.'

Then St Benedict invokes two verses of Ps. 73. 'I am reduced to nothing.' This is the undoing of creation from which re-creation springs. According to St Paul, in one of his most famous passages, Christ Jesus 'emptied himself' (Phil. 2:6). Some translate, he 'made himself nothing'. At this point, the monk is aligned with the Nothing of Nothings, who, in Roman eyes, was allotted the death of a rebellious slave; in Jewish eyes that of someone cursed by God. And it is God who has done this: *redactus sum*. 'My taste was me,' said the poet Hopkins. I may have inflicted it upon myself; it may have come to me from nature, from disease, from an accident; it may have been done to me by people. It little matters in the last resort. Or it may just be a conviction borne in upon me by accumulating circumstances. Some years ago a survey was made among retired American abbots. What did being abbot teach you? was one of the questions. And more than one of the answers was, It showed me I was nothing. *Ad nihilum redactus sum*.

Ut iumentum factus sum apud te (Ps. 73:22). A *iumentum* is a beast of burden, par excellence a donkey. How delightful that in the middle of this desperately serious chapter, in the midst of this series of cartoons, we are shown a donkey! Patient under adversity (one patristic interpretation), accepting of any task given (another), ready to be led wherever its master thinks best (yet another). 'I shall no longer misunderstand your judgements,' comments Theodoret of Cyr,

> nor bring myself to make any inquiries or busy myself with the arrangements of your wisdom; instead like a beast I shall follow your decisions, in this way not likely to be cut off from your providence. In other words, as the beast follows the one leading it, not concerned about where it is led, so shall I also follow when guided by your grace, not inquisitive about your providence.[5]

And yet it's a donkey the Lord rode into Jerusalem.

Et ego semper tecum. The positive conclusion, the up-turn. 'Always with you': 'the unique desire of the monk', as de Vogüé says, now realized. Is there any piece of Gregorian chant equal to the Introit of Easter Sunday, Christ waking from the tomb, as it were, and addressing his Father awestruck at the experience: *Resurrexi et adhuc tecum sum, alleluia: posuisti super me manum tuam, alleluia: mirabilis facta est scientia tua super me, alleluia, alleluia*, from Ps. 138? 'I have arisen, and I am with you still, alleluia. You have laid your hand upon me, alleluia. Too wonderful for me, this knowledge, alleluia, alleluia!'

The **7th Step** would, again, follow on naturally. There would be a spontaneous, interior sense of others, of each other, being 'superior' and 'dearer'. The clarifying Scripture here is Philippians 2:3: 'in humility count others better than yourselves.'

And if our man has been brought this far, has accepted Reality to this depth, again everything that follows on **Steps 8 to 12** makes spontaneous sense. It is as if on these steps a great stillness, quietness, peace envelops the monk. He has been, in a lovely phrase of the poet Wordsworth, 'insensibly subdued to settled quiet'.[6] He is unobtrusive, equable, his whole being iconic, even while he is, in his own heart and mind, constantly asking mercy at the judgement seat of God.

The final verses (67–70) are simply the other side of what's shown on **Step 12**. The Trinitarian side, if you like, the side of grace. Fear is dissolved by love, toil by good habit. There is love, delight, the flowing life of the Holy Spirit. This is the Resurrection and Pentecost in one, inwardly appropriated. Humility yields its final fruit of love. The love of Christ brings about a resurrection and a Pentecost, taking the monk beyond the fear of punishment and into delight in virtue. The cross-bearer is revealed (*demonstrare* is the chapter's last word) as bearer of the Spirit, and *Quisquis* is now indeed the Lord's 'workman'.

There is a parallel passage towards the end of Walter Hilton's *Ladder of Perfection*:

> See then what divine Love does within a chosen soul which He reforms in feeling to His likeness, when the understanding is partially enlightened to know Jesus and to experience His love. Love brings all the virtues into a soul and renders them pleasing and congenial without any action by the soul itself. For the soul does not struggle painfully to acquire them as it did formerly but obtains them easily and enjoys them peacefully through the gift of divine Love alone, that is the Holy Spirit. This is supreme consolation and unspeakable joy when it suddenly discovers without understanding how, that humility and patience, temperance and restraint, chastity and purity, brotherly love and all the other virtues that were formerly so burdensome, painful and difficult to

practise have now become attractive, pleasant and wonderfully easy. So great is the change that the soul no longer finds any virtue exacting or difficult, but very pleasant. And all this is the work of divine Love.

Seek this gift of divine Love above all else, as I have said, for if God of His grace will give it you, it will open and enlighten your spiritual understanding to see truth, that is God, and spiritual things. It will kindle your affection to love Him wholly and truly, and He will work within your soul entirely as He wills, so that you will contemplate Him with worship and love, and understand what He is doing within you. God tells us through His prophet what we must do saying, Be still and see that I am God (Ps 46:10). That is, you who are reformed in feeling and whose inward vision is clear to see the things of the spirit, cease from outward activity for a while and see that I am God. In other words, Look only at what I, Jesus, God and man, am doing; look at Me, for it is I who do everything. I am Love, and all that I do is done out of love. I will show you how this is true, for you can neither do nor think anything good except through Me, that is, through My power, wisdom, and love, for otherwise it is not wholly good. The truth is that I, Jesus, am both Might, Wisdom, and holy Love: you are nothing, and I am God. Recognize, therefore, that it is I who am responsible for all your good deeds, good thoughts, and holy desires, and that you do nothing of yourself. Notwithstanding, all these good deeds are called yours, not because you are primarily responsible for them, but because I make them over to you out of the love that I bear you. Therefore, since I am God and do all this for love, cease to think about yourself look at Me and see that I am God, for I do all this.[7]

Notes

1. Aphraates, *Demonstratio,* 4, 5.
2. Zeno of Verona, *Tractatus,* I, 37; V, 15.
3. Michael Casey, *Truthful Living* (Leominster: Gracewing, 2001), p. 12.
4. Joseph Ratzinger, *Milestones* (San Francisco: Ignatius Press, 1998), p. 131.
5. Theodoret of Cyr, *Commentary on Psalms,* 73:22-23.
6. William Wordsworth, 'Animal Tranquillity and Decay, a Sketch'.
7. Walter Hilton, *The Ladder of Perfection,* Book II, ch. 36.

12

Wells of Prayer

In his Rule, St Benedict coined the formula . . . 'our mind must be in accord with our voice'. Normally, thought precedes word: it seeks and formulates the word. But praying the Psalms and liturgical prayer in general is exactly the other way round: the word, the voice, goes ahead of us and we must adapt to it. For on our own we human beings do not 'know how to pray as we ought' (Rom. 8:26) - we are too far removed from God, he is too mysterious and too great for us. And so God has come to our aid: He himself provides the words of our prayer and teaches us to pray. Through the prayers that come from him, he enables us to set out toward him; by praying together with the brothers and sisters he has given us, we gradually come to know him and draw closer to him.[1]

We come to chapters 8 to 20 of the Rule. As a section of the *Rule for Monasteries*, they present (at least chs 8 to 18) St Benedict's Order for the Divine Office, an order which, the historians tell us, was a reworking of the kind of office found in the basilican monasteries in Rome. As a section of the *Rule for monks*, on the other hand, we can see these chapters as continuing the *Tale of Quisquis*. He has been called by the Lord, has entered the monastery, has been humbled and exalted and now prayer and praise spring up within him. 'And I am always with you' (7.50). He has joined the disciples, gone up to Jerusalem, appropriated the mysteries of Easter, and now, like the believers in Acts, is fitted to persevere in prayer. I have mentioned already the symbolism of this *rising* to pray which we find in ch. 8.

Throughout his Rule, St Benedict sinks *wells of prayer* like the patriarchs. It is up to us to go to them and draw the water. I think he offers us much more than a few phrases concerning prayer. Every chapter is a chapter on prayer. For example, chapter 35, *Whether all should receive necessaries in like measure*. Where temporal necessities are supplied according to true need, there will be thanksgiving to God, the absence of murmuring, peace in the community; in other words, prayer. And to say that every chapter is a chapter on prayer is to say that the whole life is a pedagogy, a mystagogy of prayer. And to say that the whole Benedictine life leads to prayer is to take us back to the Prologue: 'Who is the man who wants life? . . . See, in his loving kindness the Lord shows us the way of life' (15, 20).

What, after all, is the origin, the source of prayer? It is striking that the first, prehistoric intimations of ritual (and therefore of prayer) are found in Neanderthal burials, for example at the cave near Shanidar in Iraq. Can one suggest that prayer is inspired by death? Or, rather, that prayer – the raising of the heart and mind to God – is what rises up within us when we, living beings, are faced by death. It is the rebellion of the 'living man' at the prospect of death. In other words, all prayer is a cry against death and for life. Therefore for eternal life, for resurrection. St Augustine suggests as much in his *Letter to Proba*. To pray without ceasing is to desire without ceasing, and what is desired is the 'blessed life'. At the beginning of their recent book *Prayer, A History*, after discussing both the prehistoric and mythological origins of prayer and then the often reductionist attempts to explain it (Frazer, Freud . . .), Philip and Carol Zaleski write as follows:

All human beings long for the beautiful, the true and the good, and every desire – for better crops or greater wisdom, for world peace or a good-night kiss – participates in this longing. We are constituted, by nature or divine gift, in such a way that this longing carries with it, as if its necessary companion, the impulse to pray, the indwelling conviction that prayer, addressed in word, movement or silence toward God, the saints, heavenly powers, earthly spirits, or the divine spark within, will allay this longing by transporting us to the threshold of our heart's desire. This is a primordial and universal event in the history of human consciousness and the life of every human being. Prayer lies in the ground of our being and connects us to its source, and every creative act bears, manifest or hidden, its imprint. Theories of prayer that fail to recognize its fundamental and perennial character are therefore bound to fall short.[2]

Easy to weave into such an etiology the notion that what is longed for is *life,* and precisely a life stronger than death. *Quis est homo qui vult vitam*? 'God's breath in man returning to his birth,/The soul in paraphrase, heart in pilgrimage,' said the Anglican poet George Herbert of prayer. In chapter 16 (v. 5), St Benedict speaks of us 'rendering (*referamus* – let us *give back*) praises to our *Creator*', to the source of life. Prayer is the seeking of life at its source.

So perhaps the first *well* St Benedict sinks for us is precisely this well of desire, of longing, of hope. This is purity and *intentio* of heart. 'To commit one's hope to God' (4.41); 'To desire eternal life with all spiritual longing' (4.4b); 'Let him look forward to holy Easter with the joy of spiritual desire' (49.7): these are all maxims of prayer.

A second *well* is *lectio divina*. 'To listen gladly to holy reading' (4.55). 'Idleness is the enemy of the soul. The brethren, therefore, must be occupied at stated hours in manual labour, and again at other hours in divine reading' (48.1). One English commentator of the Rule calculated that St Benedict provides 1,265 hours a year for *lectio*! We all have a bad conscience here. *Lectio is* always the easy victim of our busyness and our fatigue, a 'soft target'. Are we, with our distractions, like King Jehoiakim cutting Jeremiah's scroll with a penknife as it's read and throwing it in the fire? 'Yet neither the king, nor any of his servants who heard all these words, was afraid, nor did they rend their garments' (Jer. 36:24).

To rescue us from this, it can help to recall the great biblical and ecclesial paradigms. There is the Lord speaking to and through Moses at Mt Sinai, while 'the people were afraid and trembled' (Ex. 20:18). There are the discourses of Moses to the people of Israel in the plains of Moab on the threshold of the Promised Land. 'Beyond the Jordan in the land of Moab, Moses undertook to explain this law, saying . . .' (Deut. 1:5). There is the discovery of the Book of the Law in the Temple in the reign of Josiah. 'And Shaphan read it before the king. And when the king heard the words of the book of the law, he rent his clothes' (2 Kings 22:10–11). Then 'the king went up to the house of the Lord, and with him all the men of Judah and all the inhabitants of Jerusalem, and the priests and the prophets, all the people, both small and great; and he read in their hearing all the words of the book of the covenant . . .' (2 Kings 23:2). There is, after the return from exile, the great scene from the book of Nehemiah: 'And all the people gathered as one man into the square before the Water Gate; and they told Ezra the scribe to bring the book of the law of Moses which the Lord had given to Israel. And Ezra the priest brought the law before the assembly, both men and women and all who could hear with understanding, on the first day of the seventh month. And he read from it . . .' (Neh. 8:1–2). There is the proclamation of the Law and the Prophets in the synagogue, Moses still speaking.

There is Jesus reading aloud from the prophet Isaiah in the synagogue at Nazareth, filling and fulfilling this Liturgy of the Word with himself. 'Today this scripture has been fulfilled in your hearing' (Lk. 4:21). There is Timothy 'attending to reading' (1 Tim. 4:13), that is, the public reading of Scripture in the liturgical assembly, as St Paul bids him. There is the Bishop of Jerusalem, as described by Egeria, giving the *competentes* and faithful three hours of catechesis on Scripture and the Creed every day during Lent. Surely these scenes are, as it were, painted on the walls of our cell when we engage in *lectio*, and St Benedict echoes them when he bids his monks 'to listen willingly to holy reading' and provides so carefully for what is read in public at Vigils, at meals and before Compline. What we call *lectio* is the extension, the personal, private appropriation, of something originally public, communal. St Paul's 'attend to the reading' becomes woe to the monk who is not 'intent upon reading' (48.18), that is, by himself. A passage of Hippolytus moves in the same direction. He is speaking about the laity:

If there is instruction being given [that is, in church], it is prefer-
able to attend it, and to do so conscious that it is God who speaks
through the mouth of the one giving instruction . . . So let everyone take care to go to the assembly; it is there that the Holy Spirit
produces fruit . . . On a day when catechesis is not being given,
let each one take a holy book home and there read a sufficient
amount of what seems profitable.[3]

When we engage in *lectio*, we take our place in this line. It
runs from public proclamation to private reading, from the
Liturgy of the Word to the word read in the cell, from Sinai
to our hearts, from God's eternal thought concerning us to our
appropriation of it. 'This scripture is being fulfilled today in
your hearing.'

'It is significant for our understanding of Israel among the
religions of the world,' writes an American Jewish scholar,
Jon Levenson,

that meaning for her is derived not from introspection, but from a
consideration of the public testimony to God. The present generation makes history their story, but it is first history. They do not
determine who they are by looking within, by plumbing the depths
of the individual soul, by seeking a mystical light in the innermost
reaches of the self. Rather, the direction is the opposite. What is
public is made private. History is not only rendered contemporary; it is internalized. One's people's history becomes one's
personal history. One looks out from the self to find out who one
is meant to be. One does not *discover* one's identity, and one
certainly does not forge it oneself. He appropriates an identity that
is a matter of public knowledge. Israel affirms the given.[4]

One thinks of Antony receiving his vocation from the Liturgy
of the Word, the Gospel of Matthew, or St Thérèse finding
hers in 1 Corinthians.

For the Bible, the goal or fruit of *lectio* is always a renewal
of the covenant – just as the Liturgy of the Word leads to that
of the Eucharist. For St Benedict, if we refer to chapter 48, it
is victory over *acedia* (cf. v. 18). There's a profound truth
there, I think. Liturgy and work need this other strand, and
without it there is something missing in us, depth and focus
(*intentio*) suffer. Reading has its own proper power to keep us

in the truth, and therefore alive. Reading the Bible always brings us back to the primacy of God's design and God's action. Within that we discover our place, our work, and energy wells up within us. And the whole of our life – and our prayer – benefits. We draw life from the well of the Word. We become a tree by the stream.

The third *well* is what we find directly in chapters 8ff.: the *opus Dei* and psalmody. It always perplexes me how often retreat-givers pass over the Liturgy!

The Book of Psalms remains the ideal source of Christian prayer and will continue to inspire the Church in the new millennium (John Paul II).

It is the task of monks to keep the psalms alive in the Church (Robert Le Gall).

Thanks to Odo Casel in the first place, we have been blessed for the last two generations with the recognition that, in liturgy, the Paschal Mystery of the Lord is made present under signs. It is made present so that we – the Church – may remember it, enter into it and hasten its fulfilment. In the Eucharist, it is the Paschal Mystery in its fullness that is made present, in the Body and Blood of the Lord; the Eucharist is 'the sacrament of the Paschal Mystery'. In the other sacraments and major liturgical actions of the Church, it is rather an aspect of the Paschal Mystery which is offered us in the Liturgy of the Hours; is it not the Paschal Mystery as prayer which opens before us? A door opens for the Church – the praying assembly – to enter into the prayer of Christ crucified and risen, into filial prayer. I read once the fine phrase, 'the Mass is the interior of the Passion'. But one can say the same of the Divine Office: it is the interior of the Paschal Mystery, the interior which is prayer. 'In the days of his flesh, Jesus offered up prayers and supplications, with loud cries and tears, to him who was able to save him from death, and he was heard for his godly fear' (Heb. 5:7). The Passion itself, from Gethsemane to the last cry, was a prayer, and the Resurrection was its hearing by the Father. And yet at the same time this prayer of Christ continues: 'he always lives to make intercession for them' (Heb. 7:25). The *Catechism of the Catholic Church* has this striking remark about the prayer of Christ: it 'accomplished the victory of salvation' (2606). Every 'hour' of the Office offers access to the 'Hour' of Jesus. It's as if, on the Cross, Christ is Cantor. The Choir is the beloved disciple, Mary his mother, Mary the wife of Clopas, Mary Magdalene, the faithful few – standing, but as yet silent. There is no antiphony. Only after the resurrection and ascension, when the Precentor is in glory before the Father, does the Church find her voice. 'All these with one accord devoted themselves to prayer, together with the women and Mary the mother of Jesus, and with his brethren' (Acts 1:14). After Pentecost the circle widens: '. . . and there were added that day about three thousand souls. And they devoted themselves to . . . the breaking of bread and the prayers' (Acts 2:41–42). And so the Liturgy of Hours is born. It comes from the prayer of the Hour and, hour after hour, takes us back into it. To 'accomplish the victory of salvation'. And perhaps, on the basis of this, we can see how Marian our vocation is: a share in the Pasch through prayer.

'The Psalter gives us the key to prayer in Christ', says the Catechism again (2606), and, at solemn profession, we are solemnly handed the Psalter, like a knight his sword. 'See that you prefer nothing to the work of God,' says the Abbot. One scene of a drama by the Orcadian poet, George Mackay Brown, *Magnus* (concerning St Magnus, a martyr and patron of the Orkneys), is set at the naval battle of the Menai Straits (between the Welsh and the Norsemen). Young Magnus, earl of Orkney, stands in his ship while the battle rages, saying the Psalms. 'Who is this young man fighting the battle with the Psalter?' someone asks. Magnus of Orkney is the answer. A coward! But no: 'A coward would be hiding under the thwart. A coward doesn't sit in the teeth of the swords.' Like Magnus, monks 'fight the battle with the Psalter', the sword of the Spirit. Abbot Le Gall once said, 'it is the task of monks to keep the psalms alive in the Church.' The Psalms, one can say, are to the Office what bread and wine are to the Eucharist, water to Baptism, oil to other sacraments. 'Psalmody', wrote Maurice Zundel, 'is . . . a sacrament by which Christ prays in the Church for His Father's glory and the salvation of the world.' On the Cross, Christ prayed the psalms – 21, 68, 31, and 'the prayer of Jesus accomplished the victory of salvation'. Rising from the dead, Christ then gave the psalms, in their Christian meaning, to the disciples and so to the Church. '"Everything written about me in the law of Moses and the prophets and the psalms must be fulfilled." Then he opened their minds to understand the scriptures' (Lk. 24:44–45).

It is the Holy Spirit who helps us to connect to the prayer of Christ through the medium of psalmody. Not without a struggle, though. 'The spiritual trumpet that summons the brethren together visibly,' says St John Climacus,

> is also the signal for the invisible assembly of our foes. Some stand by our bed and encourage us to lie down again after we have got up. 'Wait until the first hymns are over,' they say. 'Then it will be time enough to go to church.' Others get those at prayer to fall asleep. Still others cause bad and unusual stomach-ache, while others encourage prattle in the church. Some inspire bad thoughts, others get us to lean against the wall as though we were weary or to start yawning over and over again, while still others cause us to laugh during prayer so as to provoke the anger of God against us. Some get us in our laziness to hurry up with the singing, while others suggest we should sing slowly in order that we may take pleasure in it. Others, by sitting on our mouths, shut them so that we can scarcely open them.[5]

Monastic life does not change much! If such is the work of the demons, what is the work of the Spirit? St Benedict gives us some clues. 'As soon as the signal for the Divine Office has been heard, let them . . . assemble with the greatest speed' (43.1).

> Let us believe this without any doubt [that God is present] when we are present at the work of God. Let us always be mindful of what the prophet said, etc. . . . Let us consider how we ought to be in the sight of the Godhead and his angels . . . let us so stand to sing the psalms that our mind may be in harmony with our voice' (19.2–3, 6–7).

Let singing or reading 'be done with humility, gravity and reverence, and by him whom the abbot has appointed' (47.3). Choir can be a cockpit, as we know. There's the Jesuit definition of 'a good liturgy': 'one in which no one is killed or wounded!' But it can also be a place where we are 'socialized' by the Spirit. Those, for example, who are musically gifted learn to use their gifts to support, not to dominate, while those who feel themselves un-gifted or are simply shy learn that they too have a contribution to make. Of St Benedict's prescriptions three are striking: that latecomers *should* come in (43.8–9), that the full Lord's Prayer twice a day 'convene' the brethren (13.13), that 'at the last prayer of the Work of God there be a commemoration of all absent brethren' (67.2). The Office is cenobitic prayer. It is the prayer of this community, and St Benedict wants the whole community to be there, at least virtually, and to be in concord. Again, this is an emphasis of Acts: 'They were all together in one place' (Acts 2:1).

So, when as individuals we 'enter within', as St Benedict says (43.7), two things happen. One has been called 'ontological shrinkage': we disappear, in a sense, in the great throng, heavenly as well as earthly, praising God. At the same time we become more than ourselves. In chapter 7, there comes the phrase, '[Scripture] says in the person of the suffering, *ex persona sufferentium*' (4.38). And when we sing the psalms, we speak 'out of a person': we personify. A voice 'sounds through' us. We personify something, someone, more than ourselves. The voice of the psalms is, as St Augustine will say, the voice of Christ and the Church. It is the voice of Israel, of the saints, of the suffering, of the people I know and carry in my heart, the people who have entrusted themselves to our prayers, even of the dead. And 'our mind is to harmonize with [this] voice', our interior with this exterior. We come back to the 'enlarged heart' of the Prologue, of the risen man. The Office is the Paschal Mystery as prayer and its arms are as wide as Christ's. And it is the Holy Spirit who widens us.

This is also why – I merely mention it – for St Benedict the Office is above all Praise. It is the affirmation of the greatness of God, 'of the judgements of his justice' (16.5), in all their fullness. It is also why – at least this is my experience – when one comes out of the Office, however distracted one may have been, one never feels one has wasted time. One always feels restored. The same is not always true of private prayer. John Henry Newman was nothing if not a man of prayer. Yet, it is not perhaps widely known that one of the great discoveries of his life, and one of the human instruments of his conversion to Catholicism, was the Roman Breviary. He came into possession of a copy of it in 1836, and it was a revelation to him of the face of the Catholic Church at prayer. Within the terms of his theological journey, it was an unexpected revelation to him of the apostolicity of the Church, of the continuity between the Church of the Fathers and the Roman Catholic Church of the nineteenth century. He studied the Breviary, he wrote one of the *Tracts of the Times* about it, he pioneered the English translation of it and, above all, he prayed it. It seems that, in his last years as an Anglican, he devoted three to four hours a day to its recitation, noting every 'hour' he was unable to say because of other circumstances. And, of course, the Office remained with him as a Catholic. It was one of the great loves of his life. And being Newman, he left us a passage of great beauty on the subject – a little romantic perhaps, but valid, and encouragement for us. It comes from his *Lectures on Justification*, written when an Anglican:

> Consider those Seven Services of the Holy Church Catholic in her best ages, which, without encroaching upon her children's duties towards this world, secured them in their duties to the world unseen. Unwavering, unflagging, not urged by fits and starts, not heralding forth their feelings, but resolutely, simply, perseveringly, day after day, Sunday and weekday, fastday and festival, season by season, year by year, in youth and in age, through a life, thirty years, forty years, fifty years, in prelude of the everlasting chant before the Throne, – so they went on, 'continuing instant in prayer', after the pattern of Psalmists and Apostles, in the day with David, in the night with Paul and Silas, winter and summer, in heat and in cold, in peace and in danger, in a prison or in a cathedral, in the dark, in the daybreak, at sun-rising, in the forenoon, at noon, in the afternoon, at eventide, and on going to rest, still they had Christ before them; His thought in their mind, His emblems in their eye, His name in their mouth, His service in

their posture, magnifying Him, and calling on all that lives to magnify Him, joining with Angels in heaven and Saints in paradise to bless and praise Him for ever and ever. O great and noble system, not of the Jews who rested in their rights and privileges, not of those Christians who are taken up with their own feelings, and who describe what they should exhibit, but of the true Saints of God, the undefiled and virgin souls who follow the Lamb whithersoever He goeth![6]

St Benedict's Divine Office, with its seven times a day and once in the night, is one example of a prayer woven into the rhythm of daily life. The Roman Office is another. So are the forms of the Liturgy of Hours found in the Eastern churches. Again, there's the common pattern among the faithful of prayer in the morning and in the evening, or of the Angelus, three times a day. There is the Jewish pattern of prayer, morning, afternoon and evening. There are the three daily *sandhyas* (devotions) of Hinduism, and the parallels among the Buddhists, Sikhs and Jains, and so on, everywhere in the religious world. Best known, most visible, most practised must be the Islamic salat – the five daily prayer sessions of dawn, noon, afternoon, dusk and night.

Yet all these practices – and certainly the monastic Liturgy of the Hours – are geared to, or at least tend naturally to, something more. In the beginning is desire; then the education of desire (by *lectio divina* and the *opus Dei*); but desire's tendency will always be to go beyond, to do more. The *opus Dei is* the school of prayer, as the monastery is the school of the Lord's service. The *opus Dei is* the soil of prayer, the womb of prayer. But summoning us always is the Pauline 'Pray without ceasing' (1 Thess. 5:17). To quote the Zaleskis again:

> To pray without surcease is prayer's Ultima Thule, seemingly unobtainable yet beckoning always with unimaginable spiritual rewards. Our first reaction, upon hearing of it, is likely to be (as it was for the Russian pilgrim) to ask how such a thing can possibly exist. How can we pray at all times, when we must sleep and eat and work and procreate and love and worship and engage in the countless other necessities and pastimes that enchain our lives?

That angels pray without ceasing we can readily accept, for they are bloodless creatures, with little to do but sing God's praises, girdled round his throne day and night. It is different for us mortals, trapped in the web of life and death. Yet traditions from around the globe affirm that ceaseless prayer can indeed be achieved.[7]

And St Benedict once again takes *Quisquis* by the hand and leads him on. 'See, in his loving kindness the Lord shows us the way of life!' In chapters 8 to 20, there is a movement from the *opus Dei* in general (chs 8–16) to psalmody (17–19) to prayer (20), and in chapter 52 St Benedict envisages a monk remaining behind after the Office to pray privately (*peculiariter*). There is in monastic tradition a strong idea of *psalmody* leading to *prayer*. One can also think of *prayer* as a fire, and *psalmody* as the wood that feeds it. With too much wood, a fire will go out; with too little, likewise.

Our praying can and should arise above all from our heart, from our needs, our hopes, our joys, our sufferings, from our shame over sin, and from our gratitude for the good. It can and should be a wholly personal prayer. But we also constantly need to make use of those prayers that express in words the encounter with God experienced both by the Church as a whole and by individual members of the Church. For without these aids to prayer, our own praying and our image of God become subjective and end up reflecting ourselves more than the living God. In the formulaic prayers that arose first from the faith of Israel and then from the faith of praying members of the Church, we get to know God and ourselves as well. They are a 'school of prayer' that transforms and opens up our life.[8]

St Gertrude's great desire was that 'her devotion might be in harmony with the Offices of the Church'. As the monk enters into the Psalms, the Psalms enter into him – as famously described by St John Cassian:

Thriving on the pasturage that they always offer and taking into himself all the dispositions of the psalms, he will begin to repeat them and to treat them in his profound compunction of heart not as if they were composed by the prophet but as if they were his own utterances and his own prayer. Certainly he will consider that they are directed to his own person, and he will recognize that their words were not only achieved by and in the prophet in times past but that they are daily borne out and fulfilled in him. . . For we find all [our] dispositions expressed in the psalms, so that we may see whatever occurs as in a very clear mirror and recognize it more effectively. Having been instructed in this way, with our dispositions for our teachers, we shall grasp this as something seen rather than heard . . . Thus we shall penetrate its meaning not through the written text but with experience leading the way. So it is that our mind will arrive at that incorruptible prayer to which, in the previous discussion . . . the conference was ordered and directed.[9]

Thus, the Divine Office is the door to the 'unceasing prayer' of 1 Thess. 5:17, the goal of the monastic life. Further still, by entering into the prayer of psalmody, the monk enters into the prayer of Christ. When he rose from the dead, Jesus gave his disciples the prayer of psalmody (cf. Lk. 24:44).

For Israel, the Psalms are largely attributed to David. In the Rule, David is called 'the Prophet', because he speaks in the name of Christ.

Jesus [cf. Mt. 26:30] prays the Psalms of Israel with his disciples: this element is fundamental for understanding the figure of Jesus. But also for understanding the Psalms themselves, which in turn could be said to acquire a new subject, a new mode of presence, and an extension beyond Israel into universality.

We also see a new vision of the figure of David emerging here: in the canonical Psalter, David is regarded as the principal author of the Psalms. He thus appears as the one who leads and inspires the prayer of Israel, who sums up all Israel's sufferings and hopes, carries them within himself, and expresses them in prayer. So Israel can continue praying with David, expressing itself in the Psalms, which constantly offer new hope, however deep the surrounding darkness. In the early Church, Jesus was immediately hailed as the new David, the real David, and so the Psalms could be recited in a new way – yet without discontinuity – as prayer in communion with Jesus Christ. Augustine offered a perfect explanation of this Christian way of praying the Psalms – a way that evolved very early on – when he said: it is always Christ who is speaking in the Psalms – now as the head, now as the body (for example, cf. *En. in Ps.* 60, 1–2; 61, 4; 85, 1, 5). Yet through him – through Jesus Christ – all of us now form a single subject, and so, in union with him, we can truly speak to God.[10]

Hence the teaching of the Council:

> Jesus Christ, High Priest of the new and eternal Covenant, taking human nature, introduced into this earthly exile that hymn which is sung throughout all ages in the halls of heaven. He attaches to himself the entire community of mankind and has them join him in singing his divine song of praise. For he continues his priestly work through the Church ... Therefore, when this wonderful song of praise [the Divine Office] is correctly celebrated ... then it is truly the voice of the Bride herself addressed to her Bridegroom. It is the very prayer which Christ himself together with his Body addresses to the Father.[11]

So we come to a fourth *well*. It has more than one name. *Meditatio, prayer of the heart* ... Perhaps one can also say, the prayer of the phrase or the prayer of repetition. It seems that, in Christian tradition, there is a range of progressively simpler (and simplifying) practices which lead from the weekly or daily patterns of communal worship to constant mindfulness of God, to prayer without ceasing: the Rosary, the psalm-verse, the Jesus Prayer, the aspiration, the single repeated word ... What, in common with ancient monastic tradition, St Benedict very discreetly offers seems to be, most of all, the second of these: the psalm-verse, the biblical phrase. We know what deep Jewish roots this has – from Joshua onwards, bidden to meditate on the Law day and night if he wished to take possession of the Land (Josh. 1:8). We know how 'Mary kept all these words pondering them in her heart'. We know how widespread the practice was among the monastic Fathers, what power such phrases could have: for help in the battle with demons, for healing and encouragement, for drawing scattered thoughts and energies into contemplative union, for entering into the purposes of God.

First, though, it bears emphasizing how gentle, non-prescriptive our own Rule is. About the content of the liturgy St Benedict is generally detailed and precise, but as to the content of private prayer – *oratio peculiaris* (49.5) – he prescribes nothing, not even a fixed time. He simply suggests, perhaps revealing his own prayer. We can be grateful for this. We owe a lot to St Benedict's silences! The prayer of the heart has to be natural, to spring up from within. 'Fish swim, birds fly, men pray.' In his essay *The Mission of St Benedict*, Newman wrote:

> St Benedict found the world, physical and social, in ruins, and his mission was to restore it in the way, not of science, but of nature, not as if setting about to do it, not professing to do it by any set time or by any rare specific or by any series of strokes, but so quietly, patiently, gradually, that often, till the work was done, it was not known to be doing. It was a restoration, rather than a visitation, correction, or conversion. The new world which he helped to create was a growth rather than a structure.

What was true of the outer work of the monasteries is true, surely, of the inner work of monks. It is a growth, not a structure; it proceeds in the way of nature, not of science. 'The earth produces of itself, first the blade, then the ear, then the full grain in the ear' (Mk 4:28). 'Pray as you can, and not as you can't' is a famous saying in English monastic circles.

That said, let me simply recall the suggestions we find in the Rule. They are found in three places: in chapter 7, in the liturgical chapters, and between chapters 35 and 58.

In chapter 7, the monk is pictured several times 'saying to himself', 'saying in his heart', 'saying with the Prophet' – and this 'always' – some phrase or other, usually from the Psalms. 'Then will I be blameless before him, if I keep myself from my iniquity' (v. 18), 'I am brought to nothing, I am all ignorance, etc.' (v. 50), 'I am a worm and no man, etc.' (v. 52), 'I have been lifted up, and humbled and confused' (v. 53), 'It is good for me that you have humbled me that I may learn your commandments' (v. 54), 'Lord, I am not worthy, I a sinner, to lift my eyes to heaven' (v. 65), 'I am bowed down and humbled on every side' (v. 66). Seven texts if one wishes to be mathematical, all of them in service of purification of the heart, a working of the field of the heart.

Then in the liturgical chapters, there are phrases which, it seems, St Benedict is especially partial to and careful to explicate. 'Lord, open my lips, and my mouth shall proclaim your praise' (9.2), 'O God make haste to help me, O Lord come to my aid' (17.3; 18.1), the *Gloria Patri* (9.2, etc.), the *Kyrie eleison* (9.10), two final phrases of the Lord's Prayer (13.13-14), and *Alleluia* (15). It would be natural for these so familiar phrases to echo in the inner ear of the monk. The 'prayer of the phrase', the 'prayer of repetition', is born from the Liturgy. Here again one could count seven, but their range is wider: from a cry for mercy, a plea for help, to glorification and praise.

Then, scattered through some four later chapters, there are prayers put on the lips of monks in ritual contexts. Again surely suggesting. 'Blessed are you Lord God, who has helped me and consoled me' (35.16) – a suitable evocation of the fiery furnace for those working in the kitchen! 'O God, come to my aid etc.' (35.17). 'O Lord, open my lips, etc.' for the reader (38.3). 'We have received, O Lord, your mercy in the midst of your temple' (53.14) at the reception of guests. Finally, the beautiful *Suscipe* for the moment of profession (58.21). In these five texts, we see again the link with liturgy. We also see how this kind of prayer is a striving for integrity. 'O God, come to my aid' prefaces both prayer and work in the kitchen, the service of God and the service of the brethren, the altar and the table. It's all one. Again, we have cries for help, but also thanksgiving and hope, and the entrusting of oneself to the Lord. The range widens still further.

If we do need an aid toward perpetual prayer, experience seems to show it does lie here: in the Word of God, in the Word of God encountered in the Liturgy and taken into the heart, where it can even take on a life of its own. 'He who sees the Book of Psalms in dreams may hope for piety,' say the Rabbis. So it has been in tradition. There is John Cassian's famous development on the *Deus in adiutorium*. Among the works of St Bede is *The Abbreviated Psalter*. From St Jerome's third version of the Psalms, the *iuxta hebraicos*, St Bede selected verses from each psalm which could be used as direct prayer or praise, as food for meditation, plea for mercy, protest, contrition, or adoration and exultation. Sometimes one verse alone was used, sometimes several. . . The *Abbreviations from the Psalter* was a turning point in the history of prayer, providing a vehicle for popular devotion for the next four centuries . . . [It] contained within it the basis for the prayer of the heart for the Middle Ages . . . It had a central place in the articulation of devotion. . .[12]

until the new age of devotion, heralded not least by St Anselm of Bec.

How many life-testimonies too throughout Christian history! St Augustine, at the end of his life, had the seven Penitential Psalms written out for him to see from his sickbed. St Basil died saying, 'Into your hands I commend my spirit.' St Paulinus died at Vespers, saying *Parabo lucernam Christo meo*: 'I will prepare a lamp for my anointed' (Ps. 131). St Bede, during his last illness, after giving his daily lessons, spent 'the rest of the day chanting the Psalter as best he could', and died saying the *Gloria Patri*. St Francis of Assisi died with verses of Ps. 141 on his lips. St Thomas More said the *Miserere*, always his favourite prayer, before putting his head on the block. St Teresa of Avila repeated over and over again, 'A contrite and humble heart, O God, you will not spurn.' Dom John Chapman, an Abbot of Downside, mentions the hold the psalm verse had on him: *Exsultabunt labia mea cum cantavero tibi, et anima mea quam redemisti*: 'My lips shall rejoice when I sing to you and my soul, which you have redeemed' (Ps. 70:23). I knew a layman dying of cancer who was greatly sustained by a verse from Psalm 4: *tu Domine singulariter in spe constituisti me*: 'You alone, Lord, make me dwell in safety.' It's now on the back of his cross in our graveyard.

I sometimes think that when we sing the Psalms and other prayers in choir, we are, as it were, putting them on disk. Then the Holy Spirit can call them forth from within when the time is ripe. The Word of God wells up within us, as music can. Among the Scottish poets of the twentieth century was one Edwin Muir. He would have had a Christian upbringing as a child, but then moved away into other realms. 'My belief receded ... to an unimaginable distance.' But, he adds, 'it still stood there, not in any territory of mine, it seemed, but in a place of its own.' And one night, early in 1939, with his wife ill, work precarious and the world darkening, it returned in the prayer learned as a child. He wrote in his diary:

> Last night, going to bed alone, I suddenly found myself (I was taking off my waistcoat) reciting the Lord's Prayer in a loud, emphatic voice – a thing I had not done for many years – with deep urgency and profound disturbed emotion. While I went on I grew more composed; as if it had been empty and craving and were being replenished, my soul grew still; every word had a strange fullness of meaning which astonished and delighted me. It was late; I had sat up reading; I was sleepy; but as I stood in the middle of the floor half-undressed, saying the prayer over and over, meaning after meaning sprang from it, overcoming me again with joyful surprise; and I realized that this simple petition was always universal and always inexhaustible, and day by day sanctified human life. Now I realized that, quite without knowing it, I was a Christian, no matter how bad a one.[13]

Some of you may remember my predecessor, Abbot Alfred. When I went through his room after his death, I found his copy of *The Cloud of Unknowing*. It was well worn, and inside he had noted whenever he had read it – about twelve times, I think, at least. It was the secret heart of the man. And *The Cloud* – anonymous, but probably by a Carthusian and composed in the East Midlands of England in the late fourteenth century – stands in this same tradition of prayer, though taking it to austere monologistic heights. To aid the 'naked intent towards God', the humble and blind stirring of love, to help keep all other thoughts beneath 'the cloud of forgetting' below us and God piercing 'the cloud of unknowing' above us, he says,

> take only a short word of one syllable; that is better than one of two syllables, for the shorter it is, the better it agrees with the work of the spirit. A word of this kind is the word GOD or the word LOVE... Fasten this word to your heart, so that it never parts from it, whatever happens. This word is to be your shield

and spear, whether you ride in peace or in war. With this word
you are to beat on the cloud and the darkness above you. With this
word you are to hammer down every kind of thought beneath the
cloud of forgetting; so if any thought forces itself on you to ask
what you would have, answer it with no more than this one word
(ch. 7).

Well, once again one has to say, 'Pray as you can and not
as you can't', yet at the same time acknowledge that this
prayer of the phrase (or simply of the *word*), indicated by St
Benedict, is a traditional, natural, valid, even profoundly transforming way of prayer. It can be, like the Gospel, 'the power
of God unto salvation for everyone who has faith' (Rom.
1:16); it can be the door into the 'inner room' and the place of
secret prayer (Mt. 6:6). The precise way of *The Cloud* is not
for everyone, but presumably none of us would disagree with
this paragraph on the worth of the work of prayer:

> This is the work of the soul that pleases God most. All the saints
> and angels rejoice in this work, and hasten to help it with all their
> might. All the devils are driven crazy when you do this, and try
> to frustrate it in all ways they can. All people living on earth are
> marvellously helped by this work, in ways you do not know. Yes,
> the very souls in purgatory are relieved of their pain by the power
> of this work. You yourself are cleansed and made virtuous by this
> work more than by any other. And yet it is the easiest work of all
> and the soonest completed, when a soul is helped by grace in the
> desire it feels. . .' (ch. 3).

With that last phrase we come to St Benedict's last *well*.
'Our prayer, therefore, ought to be short and pure, unless
perhaps it be prolonged by a feeling inspired by divine grace'
(20.1). St Augustine's *Letter to Proba* is behind this passage,
his distinction between 'much speaking' (to be avoided) and
'prolonged devotion' (to be commended, when appropriate).

> Away with much use of words in prayer, yes; but let there be
> intensive prayer if fervent concentration perseveres. Saying much
> when we pray means doing a necessary thing with superfluous
> words. Intensive prayer means beating on the door of him to
> whom we are praying by long and devout stirring of the heart.

Often this task is carried on more by groaning than by speaking, with more tears than breath. He sets our tears in his sight, and our groaning is not hidden from him who created all things by his Word, and does not require the words of men (*Ep.* 130, 20).

Here, in a real sense, we come back to the beginning: desire, even wordless desire. 'Who is the man who wants life?' Now it is clear that the deepest source of this desire is the Holy Spirit, or that this desire is 'overwhelmed' by the Desire of the Father for the Son and the Son for the Father. 'For we do not know how to pray as we ought, but the Spirit himself intercedes for us with sighs too deep for words' (Rom. 8:26). Cardinal Basil Hume coined the phrase, 'the prayer of incompetence', but underneath it there can flow the 'competence' of the Spirit. 'God gives prayer to the one who prays', says Evagrius. At the human level, we will never 'succeed' in prayer. To take up a life of prayer is to be committed to failure, to being 'reduced to nothing'. Yet we can say what St Paul said: 'I am sure that he who began a good work in you will bring it to completion on the day of Jesus Christ' (Phil. 1:6).

At the end of the Prologue, St Benedict points to the 'unutterable sweetness of love' and the 'expanded heart'. At the end of chapter 2, he talks of the abbot 'being cleansed of his faults'. The end of chapter 7 we know. At the end of whole Rule, he points us beyond the 'little Rule for beginners'. And at the end of these chapters on liturgy, psalmody and prayer, he points to 'the inspiration of divine grace'. All these passages can be read pneumatologically. All of them point to the freedom of the children of God, to which every structure, method, aid, teaching is subordinate.

Or to say the same thing another way: St Benedict's Office would have ended with, climaxed in, not the Collect as with us, but with the Lord's Prayer, the prayer of the children of God. And so his few words on prayer, by their final allusion to the Spirit, point the same way: to the full freedom of a filial relationship with God. The much-commented phrases in chs 20 and 52 can all be read, as de Vogüé has said, in the light of Matthew, chapter 6 and the presentation of the Lord's Prayer.

'And because you are sons, God has sent the Spirit of his Son into our hearts, crying, "Abba! Father?" So through God you are no longer a slave but a son, and if a son then an heir' (Gal. 4:6–7). St Benedict leads us to this, bows out before this.

We all know the famous Desert Father story. 'What more can I do?' 'And the old man lifted up his hands, and they became flame.' We know the passage of Isaac of Nineveh: 'When the Spirit dwells in a person, prayer never from then on departs from his soul.' We know the story of the transfiguration of St Seraphim in the snows of Russia. In all these, I presume, the vision is of someone become prayer. And, when we turn to our old, sick monks – who sometimes no longer seem to pray at all – we perhaps see what these rather 'glorious' passages really mean, in the humility of the flesh and the poverty of the spirit. The old, more than any, are in that privileged place between the cloud of forgetting and the cloud of unknowing. They are simply waiting. They are simply an emptiness waiting to be filled, a 'lowly body' waiting to be 'changed' (Phil. 3:21). Many things about prayer I haven't touched on, I'm aware: intercession, contemplation – great themes. And how will I see Christ in prayer if I'm refusing to see him in my brother? And the Eucharist, what an omission! It is the daily bread of prayer. It keeps our hunger for God alive. And yet it, and any other aspect only in the end, I think, brings us back to that one same place, the place where our old brethren are: on the cross of prayer, between incompetence and the Spirit, forgetting and unknowing, engaged in a supremely useful and utterly impossible enterprise, fed by hunger, happy desiring, waiting ...

If there is one line in the Bible that – for me at least – sums up the mystery of Christian prayer, it is from the end of the Apocalypse. 'The Spirit and the Bride say, "Come."' Our desire is for Christ, for Christ to come, for grace to come and this world to pass away. And it is the Spirit and the Bride, the Church, who have this desire and pray this desire within us. We have only to consent to it: 'And let him who hears say, "Come." And let him who is thirsty come, let him who desires take the water of life without price' (Rev. 22:17).

Notes

1. Benedict XVI, *Jesus of Nazareth*, Vol. I (London: Bloomsbury, 2007) p. 131.
2. Carol & Philip Zaleski, *Prayer, A History* (Boston: Houghton Mifflin Harcourt, 2006), p. 31.
3. St Hippolytus, *Apostolic Tradition*, 35.
4. Jon Levenson, *Sinai & Zion* (San Francisco: Harper Collins, 1987).
5. St John Climacus, *The Ladder* of *Divine Ascent*, 19.
6. John Henry Newman, *Lectures on Justification*, XIII, 8.
7. Zaleski, p. 151.
8. Benedict XVI, *Jesus of Nazareth*, I, p. 130.
9. St John Cassian, *Conference*, X, XI, 4, 6.
10. Benedict XVI, *Jesus of Nazareth*, II (San Francisco: Ignatius Press, 2011), pp. 146–7, cf. also, pp. 153, 215.
11. Second Vatican Council, *Sacrosanctum Concilium*, 83, 84.
12. Benedicta Ward, *St Bede and the Psalter* (Oxford: SLG Press, 2002), pp. 16, 17, 22.
13. Edwin Muir, *An Autobiography* (London: Methuen, 1964), p. 246.

13

Intercession

Quisquis has shared in the Paschal Mystery through humility and charity, and his heart has been / is being enlarged, so that he can run in the way of the commandments. So first of all, with his brethren, in the cenobitic prayer of the Office, he is happy to praise God. What about the prayer of the heart? According to St Benedict, 'prayer should be short and pure, unless it is prolonged by the inspiration of divine grace' (20.4). This language of 'inspiration' and 'grace' suggests the Holy Spirit. It is as if the monk is experiencing here a little Pentecost. And one way the Spirit may prolong prayer is in intercession.[1]

I think it's too easy to look down on intercession, seeing it as a low-level prayer in comparison with meditation and contemplation, or as petty, even manipulative, magical. We may resent, as monks and nuns, being boxed up as intercessors. But still, intercession is nothing to be ashamed of. A woman once said to me she became a nun because she never felt so close to God as when she was interceding. The prayer of Christians is surely 'graded' by the charity it expresses and arouses, more than by its type. And there is something deeply human as well as Christian about intercession. There's a natural acknowledgement, recognition of intercession, in the human heart and human society. And if, as some think, the finest expression of man's spirituality and religiousness is to be found in Buddhism, certainly Buddhism contains a summons to universal intercession. There's a deep wisdom in the old three-fold allotment of function in Indo-European society: the

aratores, bellatores, oratores. There are those who must cultivate, educate, develop the good; there are those who must
watch, and protect us from evil; and finally there are those
who must keep open the lines of communication between the
society and the gods or God, sacrificing and pleading. 'Unless
the Lord keep the city . . .'

So, at the very least, intercession is an expression of human
solidarity and, for us, of Christian charity. 'The sin city
obliges us to pray for ourselves'; and we find in a homily once
attributed to St John Chrysostom, 'fraternal charity urges us to
pray for others. The prayer flowing from fraternal charity is
sweeter to God than that which is the outcome of necessity.'
Intercession, says the Catechism (2635), is the 'characteristic
of a heart attuned to God's mercy'. It is, wrote Evelyn
Underhill, thinking of Abraham, 'a particular way of exerting
love and thus of reaching and using spiritual power.' Is it
enough to say that petition and intercession only affect the one
praying, opening the mouth of the sack so that God can pour
the good things in? Or isn't it the case that God the Father has
freely exposed Himself to the desires of His children, and
therefore yields to their influence, doing what otherwise He
would not have done? If so, we should not underestimate our
responsibility.

Intercession is a prayer of human solidarity, of Christian
charity, of 'filiality'. And more, it 'is a prayer of petition
which leads us to pray it as Jesus did' (*CCC* 2634). It is a way
of sharing in the sufferings of Christ, of being with Christ on
the cross, his outstretched arms 'lengthening' ours. Christ

> died to bestow upon [man] that privilege which implies and
> involves all others, and brings him into nearest resemblance to
> himself, the privilege of intercession. This, I say, is the Christ-
> ian's especial prerogative and, if he does not exercise it, certainly
> he has not risen to the conception of his real place among created
> beings . . . He is made after the pattern and in the fullness of
> Christ – he is what Christ is. Christ intercedes above, and he
> intercedes below. Why should he linger in the doorway praying
> for pardon, who has been allowed to share in the grace of the
> Lord's passion, to die with Him and rise again? He is already in
> a capacity for higher things. His prayer thenceforth takes a higher

range and contemplates not himself merely, but others also. He is taken into the confidence and counsels of his Lord and Saviour.[2]

'No longer do I call you servants, for the servant does not know what his master is doing; but I have called you friends, for all that I have heard from my Father I have made known to you' (Jn 15:15). Intercession is an aspect of this intimacy. In our prayer Jesus makes known to us what he is hearing from the Father about the good of souls, the needs of the Church and the world, and that 'making known' provokes our intercession. The Holy Spirit, 'who intercedes for the saints with sighs too deep for words' (Rom. 8:26), presides over our intercession and links it to that of Jesus. 'He will take what is mine and declare it to you' (Jn 16:14). The Holy Spirit brings us the mind of Christ in our intercession, and, as the heart expands, our petition 'will become more and more a means of returning to God all the things that have ever been his or that ought to belong to him. It will be like an attempt to involve God afresh in his creation, his Church, his people, his faithful.'[3] It's not too much to talk of a mission here, especially if we are contemplative religious.

Someone once observed, with truth I think, that in the 'active life' the first movement is to people and so through people to God, whereas in the contemplative life the movement is first to God and then from God to people. The Lord 'sends' us to others in prayer. And the more delicately responsive we can be to the Lord's guidance, the better. May not too many opportunities pass us by? We know the phrase, 'no salvation outside the Church', best interpreted as, 'where salvation is, there is the Church'. But how? Not necessarily, not surely – statistically speaking – normally, through preaching and the administration of the sacraments, but through the prayer of intercession. 'The intercession of Christians,' says the Catechism (2636), 'recognizes no boundaries.'

Intercession, if we pause to think about it, runs through the whole economy of redemption, from Abraham through Moses and the prophets and the Temple liturgy to Our Lord and his mother and his Church and the chorus of the saints. It won't lay down its sword until the glorification of the last of the elect.

What about intercession in the Old Testament? It's there in plenty. Abraham, Moses par excellence, Aaron, Joshua, Samuel (with his great line, 'as for me, far be it from me that I should sin against the Lord by ceasing to pray for you', 1 Sam. 12:23), David, Solomon, Elijah, Elisha, Amos, Hezekiah, Jehoshaphat, Jeremiah, Ezekiel, Job, and so all the way through to the final chapter of 2 Maccabees where the curtain is for the first time pulled back on the posthumous intercession of the righteous. Judas, before battle, is encouraged by a vision of Onias the deceased high priest 'praying with outstretched hands for the whole body of the Jews', and then of 'a man who loves the brethren and prays much for the people and the holy city, Jeremiah, the prophet of God' (2 Mac. 15:12, 14).

And through the succession of stories and episodes, the Old Testament gives us a first 'theology' of intercession. There is a pattern. The people have sinned and therefore stand under the justice of God; disaster threatens. The *Lord Himself* reveals this to the mediatorial figure ('Shall I hide from Abraham what I am about to do?' Gen. 18:17) This latter in turn is provoked to pray ('Turn from your fierce wrath; change your mind and do not bring disaster on your people', Ex. 32:12). The Lord listens to his servant, the interceder; the people are spared; mercy triumphs. Old Testament intercession is always against an immediate horizon of wrath, always in view of 'sparing'. It is the conversion of wrath into mercy, almost the teasing out of God's real, inmost, merciful attitude temporarily concealed under the sound and fury of his righteous anger. Hence the chilling force of what's almost a refrain in the prophecy of Jeremiah: 'As for you, do not pray for this people and lift up cry or prayer for them, and do not intercede with me, for I do not hear you' (Jer. 7:16; cf. 11:14; 14:11; 15:1).

Among all the intercession studies, there is one that stands out: that of the intercession of Moses after the apostasy of the Golden Calf. It is told in Ex. 32–34 and Deut. 9:7–10:11. It is the essential moment in the Exodus story and therefore Israel's story, and Moses' intercession is central to it. One old Jewish commentator on the episode equates Moses here with the suffering servant of Isaiah 53 and says, 'He offered his own life to God on behalf of Israel' (Nachmanides). It is a proleptic identification with the crucified Christ. To appreciate fully what is happening here, one must appreciate the truly appalling nature of Israel's sin: the turning of the back it involved or, if you like, the frontal rejection. The worship of the Golden Calf is the original sin of the people of the Exodus, the sin, which re-enacted over and over again, will bring first the northern kingdom and then Judah and Jerusalem to destruction and enslavement. It is thanks to the intercession of Moses that destruction is averted on this occasion. It is how Moses' heart is expanded through his wrestling with God on behalf of the people. Through his intercession he grows, he lives his vocation as God's leader and instrument, he reaches perfect love. He moves from the noble refusal to be the father of an alternative people (a second Abraham, Ex. 32:10) to the total self-abnegation of asking to be blotted out of the book of the Lord (32:32). That is, he first refuses a good and then volunteers for an evil. And what follows can't be coincidence: not just the renewal of the covenant and the resumption of the onward march of salvation history, but the crowning revelation to Moses himself, on the mountain, of the glory and Name of the Lord, a high point of biblical revelation prior to the Incarnation (34:6ff.). And even then Moses doesn't forget the Israelites. Twelve times at least Moses intercedes, but this time supremely. And so the Catechism can say (2574), 'the prayer of Moses becomes the most striking example of intercessory prayer which will be fulfilled in the one mediator between God and men, the man Christ Jesus.'

Which brings us to him . . . Israel's champion intercessors – Moses, Samuel, Jeremiah – *were* Israel, personified Israel. And so one finds Our Lord's Alexandrine contemporary Philo, for example, claiming an intercessory role for Israel vis-à-vis humanity as a whole. And this pre-eminently through the liturgy of the Temple, which in Jewish tradition, stands at the centre of the world. This points to the role of the Church, Christ's Body, surely, but also in the first place to the Head, to Christ himself. Israel's line of intercessors culminates. He is *the* intercessor. More, of course, and one in a series; rather, the one who makes the series possible. Outside him, there's no intercession. Any intercession that there is, is 'in him'.

Yes, he is intercession constitutionally, ontologically, the one mediator between God and man, two natures united in one person, Son of the Father and son of Mary, doubly consubstantial. Therefore he carries us all and when he prays as man, in his life, 'existentially', 'he includes all men in his prayer for he has taken on humanity in his incarnation, and he offers them to the Father when he offers himself' (*CCC* 2602).

This life of intercession comes to its paradoxical climax in his passion and death. On the cross, he fulfilled the intercessory mission of the Isaian servant: 'he bore the sin of many and made intercession for the transgressors' (Is. 53:12). There, 'prayer and the gift of self are but one' (*CCC* 2605). There, says the Catechism again (2606), 'the prayer of Jesus accomplished the victory of salvation', and in his last agonizing cry 'all the troubles, for all time, of humanity enslaved by sin and death, all the petitions and intercessions of salvation history are summed up' (ibid.). Old people, dying people, often can't say prayers any more, but they can be, they are prayer. And Jesus on the cross, arms outstretched, crying out, is prayer. His intercession is his blood.

Yet the New Testament, when it does speak explicitly of Christ's intercession, speaks of it as that of the ascended, heavenly Christ, before the face of the Father. This is the intercession of the cross turned inside out and lifted from earth to heaven. 'Raised from the dead ... at the right hand of God [he] intercedes for us' (Rom. 8:34); 'he always lives to make intercession for us [those who donated to God through him] (Heb. 7:25); and like-mindedly if differently worded: 'we have our advocate with the Father' (1 Jn 2:1). Jesus, in heaven, isn't 'retired' or 'emeritus'; rather, he's now mediator, priest, intercessor in full flood. Just as his very dying was intercession, so is his risen living. His presence before the Father *is* intercession and if, as the Old Testament reveals, where there is an intercessor, there is mercy, then we know now with a new certainty and joy that mercy is assured and will have the last word over wrath. 'He is said to intercede for us in two ways,' says St Thomas: 'one, by his will for our salvation, two, by re-presenting to the eyes of the Father the humanity assumed for us and the mysteries celebrated in it.'

And what, in a name, is the effect of this intercession? Very simply, the Holy Spirit. 'And I will ask the Father, and he will give you another Advocate, to be with you forever' (Jn 14:16). The Advocate is the Father's answer to Jesus' asking. Pentecost follows the Ascension, and just as Jesus is always ascended, so the Spirit is always coming. 'Jesus Christ, having entered the sanctuary of heaven once for all intercedes constantly for us as the mediator who assures us of the permanent outpouring of the Holy Spirit' (*CCC* 667).

A footnote to this: in the Old Testament, the prophet intercedes for the aversion of wrath: 'O Lord, spare your people.' In the New Testament, the intercessor bears more on the greatness of the gift, on grace pure and simple. 'I pray that, according to the riches of his glory, he may grant that you may be strengthened in your inner being with power through his Spirit, and that Christ may dwell in your hearts ... I pray that you may have the power to comprehend, etc. ... to know the love of Christ that surpasses knowledge, so that you may be filled with all the fullness of God' (Eph. 3:16-17, 18-19).

I've said something about intercession in general, about intercession in the Old Testament, about the intercession of Christ. And this, of course: the Holy Spirit, the fruit of Jesus' intercession, is the root of ours.

> Likewise the Spirit helps us in our weakness, for we do not know how to pray as we ought, but that very Spirit intercedes with sighs too deep for words. And the one who searches the heart knows what is the mind of the Spirit, because the Spirit intercedes for the saints according to the will of God (Rom. 8:26-27).

The Holy Spirit introduces 'the saints', those made holy by faith and baptism, into the mystery of intercession. He takes them / us into the intercession of Christ. He intercedes for the saints, says St Augustine, by making the saints intercede. And the more the holiness of our baptism blossoms into charity, the more availing the intercession will be.

It is the saints as a whole who co-intercede, that is the Church as Church: the Body of Christ, his extension and agent; the Bride of Christ, his complement and helpmate. The Spirit and the Bride together say 'Come' (Rev. 22:17). And 'saints' here means the saints of earth and of heaven, of the Church militant and the Church triumphant.

The witnesses who have preceded us into the kingdom, especially those whom the Church recognizes as saints, share in the living tradition of prayer by the example of their lives, the transmission of their writings and their prayer today. They contemplate God, praise Him and constantly care for those whom they have left on earth. When they entered into the joy of their Master, they were 'put in charge of many things'. Their intercession is their most exalted service to God's plan... (*CCC* 2683).

And it is, of course, 'holy' Mary, 'saint' Mary who is especially identified with this 'service' of intercession, who joins the Spirit in saying 'Come'.

'First of all, then, I urge that supplications, prayers, intercessions, and thanksgivings be made for everyone' (1 Tim. 2:1). So St Paul to Timothy and through Timothy to the whole Church, all the saints. It is in *common* prayer especially that the Holy Spirit empowers the holy Church to intercede. We think of the intercessions of Good Friday, the 'litanies' of the Divine Office, the bidding prayers that conclude the liturgy of the Word. And above all the intercessions of the Eucharistic prayers, of the Eucharist itself. 'In the Eucharist, the Church is as it were at the foot of the cross with Mary, united with the offering and intercession of Christ' (*CCC* 1370). It is also united with the angels and saints before the throne of God and of the Lamb.

These are just a few thoughts on this Spirit-driven mystery of ecclesial intercession, something simultaneously personal and communal, earthly and heavenly, baptismal and Eucharistic. We shouldn't be blind to it. It has a real part in the economy of salvation. 'I harbour no doubt,' wrote the early Christian apologist Aristides, 'that it is only because of the prayers of Christians that the world continues to exist.'

But there is something else still to say, isn't there? With this common intercessory call and action, there is space for particular vocations to intercession. *The* great New Testament champion of intercession, the Moses standing our side of Christ the centre, is St Paul. He embodies the intercession of the apostle, of the bishop and priest, and more widely of all those exercising a Christian responsibility towards others. There's a vast theme in itself. And there are also folk such as our poor selves, dedicated publicly to the way of holiness, representing the bridal and praying Church with a particular intensity. There is such a thing as the monastic / contemplative ministry of intercession. All that I have said about praise is true, but intercession has its place too: St Benedict's Office has the litanies of Lauds and Vespers, and much mutual prayer within the monastery: at profession for example, at the beginning of the weekly services, for the absent brethren, and especially for those under threat from their own waywardness. If all else has failed 'let [the abbot] employ a greater thing still (*quod maius est*), namely the prayer of himself and all the brethren, that the Lord, who can do all things, may effect salvation for the brother who is sick' (28.4–5). Intercession, in any situation, is *id quod maius est*. (Scriptural root: 'pray for one another that you may be healed' (James 5:16).

Our contemplative life – God forbid it should be a purely private thing. It is a form of charity, as I've said. And so it has been recognized – by the faithful, by the Fathers, by the teaching of the Church. 'They give thanks for the whole universe as if they were fathers of the whole of humanity; they thank God for everyone and draw them into a true brotherhood', wrote St John Chrysostom.[4] 'They are lights giving light to the whole world, ramparts surrounding and protecting the cities.'[5] The law code of the sixth Byzantine Emperor Justinian includes this: 'The monk's life and his contemplation are holy things and urge the soul towards God. It not only helps those who follow this form of life, but is immeasurably useful to all because of its purity and the intercession it offers to God.' 'Teeth chew for the good of the whole body', wrote Guerric of Igny, 'and monks are established to pray for the whole body of the Church.' 'At the heart of the Church, my mother, I will be love,' said St Thérèse. 'A monk is one who prays for the whole world,' said Staretz Silouan.

Each of us and each of our communities.

It is 'expanded hearts' that save the world, that carry it. Jesus' heart expanded to breaking point on the cross, the hearts of Mary and all those one with the Trinity in eternal life are expanded hearts. And the life we lead, and everything in it, has meaning solely in the measure that it leads to and flows from this widening of the heart. 'Enlarge the site of your tent and let the curtains of your habitations be stretched out; do not hold back; lengthen your cords and strengthen your stakes' (Is. 54:2). André Louf talks of a heart enlarged 'progressively to the limits of the universe', and St Isaac of Nineveh of

> a heart that burns for all creation, for the birds, for the animals, for the devils, for every creature. When he [the compassionate man] thinks about them, looks at them, his eyes fill with tears . . . He even prays for snakes in the boundless compassion that wells up in his heart after God's likeness.[6]

One begins with intercession and one comes back to purity of heart. It's always the way. Intercession is one spoke of the monastic wheel and like every spoke it joins us to the hub. It's a part containing the whole.

Let us pray, then, for others, explicitly sometimes, certainly, but above all that we realize that our whole Christian and monastic life can be, is intercession. Let us turn to God. Let me end with *The Cloud of Unknowing*, ch. III:

> Lift up your heart to God with humble love, and mean God himself not what you get out of him. Indeed, hate to think of anything but God himself, so that nothing occupies your mind and will but only God. Try to forget all created things that he ever made; and the purpose behind them, so that your thought and longing do not turn or reach out to them be that in general or in particular. Let them go and pay no attention to them. It is the work of the soul that pleases God most. All saints and angels rejoice over it and hasten to help it on with all their might. All the fiends however are furious at what you are doing, and try to defeat it in every conceivable way. Moreover, the whole of mankind is

wonderfully helped by what you are doing in ways you do not understand. Yes, the very souls in purgatory find their pain eased by virtue of your work. And in no better way can you yourself be made clean or virtuous than by attending to this ... Do not give up then, but work away...

Notes

1. There are many tales of effective intercession. One came my way from a parish priest. A teenage girl in his parish was in a coma as a result of an accident. It was unclear whether she would ever rally. He and others prayed very much for her, especially at Mass. She did recover. And one of her first acts on doing so was to tell how, when in the coma, she had 'seen' the priest standing at the altar praying for her.
2. John Henry Newman, *Parochial and Plain Sermons,* III, XXIV.
3. Adrienne von Speyr, *The World of Prayer* (San Francisco: Ignatius Press, 1985), pp. 217–18.
4. St John Chrysostom, *On Matthew, Hom.,* 55.5.
5. Ibid., *Hom.* 72.4.
6. Isaac of Nineveh, *Ascetic Treatises,* 81.

14

The 'Ordinary' Life

The final verb of chapter 20 is *surgere*, to rise. In chapter 8, *Quisquis* rose *for* prayer. Now he rises *from* prayer, to serve his brethren and others. This is the hidden story-line of the next 51 chapters. 'Let the rest serve one another in charity' (35.6). This is an echo of Gal. 5:13: 'For you were called to freedom, brethren; only do not use your freedom as an opportunity for the flesh, but through love be servants of one another.' The freedom of humility, expressed first in filial prayer, is now expressed in fraternal service. This is the essential call of these chapters.

If love of God is expressed in the Work of God, so love of neighbour is expressed in the service of others. We can say, without too much over-organisation, that in these chapters St Benedict offers the individual en route 'to God and eternal life' (72.2) a fourfold way of love:

- that of 'bearing one another's burdens' (Gal. 6:2), brotherly concern for the wayward in the community, pastoral care for the spiritually sick (chs 21–30);
- that of practical service of the brethren, work, with kitchen and table as a particular focus, and hospitality as a natural extension (chs 31–57);
- that of spiritual fatherhood, the generation of new members within the community (chs 58–66);
- that of a whole-hearted gift of oneself to the brotherhood (chs 67–72).

All the works of the Church are found within the monastery (St Bernard).

For all the limitations of enclosure (66.7), there is a totality of Christian service being made available here, according to the gifts of each. It is not by chance that chapter 57 ends by quoting 1 Peter 4:11, which has become a Benedictine motto. The full context is worth remembering:

> Above all hold unfailing your love for one another, since love covers a multitude of sins. Practise hospitality ungrudgingly to one another. As each has received a gift, employ it for one another, as good stewards of God's varied grace: whoever speaks, as one who utters oracles of God; whoever renders service, as one who renders it by the strength which God supplies; in order that in everything God may be glorified (1 Pet. 4:8–11).

It is likely, of course, that along this path of service and care (*cura*), the individual monk may be called to act as a Dean or Cellarer or Infirmarian or Guestmaster or Novice Master or Abbot or Prior, or in some other position of responsibility. Even more, though, he will be called to welcome the service of these and his brethren into his life, as himself a needy brother, and at times a delinquent one, needing to be called to healing and repentance. Love lies in receiving as well as giving. This reciprocity emerges especially in the final chapters.

It is also noticeable how, scattered throughout this section of the Rule, there are references 'back', as it were, to the Liturgy (e.g. chs 47, 50), prayer (e.g. ch. 52), personal asceticism (e.g. ch. 49). Benedictine life is a unity.

Community life is a 'furnace' (1.6), a 'school' (Prol. 45), where the individual monk is turned to gold and begins to be a disciple.

> Religious community is the place where the daily and patient passage from 'me' to 'us' takes place, from my commitment to a commitment entrusted to the community, from seeking 'my things' to seeking 'the things of Christ'.[1]

We come to chapters 21ff. From the point of view of the
Rule for monasteries, they treat of the 'ordinary' life of the
monastery: its life and work, its discipline, its relations with
the outside world, its reception of new members etc., all the
way to chapter 72, which is a kind of capstone to this great
part of the Rule. It is fair to say that these chapters defy ordering. But for those of us who have a compulsion for order and
sequence, there is perhaps one suggestion to be made. It is
possible to consider the earlier chapters, 4 to 7, as a summary
of the teaching the *abbot* (presented in ch. 2) should give his
brethren as they seek God. It is also possible to think of chapters 8 to 20 as a guide, for the *abbot* again, as to how the *opus
Dei* and the life of prayer in the monastery should be regu-
lated. In chapter 21, however, St Benedict turns to the *deans*
of the monastery. And it is possible to take chapters 21 to 30
– mostly concerned with the misnamed 'penal code' – and put
them under, so to speak, the 'heading', the competence, of the
deans. In chapter 31 it's the turn of the c*ellarer*. And it is
possible to consider the chapters that follow, up to chapter 57,
'On the Artisans of the Monastery', as covering in a special
way, apart from some *'blocs erratiques'*, the domain of the
cellarer. Chapters 58 to 63 then deal with the reception of new
members. Here we can say, at least in the light of later Benedictine history, that we are in the realm of the *novice master*.
In chapter 64, St Benedict returns to the *abbot*, in chapter 65,
he adds a *prior*, in chapter 66, as a first conclusion, he presents
the *porter* – a great symbolic figure! Then (later) in chapters
67 to 72 he turns to the *brethren* as a whole. So, perhaps in
these chapters we can see an order formed around *persons*.

What I want to do in this conference is select one chapter
from all of these. But first just some thoughts on some of the
others. In chapters 23 to 30, St Benedict is concerned with the
pastoral care of the 'erring brothers' (27.1), the 'fluctuating
brother' (27.3). What a central and delicate aspect of our life
these chapters touch on!

'Let the abbot know that he has undertaken the charge of
weak souls, not a tyranny over the healthy' (27.6). There are
always brethren whose psychological and moral weaknesses
master them, who in a special way cry out 'to be healed'

(30.3). And one can regret we no more have such a clear, biblical and ecclesial 'procedure', as we find in these chapters, for the care of such brethren. A strange contrast with the clear procedures that prevail often in our Western health services! For there's much to learn from these chapters. For example, from the underlying reference to St Paul and his relations with the church in Corinth. I just want to mention one thing, speaking as an abbot. In these chapters we are, in a sense, at the heart of an abbot's ministry, at its most sensitive, painful, even anguishing, yet also potentially joyful point. And it is especially here the abbot needs those 'with whom he can confidently share his burdens' (21.3), he needs indeed the discreet collaboration of all the brethren. The abbot alone cannot do everything. He may do the wrong things. His emotions, including negative ones, may be so aroused, that it is essential he be steadied by counsellors and act through others. In the opening verses of chapter 27, there is, so to speak, an orderly mobilization of the whole community in care of the sick brother. The abbot is called to put on the clothes of a physician of souls (1–2), but this means in the first place sending in *senpectae*, acting through others (2–3), and in the second place the love and prayer of all (4). Ultimately, the psychologically, morally sick and suffering brother is the concern of all (cf. 28.4). When he is not, the likelihood of a sad ending is increased. When he is, there can be a sure and certain hope of a happy ending. Love will be 'strengthened towards him' (27.4) and come back to life in him. A healthy community communicates health. As the moral health of our communities can be judged on their care of the physically sick, so as regards the 'erring brethren'.

Then there follow the chapters which, I've suggested, belong in a special way to the cellarer, chapters 31ff. He is, says St Benedict, 'to be like a father to the whole community' (31.2). Abbot Denis Huerre once wrote that, in the monastery, there are 'three poles of spiritual fatherhood', that of the abbot, the cellarer and the novice master. In a sense, the fatherhood of the cellarer is exercised in the material realm. It is centred on the *table*. It consists in 'offering' (interesting word!) 'the brethren their appointed allowance of food without any arrogance or delay' (31.16), in distributing material necessities to each according to need (34), in arranging much of the daily work perhaps, in being 'the centre of the whole domestic economy' as our Constitutions say. But all that is more than merely material. The biblical profile of the cellarer is found in the deacon of the Pastoral Epistles, those Epistles so conscious of the Church as the 'house of God' (1 Tim. 3:15), the living God. The ministry of the cellarer and his assistants is ordered to the welfare of this house, to its freedom from disturbance and sadness (31.18), in other words its building up in peace and joy. In the centre of the chapter on the cellarer comes the saying that 'a good word is above the best gift' (31.14). This is an exercise of fatherhood in a full sense.

Looking at these chapters as part of the *Rule for monks*, they continue – needless to say! – the *Tale of Quisquis*. His heart has been expanded, he has emerged from the crucible of humiliation, he has become a man of praise and prayer. And now he is also inwardly free to serve his brethren in love – according to Galatians 5:13, to wash feet. He can give himself not only to the first impossible command that presides over the life of the cenobitic monk: 'pray without ceasing', but to the second one too: 'love one another as I have loved you' (Jn 13:34). And in these chapters it becomes clear what this love entails: honour and service.

This leads to chapter 53, 'On the Reception of Guests'. A beautiful chapter, a very contemporary chapter also, in the sense of one to whose values we are especially sensitive. So, the last of the five calls recognized by the General Chapter was that of making our monasteries clearly identified, clearly Christian places of hospitality.

Since the nineteenth-century restoration of monastic life, how many literary people and philosophers have been marked, sometimes profoundly, by a connection with a monastery, by the experience of being a guest in a monastery – even Tolstoy and Dostoevsky. How many 'ordinary' people have been sustained, or simply transformed, by the experience. It has been a *blessing* for them, and yet at least as much a blessing for us. Hospitality is a mystery of reciprocity; it is – in St Augustine's astonishing phrase – 'the one Christ loving himself' (*unus Christus amans seipsum*). 'Welcome one another, therefore, as Christ has welcomed you, for the glory of God' (Rom. 15:7). Rightly practised, it does not erode, but confirms our monasticity. It is an instance, not of a vicious circle, but of a virtuous one. Great is the mystery of hospitality!

The chapter begins with a statement of principle: 'Let all guests that come be received like Christ, for he will say: "I was a stranger and you took me in." And let fitting honour be shown to all, especially to those of the household of the faith and pilgrims' (1–2). There is an emphasis on 'all'. The word opens each of the first two verses. If there are distinctions to be made within the 'all', they are Christological rather than conventional. Those of the household of the faith that is, clergy and religious, pilgrims (or better, foreigners, people away from home) and the poor (15) are to be 'especially' received. Why? Because of their objective closeness to Christ.

Three things strike me here. First, courage. Sixth-century Italy was a disturbed place, the monastery would not have had means of defence, there were no police to summon ... Sometimes our African monasteries are in similarly vulnerable situations. Yet 'all' are to be welcomed. And what of the economic aspect? Would there be enough food? In the West, hospitality generally 'pays'; it is lucrative. At Pluscarden, we do not make a formal charge, and several give nothing, but still the guesthouse brings us 20% of our income. I doubt if that would have been the case in sixth-century Italy. It's not in Africa now. The 'all' was not a passport to wealth. Secondly, there is something eschatological here. The openness is not any openness, nor a merely human openness. As a matter of fact, it is unlikely that St Benedict would have received the heretics, the Arians, of his day. It is an openness to Christ, and specifically to the Christ who will come. Intriguingly, the text does not say, 'for Christ said, "I was a stranger ..."', but 'for he will say (*dicturus est*)' (1), that is when he 'comes in his glory, and all the angels with him' (Mt. 25:31). On the twelfth step of humility, the monk is seen already inwardly present at the judgement (7.64). Here, in a sense, the whole community is called to stand ready for this judgement, for the parousia.

Hospitality is eschatology in practice. 'I was a stranger and you welcomed me' (Mt. 25:35). Any guest may be the last we see of Christ in this life, the last before he comes in person. Hospitality is the sign of our vigilance. It's a sign that we haven't, with our 'Benedictine order', taken Christ prisoner, that we have left him his freedom. 'It is not for you to know times or seasons' (Acts 1:7). 'Watch, therefore – for you do not know when the master of the house will come, in the evening, or at midnight, or at cockcrow, or in the morning – lest he come suddenly and find you asleep' (Mk 13:35-36). It is even possible to read the 'liturgy of welcome' which follows in vv. 3-15 as a rehearsal for the welcome due the Christ of the parousia. Third, a word on 'those of the household of the faith'. They are to be 'especially' received. Among them are priests. It was Paul VI, on the basis of his own experience with the French monks in exile, during his youth, near Brescia, who encouraged us to be especially welcoming to priests. I think he's right. 'Let honour be shown.' In the past, the clergy perhaps received too much honour. But not now. For them just to have the gift of their priesthood acknowledged, honoured, welcomed can be a very healing thing.

We next come to what I've called the 'liturgy of welcome' (vv. 3-14). It should be looked at as a whole. It unfolds in three stages:

- at the monastery door (presumably), with a greeting, prayer, the kiss of peace;
- in the oratory, with prayer, and reading;
- in the refectory, with washing of hands and feet, accompanied by song, and followed by a meal.

This liturgy – the word is legitimate, I hope – seems to echo that of the Eucharist: introductory rites, reading, meal. The meeting of the guest takes the form of the meeting of Christ. And, as I say, it anticipates the final going forth to meet the coming Lord.

Nowadays, of course, we do not, cannot celebrate this liturgy *tel quel*, but it still has much to teach us. What the Rule concentrates in one hour, it seems to me, is what is now to be offered and received during the whole stay of a guest. That is one way, anyway, to 'read' this text. At the same time it is striking how St Benedict does concentrate everything into this first moment; there is no doubt that the first encounter, first impressions are decisive. Afterwards though – again it's remarkable – he *leaves the guest free*. Nothing is asked of him. And there is a lesson for us in this silence. We need to echo it in our reception of the guest.

Behind this liturgy stands Abraham, the great biblical icon of hospitality, celebrated so eloquently by St John Chrysostom, for example. Even though he was in his 90s, even though it was the hottest time of the day, he, like the brethren in this chapter, ran to meet the three men, prostrated before them, washed their feet, brought them to a meal (Gen. 18:1ff.). And yet this visit brought him fatherhood. Once again, reciprocity.

Behind this liturgy stands also the practice of the Desert Fathers, especially as recorded in the *Historia Monachorum*, and especially as practised by Abba Apollonius. In Judaism and Christianity, we see a human, Oriental, Bedouin 'good' taken up and filled by the presence of the living God, and of Christ. Hospitality is a place where the human and divine meet.

In the first stage of his welcome, St Benedict calls, among other things, for prayer before the peace, 'because of diabolical illusions' (5). This was good monastic tradition. It is a reminder that a discernment is always needed. 'Test the spirits to see if they are of God.' A briefer discernment than in the case of the novice in chapter 58, but still a discernment. The devil can try to visit monasteries, to 'disturb the brethren' (16). In other words, the meeting must really be with Christ. There can be no peace with the Adversary. There are also certain forms of behaviour, approved by society perhaps, but which we cannot endorse in a Christian place.

In the second stage (8–9), there is mention of the superior, or the one appointed by him, *sitting* with the guests (8). That means being with, being on the same level as, giving time to them. There is mention of prayer and the reading of the 'divine law'. The question for us is, how do we 'lead' our guests, induct them, into our liturgy and into *lectio*?

'And afterwards let all humanity be shown him' (9b). This is the third stage. 'Humanity' is what the Maltese showed Paul and his companions after their shipwreck (Acts 28:2) – the guest may be an apostle as well as Christ! *Humanitas* is a meal – we are in the refectory now – and it follows a reading of the *divine* law. So something divine and something human is to be shown the guest. We come back to reciprocity. On the one hand, the guest is Christ, yes. On the other, the receiving community too must be Christ, divine and human, God and man. Christ meets Christ, the 'one Christ loving himself'. And both the divinity and the humanity, so to speak, of the Church's mission are to enfold the guest: prayer and the word on the one hand, washing and food on the other, the spiritual and the physical. Julian of Norwich, whom Thomas Merton called the 'most charming of the English mystics' and the greatest, used two English words especially to describe Christ, one of French origin and knightly, the other of Germanic origin and domestic. Christ is at once 'courteous' and 'homely' (that is, friendly, familiar), at once the gracious Lord and the intimate Friend.

> For our courteous Lord willeth that we be as homely with him as heart can think or soul can desire. But we must beware lest we take this homeliness so recklessly as to forsake courtesy. Our Lord himself is sovereign homeliness. But as homely as he is, even so courteous he is: for he is very Courtesy. And he wants the blessed creatures who will be with him in heaven for ever to be like himself in all things.[2]

And it seems St Benedict wants monastic hospitality to be like this too, to be like Christ, to combine these apparent opposites. And so lead the guest into an experience of the homely courtesy of Christ. Indeed, Julian – a quite extraordinary figure, really – may be a good guide here, for in fact her emphasis falls more particularly on the 'homely love' of Christ. And perhaps now, when so many people are *déracinés*, a monastic community can provide a stable experience of the 'homely love' of Christ, can provide what Martha, Mary and Lazarus gave Jesus in Bethany. 'You are my family,' a guest of ours once said. We remember the Togolese teenager who

visited Dzogbegan in its early days, and who was, to his aston-
ishment, simply asked to sit down and eat with the white
monks of En-Calcat. He is now Père Martin. How can we
wash the feet of guests? For the ancients, this was not just a
practical courtesy, but a sacramental for the soul as well – in
the beautiful words of the *Historia monachorum* 'washing
away the hardships of human life by a traditional mystery'
(XXI). We can try that, can we not?

There is also the passing note on fasting (10–11). It too, it
seems to me, holds deeper meanings. There are some days of
fasting, mentions St Benedict, that not even the superior can
break – that is, those days that belonged to the whole Church.
As our hospitality must be in accord with Christ, so it must be
in accord with the Church. And as it can show the 'homely
love' of Christ, so often it can show a face of the Church that
is less easily seen, perhaps, in the parish or on the news. The
monastery, at its best, reveals the Church as a communion of
love and prayer.

Then comes the climax of it all: the entire community
gathered around the guest, singing, 'We have received, O
Lord, your mercy in the midst of your temple' (14; Ps. 47:10).
What an experience this whole ritual must have been for a
simple, rough sixth-century visitor to Subiaco or Monte
Cassino! This is, I think, the only time in the Rule the
monastery is called God's Temple. And it is the reception of
the guest that makes it such! Many guests, so to speak, sing
this psalm-verse to us after their stay; they say they have
received God's mercy in God's house. And, thank God, it is
true. It's sometimes said that if a monk doubts the value of the
monastic life, let him go and work in the guesthouse and listen
to the guests. But we too, when we receive a guest, receive
God's mercy, and the monastery at that moment becomes the
dwelling-place of God. 'Today salvation has come to this
house', and we are 'sons of Abraham' (Lk. 19:9). Truly, great
is the mystery of hospitality!

On the verses that follow (16–24) I just want to say, against
one interpretation, that they should not be read as virtually
contradicting what has gone before, as if St Benedict lost his
enthusiasm. Rather, they follow, I believe, the pattern of

chapter 36 on the care of the sick. There, after general principles, come practical provisions: an infirmarian, an infirmary,
baths, meat. Here come a 'table' (16), a guesthouse (21–22),
a guestmaster (21). And the aspect of protection of the life of
the community: of its fasting (11), of its regularity (16), of its
silence and separation (23–24), is also, of course, part of
hospitality itself. Guests are looking for a house of God, not a
guesthouse; they want to share a life, not diminish it.

At the very end (24), there is this almost charming vignette:
if one of the brethren should meet or even see a guest, he is
to greet him humbly, ask a blessing and explain the restraints
he is under. And there is this wonderful Latin phrase: *et petita
benedictione pertranseat*, 'he asks for a blessing and continues
on his way'. We connect back to *Quisquis*! He *asks* for a blessing from the guest; it is the guest who blesses the monk, not
vice versa. And strengthened by that blessing *pertranseat*, let
him pass on. He continues his *transitus* from this world to the
Father, but he continues it now – *pertranseat* – with more
energy thanks to the sustenance received from the guest. This
is beautiful! Here we have the whole meaning for us monks of
friendship and of hospitality: it blesses, vitalizes us so that we
may continue our monastic life, our own, quite personal,
search for God, our journey, as a poor pilgrim, with Christ to
the house of the Father, where one day we too hope to be
welcomed. *Suscipe me, Domine*!

In the daily life of the community, 'increase of reward and
charity is acquired' (35.2), and many transitions take place.
Quisquis is given the opportunity to move

- from the illusion of omniscience and omni-competence to a
  recognition of the need for others;
- from isolationism to brotherhood;
- from narcissism to self-forgetfulness;
- from self-defence to availability;
- from insistence on 'talents' to an inwardly free use of 'gifts'
  (Jean Vanier);
- from immaturity to a sense of responsibility;
- from barrenness to unexpected fruitfulness;
- from negativity to balanced assessments;

- from anger to patience;
- from judgementalism to compassion;
- from envy to appreciation of the gifts of others;
- from possessive anxiety over material things to dependence, trust and sharing;
- from murmuring to blessing (40.8);
- from the worship of the Christ of the Liturgy to the adoration of Christ in others (53.7).

> Whose feet then will you wash? Who will you care for? If you live by yourself, in comparison with whom will you be last? How will that good and pleasant thing, the dwelling of brethren together (compared by the Holy Spirit to ointment flowing down the high priest's head), be realised by living alone? So the living together of brethren is an athletic arena, a method of travelling forward, a continual exercise and practice of the Lord's commandments. It has as its object the glory of God.[3]

To conclude. When Simone Weil visited Solesmes, a young Englishman pointed her to what we call the Metaphysical poets, English Christian poets of the seventeenth century. So she came to know and cherish the poem *Love* of George Herbert (1593–1633). It is a conversation between Christ the Host and man the Guest. We all need the hospitality, the homely love, of Christ.

> Love bade me welcome: yet my soul drew back,
> Guilty of dust and sin.
> But quick-eyed Love, observing me grow slack
> From my first entrance in,
> Drew nearer to me, sweetly questioning,
> If I lacked anything.
>
> 'A guest, I answered, worthy to be here.'
> Love said, 'You shall be he.'
> 'I the unkind, ungrateful? Ah my dear,
> I cannot look on Thee.'
> Love took my hand, and smiling did reply,
> 'Who made the eyes but I?'

'Truth, Lord, but I have marred them: let my shame
Go where it does deserve.'
'And know you not,' says Love, 'who bore the blame?'
'My dear, then 1 will serve.'
'You must sit down,' says Love, 'and taste my meat.'
So I did sit and eat.[4]

Notes

1. Congregation for Institutes of Consecrated Life, *Fraternal Life in Community*, 39.
2. Julian of Norwich, *Revelations of Divine Love*, ch. 77.
3. St Basil, *Longer Rules, 7*.
4. George Herbert, 'Love Bade me Welcome'.

15

Receive Me, Lord

Suscipe me, Domine, secundum eloquium tuum, et vivam; et non confundas me ab expectatione mea. 'Receive me, Lord, according to your promise, and I shall live; and do not disappoint me in my hope.' (Ps. 118:116)

Last time, we looked at the reception of guests, according to chapter 53. This time, I would like to look at chapter 58, the reception of brethren. Chapter 53 begins with a liturgy of welcome; chapter 58 ends with a liturgy, the liturgy of reception into the community. As regards the deeper story line or plot, both of these chapters have to do with building the house of God (*Rule for monasteries*) and with the enlarging of the heart (*Rule for monks*).

I will focus on the second half of chapter 58, vv. 17ff., that is, the liturgy of profession. St Benedict does not quite give us a liturgical order of profession – there are some things we would like to know that he doesn't tell us – but still there is an outline, a movement. For what follows, I am much indebted to Sr Aquinata Böckmann.

To begin with the context. The context of time, first of all. Earlier in chapter 58, we find several indications of time, of duration: four or five days, a few days, two months, six months, four months, the year of novitiate, but then these cease, and all we hear, three times, is 'from that day', that is, of profession (vv. 15, 23, 25). So, clearly, this day marks a new beginning, like the day of birth, of baptism, of marriage, of death. It marks a certain overcoming of succession. It is rather like the 'henceforth' of the *Magnificat*. It suggests the 'fullness of time'. From now on the monk lives *from/ex* this day, from its strength. Something similar happens as regards place. First outside the monastery door, then the guesthouse, then the novitiate, but now the oratory and the altar. The one to be received has come to the praying heart of the monastery. And then, of course, we remember how, for the Fathers, both 'altar' and 'day' conjure up, represent Christ. From now on, the monk's place is Christ and his light is Christ. 'Abide in me and I in you' (Jn 15:4). 'I am the light of the world; he who follows me will not walk in darkness, but will have the light of life' (Jn 8:12).

In what follows, in the rite St Benedict describes, it's possible to see seven stages.

1. The first is the **promise**. 'In the oratory before all he will *promise* ...' (17–18). A promise is a pledge regarding the future, an extension of responsibility through time, in this case *usque ad mortem*. G. K. Chesterton once wrote: 'The vow is to the man what the song is to the bird, or the bark to the dog; his voice whereby he is known.' He also wrote this:

> A man's soul is as full of voices as a forest; there are ten thousand tongues there like all the tongues of the trees: fancies, follies, memories, madnesses, mysterious fears, and more mysterious hopes. All the settlement and sane government of life consists in coming to the conclusion that some of these voices have authority and others not. You may have an impulse to fight your enemy or an impulse to run away from him; a reason to serve your country; a good idea for making sweets or a better idea for poisoning them. The only test I know by which to judge one argument or inspiration from another is ultimately this: that all the noble necessities of man talk the language of eternity. When a man is doing the three or four things that he was sent on this earth to do, then he speaks like one who shall live for ever. . . There are in life certain immortal moments, moments that have authority.[1]

So this promise is made 'before all', 'before God and his saints'. It is a true 'profession', that is a 'speaking' (*fati*) 'in front of' (*pro*) others. It is a *homologia*. 'Every one who acknowledges me before men, I also will acknowledge before my Father who is in heaven' (Mt. 10:32), whereas 'if at any time he should do otherwise, let him know that he will be condemned by the one he mocks' (18).

It is a promise of stability, conversion of life and obedience. Surely the exegetes of the Rule are right to emphasize the mutually inclusive meanings of these words; each in its own way expresses the whole and implies the others. At the same time, the definitions given in our *Constitutions* – which distinguish more – are truly useful. At the same time too the understanding of the vows grows with the monk. They reveal fresh patterns.

A word on stability. It lends itself to many beautiful developments, certainly, even at the level of 'stability of place'. Perhaps, in an age of dislocation, *especially* at the level of stability of place. The monk is called to be a tree beside the waters, his roots going deep and taking up that water into his life and his prayer. The Liturgy, we say, sanctifies time; there is a holy chronology. Stability sanctifies place; there is also a geography of God. In the music of Sibelius, Finland sings; in the novels of Charles Dickens, London's many voices speak; in Gauguin, Tahiti. 'If the roots of your art are firmly planted in your own soil and that soil has anything to give you, you may still gain the whole world and not lose your own souls,' said Vaughan Williams, a British composer of the twentieth century. In a monastery, a definite *land* comes before God and becomes prayer before him. Especially after a monk has died, one looks back and sees how he incarnated something of the spirit of this place. In each monk, a corner of creation is brought back to God. (In the oldest version of our *Constitutions*, there was the delightful prescription that the cellarer was not to cut down a tree without the permission of the abbot!).

Then there are the martyr-monks of Tibhirine (Mt Atlas). For them stability grew to mean persevering in the monastic life *among the people* to whom one has been sent. Jesus could have gone to the Gentiles, and might not have been crucified, but 'I was sent only to the lost sheep of the house of Israel' (Mt. 15:24). The Trappists chose to stay with their Algerians, even at the risk of death. But what has grown on me is the equation of stability and love of the brethren, *stabilitas in congregatione*. What was the stability of Jesus? Stability in the will of the Father: 'the Father is in me and I am in the Father' (Jn 10:38). Yes, but this translated into 'having loved his own who were in the world, he loved them to the end' (Jn 13:1): these Twelve, 'those who have continued with me in my trials' (Lk. 22:28). And so for us. Stability is perseverance in the monastic life, not to shake one's neck from the yoke of the Rule, *stabilitas cordis*, 'stability of heart', but this life and this Rule are the life and Rule lived here; they are intrinsically cenobitic. So St Anselm will speak of 'setting down roots of love' in the monastery of one's profession, and there 'refraining from judging the behaviour of others' (*Letter* 37). Stability is love of the brethren, and Benedict, who began as a hermit, died with his failing limbs supported by the arms of his brethren.

By the promise of stability, I attach myself to this monastic family; by the promise of conversion of life, I strive to walk to God through the way of life lived by this community, with brethren, as a cenobite; by the promise of obedience, I make myself available to serve among my brethren in whatever way is allotted me. If I ask myself, why do I want to continue as a monk, it does, I think, come down to these things. It would be an act of violence to separate my poor, small faith, hope and love of Christ from this place, these faces, this life, this work.

2. There comes next the writing of the **petitio** (19–20), the promise put on parchment, and therefore with its solemnity and seriousness underlined. What is also suggestive here, though, is the very word *petition*. The one promising is a petitioner. The one promising is coming before God *asking*, with a prayer. The promise, the first act, now becomes a prayer. Profession is not the act of a moral Titan, so to speak: lifting up his life and putting it where he chooses. It is not simply an act of self-consecration motivated by charity, as our modern theology likes to say. It is, for St Benedict, above all a prayer, therefore above all a hope. And so . . .

3. The petition is placed on the altar; there is a **deposition** (20b). This surely is the central act of the rite. The altar is

Christ, and the petition, the hope of the soul, is placed upon him. It is placed 'by his [the novice's] hand.' 'Christ is held,' said Paschasius Radbertus, 'by the hand of hope. We hold him and are held. But it is a greater good that we are held by Christ than that we hold him. For we can hold him only so long as we are held by him' (*On Faith, Hope and Charity*, II, 1). The novice puts the petition, his aspiration, on the altar, so that it be taken up by Christ, consecrated by him, acknowledged by him before the Father.

4. Then he sings the *Suscipe* . . . (21–22), and three times the 'whole congregation' repeats the verse. The promise has become a petition, the petition has been placed on the altar and now is confirmed by a prayer. Here even more explicitly profession is revealed as a prayer, as a hope: 'And do not disappoint me in my hope.' It is the prayer and the hope of one bringing an offering so as to be at peace with God. The *Suscipe* is a Prayer over the Gifts, an Offertory prayer. (One has only to consult a concordance of liturgical Latin to see the link.) It is therefore expressing the hope of a transforming action of God and of eventual communion with him. It is also the prayer of the child, of the poor, of the stranger. 'I was a stranger and you took me in, *suscepistis me.*' It is asking Christ the Father to stoop down and pick up this child, this poor man, this stranger, this lost sheep – to acknowledge him – to take him into his house, his family, not to leave him to die outside, alone and hungry in the cold. 'And I shall live.' It is asking Christ to lean against us (the sense of the Hebrew), uphold us, carry us through the ups and downs of our journey to the house of the Father. The *Suscipe* is a prayer into which a monk can put his whole heart, his whole life; it sums up everything. It opens up, at the end of each day, at the end of our life, the possibility of entering into Mary's *Magnificat* and singing with her: *Suscepit Israel puerum suum.*

You know perhaps this beautiful prayer from St Ambrose:

Seek me, because I search for you. Seek me, find me, lift me up, carry me. You are able to find the one you seek. In kindness lift him up when you have found him; and when lifted up, place him on your shoulders... So come, and seek your sheep no longer through mere servants, nor hirelings, but through yourself. Lift me up in that flesh which fell in Adam. Lift me up, not from Sarah, but from Mary: who is not only a pure virgin, but a virgin who, through grace, is perfectly free from every stain of sin. Carry me on your cross... [And I shall live] because the person whom goodness carried on his shoulders cannot die.[2]

How can he not live, when eternal life has lifted him up, when Christ has assumed him totally to himself, when he belongs totally to the Word and his life is hidden in Christ Jesus?[3]

We are here at the climax of this whole liturgy: the petition on the altar, the novice singing the *Suscipe*, the whole community responding, the common *Gloria* – the praise of the Trinity. 'Who is the man who wants life? ... See, in his loving kindness the Lord shows us the way of life ... Uphold me, Lord, and I shall live.'

5. Up to this point in the rite, the novice has had the initiative: promising, petitioning, putting on the altar, praying. It has been an upward and Godward movement, a going up to the altar. Now the movement changes. The monk-to-be turns to the brethren, prostrating at the feet of each, and in answer the action of others, the brethren, the abbot, comes to the fore. And in a sense what happens in the final three actions represents a response to the prayer of the first four. There is a descending movement answering the ascending one. First comes the **prayer of the brethren** (23). In a modern rite of profession, there is a prayer of consecration said by the abbot. Here each of the brothers is asked for prayer. This prayer of the brethren represents the acceptance on the part of the brethren of the new member; it is a sacramental sign, even, of the acceptance on the part of Christ.

As with the liturgy for the reception of a guest, so with the liturgy of the reception of a monk. It is, in one sense, the liturgy of an hour, but in another the liturgy of a life. So we are always to carry one another in prayer, and by doing so echo the acceptance of Christ. In chapters 27 and 28, in relation to the errant brother, there is the prayer of abbot and community for him. In chapters 44, when the errant, excommunicated monk is returning to the fold, he is to 'throw himself at the feet of the abbot and then of all, so that they might pray for him' (44.4). His acceptance is renewed. To love someone is to accept them, to welcome them into our life. And therefore into our prayer. The novice makes profession, as I said, at the praying heart of the community, in the oratory. The setting of the rite is a sign of what is happening. But just as each of us must confirm, even daily, the choice of an abbot, so each of us must confirm the profession of a brother (even if we did not vote for him!). We confirm the election of our abbot by listening to him, by obedience. We confirm the profession of a brother by praying for him, by allowing him to enter the sanctuary of our prayer. Already, we had echoed his *Suscipe*, praying with him. We do that again every time we stand next to each other in choir. But now, we pray for him.

There is here a vital question of translation. For the first time in this chapter (leaving aside the title) the word 'brother' is used. The question is what does the following word *novicius* mean? Does it mean 'novice'? No, it seems it means 'new'; it is an adjective. In which case, it is *at this moment*, before the altar, in the midst of the prayer of his brothers, that *Quisquis*, a 'new brother', is born. As human beings, we are brothers and sisters thanks to our common humanity. As Christians, we are brothers thanks to the font, to baptism. As cenobitic monks, we are brothers thanks to the altar, to profession. And our prayer for one another is the living confirmation of that, the prime expression of brotherly love. 'And from that day let him be accounted one of the community'.

6. There follows the **change of clothing** (24–28). We know the significance of this in liturgical tradition. It is the original act, sign, symbol of becoming a monk. It is a putting off of the old man, a putting on of the new, of Christ. What is peculiarly striking in St Benedict's presentation is his phraseology. The new brother 'puts off his *own things* ... and is clothed with *the things of the monastery*' (26). Earlier, in chapter 33, the monk was told 'to look to the father *of the monastery* for everything' (33.5). This is the heart of monastic poverty. It is

not deprivation; it is dependence. It is not starvation; it is eating from the common table. As the prayer of the brethren is a sacrament of the good will of Christ, so the provision of the monastery is a sacrament of the providence of the Father. And as I am willing to 'put on' the things of the monastery, so I am happy to 'put off' my own desires in order to serve my brethren, to wash their feet, knowing that 'from this day I do not have authority over my own body'. This is why every failure in poverty is a failure in fraternal charity; it is tacit contempt.

7. Lastly, almost surreptitiously, there is an act of the abbot: the **taking of the petition from the altar.** It is only the second mention of the abbot in this whole rite. He takes the petition – symbol of the gift, the prayer, the hope of the monk – and keeps it in the monastery. Perhaps one could see in that a symbol of the role of the abbot. This 'taking' represents his – and, yes, Christ's – acceptance of the brother, as did the prayer of all above. As the abbot takes and preserves the petition, so he must take and preserve in his heart the 'new brother', and above all the essence, so to speak, of this brother, the best of him: his hope, his expectation. In a sense, the first *abba* in St Benedict's life was Romanus who discovered him in his solitude. And Gregory says this of him: 'And when he had come to know of his [Benedict's] desire, he both kept the secret and gave help' (*Dialogues* II, 1). It is the task of the abbot from the moment he takes the petition from the altar. This is how he joins in the *Suscipe* of this monk, this man, this soul.

So there is one outline of these verses, with their seven steps, their ascending and descending, their going up to the altar and their coming down. What is so striking is how much, for the Rule, profession is a prayer, and is therefore the expression of a desire to live, a looking forward to eternal life. In fact, the word profession is not found in this chapter, and the word used for the one making profession is simply 'the one who is to be received' (*Suscipiendus*, v. 17), ultimately into the house of the Father. And what is striking, secondly, is how this prayer is sustained by the response of the community: the prayer of the brethren, the provision of clothing, the responsibility of the abbot. One could say these are provisions for the journey.

At the same time, a silence remains, does it not? The silence of God's patience, God's expectation. A silence for our hope, our conversion, our perseverance.

There is one last thought, going back to context. The context, everything suggests (as in chapter 59), is the celebration of the Eucharist. 'From this day' the monk is in a new relation with the altar, with the Eucharist. It becomes, in a new way, light and food for his journey, daily bread, comfort, sustenance. It becomes, like Mary, his life, his sweetness and his hope. Christ accepts, receives us in the Eucharist.

There are three levels. At a first, the Eucharist is the Church's (and monastery's) daily deed in memory of Jesus, in imitation of the Supper. At a second, it is, as it were, a daily 'exaltation of the Holy Cross', proclaiming his death until he comes. It's the tree of life set up at the heart of the community. It shows us the way of life: 'Walk in love, as Christ loved us and gave himself up for us, a fragrant offering and sacrifice to God' (Eph. 5:2). Then at the third, for each and all of us who gather round this tree, it is *life*. 'And the bread which I shall give for the life of the world is my flesh' (Jn 6:51). 'Life' was the simple name for the Eucharist among the North Africans of St Augustine's day. Here is the sweet succour the monk needs:

> The mother can give her child to suck of her milk, but our precious Mother Jesus can feed us with himself, and does, most courteously and most tenderly, with the blessed sacrament, which is the precious food of true life; and with all the sweet sacraments he sustains most mercifully and most graciously... I am He [He said to Julian] whom Holy Church preaches and teaches to you. That is to say: All the health and the life of the sacraments, all the power and the grace of my word, all the goodness which is ordained in Holy Church for you, I am he.[4]

Let St Ambrose have the last word, concluding his comments on Ps. 118, v. 116, our *Suscipe*, our song of hope. For him too it is the Eucharist that sustains it.

If someone should say to you, 'What earthly use has your daily fasting been to you, your chastity of body, your purity of mind? You have been hurt just as much as the wicked and the godless', do not lose faith. For even when you are weak, faithful Christ is concerned for you. He says this to his disciples, 'Give them something to eat yourselves.' He was worried for fear that they might faint on the way. In Scripture [i.e., in the Liturgy of the Word] you have the food of the apostles. If you eat that, you will not faint. Eat it beforehand and then come to the food of Christ; to the food of the Lord's body, to the banquet of the Sacrament; to the cup by which the faithful soul is inebriated. In the Sacrament the soul is clothed in joy because her sins are forgiven. She shakes off the cares and anxieties of this life and the fear of death. Being drunk in this Sacrament does not make the soul stagger, but rise. The mind is not confounded, but consecrated.[5]

Suscipe me, Domine . . .

Notes

1. G. K. Chesterton, *The Uses of Diversity*.
2. St Ambrose, *Commentary on Ps 118*, XXII, 29–31.
3. St Ambrose, XV, 26.
4. Julian of Norwich, *Revelations of Divine Love*, 60.
5. St Ambrose, XV, 28

16

The Monastery and the Local Church[1]

Thank you for the opportunity to address this subject, and especially on such a memorable occasion – the golden jubilees of Abbot Albert and Br Egilhard.

For nineteen years I was Abbot of a Benedictine monastery in the diocese of Aberdeen in Scotland. Now I am the Bishop of the same diocese. So perhaps I have two eyes. It is also encouraging that, according to the *Dialogues* of Pope St Gregory the Great, St Benedict was the friend of a bishop, Germanus of Capua. When the latter died, St Benedict saw his soul on its way to heaven. Perhaps we can take this as a symbol: when there is a good relationship between a monastery and a local Church, it becomes possible to see something essential – the 'soul' of the matter. What follows is a small attempt to seek for this essential.

The Rule of St Benedict as Point of Reference

Let us look first at the Rule of St Benedict.

The word 'diocese' occurs once in the Rule (64.4). It's enough here to recall that the word 'diocese' is etymologically linked to the Greek word for 'house' (*oikos*). In the very next verse, St Benedict himself calls the monastery a 'house of God' (64.5). This immediately suggests that the diocese and monastery have something in common. In both, the mystery of the Church – the 'spiritual house' (1 Pet. 2:5), the 'dwelling place of God in the Spirit' (Eph. 2:22) – is realised, becomes visible.

In this passage from chapter 64, On the Appointment of an Abbot, St Benedict is speaking immediately about the election of the abbot:

> But if (which God forbid) the whole community should agree to choose a person who acquiesces in its vices, and if these somehow come to the knowledge of the bishop to whose diocese the place belongs, and to neighbouring abbots or Christians, let them foil the conspiracy of the wicked and set a worthy steward over God's house. Let them be sure that they will receive a good reward if they do this with a pure intention and out of zeal for God, just as, on the contrary, they will incur sin if they neglect to intervene (64.3–6).

Clearly the well-being of the monastery is a concern of the whole local Christian community: the bishop, other abbots, laity. The monastery is sick, it is in danger, and it is the duty of the local Church to come to its rescue, to heal it. This must certainly be done for the right motives. But the duty is so serious, it would be a sin to neglect it. One thinks of 1 Cor. 12:26: 'If one member suffers, all suffer together.' The implied link between monastery and local Church is here a very close one. They cannot be indifferent to one another. They are bound together in health and sickness.

In the Rule, the Bishop is mentioned three times: in the passage just quoted (64.4), in connection with a bad monastic priest (62.9), and in connection with the appointment of the Prior (65.3). I would like to touch on two aspects here.

First, in both chapters 64 and 65, the context is *ordinatio*. This word may refer to the Sacrament of Ordination, or more generally to any appointment. Its literal meaning is: insertion into an order. The Rule suggests that a Bishop is intimately involved in this whole reality of *ordinatio*, that he has some role to play in the *ordo* of the monastery.

In St Benedict's time, few abbots were ordained as priests. Nowadays it is a canonical requirement. And a Bishop becomes involved in the life of the monastery at two moments particularly:

- the ordination of any members to the diaconate or priesthood. Here is a reminder to the monastery that it is not a self-sufficient entity. It is an *ecclesiola in ecclesia*. It belongs to a greater whole. The word 'Catholic' etymologically means 'according to the whole' (*kath holon*). The coming of a Bishop to a community to ordain one of its members enables the monastery to experience its belonging within the 'great *ordo*' of the Church. It is a reminder of the ecclesial nature of the monastic mission.
- the liturgical blessing of an abbot or abbess. This is normally celebrated by the local Bishop. Of the Sacramentals (as distinct from the Sacraments) which a Bishop celebrates, the first listed in the *Ceremonial of Bishops* (1984) is precisely this Blessing. And n. 668 of the *Ceremonial* says this: 'The blessing of an abbot is usually celebrated by the bishop of the place where the monastery is situated. In this way the bishop has a part in one of the high points of monastic life. By example, work, and prayer, monasteries should contribute solid support to the life of the particular Church; correspondingly, the bishop should regard the monasteries of his diocese as an important part of his pastoral office, even though he must not interfere in their internal government.' In the liturgy of Abbatial Blessing, a Bishop prays for the new Abbot that he will have the qualities necessary for his mission. It has been said that the grace given through this rite is that of spiritual fatherhood. And the Bishop hands him the Rule, a ring, a mitre and a crozier. And thus the Abbot enters the *ordo* of abbots and the monastery is strengthened. The house of God is built up, and once again the monastery is reminded of its 'ecclesiality'. It is not an insignificant part of a Bishop's ministry.

Secondly, I'd like to underline a final phrase from the Rule: *episcopi ad cuius diocesim pertinet locus ipse* (64.4) – literally, 'the bishop to whose diocese the place itself belongs'. I notice that one renowned English translation makes no attempt at all to translate *pertinet*, and simply says 'the local bishop', omitting 'diocese' too! One German translation has, 'die betreffende Dioezese', 'the diocese concerned' one would say in English. But in Late Latin the word *pertinere* means 'to belong'. So, for St Benedict, the monastery – the place itself – 'belongs' to the diocese. We are not talking about property or ownership here, but something more profound; in the first place a responsibility and, underlying that, the mystery of common life. At the very least, the monastery is an integral part of the diocese in which it is placed

Canonically most contemporary Benedictine monasteries are what is called 'exempt', that is withdrawn from the jurisdiction of the local Bishop and subject to that of the Pope (*Lumen Gentium*, 45, *Christus Dominus*, 35, *Code of Canon Law*, 591, 732). The Bishop, consequently, should not interfere in the interior workings of a monastery. And correspondingly, monks by their vow of obedience, submit themselves to their Abbot, not to the local Bishop. However, as regards 'the care of souls, public worship and works of the apostolate', monks are subject to the authority of the local Bishop (*Christus Dominus*, 35, *Code of Canon Law*, 678, 738/2).

What, however, the whole ecclesiology of Vatican II suggests, what the phrase of 64.4 and especially the use of the word *pertinere* suggest, and what other indications of the Rule point to is something deeper. The relationship between a monastery and a local Church is best seen in the light of the Pauline understanding of the Church as a body with many members, each with their specific function, but working in harmony one with another and, more essentially still, *belonging* to each other.

We are led especially to Romans 12:3–8 and to 1 Corinthians 12:12–26.

Perhaps most pertinent is Rom. 12:5: 'So we, though many, are one body in Christ and individually members one of another', or as the Jerusalem Bible has it: 'So all of us, in union with Christ, form one body and as parts of it, we *belong* to each other.'

By virtue of their common belonging to / membership of Christ, the local Church and the monastery also belong to one another. 'In the mystery of the Church, unity in Christ implies a mutual communion of life among the members' (*Mutuae Relationes*, 1978, n. 2). There is a clear distinction between the monastery and the local Church, but not an opposition; rather a mutual indwelling made possible by the Holy Spirit. The external expression of this within the monastery itself lies in the celebration of the Eucharist. In the Eucharistic Prayer, day after day, the name of the Bishop of the place is mentioned.

Living Out Mutual Belonging

Out of this ontology there flows action; out of the mutual indwelling a common cooperation; out of the mutual belonging a mutual service. We pass now from the 'contemplative' to the 'active', to the practical.

What gifts, what services, does a monastery offer the local Church to which it belongs, and vice versa? Naturally, every local Church and every monastic community has its own situation which affects the ways in which it lives this relationship. Still, it is possible to make some generalizations.

First then, what might a monastery offer a local Church? Perhaps this question can be answered along the lines of the three monastic vows of stability, *conversatio morum* and obedience. Perhaps we can say that it is these a monastery offers.

1. The first vow of a monk is stability, and the first gift of a monastery to its local Church is its own stability. Much is implied in this: a simple 'being there', a fixity of place and buildings, the constancy of the life lived there, the perseverance of the brethren, the regularity of the liturgy. We are mobile creatures; modernity prioritizes movement and change. A monastery speaks rather of the 'still centre', or the *Stat Crux dum volvitur orbis*. It speaks of the things that do not pass away. For the clergy and laity of a diocese, it offers a stable point of reference, something familiar and known. The fact that monks remain there over a long period makes possible a continuity of relationship and a depth of friendship. A monk,

by his stability, is able to give a witness to a long, but, we trust, ultimately victorious struggle. It is a reminder that not everything good, true and beautiful can be accessed immediately, or even need be. So even the cemetery can be significant. Life can be seen as a whole. At a very practical level, a monastery may be able to offer facilities for meetings more easily than many other institutions in the diocese. It may well have a better library or bookshop. It may, like many monasteries in Italy and Spain and elsewhere, be a place of Marian pilgrimage, a focus of prayer and reconciliation for a wider area. A monastery often incorporates more of the world of nature than other ecclesiastical entities. Incorporating nature, it incorporates time, for nature is more patient than humanity. And good monks have time to listen to the Lord and to others.

2. The second vow of a monk, and the second gift of a monastery, is *conversatio morum*, that is, a striving for holiness. The Church can often appear as a 'business'; alas a monastery can too. But if good zeal reigns, what becomes visible in a monastery, in the very human humanity of its members and life, is the search for God, the primacy of discipleship, the universal call to holiness. And this becomes contagious. I knew of one diocese in which every seminarian had found his priestly vocation thanks to the local monastery. In 1 Corinthians 4:9, St Paul speaks of the apostles being 'a spectacle to the world'; so in a sense is a monastery. And so in a sense is each monk. Hence the huge offence or scandal caused when certain sins of monks are revealed. On the positive side, I recall the story of a young man driving past a monastery and deciding to pause and look in. It was all very quiet, deserted. He entered the church and saw one monk curled up in prayer in a corner. That was all he saw. Forty years later, he was driving past again. He broke his journey again. He entered the church. There in the same place and same posture was the same monk praying. I recall a young woman who suffered from depression. When this became acute she would ask her parents to take her to the monastery. The family never spoke to a monk. They did not attend the liturgy. They simply walked up and down the drive. And then she would say, 'I am better now. We can go.'

3. The third vow a monk takes, and the third aspect of the monastic gift to the local Church, is obedience. It may sound strange to suggest this. But obedience means listening and, on the basis of that listening, acting in communion with others.

But let me come at this from another angle. What a monastery offers to many Christians and non-Christians, to religious persons and those suspicious of religion, is a kind of discreet alternative. One might say – to use a contemporary phrase – that while in the parish there reigns the 'ordinary form' of the Church life; in the monastery, something other, a kind of 'extraordinary form'. In a monastery, the one Church shows a different face. The style of liturgy, the manner of preaching, the form of spiritual accompaniment may be other than that provided in parishes. Many feel quite at home in the latter, but others may not, and can find an ecclesial alternative in a monastery. Liturgy is especially an issue here.

But I am not thinking of liturgy only. In general, a monastery tends to attract a particular 'constituency'. It has a ministry and mission distinct from that of a parish. It can often be a sanctuary for those disaffected with the Church in general, or with the local Church, or simply with the local parish. These disaffected may be liberals impatient for change, disappointed at the conservative 'turn' within the Church, or they may be those of the opposite persuasion, who feel disinherited of rightful Tradition and still exposed to a fashionable liberalism which has now run out of steam. More widely, a monastery offers shelter to all sorts and conditions of men: tramps or alcoholics or the abused, seekers of the truth, or simply those hungry for quiet.

What a monastery offers here is a listening ear – at its best the fruit of the monks' own listening to the Word of God. The audibility of the latter – its proclamation in the church and the refectory and in the silence – is something very striking. And out of the listening to God's Word comes a capacity to listen to the human word, and to attune the latter to the former. A monastery can offer a listening that creates communion. It builds the unity of the Church, not by power or law or programmes, but by humility and respect for the truth. A monastery offers an ear, and this hearing leads to belonging. It creates communion. This is what I mean, here, by the gift of obedience.

What, on the other side, can a local Church offer a monastery? Anything? Or is the traffic all one way? Surely not! The Church, local and universal, is a mother. And she is a mother of, and to, monasteries. Let me just touch on a few aspects of this: this service which a local Church can offer to a monastery.

It is sometimes bishops who call for the setting-up of monasteries in their dioceses, and must at least always approve any new foundation. In this sense, monasteries are born, not just of the monasteries from which they come, but of the diocese where they come into being.

Then, there is a danger that monasteries think too highly of themselves, take on the face of the Pharisee more than the Publican. They can become overly preoccupied with their own life, perhaps especially their difficulties. They can become isolated, forgetting that in the Eucharistic Prayer they pray daily, it is not only the Pope who is mentioned by name but the local Bishop too, or forgetting both Pope and Bishop, and becoming a Church unto themselves! A healthy relation with the local Church prevents a monastic community becoming a sect.

At the same time, there is a danger that monasteries think too little of themselves. They see nothing but their problems: the empty choir stalls, the ageing, the diminishing, the lack of vocations. They can develop a death-wish. At this point, the intelligent (not just routine!) affirmation, the word that can come from local clergy and laity and religious or from the Bishop himself, can restore confidence to a community, if it will listen.

'I want to urge each one among you not to exaggerate his real importance. Each of you must judge himself soberly by the standard of the faith God has given him' (Rom. 12:3). It is part of the maternal function of the local Church to help a monastery find that sober judgement, between presumption and despair. We come back to the image of the Body and its members. The phrase *gaudium de veritate* – joy in the truth – comes to mind.

Then there is the sacramental aspect. I have already mentioned the need for a Bishop to ordain members of the community to the diaconate or priesthood or to bless a new abbot. The local Church is, in a sense, the mother of the sacramental life of the community. One could mention also the provision of faculties for the Sacrament of Reconciliation which come to the individual priest-monk through his abbot but ultimately from the Bishop. Again, local priests may function as external confessors to a community, and they or religious or lay persons provide spiritual guidance or support for monks.

Here too the local Church frees the monastery from the illusion of self-sufficiency. It allows it to take its true place, at once humble and special, within the totality of the Church.

I mentioned the role of a local Church and a bishop in the birth of a monastery. But monasteries die too. And it is when they are dying, reaching the end of their life-cycle, that a healthy relationship between the monastery and diocese, superior and bishop especially, is vital. Canonically, a bishop must be consulted before a monastery is closed (c. 616/1). But ideally the involvement will be greater. Questions will arise over the disposal or use of property and financial assets, over the dispersion and future mission of the monks. These are matters where disputes naturally arise and where healthy relationships can help avoid much pain.

In life and in death, we belong to the Lord and in the mystery of his Body we belong to one another in life and in death also. Let us say, *for* life! There, very simply, we glimpse the essence, the soul, of the relationship between monastery and local Church, abbot and bishop, Benedict and Germanus.

Note

1. Talk given at the Benedictine Monastery of Kornelimünster, Germany, 26 August 2012.

17

Mutual Obedience

Obedience is a blessing to be shown by all, not only to the abbot but also to one another as brothers, since we know that it is by this way of obedience that we go to God (71.1–2)

How does the chapter 71, On Mutual Obedience, work?

The first point is that this is a chapter in two parts. Only the first part – vv.1–5 – is strictly about mutual obedience. The second part, beginning from v.6, is about making satisfaction when reprimanded.

Each part, interestingly, ends with a penal clause: 'But if a person be found to be contentious let him be corrected.' In chapter 3, St Benedict had urged the monks not to 'contend' with their abbot. Here the point is extended: being contentious about obeying any senior deserves correction. Such a 'good' is obedience. Naturally if someone is going to be awkward about it, he must be sanctioned. Similarly, at the end of the second half, we hear 'Should he despise to do so, either let him be subjected to physical punishment, or if he be rebellious, let him be expelled from the monastery.' Such a good is making satisfaction when corrected – making up, reconciliation – that if someone despises it, well, if he does so contumaciously, he has no place in the monastery.

The two values it proposes: obedience and satisfaction, the two attitudes it encourages: willingness on a junior's part to obey any senior or to make satisfaction to any senior who actually or potentially corrects him, are both essential to monastic life, to community life.

This is the chapter before chapter 72 which is St Benedict's hymn to charity *à la* 1 Cor. 13. And it is already very close to it.

They are so essential to it that St Benedict is extending them beyond their primary meaning or reference. 'The good of obedience' is to be shown not only to the abbot but to all, or at least by any junior to any senior. And satisfaction is to be made to the abbot, certainly, but also to any senior whomsoever who corrects a junior, in whatever way, public or private. This, we know, is the almost revolutionary ménage of this chapter.

And this is worth dwelling on. It seems adequately proven that St Benedict made much use of the Rule of the Master: RB follows RM. At the same time RB emancipates itself progressively from RM. From the beginning to chapter 7 the dependence is literal and practically total. From chapter 8 to chapter 66 the dependence is still there, but is far less marked. St Benedict is reworking in a free way, chapters 11 to 9 of the Master. He even feels moved to have another go, as it were, at topics he had already treated under the Master's tutelage. So, there is a second chapter on the abbot – by common consent, the richer of the two. Then finally, in the chapters 67 – 73, St Benedict's Rule loses all connection, and thematic, with RM. One can't help but think of the way in which many an artist has developed: at first he may imitate a master most closely, then progressively he emancipates himself, finding his own unique mode of expression. It's tempting – and a temptation one can yield to – to think of St Benedict as he writes his Rule progressively becoming, in the good sense, his own man. Add to this another thesis of the scholarship of the last forty years; viz that chapters 67 to 72 of the Rule are an 'appendix' written after the original Rule closed at chapter 66 (with probably the present chapter 73 attached). So the Rule went through more than one edition. And it is arguable that at the time of the second edition St Benedict did some touching up of the earlier chapters. So, once again, we can see that Benedict developed as a monastic thinker or legislator, as an abbot, that is.

Benedict had learnt his monasticism at the feet of the

Master, one – perhaps rather idiosyncratic – mouthpiece of tradition. But with the years and with experience came an enlarged awareness of the traditions. For example, there is no doubt that the monastic writings of St Augustine – very different in emphasis from that of the Master – came to loom larger in Benedict's mind. It is not that late Benedict contradicts early Benedict. The Rule is coherent from beginning to end. Benedict remains committed to the values he assimilated from the Master: the flight from sin, renunciation of one's own will, obedience, humility, patience, daily office, daily work, daily reading. What happens is that his understanding of these values extends. And more than that, I think: his understanding becomes increasingly Biblical and evangelical ('Gospel'). Benedict's monasticism, as the years pass, is evermore lit up from within by the Gospel, permeated by it. St Dominic: 'His spirit of fervour lent dynamism to all the observances'; he wanted the friars to see these 'as ways of living the Gospel'.

And here's a thought. Might not this development of Benedict be somehow a pattern for us, for the disciples of Benedict? Mightn't it be that his experiences are ours too? What holds a community like ours together is a common commitment to the monastic values and the basic monastic practices. Young, old and middle aged are bound into one by that. But the perceptions of each age-group, and of each individual, will vary; will, ideally (or spirally, as I said in another context), grow and develop; will, that is, enlarge and enlarge because ever more exposed to the light of the Gospel, under whose guidance we make our way.

To return to chapter 71. It illustrates what I've been trying to say. This is 'late' Benedict. Still intent on the journey to God, still keenly aware of human frailty, still committed to obedience. But at the same time there is a shift. 'The good of obedience', Benedict says. At the beginning of the Rule we have the phrase 'the labour of obedience'; at the end the phrase 'the good of obedience'. One could develop that. But so good does Benedict know obedience to be, that he wants to extend it as widely as he can: *non solum abbati exhibendum est*, 'it is to be shown not only to the abbot'; there is no precedent for this in the Master. Likewise, so much does he cherish the humble acknowledgement of one's failings, that he wants to extend this as widely as possible too: private satisfaction. And again, so much does he cherish the value of honouring, reverencing others that he wants every junior, by obedience and by acceptance of correction, to reverence every senior.

And these extensions, I think, are really an evangelization. Asceticism is not proper to the Gospel, love of brethren is. There is the famous picture of the old apostle John with nothing to say except, 'Little children, love one another.' St Thérèse of Lisieux said, towards the end of her short life, that only now was she beginning to realize the full meaning of mutual love. You may remember how Abbot Denis, on his deathbed, spoke of coming to see the brethren as the angels see them – a transfiguration. At least it was at the end of his life, in the Last Discourse, that the Lord spoke most explicitly about the mutual love of the brethren and about the Three Persons of the Godhead.

It seems to me that this is the Gospel light shining under, in and through the sentences of chapter 71. 'For the rest, that all the juniors obey their elders with all loving solicitude' . . . 'let him lie . . . doing satisfaction, until this upset is healed by a blessing' – a lovely phrase in the Latin, *usque dum benedictione sanetur illa commotio*, a healing, distilling of the waters in the power of a blessing. Imagine the junior rising to return to his work, energized and at peace.

But it is where we go back to the two patristic parts of this chapter that its full New Testament depth can emerge. They are the *Regula Basilii* (Latin edition), nos.13 and 64 and, more importantly, Cassian's Conference 16. *R. Bas.* is entitled: 'If we should obey anybody or everybody?' The text to which it points is Eph. 4:16 (via quote Eph. 4:2 in v.7). *R. Bas.* 64 is entitled: 'How should we obey one another?' The texts to which it points are Mk 10:43–45 and Gal. 5:13–16. When we come to Cassian we are in deeper waters. The Conference is on 'friendship', effectively on mutual harmony. 'Remaining in harmony is so lofty a good that nothing is to be preferred to it. God is love and nothing is to be put before love, just as nothing is to be put below anger. No sacrifice is too great to preserve the supreme good of love and to avoid the supreme evil of anger. One's own will must be given up, what seemed useful and necessary must be forsaken, even at the spiritual level. If one's brother is angered with one, even without reason, he is to be appeased by every means, with as much delicacy as we use in the healing of our own anger . . . Cassian, speaking from experience, doesn't baulk on this theme of the 'zeal and sincerity with which one must make up for the least offences.' Basil seems to provide the background to the chapter's first half, Cassian to the second.

Anyway, as de Vogüé says, Cassian's sixteenth conference is a 'long and beautiful commentary' on RB 71. We could do worse than reread it.

The Scriptures to which Cassian refers:

[Ch. 6] Acts 4:32: 'Now the whole group of those who believed were of one heart and soul, and no one claimed private ownership of any possessions, but everything they owned was held in common.'

Jn 6:38: 'I have come down from heaven, not to do my own will, but the will of him who sent me.'

Mt. 26:39: 'Not what I want, but what you want.'

Jn 13:35: 'By this everyone will know that you are my disciples, if you have love for one another.'

Mt. 6:23-24: 'So when you are offering your gift at the altar, if you remember that your brother has something against you, leave your gift there before the altar and go and first be reconciled with your brother and then come and offer your gift.'

[Ch. 11] Phil. 2:1-3: 'If then there is any encouragement in Christ, any consolation from love, any sharing in the Spirit, any compassion and sympathy, make my joy complete: be of the same mind, having the same love, being in full accord and of one mind. Do nothing from selfish ambition or conceit, but in humility regard others as better than yourselves.'

Rom. 12:10: 'Love one another with mutual affection; outdo one another in showing honour.'

[Ch.13] 1 Jn 4:16: 'God is love and those who abide in love abide in God, and God abides in them.'

Now it's not my purpose to dwell on how far, individually and collectively, we fall short of the ideal. Nor do I want to

explore how we, now, can take up Benedict's recommenda-
tions. Suppose you have been out shopping and, apart from all
else, spend one and a half hours in pouring rain trying in vain
four establishments for Br X's 18 in. power-driven, green-
painted grunching iron and on returning empty-handed are
abruptly called a lazy b. who has effectively reduced the
monastic economy to a standstill. Does one just flop to one's
knees? Or take it from a superior's point of view. Is there a
single monk whom he wouldn't like to take aside and say,
'Brother, I wonder if you have ever considered . . .'? But how
would the superior feel if his every slight irritation provoked
an immediate prostration? Again, when do we just let a misunderstanding remain, and when do we try to explain or
dialogue? When do we just put up with a defective relationship, and when do we try to repair it? It's an extremely difficult, delicate area. It's striking though that Cassian devotes a
fair chunk of Conference 16 to 'false patience' – by which he
means, in modern terms, sweeping relational difficulties under
the carpet often on pious pretexts: persisting then going to the
altar unreconciled. And certainly the difficulties in realizing
the ideal, or the prudence required, shouldn't in practice annul
it. If we don't as a community witness to the Trinity, what the
hell . . .

Chapter 71 is true, even humanly. Where there is true
mutual love, there will be mutual obedience and mutual
apology.

We can ask ourselves: how do I react when I'm presented
with a request (or have I perhaps made it quite clear that I'd
rather not be approached?)? How do I react when it's clear that
I've irritated someone, or when I realize a relationship is
getting distinctly sticky?

Chapter 71 is a call: to give way to one another, to restore
relationships that have been ruptured; to be attentive one to
another, to be sensitive to the needs and feelings of those we
live with. Not from self defence, not in order to manipulate by
kindness, but from 'solicitude' (the right kind of anxiety) and
love. Chapter 71 asks us to take the word of God and the
example of Christ seriously, and translate them into real, clear,
daily acts of self-giving and self-effacement. 'Quickly. Imme-

diately. Now' (Joan Chittister). And it can happen. It can catch on. It's possible, as Cassian says, for anger to evaporate in the ample chambers of an enlarged heart. It's possible to seek peace and pursue it.

In the last resort chapter 71 is Eucharistic and Trinitarian. The twentieth century has yielded death camps, enclosures which are hell on earth. The Balkans are two/three hours away. More Rwandans lost their lives in the recent genocide than Britons in World War II. So we ought to try and live the Gospels.

18

The Good Zeal of Monks

Just as there is a wicked zeal of bitterness which separates from
God and leads to hell, so there is a good zeal which separates from
evil and leads to God and everlasting life (72.1)

We come to chapter 72. It is something, we feel, of a Last
Testament, St Benedict's *Tempest* or Last Quartets or *Duino
Elegies*. It is almost a second edition of chapter 7.

It has always touched me that, here, at the end of his Rule
and perhaps of his life, St Benedict can still surprise. There is,
so to speak, a familiar Benedictine 'lexicon': obedience,
silence, humility, the fear of God, patience, stability, *opus
Dei*, *lectio divina*, manual work, etc. Then suddenly, a fresh
element appears: the *good zeal* which monks ought to have.
Previously, with one exception (64.6), zeal had only appeared
in the pejorative sense of jealousy. But now the positive sense
predominates, and claims a whole chapter. If St Benedict was
old when this came to him, it is comforting. God can still give
fresh perspectives whatever one's age. 'Planted in the house of
the Lord they will flourish in the courts of our God, / still
bearing fruit when they are old, still full of sap, still green'
(Ps. 91:14–15).

At the same time, this amazing chapter contradicts nothing
of what has gone before. Everything is seen through the lens
of love, or lived in love, but there is still need for patience,
obedience, chastity, fear of God, even an abbot. Above all, the
idea of life as a journey to Life, 'eternal life', still rules: good
zeal 'separates from vice, leads to God and to everlasting life'

(2), and at the end of the chapter we pray Christ will take us to the same (13). The fraternal relations which are so emphasized are integrated within the already established search for God. So, freshness and consistency; fresh fruit, old roots. There again comforting.

One can see three 'fields' in this chapter. First, zeal (1–2). What is this 'zeal', good or bad? It's not easy for us, I think, to enter into all the resonances the word had for St Benedict. *Zelus*, and Greek *zelos*, had a wider range than our modern 'zeal'. They conjured up *jealousy*, and thence *rivalry, emulation*. Hence the need to distinguish 'good' zeal from 'bad'. And then, yes, they could have our modern sense. According to *Robert*, 'Vive ardeur à servir la cause de Dieu et de la religion, ou Vive ardeur à servir une personne ou une cause à laquelle on est dévoué.' 'Live ardently to serve the cause of God and religion or live ardently to serve a person or a cause to which one is devoted.' It is probably fair to say that the idea of emulation is not entirely absent from this chapter, even if, as de Vogüé says, it 'passes to the second level'. But there is no doubt too, as becomes clear from what follows, that 'good zeal' is simply love of a certain quality, love become intense, ardent, passionate, love – following the etymology of the Greek – 'on the boil', or, if you prefer, love aflame. According to Ps-Denys, the Lord is called a 'Zealot' in the Greek of Exodus 20:5 'because of the great love he has for existent things.'

Yet St Benedict actually begins with 'the bad zeal of bitterness, which separates from God and leads to hell' (1), a terrible, evil power. What was he thinking of? Probably of the 'I belong to Paul' or 'I belong to Apollos' or 'I belong to Cephas' or 'I belong to Christ' (1 Cor. 1:12) rending the Church of Corinth, of 'the bitter jealousy and selfish ambition' causing disorder in the churches St James was addressing (Jas 3:14), of the jealousy and envy causing havoc at Corinth again in the time of Pope Clement, and later in North Africa prompting St Cyprian's *De Zelo et Livore*. In other words, the kind of situation he had warned against in his chapter on the Prior, the spirit that divides and demolishes a community. We, with another nuance of zeal in mind, might think instinctively of contemporary terrorism. Such zeal is a two-edged sword. Even the 'good zeal' of Phineas, Elijah, Mattathias – the three great biblical examples – wrought death. 'When love therefore is fervent, and is come to that height that it would take away, remove and divert, what is opposite to the thing beloved, it is termed zeal,' says St Francis de Sales.[1] Religious zeal is a passionate dedication to the 'cause of God', to the first commandment, to worship, and therefore rises up in wrath against the worship of Baal. When zeal took hold of our Lord, he took hold of a whip. But how easy, in us, for the destructive urge to take control. Such zeal 'leads' to hell, says St Benedict. It rejoices in the destruction of the Twin Towers, in the shedding of blood. And so the great question put to religions that repose on revelation, Judaism, Christianity, Islam: how reconcile an affirmation of 'divine truth' with human vagary, diversity, freedom? We find ourselves between a rock and a hard place. To say 'I believe' is a scandal to the secular. To say 'I accept you are different' is hard for some believers. At a smaller level, doesn't the same question arise within the heart of the monk? In *The Brothers Karamazov*, there is Fr Ferapont as well as Fr Zosima. We all know the tactless zeal of the young monk, the ravaging monastic mobs of the early Church, the strong resistance to ecumenical openness among often the most fervent monks of the East ... 'We notice therefore,' says St Ambrose, 'that there is a certain measure and discipline to be observed with regard to zeal.' Indeed! And yet, if we have not felt bitter zeal, have we felt any zeal? Are we zeal-less? Relativists? How be zealous (1) and tolerant (5)?

What St Benedict offers, in a monastic microcosm, is the reconciliation of apparent contraries, the sanctification, if you like, of zeal. It is topical. It surely is a service our times call our communities to offer: the combination of an unequivocal theological, Christian, Catholic loyalty with an immense tenderness of heart – even, miracle of miracles, within the community! In the end, it echoes the reconciliation of the two natures in the one person of the Lord, the miracle of the Incarnation; in the Spirit, therefore, it must be possible. St Benedict's good zeal can only be the inverse of his bad. It is a single-minded ardour that unites and builds. In St Ambrose's words, 'it gathers the Church'. It holds a whip in its hand, it 'separates from vices', certainly, but only to unite to God and in God. 'He was speaking of the temple of his body' (Jn 2:21). Chapter 72 is monotheistic zeal taken over by the Trinity.

'This zeal, therefore, let monks exercise with the most fervent love' (3). We move into the second 'field': that of love, of charity, of fraternal charity above all, articulated in eight maxims, eight beatitudes one could say.

By way of an induction, St Augustine on the two loves:

> one holy, the other impure; one social, the other private; one consulting the common good for the sake of heavenly fellowship, the other even bringing the common good under its own sway for the sake of arrogant domination; one happy to be subject, the other envious of God; one tranquil, the other turbulent; one peaceful, the other seditious; one preferring the truth to the applause of the misguided, the other avid for any kind of praise; one friendly, the other envious; one wanting the neighbour to have what one has oneself, the other wanting to subject him to oneself.[2]

By way of another induction, two unusually sensitive people having two contrasting visions in strangely parallel circumstances, at about the same time around World War I. In a way, these are the two visions that were before twentieth-century man like prophecies, and are, in their way, before us.

The first is from the Scottish poet already mentioned, Edwin Muir. It is set in Glasgow:

> I did not believe in the immortality of the soul at that time: I was deep in the study of Nietzsche, and had cast off with a great sense of liberation all belief in any other life than the life we live here and now, as an imputation on the purity of immediate experience, which I had intellectually convinced myself was guiltless and beyond good and evil. I was returning in a tramcar from my work; the tramcar was full and very hot; the sun burned through the glass on backs of necks, shoulders, faces, trousers, skirts, hands, all stacked there impartially. Opposite me was sitting a man with a face like a pig's, and as I looked at him in the oppressive heat the words came into my mind, 'That is an animal.' I looked round me at the other people in the tramcar; I was conscious that something had fallen from them and from me; and with a sense of deso-

lation I saw that they were all animals, some of them good, some evil, some charming, some sad, some happy, some sick, some well. The tramcar stopped and went on again, carrying its menagerie; my mind saw countless other tramcars where animals sat or got on or off with mechanical dexterity, as if they had been trained in a circus; and I realized that in all Glasgow, in all Scotland, in all the world, there was nothing but millions of such creatures living an animal life and moving towards an animal death as towards a great slaughter-house. I stared at the faces, trying to make them human again and to dispel the hallucination, but I could not. The experience was so terrifying that I dismissed it . . . I could not have endured it for more than a few minutes. I did not associate it at the time with Nietzsche.[3]

The second vision belongs to an English Catholic laywoman, poet, writer, Caryll Houselander. It is set in London.

I was in an underground train, a crowded train in which all sorts of people jostled together, sitting and strap-hanging – workers of every description going home at the end of the day. Quite suddenly I saw with my mind, but as vividly as a wonderful picture, Christ in them all. But I saw more than that; not only was Christ in everyone of them, living in them, dying in them, rejoicing in them, sorrowing in them – but because He was in them, and because they were here, the whole world was here too, here in this underground train; not only the world as it was in that moment, not only all the people in all the countries of the world, but all those people who had lived in the past, and all those yet to come. I came out into the street and walked for a long time in the crowds. It was the same here, on every side, in every passer-by, everywhere – Christ. . . The 'vision' lasted with that intensity for several days, and each of them revealed the mystery and its implications for me a little more clearly. Although it did not prevent me ever sinning again, it showed me what sin is, especially those sins done in the name of 'love', so often held to be harmless – for to sin with one whom you loved was to blaspheme Christ in that person; it was to spit on Him, perhaps to crucify Him. I saw too the reverence that everyone must have for a sinner; instead of condoning his sin, which is in reality his utmost sorrow, one must comfort Christ who is suffering in him. And this reverence must be paid even to those sinners whose souls seem to be dead, because it is Christ, who is the life of the soul, who is dead in them; they are His tombs, and Christ in the tomb is potentially the risen Christ. For the same reason, no one of us who has fallen into mortal sin himself must ever lose hope.[4]

It is out of a vision such as this second one that St Benedict speaks in this chapter. It is also out of the vision that, especially, SS Peter and Paul have for the Christian communities to which they write. 'We are all one in Christ.' It is a Eucharistic vision, one can also say, a vision from the altar. And a vision of Christian friendship.

Eight maxims follow, as we know. As in the first part of the chapter, there is a movement from bad zeal to good zeal, here there is a movement from expressions of love (the first 4) to love itself (the second 4). Also, a movement from the brethren's mutual loving to their loving of God, the abbot, and Christ. Maybe these eight phrases even form a ladder.

If we wish to examine our conscience in approaching the Sacrament of Reconciliation, we can do worse than choose these eight maxims.

First, 'let them anticipate one another in showing honour' (Rom. 12:10), already quoted in chapter 63. Once, three Capuchins stayed with our community for an extended time. On leaving, they said two things had impressed them above all: the divine office and the respect the brethren showed to one another. I was astonished! And gratified too. That St Benedict should begin with honour is in character. Honour is, after all, fundamental. 'I can no longer respect him' is always a terrible thing to hear; it is the death certificate of a relationship. In chapter 53, honour consists in the ritual of meeting, welcoming the guest. Honour is translated into the ceremonies of courtesy, and especially the ceremonies of encounter, beginning with the name. In chapter 63 it consists in naming the brother reverently, in asking his blessing, in yielding one's place – all things to do with first meeting the other. The Russian poet, Irina Ratushinskaya, a dissident who spent time in prison, even under Gorbachev, tells an interesting story in her autobiography, *Grey is the Colour of Hope*. She was in detention with other women. When the guards – men – came in, they would always *tutoyer* the women. When they did, the women refused to respond, until the men were forced to use the respectful form. What is more, the women realized that, living so closely together, and in an atmosphere of degradation, it was all the more essential to preserve the ceremonies of honour among themselves. And so they resolved not even to *tutoyer* each other. (I am not making a point, you understand, about one particular form of address, but, I suppose, about language – and whatever else – as a vehicle for reverence.)

How do we show honour? Cassian quotes Romans 12:10 in *Conference* XVI, and adds, 'so that each person may ascribe more knowledge and holiness to his fellow and may believe that the height of true discretion lies in another's judgement rather than one's own' (XVI, 11, 2). It seems that for St Benedict it has to do with welcoming, meeting. Can we say that 'to anticipate one another in honour' means, essentially, to acknowledge and receive the other? Therefore perhaps, first of all simply to be ready to listen?

Then, 'let them bear with the greatest patience one another's weaknesses, whether of body or character' (5). After respect, patience. Prayer and patience: the monastic life in two words! We have already been told that it is by patience that we share in the sufferings of Christ (Prol. 50) and that the sick are to be patiently borne with (36.5). But now both the full scope of patience is spelled out: weaknesses of character as well as of body, and the degree of it: *patientissime* is a superlative and, says Lentini, 'not rhetorical'. Here everything purely 'natural' in our zeal fails. Here too we see, of course, the path of the suffering Servant, the Lamb of God. 'Tolerance' is not a question of being indifferent to our own or others' faults; it is a question of carrying them so as, in some mysterious way, to carry them away. It is a question of not succumbing to and perpetuating them, but of absorbing and transforming them into patience and prayer, or of entering with our brethren into the mystery of human frailty. In the end, we are left waiting in hope for God to act, not imposing our time on His. 'Community life,' Enzo Bianchi has said, 'is always the fruit of bearing together each member's poverty and weakness, rather than the sum of the strength of all'.[5] So easy to say, so hard to live!

Some weaknesses do not bother us, or simply amuse us. But others, or other temperaments, 'get to' us, frighten, anger, disturb us. With the best will in the world, we cannot cope, we always find ourselves reacting in ways we would rather not. Cassian has the image of the waves of anger being reduced to calm in the harbour of the enlarged heart.[6] But sometimes it seems as if every vessel in the harbour is simply overwhelmed. Perhaps there is one key recognition which can help: my brother is my salvation. Each brother is my salvation. This brother is my salvation. The Lord has set him beside me precisely to enlarge my heart. Every brother is a bringer of grace, and therefore of peace, to me. Every brother, even *this* brother ... And it is true: 'the quality of our monasteries is the quality of our fraternal life' (P. Thierry).

To jump to v. 7: 'Let no one follow what he judges useful for himself, but rather for another.' Sr Aquinata points out that, syntactically, this verse has another form than the other maxims. It breaks the flow in that sense. And so, she wonders, was it inserted later? Did the monks come to St Benedict and say, 'All you say about good zeal and love is very beautiful. But what does it mean in practice?' And this was his answer. It is a call to self-forgetfulness, to self-sacrifice, to *preferring the good of the other*. It could not be more practical. There are every day opportunities for this, in matters small and great. It echoes, most of all, St Paul. 'Love ... does not insist on its own things/way' (1 Cor. 13:5); 'Let each of you look not only to his own interest, but also to the interests of others' (Phil. 2:4); 'Let no one seek his own good, but the good of his neighbour' (1 Cor. 10:24). Paul himself did no less: 'I am not seeking my own advantage, but that of many that they may be saved' (1 Cor. 10:33). And in so doing was only trying to imitate Christ: 'We who are strong ought to bear with failings of the weak, and not to please ourselves; let each of us please his neighbour for his good, to edify him. For Christ did not please himself ...' (Rom. 15:1–3). Cassian, with these texts in mind, speaks of 'apostolic charity'; St Basil sees here the great value, the great opportunity of cenobitic life. Conversely, as Abbot Marcel Rooney once said, 'Monasteries close for lack of love.'

In a certain sense, with this and the following verse: 'Let them devote themselves (*impendant*) chastely to brotherly love' (8), we are at an ultimate point. After honouring (4), bearing (5), obeying (6), we come to the apostle's self-giving for his churches, Christ's self-sacrifice for the Church, the monk's gift of self. 'I will most gladly spend and be spent (*impendam et superimpendar*) for your souls' (2 Cor. 12:15). Sr Aquinata tells the story of explaining v.7 to a novice, and his pale-faced reply: 'But then there's nothing left for me.' No, nothing. But everything too.

Jumping again, we come to v. 10: 'Let them love their abbot with a sincere and humble charity.' It's another shock! St Benedict's last word on the abbot, the 130th!, unique in monastic tradition. But it is beautiful that in this 'dance of love', which embraces all the brethren, God and Christ, the abbot is not excluded. The honouring, bearing, obeying, preferring already mentioned must include him too. Notice that he is not simply '*the* abbot', but '*their* abbot'. The verb used for 'love' is *diligere*. It suggests a choice, not a transport of the heart, and yet we have the noun *caritas* ('holding dear') and the adjectives, 'sincere and humble'; there is warmth too. 'Sincere': it is not to be a manipulative love. In English, there is an expression 'cupboard love', that is, an insincere show of affection towards someone in return for some kind of material or emotional gain. The person is loved merely because he has access to the 'cupboard', the place of provisions. So, not this love, nor a patronizing love, but a genuine and humble, appreciative love. And it is worth repeating that everyone needs such love, and that being so loved brings out the best. It is in a climate of love that the delicate flower of the abbot will blossom! And such love will reduce his temptations to excessive external activity or taking refuge in his computer.

Then, the climax: 'Let them prefer altogether nothing to Christ, and may he bring us all alike / together to eternal life' (11–12). This both concludes the second 'field' and brings us to the third. First zeal, then love, finally Christ. It is the third and final call to prefer nothing to Him: *nada, nada, nada*. And then it turns to prayer. At the beginning of the chapter, zeal 'leads' (*ducit*), now Christ does so (*perducat*). He becomes the subject. And he leads us, we pray, 'together' – together or not at all. At the beginning of the Rule, there is the key adverb, *libenter*; at the end, this *pariter*. And surely the Christ who appears here, who leads us to eternal life, is the Christ of the Ascension. This too would connect back with the first glimpse of Christ in the Prologue: Christ the King. There we were called to serve the risen and ascended Lord. Now, as it were, he is turned towards the Father and takes us with him. The monk, the monastic community is, I think, in a special way linked to the mystery of Christ in his ascension.

May I conclude with a little fantasy ... It's to see in this chapter, as in chapter 7, the whole story / journey of the monk, of *Quisquis*, and a story / journey in three stages.

Verses 1–2 take us from bad zeal to good, separate us from vice and set us on the path to God and life eternal. Isn't zeal itself something we instinctively link with the young? The young Antony 'he emulated in goodness' the older monk.[7] It's suggestive that, in the Rule, 'zeal', good or bad, is the subject of the sentence. Isn't that, too, part of the experience of youth, of beginning: a force or forces are more in control than one is oneself? So here, we may imagine, in this first brief sentence, in its movement from bad zeal to good, in the separation from vice and the finding of the way, is the first conversion, the novitiate, the beginning of a monk's journey, in a nutshell. It's true: good zeal is the necessary point of departure, a separation from vice, from bad habits, and a focus on God and eternal life, God alone, obedience to his will whatever it asks, commitment to prayer above all, a 'determined determination' as St Teresa of Avila called it. That is the grace of the beginning. It is essential.

What happens to this zeal, though, as the years pass? Sometimes it fades away; sometimes it is clouded over; sometimes it goes in the wrong direction. What the great portion of this chapter is concerned with, one could say, is its conversion, a second conversion. 'Let the monks then exercise this zeal with the most fervent love' (3). It is the conversion of zeal into the loving, especially the fraternal loving, indicated in the following verses. This zeal-love is, it becomes clear, the true 'exercise' – the asceticism, the athleticism, the military service – of 'monks', those set on God alone. And this can be a shock for the young monk. He had had other expectations of how his monastic life would unfold. Instead what is asked of him is honouring, bearing with, etc., etc. What is asked of him is a sacrifice of himself for the good of the community. 'You will not serve; you will be taken into service.' Hopes of doing this or that have to be set aside. But, please God, he will realize that it is precisely here, in this 'field', that he is a monk (v. 3), that he becomes himself a subject, with others, of this long sentence, writing his own small line of history; he will realize, more importantly, that he may be beginning to be a Christian, to live as Peter and Paul, as the New Testament, urge us. At least, he sees more clearly what is asked. These are, at their best, the middle years of the monk. He is, broadly speaking, doing the will of God.

But then there is something more. 'Truly, truly, I say to you, when you were young, you girded yourself and walked where you would; but when you are old, you will stretch out your hands, and another will gird you and carry you where you do not wish to go' (Jn 21:18). With age, the surrender of *propria voluntas* already made will be taken to a new depth. Energy and strength will be in short supply, the mental faculties may even be more or less lost, or there may simply be another generation pushing up and taking over, with little room left for oneself. And here there lies in wait the grace of the third conversion: 'and may he bring us together to eternal life' (12). It is the grace of Christ becoming the subject of the sentence – not zeal, not oneself, but Christ. It is the grace of becoming nothing, having nothing, but expectation of eternal life. There is nothing left the monk but to wait for eternal life, which is Christ's gift, and his alone. And that empty waiting, in hidden faith and hope, is his greatest gift to his brothers and to the Church. Perhaps it is even the hidden channel of the zeal of the young and the active loving of the mature. In any case, Christ is everything. That is St Benedict's real last word.

Notes

1. St Francis de Sales, *On the Love of God*, X, XII.
2. St Augustine, *De Genesi ad Litteram* 11, 15, 20.
3. Edwin Muir, *An Autobiography* (London: Methuen, 1964), p. 52.
4. Caryll Houselander, *A Rocking-Horse Catholic* (London: Sheed & Ward, 1955), pp. 137–9.
5. Enzo Bianchi, *Words of Spirituality* (London: SPCK, 2012), p. 103.
6. St John Cassian, *Conferences,* XVI, 27, 2.
7. St Athanasius, *Life of Antony,* 3, 3.

19

A Beginning of Perfection

Chapter 73 is a surprising chapter. In it, St Benedict humbly bows out, and hands us over to Scripture, the Fathers of the Church, the monastic Fathers. But have we not been trying to follow these already?

A 'spiritual' reading of this chapter could see in it a call to the monk to immerse himself ever more deeply into the life of the Church on her pilgrim path through time to the heavenly homeland, to throw himself more fully into the currents of the Word and the Spirit which carry us back to the Father, to connect more closely with the tradition of holiness which is the best and truest history of the Church. We are pointed to another, fuller, simpler, more demanding 'rule', the rule of faith and holiness. Perhaps we can say, we are pointed – *sine nomine* – to Mary.

> In the world as it is, torn with agonies and dissensions, we need some direction for our souls which is never away from us; which, without enslaving us or narrowing our vision, enters into every detail of our life. Everyone longs for some such inward rule, a universal rule as big as the immeasurable law of love, yet as little as the narrowness of our daily routine. It must be so truly part of us that it makes us all one, and yet to each one the secret of his own life with God. To this need, the imitation of Our Lady is the answer; in contemplating her we find intimacy with God, the law which is the lovely yoke of the one irresistible love.[1]

It does, in many ways, correspond to the Prologue. It mentions for the last time our friend *Quisquis*. *Quisquis ergo ad patriam caelestem festinas* ... 'Whoever you are, therefore, who are hastening to the heavenly fatherland...' (73.8). The whole chapter is a call to continue seeking for God, not to grow weary, not to think one has arrived; to keep running, hastening 'to the perfection of *conversatio*' (73.2). There is one last rebuke of the 'lazy and ill-living and negligent' (73.7). There are, repeatedly, these strong, hortatory words with the prefix *per*: *perfectio, perducere, pervenire, perficere*, climaxing in the final *pervenies*, 'you will arrive'! We are being called, in the English idiom, to 'see' the venture 'through'.

The central message is clear, and we are indeed reminded of the Prologue. 'Who is the man who wants life?' Life is, by definition, movement, self-movement. It is never static. It is either failing or growing, in Newman's terms either corrupting or developing. When it is a question of the 'true and perpetual life', this can only mean growing towards God. The very word 'perpetual' has 'peto' – to seek, to endeavour to reach – as its root. This Christ-life the Holy Spirit has given us is always endeavouring to reach, to return to, its source: the Land of the Father, the *patria caelestis*, where the original fountain flows. It is a question of surrendering ourselves more thoroughly to this movement, the 'spring of water welling up to eternal life' (Jn 4:14), hearing the 'murmur of living water which whispers within [us], "Come to the Father"'.[2]

Here is a fine text from Walter Hilton:

> Although it may happen that you feel [Jesus] in devotion or in knowing, or in any other gift, whatever it may be, do not rest in it as though you had fully found Jesus, but forget what you have found, and always be longing for Jesus more and more, to find him better, as if you had nothing at all. For know well, whatever you feel of him, however much – yes, even if you were ravished into the third heaven with Paul – you have not yet found Jesus as he is. However much you know or feel of him here in this life, he is still above it. And therefore if you want to find him fully as he is in the bliss of loving, never cease from spiritual desire as long as you live.[3]

This conference is (once again) a rag-bag – the final rag-bag! It falls into three parts.

I

The life we live we live in community – *pariter* – and we and our communities live in the Church. And our communities and the Church live in time, in history. Christ shepherds the Church through history. So Moses sings at the Red Sea, 'In your steadfast love you led the people whom you redeemed; you guided them by your strength to your holy abode' (Ex. 15:13). And so David the Psalmist, 'The Lord is my shepherd.' Because of this, because Christ is alive in His Church, and because history itself is not static, because we too are alive, the question is always arising, What – in the present circumstances, in the contemporary situation – does it mean to be a believer, a Christian, a Catholic, a monastic community, a monk? Essentially, indeed, it will mean what it always means: 'Let us follow his paths under the guidance of the Gospel.' But, in response to our inner and outer circumstances, certain emphases will be called for at certain times, certain potentialities will be summoned forth. For example, the Gospel always guides us to the poor, but who, today, are the poor? Where are they? They are sometimes, by definition, invisible. We need eyes from the Holy Spirit. And so the perennial witness to charity, un-relinquishable, will take on a new, a specific form according to circumstances. And then there are the inner changes as well, the changes of mentality, sensibility. The expressions of 'piety' find new forms. G. K. Chesterton once compared the Church to a large farm. In that farm, some fields are cultivated, others lie fallow. But then it is time to rotate, to change ...

I should mention a certain Commission here, and its conclusion at our last General Chapter. For this was precisely the question being asked, What does it mean for us as communities and individuals to live our monastic life in the present circumstances? And I think that the conclusions arrived at – the five 'calls' – do reflect the 'mind' of our communities. The calls to deepen monasticity, to live true community, to face our situations with realism, to intensify solidarity between our communities, to practise hospitality in the wide sense ... 'See, in his loving kindness the Lord shows us the way of life' (Prol. 20).

But I would like to speak more immediately of the Church as a whole. To repeat, we ourselves and our communities live in the Church, live with the life of the Church. There is that other set of five principles in n. 2 of *Perfectae Caritatis*, of which the third is:

> All institutes should share in the life of the Church. They should make their own and should foster to the best of their ability, in a manner consonant with their own natures, its initiatives and undertakings in biblical, liturgical, dogmatic, pastoral, ecumenical, missionary and social matters (*PC*, 2c).

'The Lord is our shepherd.' It is Christ who leads His Church. And how? We remember the fine text from chapter 2 of *Dei Verbum*, on the transmission of divine revelation:

> The Tradition that comes from the apostles makes progress in the Church, with the help of the Holy Spirit. There is a growth in insight into the realities and words that are being passed on. This comes through the contemplation and study of believers, who ponder these things in their hearts (cf. Lk. 2:19, 51), from the intimate sense of spiritual realities which they experience, from the preaching of those who have received, along with their succession in the episcopate, the sure charism of truth. Thus, as the centuries go by, the Church is always advancing towards the plenitude of divine truth, until eventually the words of God are fulfilled in her (*DV*, 8).

[A footnote to that text: It reflects very much the thought of Yves Congar. But it also reflects that of Newman. On 2 February 1843, while still an Anglican, he preached before the University of Oxford on the development of doctrine – a first sketch of what would become his famous book. And his text was, 'And Mary pondered all these things in her heart'; he presented Mary as the type of the Church entering ever more deeply, through pondering in the heart, into the mystery of Christ.]

There is a triad in that passage from *Dei Verbum*. There is another – compatible with it – in 1 Corinthians 12:27: 'And God has appointed in the church first apostles, second prophets, third teachers.' This 'appointment' remains. The apostles live on in our bishops, the prophets in our saints and spiritual guides, the teachers in our Christian thinkers and theologians. And when we are looking for confirmation of what we feel the Holy Spirit has put into our hearts, when we are seeking an answer to the question, What does it mean here and now to be Christian, Catholic, monks etc., we can find the guidance of Christ, it seems to me, in these three places. When we are wanting to progress, St Benedict points us to Scripture, the Fathers and the monastic Fathers. When we are wanting to develop as the Church, we can refer to the successors of apostles, prophets, teachers.

To develop a thought as regards the first mentioned by St Paul (and the third in the passage from *Dei Verbum*): the preaching of the bishops, the famous Magisterium! We speak, as Catholics, of Scripture, Tradition and the Magisterium, this last at the service of the Word transmitted by the first two. Since the nineteenth century, there has been a marked inflation, or (less pejoratively) intensification of the Magisterium, especially that of the Pope and the Holy See. The Conciliar Magisterium has also enlarged. No Council ever said as much as Vatican II! One can consider this excessive, and it seems that Benedict XVI is of this mind and intends to say less. One might also wish, at the same time, that individual bishops proclaimed the Gospel and taught the faith more effectively within their dioceses ... But, leaving those details aside, can one suggest that this growth or expansion of the Magisterium represents a response to the acceleration of history? If so, one could see its purpose, glimpse the shepherding of Christ. The Magisterium is one way – one along with the others – in which the whole Church – *pariter*, corporately – is here and now enabled to follow Christ's paths under the guidance of the Gospel. If, as *Gaudium et Spes* remarked, 'ours is a new age of history with critical and swift upheavals spreading gradually to all corners of the earth' (*GS*, 4), then perhaps it is *au fond* the Holy Spirit inspiring the successors of Peter and the other apostles to fill so many pages with their words! Conversely, one might wonder if the Orthodox Eastern Churches, so rich in 'prophets' (holy men) and 'teachers' (Christian thinkers, the

Russian emigrés, for example), do not suffer from a certain deficiency at the hierarchical level, and therefore cannot always corporately – *pariter* – respond effectively to the demands. Perhaps then, as monks, as communities, we can indeed find real guidance in what the Council, the Popes, the bishops offer us.

A suggested application. Towards the end of *Novo Millennio Ineunte*, John Paul II said this:

> With the passing of the years, the Council documents have lost nothing of their value or brilliance. They need to be read correctly, to be widely known and taken to heart as important and normative texts of the Magisterium, within the Church's Tradition. Now that the Jubilee has ended, I feel more than ever in duty bound to point to the Council as *the great grace bestowed on the Church in the twentieth century*: there we find a sure compass by which to take our bearings in the century now beginning' (*NMI, 57*).

But the documents of the Council are something of an immensity. How get to grips with them? Gregory the Great famously connected the first four Ecumenical Councils with the four Gospels. Perhaps we can take a further step and focus on the four Constitutions of the Council: *Sacrosanctum Concilium, Lumen Gentium, Dei Verbum, Gaudium et Spes*. These are the pillars of the house. They can also be pillars of our Benedictine communities. They are also 'calls' on our communities. Could we put it like this:

- that *Dei Verbum* calls our communities to a culture of the Word,
- that *Sacrosanctum Concilium* calls them to a culture of the Liturgy,
- that *Lumen Gentium* calls to a culture of communion,
- that *Gaudium et Spes* calls to a culture of humanity?

II

Let me return to chapter 73 and to ourselves as individuals. In this chapter, St Benedict bows out. His Rule is indeed 'a chain loose at both ends' and he is only a servant of something greater than himself. His Rule is only a pedagogue, to lead us away from the 'Rule of the flesh' and hand us over to the 'Rule of the Spirit'. 'For neither circumcision counts for anything, nor uncircumcision, but a new creation. Peace and mercy be upon all who walk by *this* rule' (Gal. 6:15–16).

Striking is the emphasis on reading. St Benedict offers a list of 'further reading'. Here we have one of the origins of the monastic culture of the Middle Ages and beyond,[4] one of the roots of Benedictine learning. Here too there is made explicit for the final time something that runs through the Rule, sometimes in a hidden way, sometimes (as in ch. 42 & 48) overtly: *lectio divina.*

Given the amount of contemporary literature on the subject, given its recommendation by Vatican II (*Dei Verbum* and elsewhere) and the lengthy treatment of it in Benedict XVI's *Verbum Domini* nn. 86–87, there's no place for saying much on the subject.

> There is certainly no monastic practice on which the holy patriarch [St Benedict] so much insisted as on *reading*. The final chapter of the Rule (the 73rd), completed by the 42nd, tells us precisely in what this reading consists: it is the reading of the Holy Scriptures, commented by the Fathers, and more particularly by the lives and sayings of the first monks, such as, for instance, those cited by Cassian. It might be said that such reading is *the* monastic practice. It should be for the monk what the *Exercises* are for the Jesuit.., contemplative prayer for the Carmelite, and so on … Nothing is more remarkable than the all-pervading, absorbing place of the divine Word in the life of the early monks.[5]

There's exaggeration here, but also truth. Some passages of the Rule are permeated by Scripture, others take Scripture as a clear starting-point (e.g. chs 36, 53, etc.), and the exposure of the monk to Scripture (and the Fathers) which the Rule provides for is immense. The 'deifying light' and the 'magisterium' / 'doctrine' of Christ mentioned in the Prologue are clear references to Scripture. The abbot is to teach or prescribe nothing 'outside the commandment of the Lord' (2.4) and is to be 'learned in the divine law' (64.9). The readings at the Divine Office – itself largely Scripture – are to be 'the inspired Scriptures of the Old and New Testaments, and also the commentaries on them which have been made by well-known and orthodox Catholic Fathers' (9.8). 'Reading is not to be lacking at the meals of the brethren' (38.1), i.e. of Scripture again, and perhaps the Lives of Martyrs and Saints. At the end of the day 'four or five pages' of 'the Conferences of Cassian or the Lives of the Fathers, or something else that may edify the hearers' are to be read (42.3) – calculated by some to take some twenty minutes. Thus in the oratory, refectory and chapter, from Vigils to Compline, the Word resounds. And then `there is the provision for private reading: after Vigils in the winter (8.3), and at other times of day according to the seasons, this reaching a surprising three hours in Lent (48.14), itself regarded as a privileged time for *lectio* (49.4) following the counsels of St Caesarius of Arles.

The Rule and its background suggest at least the following observations:

Everything monastic is first of all ecclesial, and this monastic attentiveness to the Word is simply an intensification of the practice of the early Church.

> If there is instruction being given [in church], it is preferable to attend it, and to do so conscious that it is God who speaks through the mouth of the one giving instruction. . .So let everyone take care to go to the assembly; it is there that the Holy Spirit produces fruit. . .On a day when catechesis is not being given, let each one take a holy book home and there read a sufficient amount of what seems profitable.[6]

The three hours of Lenten reading, found in chapter 48 and in other Western Rules, has been connected to the three-hour catecheses the Bishop of Jerusalem would give the catechumens and faithful during Lent (cf. Egeria). For St Benedict, the listening and reading to which he calls his monks could be described as on-going catechesis. For St Benedict, the 'divine authority' and orthodoxy of what his monks read is a primary concern.

For St Benedict the goal of *lectio* is nowhere described as 'contemplation'. It is understood either as a practical means of self-instruction for the Office (8.3; 58.5), or more generally as an aid to virtue, that is, to *praxis*. Scripture and the Fathers offer the monk 'a most straight norm for human life', enable us 'to attain to our Creator by a straight path' (73.3, 4). Key is the concluding couplet: *doctrina* acquired by reading and *virtus* shown in its living out (73.9).

> The attraction towards Christ as fullness also influences our daily life in *lectio divina*. The amount of time daily that St Benedict, in line with early monastic tradition, devotes to this activity is impressive. It shows a sense of the vastness of the object of study. It is not just a matter of getting a little daily nourishment for the spiritual life. That is to say, we are not so much bringing something into our life, as immersing ourselves in another life that is becoming ours. Our reading is to fulfil the prayer of St Paul: 'Let the word of Christ dwell in you richly' (Col. 3:16) (Abbot Anselm Atkinson).[7]

This gives force to the opening phrase of chapter 7: 'Holy Scripture *shouts* at us, brethren', and to the French understanding of the monastery as a place of 'la circulation de la Parole'.

> If there is to be any shouting in the monastery, it is Scripture that does it (Abbot Gilbert Jones).

It is somewhat remarkable, then, that St Benedict should, as it were, give us this final bibliography, this list for 'suggested further reading'. Surely his monks have already been reading and hearing read Scripture, the Fathers, the monastic Fathers? Be that as it may, at the centre of this chapter are three questions – the first questions, if I'm right, since the two great questions of the Prologue: 'Who is the man who wants life and longs to see good days?'; 'Lord, who shall dwell in your taber-

nacle or rest on your holy mountain?' (vv. 15, 23) Now it is,
'What page or what word of the divinely inspired Old and New
Testament, etc.? Or what book of the holy Fathers, etc.? Then
the Conferences of the Fathers, etc., what else are they but
...?' (vv. 3–6) We are handed – it is the final *traditio* – Scripture, the Fathers, the monastic Fathers, a threefold gift. And
three times their utility, their goal, is described: 'a most
straight norm of human life ... so that, by a straight course,
we may come to our Creator ... tools of the virtues for good
living and obedient monks' (vv. 3, 4, 6).

What is St Benedict really saying here? Surely something
more than recommending books. He is asking us to immerse
ourselves in the living water, welling up to eternal life. 'By the
rivers of Babylon we sat down and wept.' 'Babylon,' says St
Bernard,

> means confusion: the citizens of Jerusalem sit and weep in
> Babylon, or in confusion, because even if they are not confused
> in their actions they are in their thoughts. They want to turn their
> mental eye toward God but cannot because they are assailed by
> futile and unwanted distractions. The rivers of Babylon are bad
> habits which are sweet to the memory. Quickly flowing, they
> sweep those whom they seduce into the sea of this world.[8]

We all know those waters of Babylon running inside us. But
there is another stream. There is the river that flows out of
Eden (Gen. 2:10), the river whose streams give joy to the city
of God (Ps. 45:4), the river 'issuing from below the threshold
of the temple toward the east' (Ezek. 47:1). It is what the angel
shows John in the closing pages of his Revelation: 'the river
of life, rising from the throne of God and of the Lamb and
flowing crystal-clear through the middle of the street of the
city' (Rev. 22:1–2). And by the side of which we are called to
put down roots, to become trees of life, our leaves for the
healing of the nations. Blessed is he who meditates on the law
day and night. 'He is like a tree planted by streams of water,
that yields its fruit in its season, and its leaf does not wither.
In all that he does, he prospers' (Ps. 1:3). St Benedict is asking
the monk to immerse himself more fully in the living stream

of Truth that comes to us from 'the divine well-spring' (*DV,* 9) through the channels of Scripture and the Fathers and the lived holiness of the Church. In chapter 7, on the eighth step of the Ladder, St Benedict bade the monk 'do nothing except what is commended by the common rule of the monastery and the example of his seniors' (7.55). It was a call to immerse oneself in the life of one's community, in its tradition. Now, the heart has been enlarged and the perspective is wider, and the call is to swim in the great river of Truth which flows through the Church, to enter in depth into the wisdom found in Scripture and Tradition.

And this stream of Truth is also a stream of holiness. Three times in this chapter, we find the adjective *sanctus,* each time attached to the Fathers or 'our holy father Basil' (vv. 2, 4, 5). This suggests how St Benedict envisaged this stream, this river of Tradition: as the succession of saints, as – another image – a chain of saints. For the ancients, more than for us (and it's a loss, I think), Scripture itself was the work of saints: Moses, Samuel, David, Solomon, *Saint* Matthew, *Saint* Paul, etc., and it tells the story of a line of saints, from Abel to John of Patmos. To read the Bible is to enter the Communion of Saints. And likewise with reading the works of the holy Catholic Fathers, and the Institutes, Conferences and Lives of the Egyptian monastic Fathers. It is a summons to enter the Communion of Saints.

In pointing us where he does, to Scripture and Tradition and the succession of saints, St Benedict is also, implicitly, pointing us to Mary. There are, in our monastic liturgy, two daily moments of communion with Mary (apart, that is, from the Eucharist, which makes a third). They are precious. There is, last thing, the *Salve* or its seasonal variants. The *Salve* is the moment we look to, meet Mary as mother – the Mother of God and therefore of the children of God, the brethren of her Son. The moment of the 'merciful eyes'. The moment for entrusting ourselves and our concerns and one another to her in hope of the day she will show us 'the blessed fruit of her womb' face to face. It's the moment of her prayer and protection, when she shows herself as, in the words of our Constitutions, the 'protectress (*tutamen*) of the monastic life' (C. 79), of our hopes and desires as monks. It's the Johannine moment, one might say, the moment of the 'mother of Jesus'. 'Woman, behold your son! . . . Behold your mother!' (Jn 19: 26, 27). That is one moment. The other – which St Benedict himself knew – is the singing of the *Magnificat* at Vespers. One could say this is the Lucan moment, the moment of 'the handmaid of the Lord' (Lk. 1:38), of Mary as 'the blessed believer' (cf. Lk. 1:45), of the one who sings the praises of God and, as St Irenaeus says, 'prophesied in the name of the whole Church'. It's the moment she shows herself as the 'example of the monastic life' (C. 79). At the *Salve*, she is turned towards us and we turn to her. At the *Magnificat*, she is turned to the Lord and we turn with her. And I think that chapter 73 implicitly, gently turns us to Mary. She is the quiet heart of Scripture and Tradition, the heart that ponders the Word. She is the centre of the Communion of Saints. Possibly St Benedict knew a remarkable sentence in the *De Virginitate* attributed to St Athanasius: 'The Holy Scriptures which instruct us, and the life of Mary, Mother of God, suffice as an ideal of perfection and the form of the heavenly life.'

She is, in other words, like Scripture, 'a most straight norm of human life' (73.3). If we are 'hastening to perfection . . . to the heavenly fatherland', we do so in her company, in her wake. Her life in some sense suffices; it is an epitome of the Gospels. Certainly St Benedict knew St Ambrose, the West's most eloquent exponent of Mary as the model for the ascetic, virginal life. 'Virginity is thus proposed to us, as if in a picture, in Mary's life . . . This is the model of virginity; in truth, such was Mary, whose life alone is sufficient to instruct everyone (*cuius vita omnium est disciplina*).'[9] In ch. 73, St Benedict looks to Rules beyond his *Rule*. He therefore looks to Mary. And each time we sing the *Magnificat*, each time we turn to the Lord and Saviour with her, we enter her expanded heart, we take a step towards 'the perfection of monastic life' and 'the heavenly fatherland'. 'Such as these fearing the Lord are not puffed up on account of their good works, but judging that they can do no good of themselves and that all comes from God, they magnify the Lord working within them (*operantem in se Dominum magnificant*)' (Prol. 29–30). The *Magnificat* is the daily moment of entering into the poverty of spirit and the joy – immense joy! – of Mary. The Lord who worked in her is also working in us! *Suscepit Israel puerum suum.*

III

It's time I finished! And I think there is one last thought which suggests itself. We need simplicity in the end, we need unity. And perhaps both what Vatican II still has to say to our communities and what St Benedict says to us in chapter 7 as individual seekers of God comes down, comes back to the one, same thing: the Holy Spirit.

It was, of course, the prayer of Blessed [now Saint] John XXIII that Vatican II inaugurate a 'new Pentecost'.

Each section of the Rule, it seems to me, concludes by alluding to the Holy Spirit. So the Prologue: 'But as we progress in our monastic life and in faith, our hearts shall be enlarged, and we shall run with unspeakable sweetness of love in the way of God's commandments' (49) – phrases redolent of the Spirit. So the conclusion of chapter 2 – consolation for the abbot: 'he himself is cleansed of faults' (2.40), a work of the Spirit. So explicitly at the end of chapter 7, and again in chapter 20: 'Prayer should be short and pure, unless it chance to be prolonged by the impulse and inspiration of divine grace' (20.4). The whole of chapter 72 is about the good zeal inspired by the Spirit. And so, by force of precedent, with chapter 73.

St Benedict always ends by handing us over to the Holy Spirit. The poverty of spirit he teaches, he teaches as preparation for the wealth of the Spirit of God. We know how St Paul's great line, 'But he who is united to the Lord becomes one spirit with him' (1 Cor. 6:17), has echoed down the monastic centuries. What does it mean, here and now, to be Christian, Catholic, monks? There is only one final answer: to be – for want of a better word – mystics. This is something the Abbot General of the Trappists has said very powerfully. And what does this mean? To live our life of faith, hope and charity, not by our own criteria, by our own rule, but under the sway of the Holy Spirit. We can at least hope for this!

'Obedient' is the last positive adjective St Benedict allots the monk (73.6), and I think obedience is for us always the surest door to life in the Spirit. *Obedientes Spiritus ad alta vexit culmina.*

To return to *Quisquis* . . . What chapter 73 suggests is another dimension to his story, the eternal revealed in time. At the beginning of the Rule, he is asked to open the ear of his heart to the teaching of the master, St Benedict. At the end of it, he is asked to open his whole life to the Word of God in all its revealed fullness. The *doctrina* of 73.9 suggests the divine Person of the Word, the *virtus* the divine Person of the Holy Spirit. The real 'story' of *Quisquis* is how the Father speaks his Word to him, and how from this Word there proceeds the power which is the Holy Spirit. And so, like Ignatius of Antioch, *Quisquis* ceases to be merely 'a (meaningless) cry' and becomes himself 'a word of God'.[10] He ceases to be mere vanity, 'a breath that passes away', and is filled instead with the power of God's Spirit. The story of *Quisquis*, outlined by the Rule, is the story of God's grace at work within him.

They magnify the Lord working in them, using the word of the prophet: 'Not to us, Lord, not to us, but to your name, give the glory' (Ps. 113:9; Prol. 30).

And so, 'under God's protection, you shall arrive. Amen'.

Notes

1. Caryll Houselander, *The Reed of God* (London: Sheed & Ward, 1944), pp. xi-xii.
2. St Ignatius of Antioch, *Letter to the Romans*, 7.
3. Walter Hilton, *The Scale of Perfection*, I, 46.
4. cf. J. Leclercq, *The Love of Learning and the Desire for God* (London: SPCK, 1978).
5. Louis Bouyer, *The Meaning of the Monastic Life* (London: Burns & Oates, 1955).
6. St Hippolytus, *The Apostolic Tradition*.
7. Abbot Anselm Atkinson, OSB, is Hugh Gilbert's successor as Abbot of Pluscarden.
8. St Bernard, *In Adventu*, 10.
9. St Ambrose, *De Virginibus*, 2, 6, 15.
10. St Ignatius of Antioch, *Letter to the Romans*, 2.

Lightning Source UK Ltd.
Milton Keynes UK
UKOW04f1048140715

255151UK00001B/32/P